NUTRITION
FOR FOODSERVICE
MANAGERS

NUTRITION FOR FOODSERVICE MANAGERS

Concepts, Applications, and Management

Mahmood A. Khan, Ph.D., R.D., F.M.P.

Department of Hospitality & Tourism Management
Virginia Polytechnic Institute & State University

JOHN WILEY & SONS, INC.
New York   Chichester   Weinheim   Brisbane   Singapore   Toronto

Library of Congress Cataloging-in-Publication Data:

Khan, Mahmood A.
    Nutrition for foodservice managers : concepts, applications, and
    management / Mahmood A. Khan.
        p.   cm.
    Includes index.
    ISBN 0-471-12951-8 (cloth : alk. paper)
    1. Nutrition.   2. Food service management.   I. Title.
TX353.K424   1998
613.2′024′642—dc21   97-36348

Printed in the United States of America

10 9 8 7 6 5 4 3 2 1

Dedicated to my wife Maryam and my children Samala, Feras, and Nufayl for their continuous encouragement, affection, and patience.

In memory of my father Habib Ullah Khan and my mother Achi Bano, for their inspiration and support.

CONTENTS

Chapter 3   CARBOHYDRATES   **41**

Chapter 4   LIPIDS: FATS AND OILS   **59**

Chapter 5   FAT-SOLUBLE VITAMINS   **73**

Chapter 6   WATER-SOLUBLE VITAMINS   **85**

Chapter 14   SPECIAL DIETS AND NUTRITIONAL NEEDS   **241**

PREFACE

This book is intended for students in foodservice management, hospitality management, dietetics, and culinary arts programs, and for foodservice managers in all types of commercial and institutional foodservice operations. As the title *Nutrition for Foodservice Managers: Concepts, Applications, and Management* indicates, this book is designed to provide basic concepts and applications of nutrition to all aspects of foodservice management. The unique part of this book is the incorporation of the recently introduced *Food Guide Pyramid, Dietary Guidelines for Americans,* and *Nutrition and Food Facts Labels* into every aspect of foodservice systems management. This book should be helpful not only to present and future foodservice managers but also to students in hospitality and dietetic curricula, especially those who are preparing for the foodservice management component of the Registered Dietitian® examination.

The information in this book is divided into 15 chapters. The first 8 chapters deal with the basic concepts of nutrition and provide a discussion of each nutrient. Efforts have been made to simplify as much as possible the scientific and technical information so that it is easily comprehended. Within each chapter is an exhaustive list of food sources and dietary requirements. Pertinent examples are provided to explain concepts and applications. Chapters 9–15 cover the application of nutrition information to every aspect of foodservice management, from menu planning, food purchasing and storage, receiving, and preparation to service. Nutrition retention and preservation are emphasized at each step. Special diets and nutritional needs are also discussed in a separate chapter. In short, this book is unique in its attempt to apply all of the current concepts and nutrition principles to foodservice systems.

One of the objectives of this book is to show how healthy meals can be provided without sacrificing taste or appeal. Effective planning, management, and marketing from a nutritional point of view are described. Most of the management information is provided in easy-to-follow steps. Menu planning and recipe modification from a nutritional point of view are covered in detail. In addition, useful information is provided in appendices, which list food composition and foods with special nutrients, glossary terms, and other pertinent information.

This book should serve as a handy reference for foodservice managers; hospitality management students; those working on food legislation; franchisors and franchisees of restaurant corporations; libraries; and anyone who is interested in nutrition. It can also serve as an aid in seminars and workshops related to nutrition.

The information provided in this book was collected and updated during the past several years utilizing a variety of sources. The final product would not have been possible without the patience, affection, and understanding of my wife and children. I would also like to thank the editor, Claire Thompson Zuckerman, for her cooperation and advice in developing this project. Also, many thanks to Donna Conte for her help during the final stages of the production of this book. Last, but not the least, I would like to thank all reviewers who have given valuable advice for the completion of this manuscript.

Mahmood A. Khan,
Ph.D., R.D., F.M.P.
Professor and Department
Head
Department of Hospitality &
Tourism Management
Virginia Polytechnic
Institute and State
University

NUTRITION FOR FOODSERVICE MANAGERS

Chapter 1

NUTRITION AND FOODSERVICE MANAGEMENT

The increasing importance given to nutrition by consumers, governments, and the private sector makes it imperative for foodservice managers to have adequate knowledge of this subject. The foodservice industry is the largest and fastest-growing industry in the United States. It consists of foodservices provided by hotels, restaurants, hospitals, nursing homes, colleges and universities, sports arenas, theme parks, attractions, tourism destinations, surface and air transportation companies, contract foodservice operations, military foodservice operations, and other institutions, to name only a few. The daily transactions in this industry average several million dollars. There are numerous reasons why it is important for foodservice managers to have adequate theoretical and practical knowledge of nutrition, some of which are as follows:

- Consumers are becoming increasingly health conscious and are making more demands for nutritionally well-balanced diets than at any time in history.

- An increasingly large number of people are eating away from home (at a variety of locations), making it necessary for foodservice managers to provide them with healthy meals.

- Public and private agencies are focusing on the nutrition and health of consumers. Recent regulations are designed to provide nutrition information to consumers; understanding these regulations requires comprehension of different nutrients and their role in health and well-being.

- Dietary guidelines for Americans are designed to provide advice for healthy persons aged two years and over about food choices that promote health and prevent disease. To understand and implement these guidelines, a foodservice manager should know the basic concepts of nutrition and their implications.

- The Recommended Dietary Allowances are based on nutrition requirements for persons of different ages. Knowledge of nutrition is imperative to understand not only these allowances but also the reasons for them.

- To meet the food-labeling requirements, all packaged foods have to include certain nutrition facts, including the percentages of nutrients provided by a serving of the particular food product. To benefit fully from these labels, a foodservice manager should have adequate nutrition knowledge.

- To provide nutritionally balanced meals, it is important to purchase foods that are of high nutritional quality. To perform this important function, nutrition information is essential.

- To preserve their nutritional quality, foods have to be handled and stored at proper temperatures and under correct storage conditions. Therefore, it is important to know the properties and shelf life of different nutrients.

- Nutrients can easily be destroyed or lost during prepreparation steps such as washing, cleaning, peeling, or coring foods. An understanding of nutrients and actions to prevent such losses are important.

- Proper methods of cooking should be selected to preserve nutrients. Thus, nutrition information is imperative to choose the most appropriate method of food preparation.

- Postproduction storage can also be a factor in preserving the nutrient contents of foods. Different foods require different methods of handling and delivery to preserve their nutritional quality.

- Nutrients can be lost while serving foods to consumers. Therefore, the manner of service and delivery requires careful planning by the foodservice manager.

- Utilization of leftovers and menu forecasting require planning to achieve optimum benefits from the nutrients present in foods.

- Nutrition is one of the primary factors that should be considered in planning menus. Without knowledge of nutrition, it is impossible to develop a well-balanced menu.

- Nutritionally well-balanced menus based on consumer demand can increase the profitability of an operation.

- Certain foodservice operations, such as those in hospitals, nursing homes, schools, and colleges and universities, require the serving of nutritionally balanced or special menus on a daily basis, for which nutrition knowledge is necessary.

As the above list demonstrates, nutrition is necessary for effective management of any foodservice operation. This book provides basic information on nutrition to foodservice managers, including the implications of good nutrition practices at various phases of the operation. The information is structured to provide the concepts and fundamentals of nutrition, the properties of all essential nutrients, and, finally, the application of nutrition principles in the management of all types of foodservice operations.

DIETARY GUIDELINES FOR AMERICANS

The U.S. Department of Agriculture (USDA) and the U.S. Department of Health and Human Services (HHS) have set Dietary Guidelines for Americans. These guidelines are outlined in the following sections. They are designed to provide advice for healthy Americans two years of age and over about food choices that will meet nutrient requirements, promote health, support active lives, prevent disease, and reduce the risk of chronic diseases. To meet the Dietary Guidelines, a diet with most of the calories from grain products, vegetables, fruits, low-fat dairy products, lean meats, fish, poultry, and dry beans is advised. Fewer calories from fats and sweets are also recommended.

Food choices depend on history, culture, and environment, as well as on energy and nutrient needs. Food choices are influenced by family, friends, and beliefs. Many genetic, environmental, behavioral, and cultural factors can also affect the health and well-being of an individual. It is therefore imperative to understand the family history of a disease and the risk factors. These risk factors may include body weight, fat distribution, blood pressure, and blood cholesterol level. Healthy diets are also important during growth and development. In addition to promoting well-being, healthy diets can increase work productivity and provide energy and zest for everyday activity. Selecting foods wisely can reduce the risk of chronic diseases including heart disease, certain types of cancer, diabetes, stroke, and osteoporosis. This may be due primarily to the fact that risk factors such as obesity, high blood pressure, and high cholesterol can be controlled by choosing healthy foods.

As noted earlier, foods contain energy, nutrients, and other components that affect health. Essential nutrients are those that cannot be manufactured by the body and have to be provided by foods. These nutrients include vitamins, minerals, certain amino acids, and fatty acids. Besides providing nutrients, foods are good sources of certain components such as fiber, which is equally important for health and is considered vital for reducing the risk of certain disease factors. Most of the nutrients work in combination. Therefore, a variety of foods that contain one or more of these nutrients and components have to be incorporated in daily dietary needs.

Recently, the number of calories provided by foods has become a common concern. Caloric needs depend on age, level of activity, physiological changes, and other factors. For example, older persons need fewer calories than young teenagers because of their decreased activity. By contrast, teenagers and pregnant women need additional nutrients to cope with physiological demands.

Healthy diets are defined as those containing the amounts of essential nutrients and calories needed to prevent nutritional deficiencies and excesses. They also provide the right balance of carbohydrates, fat, and protein to reduce the risk of chronic diseases and to promote a full and productive life. Since different nutrients and components are involved, a healthy diet can be obtained only by eating a variety of foods that are available, affordable, and preferable. To provide guidelines for selecting foods based on nutrient contents required by the body, Recommended Dietary Allowances are set. **Recommended Dietary Allowances (RDAs)** represent the amounts of nutrients that are adequate to meet the needs of most healthy people. Diets that meet RDAs are almost certain to ensure the intake of enough essential nutrients by most healthy people. The Dietary Guidelines describe food choices that will help meet RDAs. Like the RDAs, the Dietary Guidelines apply to diets consumed over several days, not to single meals or foods. Diets that are high in total fat, saturated fat, cholesterol, and salt need restriction. Diets that contain more calories than the body can use result in a surplus of calories that accumulate as fat. A healthy diet contains foods that provide an adequate number of calories and consist of grain products, vegetables, fruits, and fiber.

The Dietary Guidelines for Americans are listed in Figure 1.1 and described in the following sections.

1. **Eat a variety of foods.**

2. **Maintain a healthy weight.**

3. **Choose a diet that's low in fat, saturated fat, and cholesterol.**

4. **Choose a diet with plenty of vegetables, fruits, and grain products.**

5. **Use sugars only in moderation.**

6. **Use salt and sodium only in moderation.**

7. **If you drink alcoholic beverages, do so in moderation.**

Figure 1.1 Dietary Guidelines

Eat a Variety of Foods

No single food can supply all nutrients in the amount needed by an individual. Certain foods are rich sources of particular nutrient(s). For example, oranges provide vitamin C but not vitamin B_{12}, whereas meats provide vitamin B_{12} but not vitamin C. However, certain foods have more than one required nutrient in desirable quantities.

Eating a variety of foods is recommended to get the energy, protein, vitamins, minerals, and fiber needed for good health. This requires a careful selection of foods. One way of getting a variety of nutrients is by using enriched foods. **Enriched foods** are those to which specified amounts of nutrients are added and that are required by the Dietary Guidelines. Enriched bread, for example, should contain thiamin, riboflavin, niacin, and iron. Dairy products are usually enriched with vitamin A; milk itself is enriched with vitamin D. Foods can be fortified by adding nutrients. **Fortification** refers to the addition of nutrients in extra amounts. Enrichment focuses on those nutrients that are normally present in foods, whereas fortified foods may contain one or more nutrients that are not naturally present but are added as extras. Fortified foods are also useful for meeting special dietary needs.

Although nutrients can also be obtained by supplements of vitamins, minerals, or fiber, they do not supply other substances that can be provided by foods and should not be used in place of foods. A person who is eating a healthy diet will seldom need vitamin or mineral supplementation. Supplementation is recommended during certain periods, such as pregnancy or during specific illnesses.

Different food groups provide enough variety to supply necessary nutrients and energy for good health. Fresh foods and vegetables add to the variety of nutrients that can be provided by foods.

Maintain a Healthy Weight; *Balance Food Intake With Physical Activity*

Gaining weight, particularly in adulthood, increases the risk of high blood pressure, heart disease, stroke, diabetes, certain types of cancer, arthritis, breathing problems, and other illnesses. Losing weight may be important for many individuals. Losing or maintaining weight requires careful control of the calories taken in compared to those expended. Physical activity is one of the best ways to use food energy. Sedentary activities result in the accumulation of calories, which leads to weight gain. Physical activities such as walking, using stairs, and gardening help to reduce or maintain weight when combined with a healthy diet. Thirty minutes of moderate physical activity, at least three times a week and preferably every day, is recommended.

High-fat foods contain many calories and result in weight gain. Even eating too many foods high in starch, sugar, and protein can result in accumulation of calories. Eating a variety of foods such as pasta, rice, bread, and other whole-grain foods, as well as fruits and vegetables, is recommended. These foods are filling, but they are also lower in calories than foods rich in fats or oils. Caloric intake is tied

Table 1.1   Desirable Weight Table for Men

Height (feet/inches)	Small Frame (pounds)	Medium Frame (pounds)	Large Frame (pounds)
5′2″	112–120	118–129	124–141
5′3″	115–123	121–133	129–144
5′4″	118–126	124–136	132–48
5′5″	121–129	127–139	135–142
5′6″	124–133	130–143	138–156
5′7″	128–137	134–147	142–161
5′8″	132–141	138–152	147–162
5′9″	136–145	142–156	151–170
5′10″	140–150	146–160	155–174
5′11″	144–154	150–165	159–179
6′0″	148–158	154–170	164–184
6′1″	152–162	158–175	168–189
6′2″	156–167	162–180	173–194
6′3″	160–171	167–185	178–199
6′4″	164–175	172–190	182–204

Note: The American Heart Association uses these guidelines set by the Metropolitan Life Insurance Company.

closely to the eating patterns of individuals. Consumption of snacks in addition to meals provides a large percentage of daily calories for many Americans. Healthy weight ranges for men and women are based on their height and age. Tables 1.1 and 1.2 show the desirable weight ranges for men and women of all ages. Body weight depends on different factors, and these tables are given only as examples. The location of body fat is also significant when considering body weight. It has been reported that excess fat located in the abdomen (stomach area) is a greater health risk than excess fat in the hips and thighs. This extra fat in the abdomen is linked to high blood pressure, diabetes, early heart disease, and certain types of cancer. Consumption of too much alcohol and smoking increases abdominal fat and thereby heightens the risk of diseases related to obesity. Vigorous exercise helps to reduce abdominal fat and decreases the risk of these diseases. Healthy diets and exercise can also help reduce weight. Caloric intake can be reduced by eating less fat and controlling portion sizes. Reducing sedentary activities and increasing physical activities are also necessary for weight reduction.

Choose a Diet Low in Fat, Saturated Fat, and Cholesterol

Fat supplies energy and essential fatty acids, as well as promoting absorption of the fat-soluble vitamins A, D, E, and K. High levels of saturated fat and cholesterol in the diet are linked to increased blood cholesterol levels and a greater risk of heart disease. A diet with less total fat, saturated fat, and cholesterol is recommended.

Table 1.2 Desirable Weight Table for Women

Height (feet/inches)	Small Frame (pounds)	Medium Frame (pounds)	Large Frame (pounds)
4'10"	92–98	96–107	104–119
4'11"	94–101	98–110	106–122
5'0"	96–104	101–113	109–125
5'1"	99–107	104–116	112–128
5'2"	102–110	107–119	115–131
5'3"	105–113	110–122	118–134
5'4"	108–116	113–126	121–138
5'5"	111–119	116–130	125–142
5'6"	114–123	120–135	129–146
5'7"	118–127	124–139	133–150
5'8"	122–131	128–143	137–154
5'9"	126–135	132–147	141–158
5'10"	130–140	136–151	145–163
5'11"	134–144	140–155	149–168
6'0"	138–148	144–159	153–173

Note: The American Heart Association uses these guidelines set by the Metropolitan Life Insurance Company.

Irrespective of its source, whether plants or animals, fat contains more than twice as many calories as carbohydrates or protein. A diet should provide no more than 30 percent of total calories from fat. The amount of fat needed depends on the total required calories. For example, at 2000 calories per day, the recommended maximum number of calories from fat is about 600. This is equivalent to about 65 grams of fat (65 grams of fat × 9 calories per gram).

Fats contain both saturated and unsaturated (monounsaturated and polyunsaturated) fatty acids. Saturated fat raises blood cholesterol more than other forms of fat. Reducing saturated fat to less than 10 percent of calories will help lower the blood cholesterol level. The main sources of saturated fats in most diets are meat, milk, and milk products. Many bakery products are also rich in saturated fats. Vegetable oils, in general, supply smaller amounts of saturated fat. Olive and canola oils are particularly high in monounsaturated fats; most other vegetable oils, nuts, and high-fat fish are good sources of polyunsaturated fats. Both kinds of unsaturated fat reduce blood cholesterol when they replace saturated fat in the diet. The fats in most fish are low in saturated fatty acids and contain a certain type of polyunsaturated fatty acid (omega-3) that is under study because of its possible association with a decreased risk of heart disease in certain persons. It is recommended that mono- and polyunsaturated fats replace saturated fats within the set limit of 30 percent of total calories from fat. Partially hydrogenated vegetables oils, such as those used in many margarines and shortenings, contain a particular form of unsaturated fat known as **trans-fatty acids.** These acids have been shown to raise blood cholesterol.

Cholesterol is made by the body as well as obtained from food. Dietary cholesterol comes from animal sources such as egg yolks, meat (especially organ meats such as liver), poultry, fish, and high-fat milk products. Many of these foods are also high in saturated fats. It is recommended that foods with less cholesterol and saturated fat be used to help lower the blood cholesterol level. The level of cholesterol recommended on food labels is 300 milligrams. This intake level can be maintained by eating more grain products, vegetables, and fruits and by limiting the intake of high-cholesterol foods.

Choose a Diet with Plenty of Vegetables, Fruits, and Grain Products

Grain products, vegetables, and fruits provide vitamins, minerals, and complex carbohydrates (starch and dietary fiber), making the diet healthy. In addition, they are generally low in fat and therefore in calories, depending, of course, on the way they are prepared. Most of the calories in the diet should come from vegetables, fruits, and grain products. These include breads, cereals, pasta, rice, potatoes, and corn. Fiber is found in plant foods such as whole-grain breads and cereals, beans and peas, and other vegetables and fruits. Eating a variety of fiber-containing foods helps to reduce chronic constipation, diverticular diseases, and hemorrhoids, and may lower the risk of heart disease and some cancers. In general, it helps to maintain efficient bowel movement. Fruits and vegetables are also generally low in fat and provide many of the essential nutrients and other food components important to health. They are generally good sources of vitamin C, vitamin B$_6$, carotenoids, and folate. Research has shown that some antioxidant nutrients found in plant foods, such as vitamin C, carotenoids, vitamin E, and certain minerals, have a potential role in reducing the risk of cancer and certain other chronic diseases.

Use Sugars Only in Moderation

Dietary carbohydrates include sugars, starches, and fiber. During the digestion process, all carbohydrates break down into sugars. Sugars and starches occur naturally in many foods and are commonly used in foodservice operations. Examples of common foods that are good sources of carbohydrates are milk, fruits, some vegetables, breads, cereals, and grains. Some sugars are used as natural preservatives, thickeners, and baking aids. They are often added to foods during processing and preparation. Diets high in sugars are linked to hyperactivity or diabetes. Some foods high in sugars supply calories but few or no nutrients. Sugars should be used in moderation by most healthy people and sparingly by people with low caloric needs. The Dietary Guidelines caution against eating sugars in large amounts and against frequent use of snack foods and drinks containing sugars that supply unnecessary calories and few nutrients.

Certain sugar substitutes, such as sorbitol, saccharin, and aspartame, are also ingredients of many foods. Most of these sugar substitutes do not provide significant calories and therefore may be useful in the diets of persons concerned about caloric intake. Sugars and starches promote tooth decay. The more often foods containing them are used, the longer they stay in the mouth, increasing the risk of tooth decay.

Use Salt and Sodium Only in Moderation

Salt, which is mainly sodium and sodium chloride, occurs naturally in foods, although in small amounts. It is added at the table as well as used commonly in food processing. It is present in most salty sauces and pickles. Although people add salt to enhance the taste of foods, their preference may weaken by eating less salt and by reducing the level of salt intake gradually.

Sodium plays an essential role in regulating fluids and blood pressure. High sodium intake has been linked to high blood pressure. Reducing weight and increasing physical activity help to reduce blood pressure as well. Consuming more fruits and vegetables also increases potassium intake, which may help to reduce blood pressure. Higher salt intake may also increase the amount of calcium excreted in the urine and therefore may increase the body's need for calcium. Americans consume more salt than they need. On food labels, the listed value is 2400 milligrams per day of sodium [2400 milligrams of sodium per day is contained in 6 grams of sodium chloride (common salt)]. Normally, a teaspoon of salt provides about 2300 milligrams of sodium.

Drink Alcoholic Beverages in Moderation

This guideline was suggested since alcoholic beverages supply calories with very few or no nutrients. The alcohol in these beverages has drug effects and is harmful when consumed in excess. The drug effects of alcohol alter judgment and can lead to dependency and many other serious health problems. High levels of alcohol intake raise the risk of high blood pressure, stroke, heart disease, certain cancers, accidents, violence, suicide, birth defects, and overall mortality (death). Too much alcohol may cause cirrhosis of the liver, inflammation of the pancreas, and damage to the brain and heart. Heavy drinkers also are at risk of malnutrition because alcohol contains calories that may substitute for those in more nutritious foods.

THE FOOD GUIDE PYRAMID

The Food Guide Pyramid (Figure 1.2) translates the Dietary Guidelines for Americans into practical eating advice. The Pyramid is based on USDA's research on what foods Americans eat, what nutrients are in these foods, and how to make the best food choices. It goes beyond the basic four food groups to help put the Dietary Guidelines into action. The Pyramid is an outline of what to eat each day. It is not a rigid prescription but rather a general guide in choosing a healthy diet. It is designed to help select foods that provide nutrients by choosing the recommended number of daily servings from each of the five major food groups shown.

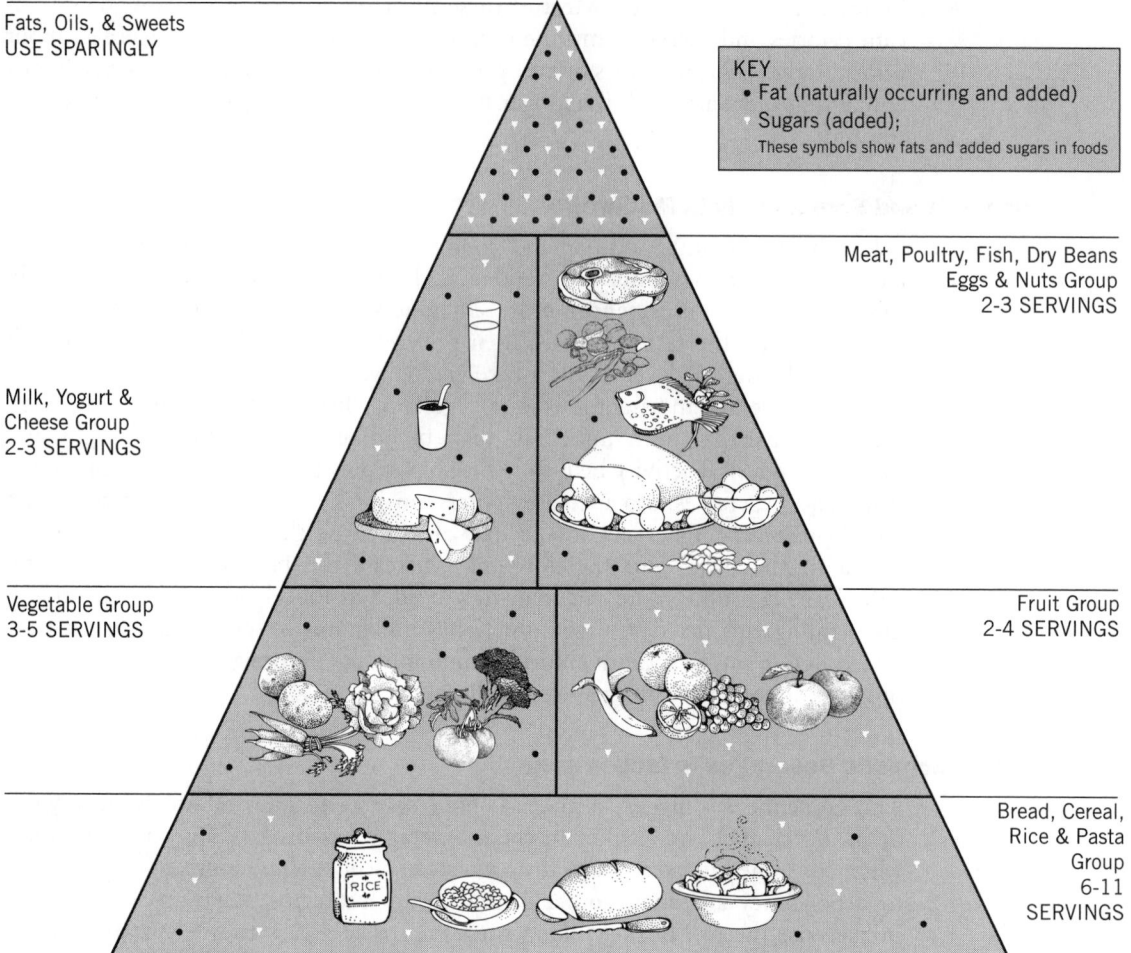

Figure 1.2   The Food Guide Pyramid

The Pyramid also focuses on fat because most American diets are too high in fat, especially saturated fat.

People often choose amounts from some food groups higher or lower than those suggested in the Food Guide Pyramid. The Pyramid emphasizes foods from the five major food groups (bread, cereal, rice, and pasta; fruits; vegetables; meat, poultry, fish, dry beans, and nuts; and milk, yogurt, and cheese) shown in the three lower sections of the Pyramid. Each of these food groups provides some, but not all, of the nutrients one needs. Foods in one group cannot replace those in another. No one food group is more important than another; for good health, all of them are needed.

Fat and added sugars are concentrated in foods from the Pyramid tip—labeled "fats, oils, & sweets." These foods should be used sparingly since they supply calories but few or no vitamins or minerals. Some fat and sugar symbols are shown in the food groups to remind consumers that some foods in these groups can also be high in fat or added sugars. When choosing foods for a healthy diet, the fat and added sugars in food groups, as well as the fats, oils, and sweets from the Pyramid tip, should be considered. In general, foods that come from animals (milk and meat groups) are naturally higher in fat than foods that come from plants. However, many low-fat dairy products and lean meats are available, and these foods can be prepared in ways that lower fat.

The symbols for sugars represent sugars added to foods in processing or at the table, not those found naturally in fruits or milk. Added sugars provide calories with few vitamins and minerals. Most of them come from foods such as ice cream, sweetened yogurt, chocolate milk, canned or frozen fruit with heavy syrup, and sweetened bakery products like cake and cookies. The amounts of added sugars in some popular foods are shown in Table 1.3.

The amount of fat that can be consumed depends on the caloric needs of an individual. The Dietary Guidelines recommend that Americans limit the fat in their diets to 30 percent of calories. This amounts to 53 grams of fat in a 1600-calorie diet, 73 grams of fat in a 2200-calorie diet, and 93 grams of fat in a 2800-calorie diet. The number of grams of fat that provide 30 percent of calories in the daily diet can be figured as follows: (1) multiply the total day's calories by 0.30 to get the calories from fat per day (example: 2200 calories $\times$ 0.30 = 660 calories from fat) and (2) divide the calories from fat per day by 9 (each gram of fat has 9 calories) to get the grams of fat per day (example: 660 calories from fat $\div$ 9 = 73 grams of fat). The Dietary Guidelines also recommend limiting saturated fat to less than 10 percent of calories, or about one-third of total fat intake. All fats are mixtures of three types of fatty acids: saturated, monounsaturated, and polyunsaturated. Saturated fats are found in the largest amounts in fats from meat and dairy products, as well as in some vegetable oil such as coconut, palm, and palm kernel oils. Monounsaturated fats are found mainly in olive, peanut, and canola oils. Polyunsaturated fats are found mainly in cauliflower, sunflower, corn, soybean, and cottonseed oils and some fish. Saturated fats and dietary cholesterol raise blood cholesterol levels in many people increasing their risk of heart disease. These fats and cholesterol are explained in detail in Chapter 4.

It is recommended that the sodium intake be no more than 3000 milligrams a day. Much of the sodium in diets comes from salt added during cooking or at the table. (One teaspoon of salt provides about 2000 milligrams of sodium.) Sodium can be found in foods such as cured meats, luncheon meats, cheese, most canned soups and vegetables, and soy sauce. Low-salt and no-salt-added products are available. Foods high in salt are listed in Chapter 8.

At the bottom of the Food Guide Pyramid is the bread group, with the recommendation of 6 to 11 servings per day. These foods provide complex carbohydrates, which are important sources of energy, especially in low-fat diets. They also provide vitamins, minerals, and fiber. Examples of one serving of this group

Table 1.3   Amount of Added Sugars in Some Common Foods (†)

Food Groups	Added Sugars
Breads, Cereal, Rice, and Pasta	
Bread, 1 slice	0
Muffin, 1 medium	* 1
Cookies, 2 medium	* 1
Danish pastry, 1 medium	* 1
Doughnut, 1 medium	** 2
Ready-to-eat cereal, sweetened, 1 ounce	* 1
Pound cake, nonfat, 1 ounce	** 2
Angel food cake, 1/12 tube cake	***** 5
Pie, fruit, 2 crust, 1/6 8 in.	****** 6
Fruit	
Fruit, canned in juice, 1/2 cup	0
Fruit, canned in light syrup, 1/2 cup	** 2
Fruit, canned in heavy syrup, 1/2 cup	**** 4
Milk, Yogurt, and Cheese	
Milk, plain, 1 cup	0
Chocolate milk, 2 percent, 1 cup	*** 3
Low-fat yogurt, plain, 8 ounces	0
Low-fat yogurt, flavored, 8 ounces	***** 5
Low-fat yogurt, fruit, 8 ounces	******* 7
Ice cream, ice milk, or frozen yogurt, 1/2 cup	*** 3
Chocolate shake, 10 fl ounces	********* 9
Other	
Sugar jam or jelly, 1 teaspoon	* 1
Syrup or honey, 1 tablespoon	*** 3
Chocolate bar, 1 ounce	*** 3
Fruit sorbet, 1 ounce	*** 3
Gelatin dessert, 1/2 cup	**** 4
Sherbert, 1/2 cup	***** 5
Cola, 12 fl ounces	********* 9
Fruit drink, ade, 12 fl ounces	************ 12

† Check product label.

* = 1 teaspoon sugar.

Note: 1 teaspoon = 4 grams of sugar.

Source: USDA.

include one slice of bread, 1 ounce of ready-to-eat cereal, and ½ cup of cooked cereal, rice, or pasta.

The next tier in the Pyramid consists of the vegetable group (three to five servings) and the fruit group (two to four servings). Vegetables provide vitamins, such as vitamins A, C and folate; and minerals, such as iron and magnesium. Examples of a serving of this group are 1 cup of raw leafy vegetables; ½ cup of other vegetables, cooked or chopped raw; and ¾ cup of vegetable juice. This tier also contains the fruit group. Fruit and fruit juices are important sources of vitamins A and C and potassium. They are also low in fat and sodium. The Food Guide Pyramid suggests two to four servings of fruits a day. Examples of one serving are one medium apple, banana, or orange; ½ cup of chopped, cooked, or canned fruit; and ¾ cup of fruit juice.

The next higher tier of the Pyramid consists of the milk group (two to three servings) and the meat group (two to three servings). Meat, poultry, and fish supply protein, B vitamins, iron, and zinc. The other foods in this group—dry beans, eggs, and nuts—are similar to meats in providing protein and most vitamins and minerals. The total amount of these servings should be the equivalent of 5 to 7 ounces of cooked lean meat, poultry, or fish per day. Two to 3 ounces of cooked lean meat, poultry, or fish is counted as one serving. A 3-ounce piece of meat is about the size of an average hamburger or the amount of meat on a medium chicken breast half. For other foods in this group, ½ cup of cooked dry beans, one egg, or 2 tablespoons of peanut butter are counted as 1 ounce of meat (about one-third of a serving).

Milk and milk products provide protein, vitamins, and minerals. Milk, yogurt, and cheese are the best sources of calcium. Examples of one serving of this group are 1 cup of milk or yogurt, 1½ ounces of natural cheese, and 2 ounces of processed cheese.

The Pyramid shows that foods from the grain products group, along with vegetables and fruits, are the basis of a healthy diet. Meals that include rice, pasta, potatoes, or bread are recommended, accompanied by vegetables, fruits, and lean and low-fat foods from the other groups. Fats and sugars added to food in preparation and at the table are to be limited. Selecting a variety of foods within and across food groups improves dietary patterns since foods within the same group have different combinations of nutrients and other beneficial substances. Choosing a variety of foods within each group also helps to make meals more interesting and reduces monotony. Some foods may contain fewer calories, yet may be rich in nutrients. Fruits, vegetables, and grain products fall into this category. On the other hand, there are certain foods that are high in calories and low in nutrients, such as fats, sugars, and alcohol. Thus, it is advisable to select foods that provide optimum numbers of nutrients and fewer calories for people who would like to reduce their weight. For many women and adolescent girls, calcium-rich foods are needed for healthy bones, which can be achieved by selecting foods low in fats and high in calcium, such as low-fat or fat-free milk products. Iron-rich foods are recommended for young children, teenage girls, women of childbearing age, and during pregnancy. Such foods include lean meats and whole-grain or enriched white bread.

The Food Guide Pyramid shows a range of servings for each major food group. The number of servings that is right for an individual depends on how many calories are needed, which in turn depends on age, sex, size, and activity level. The following calorie-level suggestions are based on recommendations of the National Academy of Sciences and on calorie intakes reported by people in national food consumption surveys: 1600 calories for many sedentary women and some older adults; 2200 calories for most children, teenage girls, active women, and many sedentary men (women who are pregnant or breast feeding may need somewhat more calories); 2800 calories for teenage boys, many active men, and some very active women.

THE IMPORTANCE OF NUTRITION

The body is made up of nutrients and needs nutrients for its existence. Nutrition has a broad influence on daily life since it deals with the survival and well-being of any living body. The methods of selecting, obtaining, preparing, serving, and consuming foods shape the culture of a society. Food is used during times of happiness and stress; during aging and disease; and as a symbol of prosperity and power. Food and nutrition are inseparable; hence, the study of nutrition is linked directly to food intake.

Nutrition is not only related to the well-being of an individual but deals with every process of survival. Nutrition is closely involved in physiological, social, economic, and technological factors. Thus, nutrition has such a broad influence that it is referred to as the result of constant interaction between food and a living organism. A considerable misconception exists about nutrition, and it has become one of the most controversial issues in recent history. It is vital that foodservice managers know the basics and applications of nutrition. Nutrition not only affects physiology and health but is also related to the consumer's food habits, social interactions, economic impact, and almost every other aspect of life.

Simply defined, **nutrition** is the study of nutrients. A **nutrient** is a substance that is used by the body for normal growth, reproduction, and maintenance of health. A nutrient can also be defined as a substance that must be taken into the body in sufficient quantity to meet the body's needs. Nutrition can also be defined as a science that deals with the relationship of life and food, which is related to all associated sciences. Finally, nutrition can be defined as the science of food and nutrients, that is, their action and interaction in relation to health and disease. It involves the sources of nutrients and all processes that deal with the intake, ingestion, digestion, absorption, transportation, utilization, and excretion of food and associated substances. The human body requires about 50 different substances that must be taken in in sufficient quantities to meet the body's needs. It is their essential nature that separates nutrients from other chemical substances. Paradoxically, it was the lack of nutrients and accompanying deficiency symptoms that led to the discovery of many nutrients. To provide nourishment, nutrients have to be obtained primarily from foods. Although foods contain nutrients, there is no one food that can provide all nutrients needed by the body; therefore, it is essential to select a variety of foods. Food selection has become very complex in modern society, due partly to the advances in technology and the refinement of foods. The most difficult task is to select or provide a balanced diet that consists mostly of desired nutrients in the right proportion. This is not easy, and it is intimately related to food habits. Body processes are not simple, and several factors have led to nutritional imbalance in the majority of the world's population. This imbalance has become a grave health problem that must be handled at individual, societal, national, and international levels.

Although nutrients are provided by foods, eating food alone cannot guarantee adequate well-being and health. Other factors, such as exercise, rest, stress, age, and disease conditions, are also important. As much as the intake of nutrients is beneficial to health, excessive intake can be harmful and, in some cases, may result in toxicity.

Nutrients are grouped into the following classes: carbohydrates, lipids (fats), proteins, vitamins, minerals and water. Nutrients that are needed in large quantities, such as water, carbohydrates, lipids, and proteins, are referred to as **macronutrients,** whereas those that are needed in small quantities, such as vitamins and minerals, are called **micronutrients.** In general, nutrients are responsible for (1) providing energy, (2) forming body structures, and (3) regulating body processes. All three functions are equally important and play a significant part during every stage of the life cycle. Carbohydrates, lipids, and protein are primary nutrients that provide energy to body cells. Energy is extremely important; without it, it is impossible for any life to exist.

Energy provided by nutrients is measured in a unit of heat referred to as the **kilocalorie (kcal** or **kcalorie,** popularly known as the **calorie).** Although calorie is commonly used in place of kcalorie, this is not technically correct since a calorie represents only $\frac{1}{1000}$ of a kcalorie. The definition of a kcalorie is similar to the one used in the physical sciences: the amount of heat required to raise the temperature of 1 kilogram of water 1°C. The number of kcalories used by humans depends on age, sex, and other physiological factors. The number of kcalories used by adults per day varies from 2300 to 3000. Kcalories provided by foods vary based on the contents of energy-providing nutrients. Not all nutrients provide equal amounts of kcalories. Carbohydrates and protein provide, on average, 4 kcalories per gram, whereas lipids provide 9 kcalories per gram. These are common averages that are used in the calculation of kcalories provided by foods. Alcohol provides about 7 kcalories per gram.

Nutrients that help form body structure are proteins, lipids, minerals, and water. Regulatory functions are carried out by several vitamins and minerals, which take an active part, directly or indirectly, in various metabolic processes. The role of nutrients in sustaining some of the most vital functions of the body is evident from the above discussion. It should be noted that both inadequate and excessive food intake can result in unhealthy consequences referred to as **malnutrition.** While millions of people throughout the world suffer from lack of food,

Table 1.4   Food and Nutrition Board, National Academy of Sciences—National Research Council Recommended Dietary Allowances,[a] Revised 1989

Category	Age (years) or Condition	Weight[b] (kg)	Weight[b] (lb)	Height[b] (cm)	Height[b] (in)	Protein (g)	Fat-Soluble Vitamins Vitamin A (μg RE)[c]	Fat-Soluble Vitamins Vitamin D (μg)[d]	Fat-Soluble Vitamins Vitamin E (mg α-TE)[e]	Fat-Soluble Vitamins Vitamin K (μg)
Infants	0.0–0.5	6	13	60	24	13	375	7.5	3	5
	0.5–1.0	9	20	71	28	14	375	10	4	10
Children	1–3	13	29	90	35	16	400	10	6	15
	4–6	20	44	112	44	24	500	10	7	20
	7–10	28	62	132	52	28	700	10	7	30
Males	11–14	45	99	157	62	45	1000	10	10	45
	15–18	66	145	176	69	59	1000	10	10	65
	19–24	72	160	177	70	58	1000	10	10	70
	25–50	79	174	176	70	63	1000	5	10	80
	51+	77	170	173	68	63	1000	5	10	80
Females	11–14	46	101	157	62	46	800	10	8	45
	15–18	55	120	163	64	44	800	10	8	55
	19–24	58	128	164	65	46	800	10	8	60
	25–50	63	138	163	64	50	800	5	8	65
	51+	65	143	160	63	50	800	5	8	65
Pregnant						60	800	10	10	65
Lactating	1st 6 months					65	1300	10	12	65
	2nd 6 months					62	1200	10	11	65

[a] The allowances, expressed as average daily intakes over time, are intended to provide for individual variations among most normal persons as they live in the United States under usual environmental stresses. Diets should be based on a variety of common foods in order to provide other nutrients for which human requirements have been less well defined.

[b] Weights and heights of reference adults are actual medians for the U.S. population of the designated age, as reported by the National Health and Nutrition Examination Survey II. The median weights and heights of those under 19 years of age were taken from Hamill et al. (1979) (see pages 16–17). The use of these figures does not imply that the height-to-weight ratios are ideal.

Source: Hamill, P.V.V., T.A. Drizd, C. L. Johnson, R.B. Reed, A.F. Roche, and W.M. Moore. 1979. "Physical Growth. National Center for Health Statistics Percentiles." *Am. J. Clin. Nutr.* 32: 607–629.

millions of others suffer from too much. Both groups suffer from malnutrition or malnourishment. Nutrient requirements change based on several factors, such as availability of foods, physiological requirements during various stages of the life cycle, bioavailability of nutrients, and safe and adequate use of nutrients. In the United States, the Food and Nutrition Board of the National Research Council has prepared Recommended Dietary Allowances (commonly referred to as RDAs) since 1941. These recommendations, which are revised periodically, are intended to reflect the best scientific judgment on nutrient allowances for the maintenance of good health and to serve as the basis for evaluating the adequacy of diets of groups of people in the United States. RDAs are defined as the levels of intake of

Table 1.4 *(Continued)*

	Water-Soluble Vitamins						Minerals						
Vitamin C (mg)	Thiamin (mg)	Riboflavin (mg)	Niacin (mg NE)^f	Vitamin B$_6$ (mg)	Folate (µg)	Vitamin B$_{12}$ (µg)	Calcium (mg)	Phosphorus (mg)	Magnesium (mg)	Iron (mg)	Zinc (mg)	Iodine (µg)	Selenium (µg)
30	0.3	0.4	5	0.3	25	0.3	400	300	40	6	5	40	10
35	0.4	0.5	6	0.6	35	0.5	600	500	60	10	5	50	15
40	0.7	0.8	9	1.0	50	0.7	800	800	80	10	10	70	20
45	0.9	1.1	12	1.1	75	1.0	800	800	120	10	10	90	20
45	1.0	1.2	13	1.4	100	1.4	800	800	170	10	10	120	30
50	1.3	1.5	17	1.7	150	2.0	1200	1200	270	12	15	150	40
60	1.5	1.8	20	2.0	200	2.0	1200	1200	400	12	15	150	50
60	1.5	1.7	19	2.0	200	2.0	1200	1200	350	10	15	150	70
60	1.5	1.7	19	2.0	200	2.0	800	800	350	10	15	150	70
60	1.2	1.4	15	2.0	200	2.0	800	800	350	10	15	150	70
50	1.1	1.3	15	1.4	150	2.0	1200	1200	280	15	12	150	45
60	1.1	1.3	15	1.5	180	2.0	1200	1200	300	15	12	150	50
60	1.1	1.3	15	1.6	180	2.0	1200	1200	280	15	12	150	55
60	1.1	1.3	15	1.6	180	2.0	800	800	280	15	12	150	55
60	1.0	1.2	13	1.6	180	2.0	800	800	280	10	12	150	55
70	1.5	1.6	17	2.2	400	2.2	1200	1200	320	30	15	175	65
95	1.6	1.8	20	2.1	280	2.6	1200	1200	355	15	19	200	75
90	1.6	1.7	20	2.1	260	2.6	1200	1200	340	15	16	200	75

^{c} Retinol equivalents. One retinol equivalent = 1 microgram (μ) retinol or 6 μg β-carotene.

^{d} As cholecalciferol. Ten μg cholecalciferol = 400 IU of vitamin D.

^{e} α-Tocopherol equivalents. One mg d-α tocopherol = 1 α-TE.

^{f} 1 NE (niacin equivalent) is equal to 1 mg of niacin or 60 mg of dietary tryptophan.

essential nutrients that, on the basis of scientific knowledge, are judged by the Food and Nutrition Board to be adequate to meet the known nutrient needs of practically all healthy persons. Nutrient needs of individuals are influenced by sex, body size, growth, and reproductive status. RDAs are set based on the body's physiological needs, and different recommendations are made for specific nutrients in certain cases. The RDAs for various groups are shown in Table 1.4.

RDAs are used for (1) planning and procuring food supplies for population subgroups (including national defense); (2) interpreting food consumption records of individuals and populations; (3) establishing standards for food assistance programs; (4) evaluating the adequacy of food supplies in meeting national nutritional needs; (5) designing nutrition education programs; (6) developing new products; and (7) establishing guidelines for nutritional labeling of foods. In foodservice operations, RDAs serve the above-mentioned purposes by being used in (1) food procurement, (2) menu planning, (3) nutritional assessment of recipes, and (4) meal management. Several private and public contractors use RDAs in setting standards for providing nutrients through meals, the most common examples being the school lunch requirements that specify providing one-third of the RDAs for specific age groups.

Since nutrition has such a broad influence, its definition is also multifaceted. As is evident from its definition, nutrition involves physiological and biochemical processes and is affected by a combination of psychological, social, cultural, geographical, economic, and technological factors. A very simple definition of **nutrition** is that it is the study of nutrients. Nutrients are basic substances making up the body. They are needed for fuel and regulatory functions. Nutrients are chemical substances that, most often in combination, provide energy; support growth, maintenance, and repair of tissues; and regulate body processes. Thus, nutrition can also be defined as a science concerned with the body's need for nutrients, the sources from which these nutrients can be obtained, and their role in maintaining body health and well-being. The science of nutrition explores the actions and interactions of nutrients that fuel the physiological activities of the body. Thus, nutrition is a blend of sciences that deals with different aspects of food as it relates to life. Animals, plants, and other living creatures all need nutrition, depending on their physiological needs. In this book, only human nutrition will be considered. All human body functions basically depend on nutrition, and many physiological processes are designed to nourish the individual cells that collectively form the human body. The study of nutrition is not related to food and eating alone; it also considers how individual body cells are fed with nutrients. The body consists of millions of cells that need energy, oxygen, and nutrients for their existence, growth, and other functions. Nutrition is the sum of all the interactions between the human body and the food it consumes. In addition, humans have the ability to influence the direction of life and the nature of the environment in which they live. They are capable of making decisions in selecting foods, manipulating foods to their liking, improving the nature of foods, and attaching different cultural and social values to foods. Thus, the study of nutrition has become more complex and will become increasingly so with technological advances in food cultivation, processing, preparation, delivery, and consumption. Since nutrition is intimately related to foods, it also examines the balance of foods and nutrients.

The human body needs several specific substances that must be taken preformed and in sufficient quantities to meet its requirements. These essential substances are referred to as nutrients. Nutrients are derived primarily from foods. It should be clearly understood that food contains substances other than nutrients that are nonessential in the sense that they can either be produced by the body or are not needed by it. Some nutrients are needed in large quantities; others are not. Based on the quantity needed, they are classified as **macronutrients** (*macro* means "large") or **micronutrients** (*micro* means "small"). Water, carbohydrates, lipids, and proteins are classified as macronutrients; vitamins and minerals, which are needed in small amounts, are classified as micronutrients. Not all nutrients are present in one food. Some foods are major sources of a particular nutrient.

THE FUNCTIONS OF NUTRIENTS

Nutrients have three major purposes: (1) providing structure to the body, (2) providing energy, and (3) regulating body functions. The structure of the body consists of nutrients. The nutrients that contribute significantly to body structure are water, proteins, lipids, and minerals. Most adult humans use 1500 to 3000 kcalories or calories per day. Since calorie is commonly used and understood, it will be used to represent kcalories in all discussions in this book. Carbohydrates, lipids, and proteins are nutrients that provide energy, are also referred to as *energy nutrients*. Vitamins and minerals do not provide energy themselves but act as catalysts in the biochemical reactions of the body. These biochemical reactions utilize the energy produced by other nutrients.

Regulation of body processes is also an important function of nutrients. Nutrients promote the biochemical reactions that take place in the body, a process referred to as **metabolism.** Proteins, vitamins, and minerals are the chief nutrient regulators. Metabolic processes are carried out with the help of **hormones,** which serve as chemical messengers to regulate enzymes. **Enzymes** are protein substances that act as catalysts for reactions that are vital for different body processes. Vitamins and minerals participate in a series of reactions that eventually generate energy. Minerals such as sodium and potassium help to regulate the distribution of water within the body. Phosphorus and chloride help to regulate the acidity or alkalinity of various body substances. All of these regulatory functions are vital for bodily health, and lack of nutrients results in malfunction. Both inadequate and excessive intake of nutrients are referred to as **malnutrition.** When some or all nutrients are totally absent, the body will malfunction, stop growing, be more susceptible to infection, be incapable of reproduction, cease to function, and eventually die. If some or all of the nutrients are present in less than adequate amounts, the consequences will be less severe but still alarming—stunted growth, increased susceptibility to infection, less energy to perform routine daily functions, loss of body weight, and other complications. Ironically, the deficiency of a nutrient is detected only by the symptoms created by its absence. The consequences of inadequate intake and deficiency symptoms of each nutrient are described in the following chapters.

Like inadequate levels of nutrients, excess amounts of certain nutrients can be damaging. Toxicity or disturbance of the body's regulatory functions can result. These dangers are greater when nutrients, particularly vitamins and minerals, are derived from supplements rather than from foods.

The effects of nutrition vary over time based on the nutrients involved. Some effects of nutrients are immediate; a sugar-containing drink can be detected in blood soon after its consumption. Lack of water in the body is felt in a short period of time. The effects of other nutrients take weeks to see, such as a deficiency of vitamin C. By the same token, curing vitamin C deficiency is a slow process. Several weeks are needed to see marked improvement in the symptoms. Some nutrients have effects after months or years. For example, heart conditions and cancers related to nutrition take several months or years to become apparent.

THE PHYSIOLOGY OF NUTRITION

Although a thorough discussion of the physiology of nutrition is beyond the scope of this book, it is important to understand some of the basic roles of nutrients in physiological processes. Food, when consumed, undergoes several changes, and the release and absorption of nutrients are very complicated processes. The main processes involved are **ingestion,** which is primarily taking in food and cutting it into smaller, palatable portions; **digestion,** which prepares food for movement through different parts of the system; **absorption,** which moves nutrients into the interior part of the body; **circulation,** which carries nutrients to the cells and eliminates their waste products; **metabolism,** during which nutrients are used; and **excretion,** which transports waste products out of the body. Digestion is the process of breaking food down into substances that can be absorbed, whereas absorption is the process of taking digested substances into the body. The digestive system consists primarily of a hollow tube referred to as the **alimentary canal** or **gastrointestinal (GI) tract.** This tube begins at the mouth and ends at the anus. Although it is a connecting tube, its diameter varies from part to part, as shown in Figure 1.3. There are several secretions in different parts of the alimentary canal. These secretions include **mucus,** a slimy material that lubricates the tract, facilitating easy movement of the food; **enzymes,** which are proteins that speed up the rate

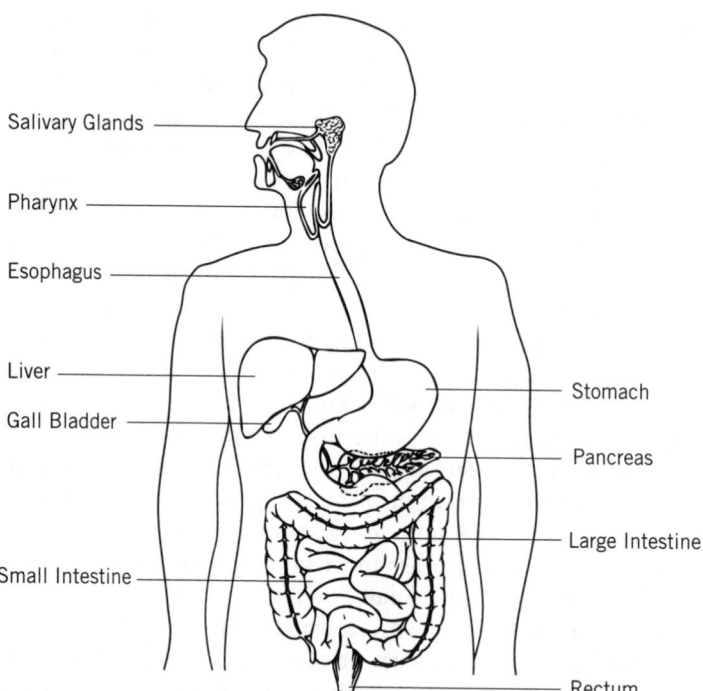

Figure 1.3 The Human Digestive Tract

of biochemical reactions; and **hormones,** which are chemical messengers that help trigger different reactions. In addition, there are different chemical compounds that facilitate digestion and produce acidity or alkalinity.

The brain starts the digestive process. The smell, sight, and sound of food trigger a reaction initiated by the brain that results in the secretion of saliva and other digestive juices. When food is ingested in the mouth, it is moistened, cut, chewed, mashed, and mixed together. This process is facilitated by additional saliva produced by the mouth. In addition to lubricating the food and the GI tract, saliva contains the enzyme **amylase,** which begins the breakdown of starch. The rhythmic movements of esophageal muscles help move food into the stomach. There the food mixes with the acidic content of the stomach, which helps digest it and breaks it down into smaller pieces, enabling absorption. Enzymes as well as other digestive juices in the stomach and small intestine help to break food down further and facilitate the absorption of nutrients. The stomach muscles squeeze and churn the contents, mixing the food with the digestive juices. The slushy blend of food at this stage of digestion is referred to as **chyme.** The digestive juices contain strong hydrochloric acid and enzymes that act on proteins. Little absorption takes place from the stomach. Chyme is emptied from the stomach over a prolonged period of time. Most of the nutrients are absorbed in the upper part of the small intestine. Carbohydrates, proteins, and fats are broken down into smaller units before absorption. Other substances, such as water, vitamins, minerals, and alcohol, are also absorbed. The **liver** secretes **bile,** a solution that is stored in the **gallbladder** until it is needed. Bile helps to keep the fats divided into very small droplets that can be digested easily, a process called **emulsification.** The **pancreas** produces secretions that contain alkali, which neutralizes the hydrochloric acid of the chyme. The pancreas also secretes enzymes such as amylases, proteases, and lipases, which acts on carbohydrates, proteins, and lipids, respectively. The structure of the lining of the small intestine promotes the absorption process. About 90 percent of the carbohydrate, fat, and protein are absorbed by the small intestine. Unabsorbed nutrients and other substances enter the large intestine and are eliminated in the feces. Water is absorbed in the large intestine. The nutrients are absorbed from the intestine into either the blood or the lymph. Both blood and lymph circulate throughout the body, picking up wastes and delivering needed products to the cells for use. Blood is composed of water, red blood cells, white blood cells that are important in providing immunity and resistance to disease, nutrients, and other components. Lymph is similar to blood but has no red blood cells and goes to areas where no blood vessels are available to feed the cells. Blood travels through the kidneys, where its waste products are released. The kidneys make and send urine to the bladder, which excretes it.

CONSUMER FOOD HABITS AND PREFERENCES IN RELATION TO NUTRITION

Managers in the hospitality industry should recognize that all consumers have knowledge of and experience with food (no matter how limited that may be), which makes them highly critical of food compared to other products. Nutritional intake is largely dependent on food habits and preferences—which, in turn, are intimately related to several complex beliefs and habits, which are very hard to change since they are acquired over a long period of time. The intake of nutrients depends on what foods are preferred, selected, and consumed. **Food preferences** may be defined as the selection of food items from among a variety of acceptable foods. Patterns of food selection may emerge as a consequence of temporary or permanent food preferences. **Food habits** may be defined as the way in which individuals, in response to social and cultural pressures, select, consume, and utilize the available food supply. Food preferences are based on sensory, social, psychological, religious, emotional, cultural, health, economic, preparation methods, and other related factors. Food habits and food acceptances are learned, acquired, and finally become a part of the self. They become a very strong form of individual expression. Several influences start acting on food preferences at birth and continue to operate throughout life. The most important factors that influence consumer food preferences should be taken into consideration when planning nutritional menus. For the intake of nutritionally balanced meals, it is vital to understand the factors influencing food intake. These factors are summarized below and presented in Figure 1.4, followed by a discussion of food characteristics.

Intrinsic Factors

Intrinsic factors include certain influences directly associated with foods, such as appearance, color, odor, texture, temperature, flavor, and quality. The way food is presented (including both desirable and undesirable attributes), the way it is arranged on the plate, and the temperature at which it is served all have an impact on food preferences. For example, standardized large-quantity food production may result in a different food preference ranking than when the same foods are prepared in a small quantity at home. Variability in these intrinsic factors affects food preferences.

Extrinsic Factors

Extrinsic factors include direct external factors that can affect food preferences, as described below.

Environment   Food preferences are affected by the environment in which food is served, such as homes, restaurants, nursing homes, and clubs. Good examples are a hospital and a candlelit restaurant, which have markedly different effects on the selection of food.

Situational Expectation   The quality of food one expects depends on the situation in which it is to be consumed. Food is expected to be good when it is associated with social, ritual, or religious occasions. Thus, the food served at a banquet or wedding party is assumed to be outstanding, in keeping with the occasion.

Advertising   It is evident, and has been proven by many studies, that advertising can influence one's attitude toward food. Many foodservice operations use adver-

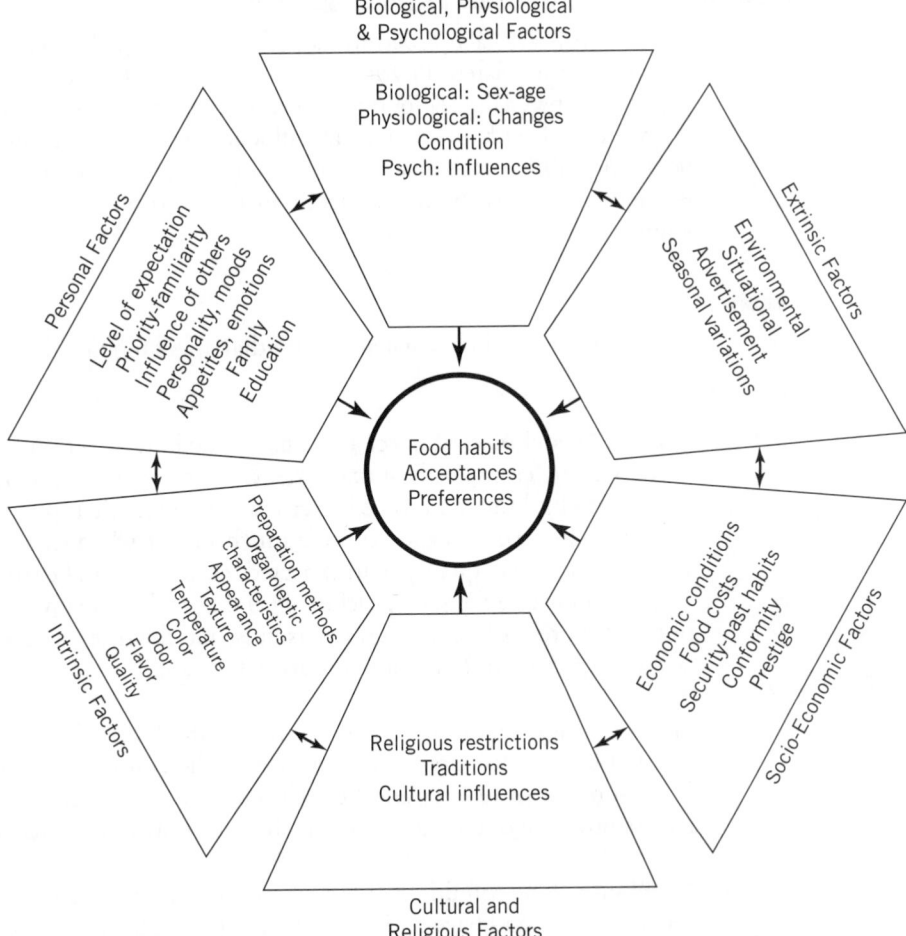

Figure 1.4   Factors Affecting Food Habits, Acceptance, and Preferences

tisements and promotions to attract customers. Consumers are tempted to try new food when it is appealingly advertised. Many restaurants advertise the specialties on their menus.

Time and Seasonal Variations   Food selections appear to be somewhat immune to the influence of certain natural phenomena, such as seasonal variations, outdoor temperatures, and the day of the week. However, the availability of certain foods, particularly fruits and vegetables, affects their selection. For example, watermelons are generally preferred during the hot summer months; hot chocolate is a winter favorite. Other factors, such as the hours of meal service and the length of meals, may also affect food preferences.

Biological, Physiological, and Psychological Factors

These factors are each broad in scope but are grouped together here because they are closely interrelated. Physiological disorders can have a profound effect on food preferences by changing food appreciation, perception, or appetite. These changes are associated with psychological influences commonly related to physical well-being. Age and sex are major demographic factors that influence food preferences. A good example is the higher acceptance of and preference for fast foods by the younger generation.

Personal Factors

The individual and personal attributes that affect food choices will now be considered.

Level of Expectation Expectations have a definite effect on food preferences and selection. For example, hospital patients have a low expectation regarding food. When they find the food to be better than expected, their preferences are favorably affected. The level of expectation is much higher when dining at a restaurant. If the food is of lower quality than expected, customers can be strongly critical. These reactions illustrate the sociopsychological theory that the lower the level of expectation, the more easily satisfied the person is, and further, that people perceive things as they expect them to be rather than as they are.

Priority Priorities are indirectly related to the level of expectations. Airline and hospital foodservices are good examples of the consumers' priority to reach their destination or to recover and be well, rather than to have gourmet meals. Thus, factors others than food are more likely to be critically evaluated.

Familiarity The conditions (both environmental and social) under which a person initially eats a food have an impact on acceptance behavior. Earlier studies showed that familiar terms on menus produced controversial results. Some research shows that menu acceptance is enhanced by the use of familiar terms, whereas other studies indicate that novel or descriptive menus may increase food appeal.

Influence of Other Persons Friends, family members, and other relatives can influence food preferences. Even those being served on a cafeteria line can influence the food selection of someone behind them. Individuals sometimes accept the selection of a person in front of them. They also accept food advice best from those they consider friends or professionals. As expected, parents are quite influential in the introduction and acceptance of foods by children.

Emotions and Moods The emotions have a complex influence on food preferences. A careless server may be spared for bringing cold food to the table when one is in a good mood; the same may not be true if one is in a bad mood. Food preferences also vary with mood. Moods are unpredictable and constantly changing, which causes problems for foodservice personnel. Moods and appetite are also influenced by physiological disorders, as well as such factors as satisfaction or dissatisfaction with work and other aspects of one's life. Food preferences may demonstrate one's personality, mood, and emotions.

Family Unit   A mother's educational achievements and employment status are associated with a familial influence on food preferences. A young family usually is more concerned with economizing than a middle-aged couple, who may be primarily concerned with reducing the calories, cholesterol, and salt in their diet.

Educational Status   The extent and type of education affect food preferences and selection. Nutrition knowledge and education also influence food preferences, but these factors alone do not ensure an adequate diet or the proper selection of foods.

Socioeconomic Factors

Socioeconomic factors operate when one is following set food patterns or is altering them temporarily or permanently to meet economic limitations. Abundant evidence in both developed and developing countries demonstrates that food choices are largely related to income. During such short-term crises as illness or unemployment, people tend to spend less on food and drink. One's sense of security can also be enhanced by retaining past food habits and resisting any change in them. Food preferences can be a means of demonstrating group acceptance, conformity, and prestige.

Cultural and Religious Factors

Cultural and religious influences on food preferences may be transmitted from one generation to another. Various religious restrictions have resulted in stable and rigid food preferences. For example, Muslims and Jews prohibit the use of pork and pork products. For nutritional planning in foodservice operations recognizing the food preferences of various population groups is very important.

The above-mentioned factors are interrelated and complex. All of them must be considered in planning nutritional menus, regardless of the type of foodservice. Food preferences must be analyzed carefully to avoid individual bias. Using informal and formal methods to analyze how consumers react to various menu items is useful. Informal observations in the dining room or the cafeteria line, comments made by consumers, what is left over, and the extent of food waste provide valuable information on food likes and dislikes, as well as nutritional intake. Formal surveys or 24-hour recall surveys can also be conducted. Food preferences of consumers should be assessed periodically to consider changes in technology, food availability, economy, and food habits. Consideration of food preferences is especially important in long-term nutritional planning of menus. Menu items have to be rotated to avoid repetition, particularly of foods that are not well liked. A method of ranking food preferences may also be developed, and when choices are provided, foods can be selected in such a way that similarly ranked items are included on the menu.

This will facilitate a balanced selection of items. Choices should be carefully weighed before inclusion since forecasting production becomes more complex with increases in the number of choices.

Food Characteristics

Probably the most important factor to be considered in nutritional planning is the food itself. Characteristics of foods, including their **organoleptic (sensory)** properties, play an important role in their acceptance. Some of the most important food characteristics are discussed below.

Color Interesting and coordinating color combinations promote the acceptance of food and, to an extent, indirectly help stimulate appetite. Planning and arranging foods so that there is a good color combination on a plate, tray, counter, or salad bar is important. Even a small garnish, like a parsley twig or a cherry, can make an enormous difference in the appearance of food. Color also emphasizes the variety available for selection and can be an indirect indication of nutritional richness. A consumer will often select food first by its eye appeal; thus, color is important in planning menus. Color also has a psychological impact on consumers. Red, orange, peach, pink, brown, yellow, and light green are considered desirable food colors, purple, violet, dark green, gray, and olive less so. Although artificial coloring may be added to enhance food colors, natural colors are preferable. Fruits and vegetables in a variety of shapes add to the colors of the menu items. Garnishing, plate decorations, and attractive counter displays add color and should be considered when planning menus.

Texture and Shape The textures and shapes of foods also affect consumers' preferences. Certain foods are preferred because of their hard or soft texture. A desirable combination of soft- and hard-textured menu items is essential. Impressions of the texture and shape of a particular food are formed even before it is tasted. Texture can best be detected by mouth feel. "Soft," "hard," "crispy," "crunchy," "chewy," "smooth," "brittle," and "grainy" are some of the adjectives used to describe food texture. Certain foods go well together. Soups are preferred with crisp crackers, soft-textured items go well with chewy steaks, and casseroles are desirable with crisp vegetables. Foods in different shapes add to the attraction of the menu, as well as to eye appeal when they are served. Vegetable and fruit carvings provide interesting shapes and add to food appeal.

Consistency **Consistency** refers to the degree of viscosity or density of a product. Like texture, consistency provides variety among food choices. "Runny," "gelatinous," "pasty," "thin," "thick," "sticky," and "gummy" are the most common adjectives used to describe consistency. Food items that have a hard texture complement those with a thin consistency. Relatively hard-textured meats go well with thin gravies, while nuts in thin items create a desirable combination of textures.

Flavor   It is obvious that the flavor has an important impact on food preferences. Foods can have sweet, sour, bitter, or salty flavors, which can be present alone or in combination. In addition, there are various off-flavors and undesirable flavors that hinder the selection of foods. A blend of flavors is desired since the predominance of one flavor in a meal is undesirable. Broccoli, cabbage, and onions, which provide strong flavors and have special nutrient contents, add to the flavor of meals.

Method of Food Preparation   Food can be prepared in many ways, and variety in preparation is preferred. Even the same food item is prepared differently by each household. Methods commonly used include frying, baking, broiling, boiling, steaming, grilling, braising, or a combination of these types. Each of these methods has an impact on food preferences, as well as on the nutritional content of foods.

Serving Temperature   Temperature is probably the most variable item when it comes to preferences. Food temperatures preferred by individuals vary with age and other personal factors. Both hot and cold temperatures are preferred for different types of food. There is no strong evidence that season or weather has an impact on the selection of particular temperatures of food.

Chapter 2

PROTEINS

The word **protein** is derived from the Greek word *protos,* which means "first." It is no coincidence that proteins get first priority in foodservice operations, since they are important from a nutritional point of view as well as represent some of the most expensive items served in any type of foodservice operation. Proteins are not single nutrients or substances. They are complex structures that include thousands of related substances. Proteins are made up of building blocks similar in structure known as **amino acids.** To understand proteins, it is essential to understand the structure and function of their amino acids. An amino acid is an organic substance consisting principally of carbon, hydrogen, and oxygen. Amino acids, unlike other organic nutrients, always contain nitrogen and sometimes sulfur. In order to understand the structure of amino acids, it is essential to know the makeup of a single amino acid. Each amino acid consists of an **amino group** that contains nitrogen; an **acid group;** and one or several connected atoms, referred to as a **side group.** Figure 2.1 shows the general structure of a typical amino acid.

Approximately 20 amino acids are commonly found in nature. Every living cell, with the help of carbon, hydrogen, oxygen, and nitrogen, can produce amino acids. However, not all 20 amino acids can be produced by cells. Ample amounts of carbon, hydrogen, and oxygen are available for the production of amino acids by cells, but the limiting elemental ingredient is nitrogen. Once all the elements are available, a living cell can produce amino acids. Amino acids can connect with each other to form protein molecules by linkages referred to as **peptide bonds.** If two

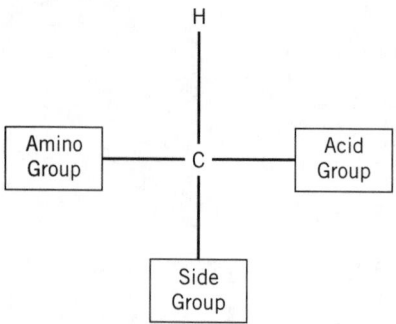

Figure 2.1 Structure of an Amino Acid

amino acids join, the resulting substance is called a *dipeptide;* if three amino acids join, they create a *tripeptide;* and a larger number of amino acids constitute a *polypeptide.* A protein structure may be complicated and may contain one or more polypeptides. It can be visualized as a long chain of amino acids that may contain anywhere from a few to several hundred amino acids. This chain of amino acids may be bent, folded, and/or coiled into specific three-dimensional shapes. The arrangement of amino acids in a protein molecule determines the type, characteristics, and properties of that particular protein. An analogy can be drawn by using different letters to form words. For example, if the letters A, E, M, R, S, and T represent different amino acids, they can be combined to form "MEATS," "STEAM," "TEAMS," "STREAM," and so on, which are different words made up of the same letters. Likewise, different proteins can be formed, although they may contain the same amino acids. Thus, amino acids found in blood may be very different from those found in foods. The human body has the ability to synthesize proteins if the right types of amino acids are available. The types of proteins made within the body are determined by the **deoxyribonucleic acid (DNA)** and **ribonucleic acid (RNA)** within the body cells. Extending the earlier analogy of words and letters, DNA and RNA direct the spelling of the "words"—the arrangement of amino acids in protein molecule. Foods contain different types of protein that may or may not be the types produced by the body. Different functions of proteins within the body are described below.

THE FUNCTIONS OF PROTEINS

Providing Body Structure

Proteins are part of every living cell and therefore are key components in the structure of the body. They are part of the cell membrane, the cytoplasm, and the nucleus; thus, they make up the entire structure of the body. The specific roles of proteins in body structure are evident from the muscles that constitute the skeleton, internal organs, connective tissue, and matrix of the bones and teeth. These muscles contain many different types of protein. The composition of body proteins varies not only from tissue to tissue but also from person to person. This variation depends on the makeup of DNA, which in turn is dependent on heredity. The content and arrangement of amino acids are crucial, and even a small disarray may result in serious diseases.

Regulating Body Processes

Proteins are responsible for regulating various processes within the body, some of the most important being **metabolic reactions. Enzymes,** consisting of special proteins, promote a variety of reactions and are critical for body processes and metabolism. For example, during digestion, various enzymes act on the foods, facilitating the digestive process. Thousands of enzymes are present within the body, each having different functions in metabolic processes. Without enzymes it would be impossible to conduct various activities, and many metabolic processes would take forever. Enzymes speed up reactions as well as carry out specific functions.

Other types of proteins also help carry out different metabolic activities. For example, **hemoglobin** is a blood protein that helps carry the oxygen needed for energy to body cells. Muscle contains **myoglobin,** a protein responsible for energy production in cells. **Hormones** are also very important proteins that are referred to as "chemical messengers." They are produced within the body and have specific functions. Hormones are responsible not only for reproduction but also for basal metabolism, emptying of the stomach, and other functions.

Proteins also act as the first line of defense for the body against invading microorganisms. Since they are part of skin and mucosal secretions, they attempt to destroy disease-causing organisms before they enter the body. They also are part of the bactericidal substances found in mucosal secretions. If disease-causing organisms enter the body, **antibodies** within the body identify and destroy them. These antibodies are body proteins. Proteins in cell membranes act as gatekeepers that control the body's **mineral balance.** Vital functions of the body, like the beating of the heart and the movement of organs, require an exact balance between electrolytes inside and outside the cells. This balance is also critical for proper functioning of muscles and nerves. Mineral ions are pumped into or out of the cells by proteins to maintain this balance. For example, sodium ions are pumped out of the cells by these proteins and potassium ions are pumped in, which keeps the muscles, such as that of the heart, beating. Proteins also help maintain the body's **fluid balance.** Like electrolytes, proteins help maintain fluid balance in the cells by equalizing the concentrations of particles on either side of the cell membrane. In the absence of proteins, this balance is difficult to maintain. In addition to providing mineral and fluid balance, proteins help maintain the **acid-base balance.** Body systems require a specific acid-base balance in different areas. Proteins help to maintain this balance due to their unique chemical makeup and characteristics. As we saw earlier, proteins contain both acidic (acid) group(s) and basic (amino) group(s), which help to maintain this critical balance. In the presence of excess acid in a system, the soluble proteins reduce the circulating acidity; if there is excess alkalinity, they decrease the pH. This action is performed by the **protein buffering system.** Without this type of buffering, it would be impossible for the body to survive. Some amino acids, like **tryptophan** and **tyrosine,** are referred to as the *precursors* of neurotransmission; they facilitate **nerve impulse transmission,** another important function of proteins.

Providing Energy

Like carbohydrates and fats, proteins can be metabolized for energy. Like carbohydrates, they provide 4 kcalories of energy per gram. This figure is an average for proteins; different types of protein provide less or more energy per gram of food consumed. As discussed earlier, proteins perform essential functions within the body, and they are needed more for those functions than for providing energy. The body tries to save proteins and to use carbohydrates and fat as the primary energy sources. If carbohydrate and fat supplies are insufficient, the body will use proteins to meet its energy needs. Within the body, proteins are continuously degraded and synthesized, turning over several times within 24 hours. In this conversion process, many amino acids are lost and have to be replenished by dietary sources. Proteins are *deaminated;* that is, the amino group is detached and the rest of the structure is metabolized, as in the case of carbohydrates. The nitrogen is excreted as urea, and the keto acids left after removal of the amino groups are either utilized directly as sources of energy or are converted to carbohydrates or fat. Carbohydrates have a protein-sparing function. On the other hand, if there is an excess supply of proteins, the body will use it for energy or will store it as fat.

DIETARY PROTEIN NEEDS

Proteins are needed for two purposes: (1) for the nitrogen they contain and (2) for the amino acids that cannot be synthesized within the body. Amino acids are required for the synthesis of body proteins, peptide hormones, and some neurotransmitters. Most important amino acids are synthesized within the body. For this synthesis to take place, the body needs enough nitrogen, which is provided by proteins. Thus, the first need is to get enough protein in the diet to provide sufficient nitrogen so that the body can synthesize the required amino acids. For the purpose of calculation, approximately 16 percent of the weight of proteins consists of amino nitrogen. The second body need is for good-quality protein. Good-quality protein has adequate amounts of essential amino acids that the body cannot synthesize. The nine amino acids that are essential in the diet are referred to as such: **essential amino acids.** Eleven other amino acids are called **nonessential** because the body can produce them. Protein quality is determined by the amount of essential amino acids that are present in a particular protein. Although the allowances are expressed as grams of protein, the biological requirement is for amino acids. The essential and nonessential amino acids are listed in Table 2.1.

Table 2.1   Essential and Nonessential Amino Acids

Essential Amino Acids	Nonessential Amino Acids
Histidine	Alanine
Isoleucine	Arginine
Leucine	Aspargine
Lysine	Aspartic acid
Methionine	Cysteine[a]
Phenylalanine	Glutamic acid
Threonine	Glutamine
Tryptophan	Glycine
Valine	Proline
	Serine
	Tyrosine[a]

[a] Cysteine and tyrosine are considered nonessential, but they can substitute in part for methionine and phenylalanine, respectively.

Due to their amino acid content, proteins in meat are of higher quality than plan proteins. Eggs and milk provide the best-quality proteins. Other good protein sources are meats, fish, poultry, and cheese. Among plant sources, soybeans are considered the best. Other sources include legumes, nuts, seeds, grains, and other vegetables. Gelatin is considered a low-quality protein. The quality of protein is evaluated by the proportion of essential amino acids provided and by their impact on weight gain. Measurement of the weight gain of a growing animal compared to its protein intake yields a value referred to as the **protein efficiency ratio (PER).** The quality of protein depends on the amino acid content, and generally enough amino acids appear in the diet so that the body's needs are easily met. Also, the proteins from plants and meat complement each other in foods when used in combination.

For digestion and absorption, proteins have to be broken down into amino acid units. Stomach acid denatures proteins, and the digestive enzyme pepsin splits the peptide bonds. Breakage of the peptide bonds shortens proteins, and other enzymes in the small intestine work further to release amino acids. The released amino acids then travel to the liver and other organs where they are needed.

Proteins as such are not stored in the body but are present only in the form of amino acids. Whenever the body needs proteins, these amino acids are pulled together to synthesize new ones.

FOOD SOURCES OF PROTEINS

Proteins, whether from plant or animal sources, provide about 20 amino acids, classified earlier as essential or nonessential. The proportion of these amino acids varies in almost all proteins except gelatin. It is estimated that about 10 to 12 percent of the kcalories come from proteins. More than half of the proteins in the diet come from meat, poultry, and fish.

As stated earlier, the quality of proteins refers to the amounts and types of amino acids present in foods. Food proteins that contain all of the essential amino acids in the proportions needed are referred to as high-quality or **complete proteins.** Animal proteins such as those in meats, poultry, fish, eggs, milk, and other dairy products are complete proteins. An essential amino acid lacking or low in a protein is referred to as a **limiting amino acid.** Limiting amino acids are like the weak link in a chain, since they limit the usefulness of a protein. Foods with limiting amino acids can be complemented by other foods that contain those amino acids. Proteins lacking one or more essential amino acid are referred to as **incomplete proteins.** Compared to animal proteins, most plant proteins are incomplete. Sources of plant proteins include legumes such as beans, peas, lentils, grains, nuts and seeds, and vegetables. Most of these are incomplete proteins. They are rich in fiber but lack one or more essential amino acids. Thus, a balance of plant and animal proteins in the diet can have a good complementary effect and help provide essential amino acids. This phenomenon is referred to as **complementing.**

The amounts of proteins in selected foods are listed in Table 2.2. As examples, the average amounts of proteins provided by selected foods are shown in Figures

Table 2.2   Protein Content of Selected Foods

Foods	Serving Size	Proteins (grams)
Ground beef	3 ounces	21
Beef liver	3 ounces	23
Beef steak	3 ounces	25
Roasted chicken	1 cup	41
Chicken breast	1 breast	27
Chicken drumstick	1 drumstick	14
Fish sticks	2 sticks	12
Cod	3.5 ounces	20
Milk	1 cup	8
Processed cheese	1 ounce	6
Whole wheat bread	1 slice	3
Green peas	1 cup	8
Soybeans	1 cup	20
Lima beans	½ cup	6
Whole eggs (large)	1 egg	6
Egg white	1 white	3
Egg yolk	1 yolk	3
Peaches	1 peach	1
Oils	1 tablespoon	0

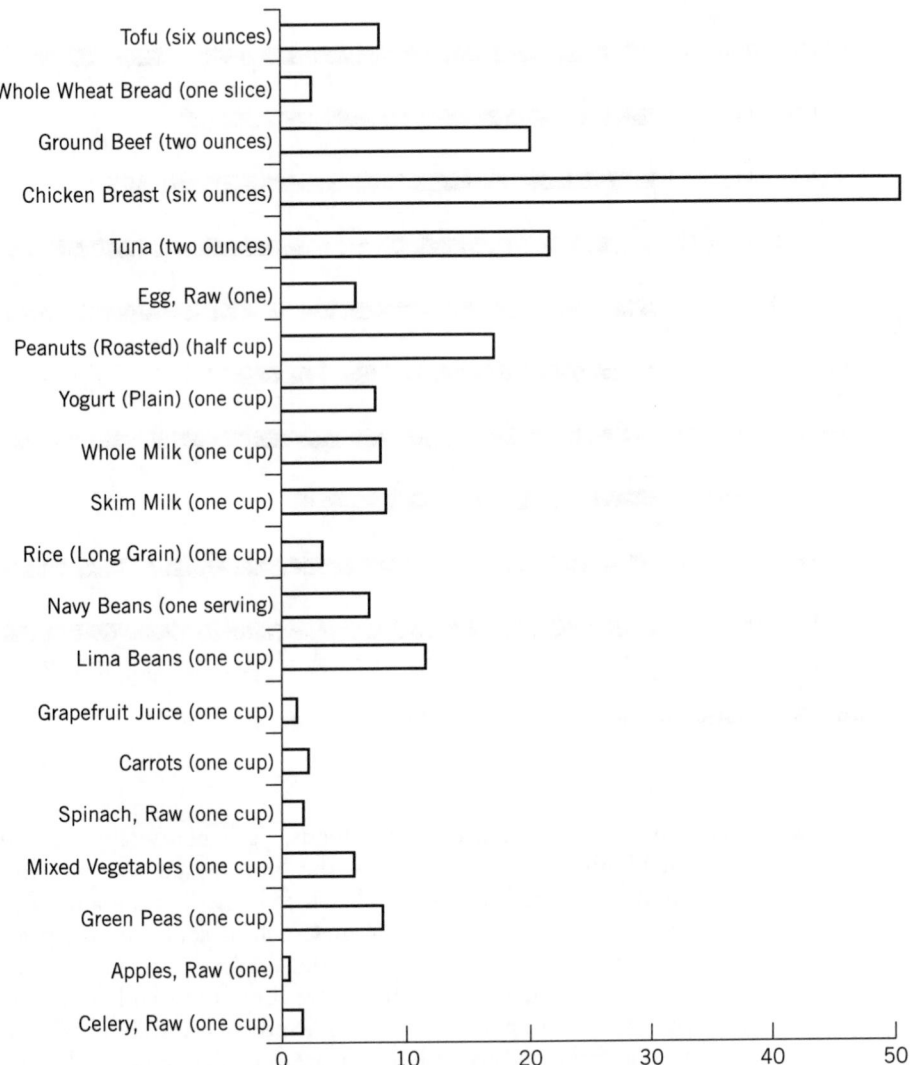

Figure 2.2 Protein Content of Selected Foods

2.2 and 2.3. In general, fruits and vegetables have incomplete proteins. With the exception of legumes, plant proteins are generally low in protein. Even legumes are incomplete proteins since they lack one or more essential amino acids. Grains and cereals contain considerable quantities of proteins, but they are also incomplete. Since most animal proteins are complete, a combination of plant and animal proteins provides good complementation. Soybeans contain protein quantities almost equal to those of many meat products and should be considered in nutrition

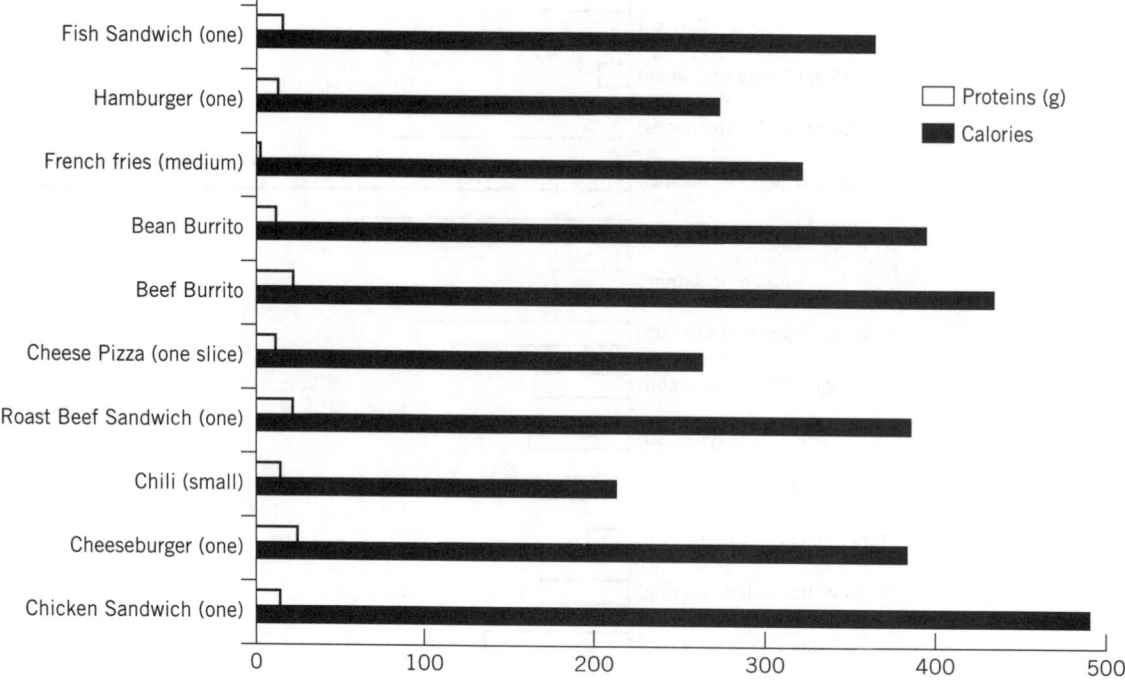

Figure 2.3 Caloric Content and Protein in Prepared Foods

supplementation. Most plant foods, particularly legumes, nuts, and seeds, have methionine and tryptophan as the limiting amino acids; in grains, the limiting amino acids are lysine and isoleucine. These limiting amino acids can be provided by other plant proteins. Legumes such as starch beans, peas, and lentils can be combined with grains or nuts and seeds to provide the limiting amino acids. Examples of such combinations are lima beans and rice, lentil curry on rice, pea soup and wheat crackers, bean chili and rye bread, bean burrito with wheat or corn tortilla, baked beans with wheat bread or rice, ground chickpeas and sesame seeds (hummus), and tofu recipes with sesame seeds.

Because of their rich protein content, soybeans are processed in many different ways. Soy proteins are separated from soybeans and marketed as soy protein isolates. These soy proteins can be spun into strands of texturized vegetable proteins. They can also be converted into cubes or shaped as hot dogs, cutlets, or meatballs. When appropriately flavored, they can be served as meat analogues. To enrich their quality, limiting amino acids are added to soy proteins, making them wholesome. For supplementation, soy protein concentrates are also available. Tofu, a curd product made from soybeans, has been used for many years. Soy foods in different combinations are used as meat substitutes, beverages, snack foods, and condiments.

PROTEINS IN FOODSERVICE OPERATIONS

Proteins have certain properties that make them extremely useful in any foodservice preparation. Most of the desirable changes in proteins result from **denaturation,** the process by which the protein chain uncoils and changes shape. Denaturation occurs in the presence of heat and acid, as well as with changes in pH. During cooking and mixing with other ingredients, proteins undergo denaturation. Exposure of the surfaces of protein-containing foods to heat determines the extent of denaturation. Sometimes, when steaks cook on high heat, the outer surface may be quickly denatured, forming a thick film, while the inside is left uncooked. This is why tossing, turning, or flipping protein-containing food is desirable for proper and uniform cooking. Another method by which proteins change is called **coagulation.** During coagulation, when proteins are denatured or when the protein chains uncoil, they get into cross-bonding, becoming coherent and firm. This cross-bonding results in a gel or semisolid formation. It occurs, for example, when egg, a rich source of proteins, is cooked or poached. If an egg is fried over slow heat, the transparent white slowly becomes opaque and finally firm and tough. Similar changes take place when meats are cooked, resulting in firming of the proteins and hardness upon overcooking. By the same process, baked custard becomes firm. The extent of cross-bonding determines the extent of solidification of proteins, with more solid formation resulting from intensive cross-bonding. Coagulation can be facilitated or delayed by adding certain ingredients, like salt or acid. However, the stability of coagulation depends on the temperature; high temperatures or cooking for a long period of time results in destabilization. This destabilization occurs when liquids escape from the cross-bonds as they become progressively tighter. This process, which is often described as "weeping," is also referred to as **syneresis.**

The properties of proteins are extremely helpful in baking. The process of hydration and kneading results in changes in protein structure, facilitating stretching and manipulation. Good examples are pasta products, which can sometimes be stretched for miles under proper conditions. The coagulation of gluten results in the rigid structure of breads. The proteins that develop during kneading and hydration of dough are solidified on baking, giving a nice texture to breads. Air can also be incorporated among these proteins. This texture, as well as the air that is incorporated in dough, is visible from holes such as those seen in toast. This sort of structure may be desirable in certain products, such as breads, or undesirable in other products, such as pastries or cakes. Thus, different methods of handling flour and baking are needed to achieve different textures in baked products. In other words, food proteins can be manipulated to produce different types of products with desirable qualities.

Proteins are useful thickening agents. When flours are used to thicken sauces, the proteins expand and provide a smooth texture. Normally, the more protein in the flour, the gummier the sauce. Proteins are also used as leavening agents. For example, when eggs are beaten, the air is incorporated in their proteins, resulting in their expansion and stretching. Upon heating, these proteins coagulate and provide texture and flavor. The resultant products are lighter and have increased volume.

To achieve the desired quality, it is therefore essential to control the amount of beating, manipulation, or blending of protein-containing foods. This property is utilized in preparing a number of products, such as soufflés, batters, doughs, and icings, in which beaten egg whites are added to provide desired volume and lightness of texture. Egg whites whip faster and achieve greater volume if they are at room temperature. Acids such as cream of tartar or lemon juice are added to foams to increase their stability. Stiffly beaten egg whites will have good volume and will stand up in peaks after whipping. However, there are optimum time, temperature, and physical parameters that should be taken into account; if they are not, proteins lose their desirable qualities.

Meat protein structures are similarly affected by heat. **Collagen** is a protein occurring mainly as connective tissue in meats. It is the white, fibrous tissue found between other meat proteins. On heating in the presence of liquids, the collagen fibers contract and break down into gelatin. Similarly, bones, when heated, form gelatin. This gelatinous material is present in stocks containing bones. Another muscle protein, **elastin,** is a yellow connective tissue. It does not break down on heating and provides the chewiness in cooked meats. The tenderness of meats thus depends on the types of proteins present and on how they are affected by controllable factors such as cooking methods, temperature, pH level, and cooking ingredients. To soften some of the hard connective tissue protein in meats, mechanical means are used. Grinding, beating, and the use of additives act on these proteins, changing their chain structure. Tenderizing agents such as enzymes are also used for this purpose. **Papain** (found in raw papaya fruits), a common enzyme found in meat surface tenderizers, acts by digesting muscle proteins. Acids, such as vinegar, and salts are also used as tenderizers. Tenderization also takes place when these ingredients are added in marinades.

Two other meat proteins, **hemoglobin** and **myoglobin,** are also affected by heat. It is interesting to note that different meat proteins react in different ways when heated, all imparting special properties to the quality of cooked meats. Hemoglobin and myoglobin, which are red in color due to the presence of oxygen, are denatured on heating and turn brown when meats are cooked.

Protein gels are made by using gelatin since they can soften when heated and solidify when chilled, thereby increasing their versatility in food preparations. This property is also utilized in the preparation of different types of sauces. Proteins also inhibit the crystallization process, whereby ice and crystals are formed in frozen foods such as desserts.

Milk proteins undergo similar changes on heating or in the presence of certain additives. The chief milk protein is **casein.** The variety of changes exhibited by proteins allows different kinds of products to be made with milk. For example, when milk is coagulated, curds are formed that separate from the liquid whey. This happens when milk is chilled too rapidly or heated too long in products such as soups, sauces, and custards. Cheeses are made from milk curds by using proteins that become tough, stringy, airy, soft, or cakelike, with different physical and chemical changes.

Proteins, due to their physical and chemical properties, are versatile in any type of foodservice operation. In fact, menu flexibility and variety are due primarily to the different characteristics of proteins. In addition, proteins are present in all food groups and therefore provide flexibility in food selection. Protein-containing food items are very expensive and need careful handling before, during, and after preparation.

Chapter 3

CARBOHYDRATES

C arbohydrates do not represent a single nutrient or a food but rather a family of very important nutrients. There is a general misconception that carbohydrates are rich in calories. The fact is that they provide 4 kcalories per gram, the same number provided by proteins and less than half of those provided by fats. Other names by which carbohydrates are commonly known are **starches** and **sugars.** From the foodservice point of view, carbohydrates are an important group of nutrients that play a significant role in practically all menu items. Carbohydrates provide not only variety in menus but also bulk in food items. They are essential for several important body functions, which are described below.

THE FUNCTIONS OF CARBOHYDRATES

Providing Energy

Carbohydrates provide energy and are considered fundamental fuel for the body. As noted above, they provide 4 kcalories of energy per gram. It should be noted that this number is an average; not all carbohydrates provide exactly the same amount of energy. For example, fibers provide a minimal amount of energy, whereas sugars and starches are major energy sources. The variation in kcalorie content among carbohydrates is an important characteristic that is helpful in planning healthy diets while balancing the caloric content of menu items. Compared to fats and proteins, carbohydrates do not leave residues that may harm the body; therefore, they often are referred to as "clean" body fuel.

Sparing Proteins

Proteins are needed by the body for different physiological functions. When carbohydrates are readily available, proteins are spared for fulfilling other important body functions, as discussed earlier. If carbohydrates are not provided in the diet, the body will use proteins, which are needed for other purposes, particularly brain and nervous system functioning.

Providing Bulk

Carbohydrates provide bulk, or solid materials, in the GI tract, facilitating the movement of intestinal muscles and food. The beneficial effect of fiber in preventing colon cancer is well established. Also, adequate amounts of fiber absorb water, some as much as 20 times their weight, and help relieve constipation by providing bulky feces.

Promoting Fat Metabolism

Carbohydrates play an essential role in the metabolism of fat. They help at different stages of fat metabolism, facilitating the digestion of fats. Metabolic processes in the digestion of fat are very complicated and will be briefly discussed in Chapter 4.

TYPES OF CARBOHYDRATES

Carbohydrates are so named because they are made up of carbon, hydrogen, and oxygen. The typical structure of a carbohydrate (glucose) is presented in Figure 3.1. As the figure shows, the molecules can be linked together to form various combinations of saccharides.

Thus, carbohydrates actually belong to a family of saccharides (commonly referred to as *sugars*). The simplest form of saccharide is known as a **monosaccharide,** also referred to as a **simple sugar.** Examples of simple sugars are glucose, fructose, and galactose. Sugars (primarily glucose) are formed in green plants by the process of photosynthesis. Monosaccharides are the building blocks of carbohydrates. Although most sugars remain in the form of glucose, some are converted to fructose. **Glucose** (sometimes called **dextrose** or **blood sugar**) is the simplest form of carbohydrate that the body uses for conversion into energy. Eventually, all types of carbohydrates are broken down into glucose for use by the body. **Fructose** (sometimes called **levulose**), is also known as **fruit sugar** since it is present in many fruits and imparts its sweetness to many plant foods. Fructose in its natural form is very sweet. **Galactose** is another monosaccharide found mainly in milk and milk products and is a component of milk sugar. It is important to become familiar with these monosaccharides, since many carbohydrates in foods

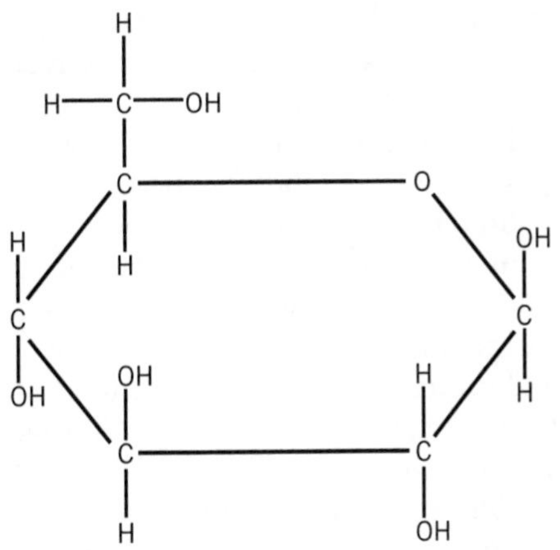

Figure 3.1   The Structure of Glucose

contain them in simple or complex form. Simple sugars have only one molecule and play a major role in baking and cooking. They can join to form **disaccharides,** which, as their name implies, are formed by the linking of two monosaccharides. For example, glucose and fructose can combine chemically to form a disaccharide, sucrose. Other examples of such combinations are:

$$Glucose + glucose \quad = maltose$$

$$Glucose + fructose \quad = sucrose$$

$$Glucose + galactose = lactose$$

Thus, two molecules of glucose can combine to form **maltose,** which is also known as **malt sugar** since it is obtained from starch in barley. Maltose is used as a sweetener in many cereals and drinks. Similarly, a molecule of glucose can link with a molecule of fructose to form **sucrose,** also known as **table sugar,** the sugar in everyday usage. In the same fashion, glucose and galactose can link together to form **lactose** or **milk sugar,** which is present in milk and milk products. Both sucrose and lactose are used extensively in food preparation and are responsible for a variety of flavors in recipes. For example, sucrose, in addition to providing sweetness, is responsible for many flavors in baked goods. Similarly, lactose can be converted to lactic acid, which imparts sour flavors to a variety of foods. Although most of these sugars vary in sweetness, they do not vary significantly in the number of kcalories provided, since these are essentially carbohydrates. There is a misconception that some sugars, such as fructose, have fewer calories than sucrose.

Like disaccharides, many monosaccharides can join to form complex structures referred to as **polysaccharides.** Polysaccharides are complex carbohydrates consisting of many monosaccharide units linked together in long chain(s). Examples of polysaccharides are starches, dextrins, and fiber. Some of the glucose produced in plants is converted to polysaccharides (such as starches), which are the insoluble, nonsweet forms of carbohydrates. They are composed of scores of glucose units linked together.

From the foodservice point of view, polysaccharides can be grouped into two types: (1) starches and (2) fibers.

Starches are very large molecules and are commonly present in plant foods. Chemically, starches are polymers of glucose. Roots, tubers, and seeds commonly contain large amounts of starches. Starches are found in plants in a granular form. The granules contain two types of sugar molecules known as **amylose** and **amylopectin.** These differ in structure, although both have glucose unit linkages. Due to the arrangement of these linkages, amylose and amylopectin have different characteristics.

Fibers are also found primarily in foods of plant origin and provide food components that cannot be broken down by digestive processes. Dietary fibers are primarily indigestible complex carbohydrates found in plant cells. In addition, a variety of gums, mucilages, and algal polysaccharides are complex carbohydrates. The linkages formed by polysaccharides are acted on only with difficulty by enzymes and cannot be broken down easily. However, they provide bulk in foods and are now considered an important ingredient to consider in planning menus. There are different types of fibers, such as **cellulose** and **hemicellulose,** both of which are present in many plant cells. Fruits, vegetables, grains, seeds, and nuts all contain these fibers. They are concentrated in the protective outer layer of grains such as wheat, sorghum, and rice. This outer layer, referred to as **bran,** is commonly used as a source of fiber in many baked products due to its fiber content. These fibers are mainly insoluble in water; however, some fibers are soluble, such as **pectins** and **gums.** Apples, guavas, and some citrus fruits have pectins that are useful in food preparations. Gums are also found in selected plants and are used primarily in processing a variety of manufactured foods. Carbohydrates are also classified as **available carbohydrates,** which are digestible, and as **unavailable carbohydrates** such as fibers.

Although sugars are naturally present in plants, there are various ways of processing and preparing them in crystalline or powdered form. Sugars are extracted or processed from natural sources to form a variety of sweeteners. In foodservices the common sweeteners used are table sugar, brown sugar, maple syrup, molasses, white sugar (pure sucrose), and honey. **Confectionery sugar** or **Baker's sugar** has different grades of texture. Sweeteners are formed from the starches found in grains such as corn, rice, and barley. Lactose is extracted from **whey,** a by-product formed during cheese making. Whey itself is added to many foods when lactose is needed. **Glycogen** is a starch that is manufactured in animal and human bodies. It is usually concentrated in liver and muscle tissues and is used as an energy reserve.

The relationship between different types of carbohydrates is outlined in Table 3.1. Through chemical combinations, carbohydrates have the unique property of either joining together or breaking apart. Monosaccharides can link to form di- or polysaccharides, and these links can be broken by hydrolysis. Thus, when

Table 3.1 Classification of Major Carbohydrates

| Simple Carbohydrates | | Complex Carbohydrates | |
| | | Polysaccharides | |
Monosaccharides	Disaccharides	Available Polysaccharides	Polysaccharides Not Digested by Humans (fibers)
Glucose	Sucrose (glucose and fructose)	Starches	Cellulose
Fructose	Maltose (glucose and glucose)	Dextrins	Hemicellulose
Galactose	Lactose (glucose and galactose)		Pectins
			Gums

carbohydrate-containing foods are consumed, sugars and starches are broken down into glucose. This glucose becomes the major source of energy for cells.

SOURCES OF CARBOHYDRATES

Most of the carbohydrates derived from foods are from plant sources. Plants can make their own carbohydrates by photosynthesis. Most plants contain sugar in some form; the sugar content varies in different parts of plants. While fruits contain a large concentration of sugar, most roots, leaves, stems, and tubers contain smaller amounts. On the other hand, fruits contain less starch than roots and seeds. Grains, nuts, legumes, root vegetables, potatoes, and sweet potatoes are good sources of starch. Compared to plants, animal tissues contain less carbohydrates. Animal sources of carbohydrates consist primarily of milk and milk products. Glucose, sucrose, and fructose are carbohydrates commonly used in foods such as ice cream, gelatin, desserts, soft drinks, sherbets, sweet baked products, cereals, cookies, and candies. Carbohydrate-rich foods are listed in Table 3.2. Good sources of dietary fiber based on selected serving sizes are shown in Table 3.3. The digestible carbohydrate and dietary fiber contents of selected fruits and vegetables are shown in Figure 3.2, and those for combination foods are shown in Figure 3.3.

Gums are used in manufactured foods and are derived from exotic sources such as seed pods, shrubs, and trees of tropical origin. These gums are referred to and labeled as **guar gum, locust bean gum, gum tragacanth, gum arabic,** and **xanthan gum.** They are used commonly in ice creams, cereals, fruit drinks, and canned foods. From seaweeds **agar, carrageenan,** and **alginates** are derived, which are used as stabilizers and thickeners in different food products. Fiber is found primarily in plant foods such as dried beans and peas.

One teaspoon of sugar contains approximately 5 grams of carbohydrates, which provide about 20 kcalories. The amount of carbohydrates used determines the total calories in foods. If the amounts of different carbohydrates are varied, calories in foods can be adjusted without sacrificing sweetness. For example, honey and molasses may be used in smaller quantities, thereby providing sweetness as well as fewer calories. Nonnutritive sweeteners usually contain other substances, such as saccharin and aspartame, rather than sugars. It is not common practice to use nonnutritive sweeteners in recipes. These are provided only as a substitute for table sugar. Some of the foods rich in carbohydrates are described below.

Wheat

Wheat is used in many baked products, ready-to-eat cereals, pasta, and similar products, largely in the form of flour. It is classified as **soft** wheat or **hard** wheat, based on its protein content. **Durum** wheat is a hard wheat with a relatively high protein content and, when grounded, forms **semolina** flour, which is used in making pastas such as macaroni, noodles, and spaghetti. Different flours are used in the preparation of a variety of baked goods, pastries, doughnuts, and so on. Whole wheat can also be used in products such as bulgar, which are steamed and dried and consist wholly or partially of cracked wheat. They provide a nutty flavor to foods and can be used in combination with other cereals, as well as in the preparation of pilafs, stuffings, salads, mixed cereals, and other recipes.

A typical serving of bread, starchy vegetables, or grains weighing 15 grams provides about 60 calories. Wheat bran is also used as a fiber source in baking or cooking. Another useful product is **wheat germ,** which is separated from the whole wheat grain. This can be added to baked goods, cereals, salads, casseroles, stuffing, and breading. Wheat germ contains oil; when used in food products, it should be kept fresh by proper refrigeration.

Table 3.2 Carbohydrate Contents of Selected Foods

Foods	Serving Size	Weight (g)	Carbohydrate Contents (g)	Dietary Fiber (g)	Kcalories
Fruits and Vegetables					
Peach	1 (medium)	87	10	1.7	37
Apple	1 (medium)	138	21	3.7	81
Carrots	1 cup	212	22	5.1	91
Spinach (raw)	1 cup	56	2	1.5	12
Romaine lettuce	1 cup	56	1	1.3	9
Peas (green)	1 cup	160	23	8.8	125
Mixed vegetables (boiled)	1 cup	182	24	4.0	140
Potato (baked)	1 (medium)	202	51	4.9	220
Sweet potato	1 (medium)	114	28	3.4	117
Celery	1 cup	213	8	3.8	34
Lima beans	1 cup	170	40	9.0	209
Navy beans	1 serving	223	19	4.4	107
Broccoli	1 cup	88	5	2.6	25

Table 3.2 *(Continued)*

Foods	Serving Size	Weight (g)	Carbohydrate Contents (g)	Dietary Fiber (g)	Kcalories
Breads					
Whole wheat	1 slice	25	13	2.2	69
French	1 slice	25	13	0.7	69
Italian	1 slice	30	15	0.9	81
Pita (whole wheat)	1	64	35	4.8	170
Rye	1 slice	32	16	2.0	83
Sourdough	1 slice	25	13	0.7	69
Bagel (plain)	1	71	38	1.5	195
Grain Products					
Popcorn	1 cup	8	6	1.2	31
Rice (white)	1 cup	165	35	1.3	162
Cornflakes	1 cup	30	26	1.0	110
Cake (chocolate)	1 slice	65	32	—	198
Cookie (chocolate)	1	16	9	—	78
Beverage					
Diet cola	1 fl ounce	30	0.01	0	0.1
Cola	1 fl ounce	31	3.2	0	13
Juice (apple)	1 cup	251	29	0.3	118
Juice (grapefruit)	1 cup	247	22	0.2	94
Combination Foods					
Corn pudding	1 serving	89	17	1.1	108
Cherry pie	1 slice	180	69	—	486
Cheese pizza	1 slice	63	21	—	140
Macaroni and cheese	1 serving	413	22	1.3	358
Hamburger	1	137	32	—	425
Beef burrito	1	206	48	2.0	432
Bean burrito	1	198	58	8.0	390
Peanuts	0.5 cup	73	16	5.9	427
Pasta (spaghetti)	1 cup	140	40	2.4	197
Pasta (noodles)	1 cup	140	32	2.2	155
Milk and Milk Products					
Yogurt (plain)	1 cup	193	46	0	306
Milk (whole)	1 cup	244	12	0	150
Milk (skim)	1 cup	245	12	0	86
Ice cream (chocolate)	1 cup	132	37	—	285

Table 3.3 Sources of Dietary Fiber Based on Selected Serving Size

Food	Selected Serving Size (at Least 2 Grams of Dietary Fiber)
Breads, Cereals, and Other Grain Products	
Bagel, whole-wheat	1 medium
Biscuit, whole-wheat	1 medium
Breads (multigrain, pumpernickel, rye, white, and whole-wheat blend, whole-wheat, or whole-wheat with raisins)	2 regular slices
Bulgar, cooked or canned	⅔ cup
English muffin, whole-wheat	1
Muffins, bran or whole-wheat	1 medium
Oatmeal	
Instant, fortified, prepared	⅔ cup
Regular or quick, cooked	⅔ cup
Rolls	
Multigrain	1 large
Whole-wheat	1 medium
Fruits	
Apples	
Dried, cooked, unsweetened	½ cup
Raw	1 medium
Applesauce, unsweetened	½ cup
Apricots, dried	
Cooked, unsweetened	½ cup
Uncooked	¼ cup
Banana, raw	1 medium
Blackberries, raw or frozen, unsweetened	½ cup
Blueberries, frozen, unsweetened	½ cup
Dates, chopped	¼ cup
Fruit mixture, dried	¼ cup
Guava, raw	1
Kiwi fruit, raw	1 medium
Mango, raw	½ medium
Nectarine, raw	1 medium
Orange, raw	1 medium
Peaches, dried	
Cooked, unsweetened	½ cup
Uncooked	¼ cup
Pears	
Canned, juice-pack	½ cup
Dried, cooked, unsweetened	½ cup
Dried, uncooked	¼ cup
Raw	1 medium

Table 3.3   *(Continued)*

Food	Selected Serving Size (at Least 2 Grams of Dietary Fiber)
Prunes, dried	
Cooked, unsweetened	½ cup
Uncooked	¼ cup
Raisins	¼ cup
Raspberries, raw or frozen, unsweetened	½ cup
Strawberries, frozen, unsweetened	½ cup
Tangelo, raw	1 medium
Vegetables	
Artichoke, globe (french), cooked	1 medium
Beans, green or lima, cooked	½ cup
Beets, cooked	½ cup
Broccoli, cooked	½ cup
Cabbage, cooked	½ cup
Carrots, cooked	½ cup
Okra, cooked	½ cup
Parsnips, cooked	½ cup
Peas, green, cooked	½ cup
Potato, boiled, with skin	1 medium
Snow peas, raw or cooked	½ cup
Spinach, cooked	½ cup
Squash, winter, cooked, mashed	½ cup
Sweet potato, baked or boiled	1 medium
Tomatoes, stewed	½ cup
Meat, Poultry, Fish, and Alternates	
Dry Beans, Peas, and Lentils	
Beans; black-eyed peas (cowpeas), calico, chickpeas (garbanzo beans), lima, Mexican, pinto, red kidney, or white; cooked	½ cup
Lentils, cooked	½ cup
Peas, split, green or yellow, cooked	½ cup
Nuts and Seeds	
Almonds or chestnuts, roasted	2 tablespoons
Peanut butter	2 tablespoons
Pine nuts (pignolias)	2 tablespoons
Pumpkin or squash seeds, hulled, roasted	2 tablespoons
Sesame seeds	2 tablespoons
Sunflower seeds, hulled, unroasted	2 tablespoons

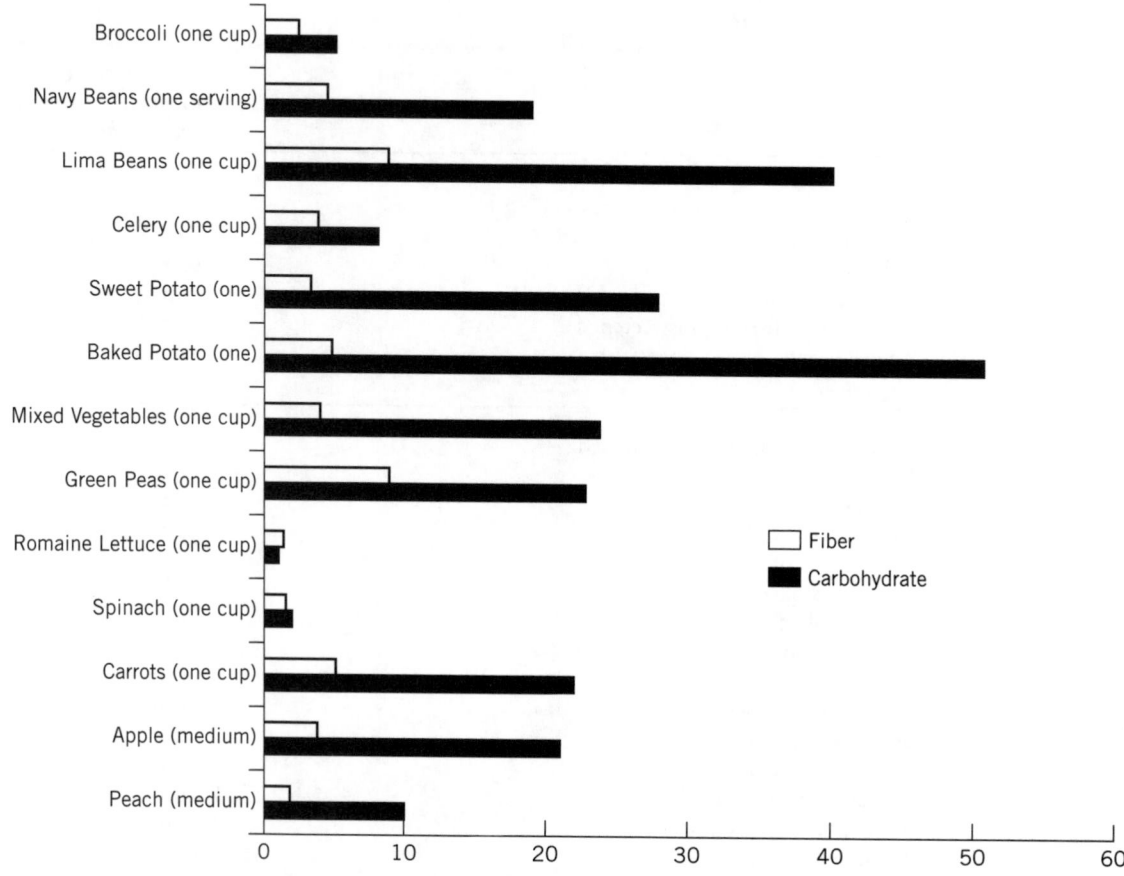

Figure 3.2 Carbohydrate Content of Selected Fruits and Vegetables

Corn

In addition to being commonly used in foods in various forms, corn is indispensable in food processing. Many carbohydrate products are derived from corn. Corn in ground form is used as cornmeal, which can be yellow or white. **Hominy** is prepared by soaking whole corn kernels after removing the germ and bran. Dried ground hominy is referred to as **grits.** Corns used as popcorn are of a special variety that pops at lower temperatures. Stone-ground whole cornmeal is used in several recipes, such as those for preparing porridge. Corn is also used extensively in making **tortillas** and chips.

Rice

Rice is commonly used as a side dish, and the recipes containing rice are numerous. Rice is also used in the forms of cereals and flours. Based on the length of

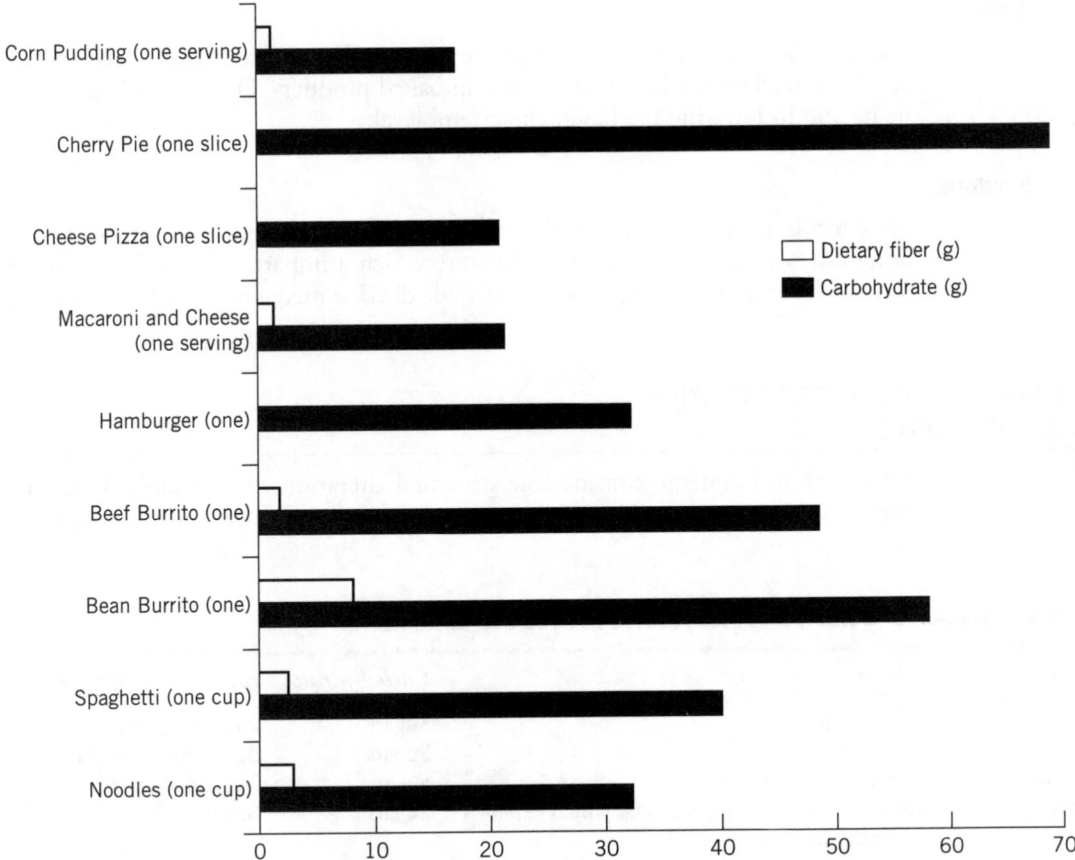

Figure 3.3   Digestible Carbohydrate and Dietary Fiber Content of Selected Combination Foods

the grain, rice is classified as long-grain, medium-grain, or short-grain. There are many varieties of rice, which on cooking provide different flavors and textures.

Rye

Rye is used as flour only in combination with other flours, as well as in the preparation of different breads. Rye flour is classified as light, medium, or dark.

Barley

Barley is commonly used in soups after the germ and bran are removed and is referred to as **pearled barley.** Barley that contains bran is a rich source of fiber. Barley is used in soups, casseroles, stews, cooked cereals, and pilafs. Malt is also produced from barley.

Oats

Oat flour is used in cereals, baked products, granolas, and some baby foods. Oats are also mixed with other flours for use in baked products. Oat bran is believed to be helpful in lowering the blood cholesterol level.

Sorghum

Sorghum is a type of millet used in many recipes in different parts of the world. Sorghum flour is used in baked products, to which it imparts a distinctive flavor. It can also be used in making porridge, as a side dish, or mixed in vegetable casseroles.

THE IMPACT OF FOOD PREPARATION ON CARBOHYDRATES

Carbohydrates undergo considerable structural alteration when subjected to heat, acid conditions, pressure, water, and other chemicals. Dry heat, such as that from

Table 3.4   Function of Selected Carbohydrates in Food Preparation

Function	Action	Carbohydrate	Examples of Applications
Sweetness	Inherent property	Sugars	Pies, cakes, drinks
Flavor	Inherent property	Sugars	Baked foods, custard
Stabilization	Stabilizes beaten egg foams	Sugars	Pies, baked foods
Volume	Incorporates air into products, which expands on baking	Sugars	Breads, cakes
Tenderization	Inhibits gluten development and delays starch glutenization	Sugars	Specialty breads
Caramelization	Surface crust formation and development of flavor	Sugars	Candies, breads
Aroma	Due to caramelization	Sugars	Breads, candies
Preservative	Takes up moisture required for some bacteria to survive	Sugars	Jams, jellies, preserves
Texture	By dissolving and mixing with ingredients	Sugars	Custard, frozen desserts
Texture	By adding soluble or semisoluble constituents	Fiber	Bran muffins, multigrain breads
Gelatinization	Absorption of water, resulting in swelling of the granules	Starches	Peas, rice
Thickening agent	By absorbing moisture	Fiber	Gums in foods
Thickeners	Thickens liquid mixtures and batters by absorbing moisture	Starches	Soups, sauces
Elasticity	Gluten development	Starches	Breads, pastas
Consistency	Thickening	Starches	Sauces, soups
Viscosity	Thickening by dissolving in water	Fiber	Jams, jellies
Moisturization	By trapping moisture	Fiber	Gums in foods

ovens, causes the large starch molecules to break down into dextrins. Some starches break down into units of disaccharides such as maltose. In this case, starches are referred to as **malted starch,** which is normally used in processed cereals. Starches have the unique ability to thicken or gel, which is used in a variety of ways in food preparation. Some starches are specially treated to enhance their ability to thicken or gel; after treatment, they are referred to as **modified starches.** They are very useful in preparing soups, sauces, puddings, and a variety of products that need thickeners.

Several compounds called **sugar alcohols** are structurally related to sugars and are used as sweeteners. Examples of sugar alcohols are mannitol and sorbitol, which are "sugarless" substances used in chewing gums and candies. As noted earlier, carbohydrates are rich source of fibers, which undergo little change during food preparation. However, fiber may be purposely or inadvertently discarded during prepreparation steps such as peeling and coring vegetables and fruits or removing bran from wheat or rice. Bran can be added to flours or cereals or even used as a topping on salads. Food processing can itself cause considerable changes in the fiber content of foods. Due to the increased significance of fiber in foods, many food manufacturers are adding it back. For example, bran is being added to a number of baked goods and breakfast cereals. Bran is also marketed separately for use in foodservice recipes. In addition to adding fiber to foods, bran helps to lower the total kcalories provided by foods. Pectins and gels are used in refined form in jams, jellies, candies, and other foods as thickeners, emulsifiers, or stabilizers. Pectins are refined from orange or apple peels and used in making jams, jellies, and candies. The functions of selected carbohydrates in food preparation are shown in Table 3.4.

CARBOHYDRATES AND HEALTH

Carbohydrates are often associated with body weight and are erroneously considered to be fattening. However, they are not fattening and do not provide kcalories that are more fattening. As indicated earlier, within the body, sugars and starches are broken down into glucose, which is a major source of energy. When more carbohydrates are consumed than are needed for energy, they are converted to fats, which are stored as reserves within the body. Thus, it is the excess caloric intake from different foods that results in weight gain; whether the calories come from fat, protein, or carbohydrates is immaterial. Carbohydrates are also linked to tooth decay due to the production of cavities. Cavities, or caries, occur when susceptible teeth are exposed to acids over an extended period of time. These acids are produced when bacteria metabolize common sugars in the mouth. Common sugars such as sucrose, glucose, fructose, lactose, and maltose are all fermentable and are almost equally cariogenic. Since they are fermentable, bacteria can convert these sugars into acids that are responsible for tooth decay. Several indirect factors in tooth decay are also associated with food, such as stickiness (which keeps the sugar in the mouth for a long time) and the amount and frequency of eating foods that are high in sugar.

Although the carbohydrates in foods do not have the importance they deserve, they are preferred sources of energy since they are efficient to use and can be easily and cleanly converted to energy. Glucose is the sole source of energy for the brain and the nervous system, which play an important role in the normal functioning of the body. Carbohydrates also play a role in the regulation of fat metabolism. Low levels of carbohydrates in the diet result in the slowdown of body metabolism. In the absence of carbohydrates, the body will use fats or proteins for energy. The use of fats may result in by-products such as ketones, which may harm the body. The use of proteins may be very costly since they may be needed for other important body functions. Fiber-containing foods such as fruits, vegetables, and grains, in addition to providing fewer calories, help reduce the risk of some forms of cancer. Dietary fiber is also known to provide laxation, lower serum cholesterol, lower blood pressure, improve glucose metabolism, and aid in weight maintenance—all of which are associated with reduced risks of heart disease, diabetes, and obesity. Dietary fibers are converted to absorbable fatty acids by intestinal microorganisms. The advantages of dietary fibers include increased satiety and softening of stools. In addition, some fiber components, such as oat bran and pectin, are reported to reduce the plasma cholesterol level. Complex carbohydrates are preferred in diets since they are absorbed relatively slowly and help maintain an even level of blood glucose. A careful assessment of all these factors shows that a diet rich in fiber is indirectly involved in the reduction of heart disease, colon cancer, and diabetes.

Caloric contents are not indicative of the concentration of sweetness; for example, 1 teaspoon of honey is sweeter than 1 teaspoon of sugar. A typical serving of bread, grains, or starchy vegetables provides approximately 15 grams, or 60 calories. A single slice of bread provides about 70 calories. Since it is desirable to reduce the intake of fats and proteins, it is important to use carbohydrates as the energy source. Thus, more than half of the energy should come from carbohydrates. For a person consuming 2000 kilocalories per day, this amounts to about 1000 kilocalories per day. Since carbohydrates provide 4 kilocalories per gram, the quantity of carbohydrate needed in the diet will be 250 grams. However, this intake should come primarily from complex carbohydrates rather than from sugars.

RECOMMENDED DIETARY FIBER INTAKE

Carbohydrates do not have an RDA, although their role in nutrition is significant. One reason for the lack of allowance is that carbohydrates can be produced by the body from proteins. There are estimates of the RDA considering their use in the body, particularly when the protein supply is limited. Daily recommendations for carbohydrates range from 110 to 200 grams. These recommendations are sometimes given as percentages of the total caloric intake per day.

Recommendations for fiber intake for adults range from 20 to 35 grams per 1000 kcalories. Many Americans consume about half of the recommended amount of dietary fiber. Some people find that dietary fiber causes increased gas and bloating, which can be attributed to the bacterial fermentation of fiber. Generally, this discomfort subsides as the body adapts to the increased fiber intake. Lactose intolerance is a condition in which digestion of lactose becomes a health problem. Menu items can be selected in such a way that the lactose content is reduced and foods that cause this condition are avoided.

THE ROLE OF CARBOHYDRATES IN FOOD PREPARATION

The role of carbohydrates in food preparation is wide-ranging, and one of the most important carbohydrate groups so used is sugars. It is not only their sweetness but also other properties that make sugars practically indispensable in foods. As frequently as sugars are used as sweeteners, starches are used as thickeners. The role of carbohydrates in foods can be understood primarily by examining the role of sugars, starches, and fibers in food preparation.

Sugars

The most common form of sugar in food preparation is the granular form, used mainly as a sweetener either at the dining table or in the kitchen. Sugar is available in white or brown form. The sweetness and other characteristics of the two sugars are comparable. Brown sugar differs mainly in color due to the presence of molasses left while processing and refining sugar. In some cases, brown sugars are preferred due to their color and their special flavor characteristics. Sugar granules are graded based on their crystalline nature. Confectionery sugars are finely ground and mixed with cornstarch. These sugars are preferred for baking since they do not cake easily due to the presence of cornstarch. Since they are finely ground, they mix well and do not remain grainy. They are used in a wide variety of confectionery items such as candies, pastry fillings, and frostings. Also, finely ground sugar is preferred for drinks and mixing since it dissolves quickly without leaving granules. Sweeteners are also available in liquid or semiliquid forms such as corn syrup, molasses, and honey. Corn syrup is widely used in food processing, and many confectionery products contain it in some form. Corn syrup provides viscosity, which prevents crystallization. When fine glazes are needed, this property is very desirable. Corn syrup also preserves the moisture in processed foods, prolonging their quality.

Apart from their sweetening properties, sugars play an extremely important role in baking. In most baked products, sugar forms a basic ingredient in addition to flour, shortening, eggs, liquids, and leavening agents. The amount and type of sugar determines the finished quality of any baked product. Sugars provide tenderness and texture to baked products. They absorb water, which maintains the texture by promoting the formation of gluten and reducing the rigidity of batters. Moisture is also needed for the thickness of gels, thereby solidifying products. Sugars are sometimes used more for its moisture-providing properties and texture than for sweetness. The moisture-retaining property of sugars calls for precise control of their content in recipes. Too much sugar can retain moisture, making it unavailable for gelling or rendering the baked product watery.

Sugars also help make baked products softer, lighter, and fluffy. When mixed with other ingredients, sugars help to create air pockets in doughs and batters. These air pockets expand when baked at high temperature, leaving a lighter product, such as is desired in many breads and cakes. In a similar manner, when egg foams are beaten, air cells are embedded in them that expand when baked. Sugars are also believed to provide food for yeast, thereby speeding the leavening action due to quicker release of carbon dioxide.

Sugars are also preferred for their help in two processes, caramelization and syneresis. *Caramelization* results in the formation of crumbs or special flavors in many baked products. It causes surface browning and provides texture and aroma, in addition to desirable color. The property of caramelization is used in many candies and confectionery products. In *syneresis*, water droplets are formed on the surface due to the rapid coagulation of egg whites in baked products. Sugars permit slow coagulation of egg proteins, creating a stable and consistent product. Sugars also act as preservatives since they reduce moisture, which is necessary for the survival and multiplication of bacteria.

Although many of the properties of sugars are helpful in food preparation, care should be taken in their use since sugars can adversely affect the outcome of a recipe, resulting in a product of inferior quality. For example, excess sugar may lead to the absorption of liquid that would otherwise be needed for expansion of starches or for the formation of gluten in flours.

Starches

Starches, in general, provide texture, stability, viscosity, and translucency to foods. The grains mentioned earlier contain large amounts of starches, which are very useful in food preparation. Starches vary in forms such as tubers (potatoes), grains (rice), and legumes (peas); thus, their role in food preparation varies considerably. They possess the property of gelatinization, which is extremely useful in food preparation. Starches undergo remarkable changes when cooked, especially when heated with water, which causes them to swell. This property is extremely helpful when using starches as thickeners in soups and sauces. Starch granules can absorb as much as two to three times their weight in water, forming gels or semisolid pastes. Starches thicken when heated to about 90°F and begin to gelatinize at about 200°F. Thus, there is a point at which thickening of starches will stop and thinning will take place. This is why careful handling of sauces is necessary to impart the desired degree of thickness, controlling the amount of starches used as well as the temperatures to which they are heated. Wheat flour and cornstarch are commonly used in food preparation. Flour-based sauces are opaque, whereas those from cornstarch are translucent.

Starch is only one of the components used in baking, acting in combination with other ingredients such as salt, leavening agents, sugar, eggs, liquid, and shortening. It is the combination of all the ingredients in the right amounts, baked under optimum conditions of temperature and time, that results in a quality product. It is very important to understand the role of starch in baking and its interaction with other ingredients.

Fiber

As discussed earlier, fiber plays a major role in providing texture to foods. There are different types of fiber and their characteristics vary considerably, some breaking down easily on cooking and others remaining fairly hard. Major fruit and vegetable fibers consist of cellulose, hemicellulose, pectin, and lignin. Celluloses and hemicelluloses are insoluble in water and remain hard to viscous, depending on the food source; for example, fibers from celery, asparagus, and parsnips are hard to dissolve, whereas pectins are easily soluble in water. Some polysaccharides, particularly gums, are used as thickeners in many processed foods. Brans are usually high in cellulose, and fruit fibers are high in pectin. Pectin is commonly used in jams, jellies, and preserves.

From the dietary point of view, fiber has become very important and is being added to different baked products and other prepared food recipes. When fiber is added, the texture and consistency of food are affected. Since fiber is not soluble, quality products require ingredients that can bind or keep the fiber from falling apart.

Chapter 4

LIPIDS: FATS AND OILS

ats and oils are normally classified as **lipids,** fatty substances that usually do not dissolve in water but do dissolve in ether. Terms such as *monoglycerides, diglycerides,* or *cholesterol,* which are commonly seen on food packages, all indicate lipids. **Fats** are solid lipids and **oils** are liquid lipids. They come in a variety of forms, which are commonly used in foodservice operations. Fats and oils, which are the most abundant lipids found in nature, have become extremely controversial due to their role in human health. Lipids have been associated with such conditions as high blood pressure, stroke, cardiovascular diseases, certain types of cancer, and obesity. Some of the claims are debatable and need further studies. Although lipids have gained a bad reputation, they are responsible for some of the delicious flavors in foods. They provide aroma, moistness, tenderness, and a sense of satiety. They can enhance palatability by absorbing and retaining flavors and by influencing the texture of foods. In addition, they provide desirable chemical and physical properties that are crucial in food preparation. They also perform a variety of functions when consumed in the diet. These functions are described below.

THE FUNCTIONS OF LIPIDS

Providing Energy

Lipids provide twice as much energy per gram as carbohydrates and proteins. They provide 9 kcalories per gram, making them the most concentrated source of energy of the three macronutrients derived from foods. Fats contain more carbon and hydrogen atoms in proportion to oxygen, which accounts for their higher energy value compared to carbohydrates and proteins. One tablespoon of oil weighs about 5 grams and provides 45 calories. The body can store unlimited amounts of excess fat in adipose or fat tissue. This creates a problem when excess fat is derived from foods. This energy reserve can be converted to fuel when the body lacks other energy sources.

Providing Essential Nutrients

Lipids provide essential nutrients for the body in the form of **linoleic acid** and **linolenic acid.** These fatty acids are essential when the body grows. They are present in abundance in plant oils.

Carrying Fat-Soluble Vitamins

The fat-soluble vitamins A, D, E, and K are absorbed by the body when they are dissolved in fats. Since these vitamins are very important, the role that lipids play as carriers is significant. Lipids carry these vitamins in foods, as well as within the body.

Providing Thermal Insulation

It is estimated that roughly half of the adipose tissue in the body is located just under the skin in a layer referred to as **subcutaneous fat.** This layer of fat constitutes a thin internal blanket that helps preserve the body's heat. This is an advantage in colder climates.

Protecting Vital Organs

Adipose tissue also surrounds vital organs and acts as a cushion against shocks and bruises.

Providing Components

Lipids are necessary components of various body parts such as cell membranes, hormones, nerve coverings, and some digestive secretions. **Cholesterol,** a lipid, performs many of these functions.

Providing Satiety

Since lipids remain in the stomach longer than other nutrients, they have higher satiety value. Thus, they indirectly reduce the appetite and probably the amount of food intake.

TYPES OF LIPIDS

Lipids are classified on the basis of their structural properties. The major types of lipids, based on their significance in foods and diets, are glycerides, phospholipids, and sterols. These lipids are discussed below.

Glycerides

Glycerides are the most common form of lipids, and most food labels show them in some form. They consist of one, two, or three **fatty acids** attached to a molecule of **glycerol.** Glycerol attached to one fatty acid is referred to as a **monoglyceride;** one containing two fatty acid is called a **diglyceride;** and one with three fatty acids is called a **triglyceride.** Fats and oils are mostly triglycerides, which account for almost 90 percent of the weight of lipids in foods. Thus, when fat is referred to in food, it is generally in the form of triglycerides. Mono- and diglycerides also occur commonly in nature. The attached fatty acid(s) give lipids their special characteristics. Fatty acids differ from each other most significantly in chain length and degree of saturation. It is therefore important to understand their structure since their characteristics depend on it. *Chain length* refers to the number of linked carbon atoms in the fatty acid structure (Figure 4.1). Length can vary from 2 carbons, as in acetic acid (found in vinegar), to 14 carbons in meats. The fatty acid components of lipids are classified as short-chain (fewer than 6 carbons), medium-chain (6–10 carbons), or long-chain (12 or more carbons). The shorter the fatty acid chain, the more likely it is that a glyceride will be liquid at room temperature. For example, milk fat has many short-chain fatty acids. Triglycerides with long-chain fatty acids are solid at room temperature. For example, red meats have long fatty acid chains. There may be anywhere from 4 to 22 carbons in a fatty acid. The temperature at which butter or margarine liquefies depends on the characteristics of these carbon chains.

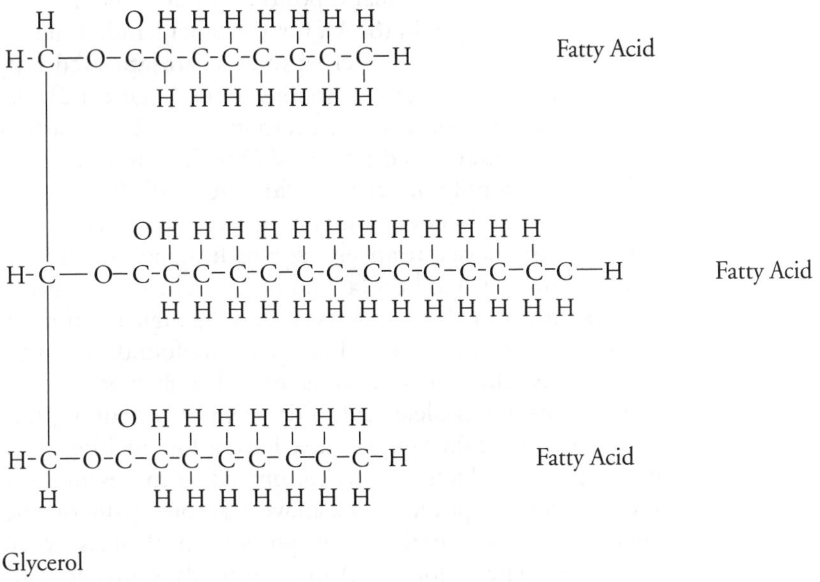

Figure 4.1   The Structure of a Triglyceride

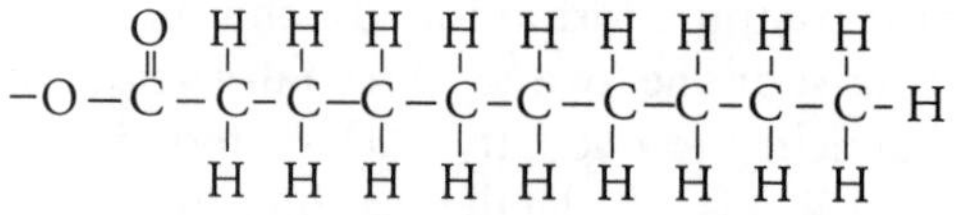

A. A Saturated Fatty Acid (SFA)—filled with as much hydrogen as it can hold

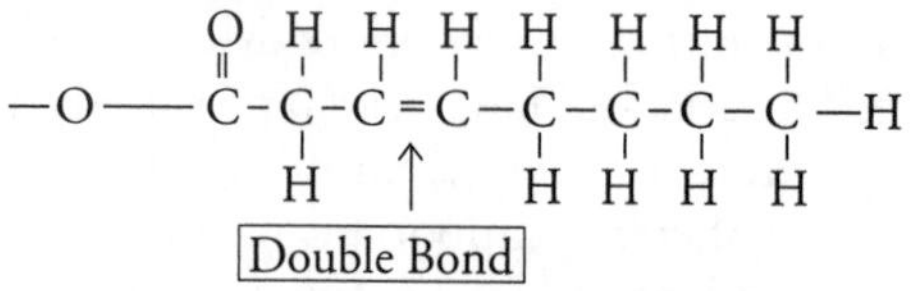

B. A Monounsaturated Fatty Acid (MUFA)—with one double bond

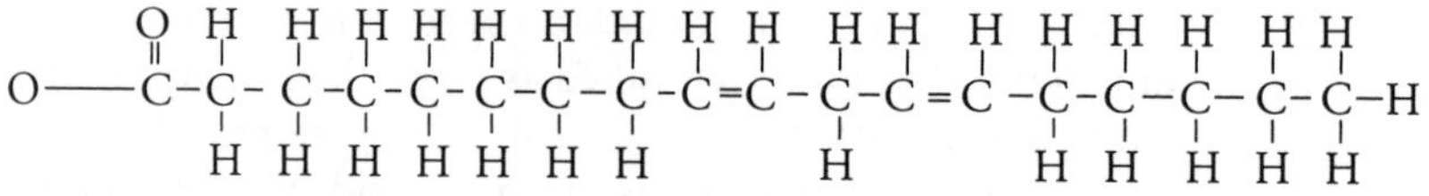

C. A Polyunsaturated Fatty Acid (PUFA)—with two or more double bonds

Figure 4.2 Different Fatty Acid Structures

From the foodservice point of view, a very important factor is **saturation,** degree to which hydrogen atoms fill all available positions in the fatty acid skeleton. When hydrogen atoms hold all available positions in the structure, the fatty acid is referred to as a **saturated fatty acid (SFA).** On the other hand, if the fatty acid has room for more hydrogen atoms, it is referred to as an **unsaturated fatty acid.** Unsaturated carbon atoms are connected by double bonds (Figure 4.2). In other words, a fatty acid with no double bond between carbons is an SFA. A fatty acid with one double bond is a **monounsaturated fatty acid (MUFA),** and a fatty acid with two or more double bonds is a **polyunsaturated fatty acid (PUFA).**

In general, triglycerides containing large amounts of SFAs are solid at room temperature and have a relatively high melting point. They are generally found in animal products such as beef fat and butter. The major SFAs in foods are palmitic acid and stearic acid. Triglycerides containing high amounts of MUFAs are usually liquid at room temperature and are generally found in plant foods such as olives, avocados, nuts, olive oil, and canola oil. They melt at relatively low temperatures. The major MUFA is oleic acid. Triglycerides containing mostly PUFAs are also usually liquid at room temperature, have a low melting point, and are generally found in plant products such as cottonseed, corn, sesame, soy, and safflower oils. There are some exceptions to the above examples; palm oil and coconut oil, which are plant products, contain a high proportion of SFAs, whereas fish oils contain many PUFAs. The major PUFA in plant foods is linoleic acid. Table 4.1 describes the contents of SFAs, MUFAs, and PUFAs in various foods.

Table 4.1. Fat Content of Selected Common Foods

Foods	Portion Size	Cholesterol (mg)	Saturated Fat (g)	Mono Fat (g)	Poly Fat (g)
Pizza—cheese	1 slice	9.45	1.54	0.99	0.49
Potato chips	1 ounce	0	1.54	5.11	2.60
French fries	Large	0	4.00	2.00	5.00
Chocolate chip cookie	One	11.2	2.25	1.32	0.73
Corn chips	1 ounce	0	1.29	2.74	4.67
Whole milk	1 cup	3.86	0.59	0.27	0.04
Chocolate ice cream	1 cup	44.90	8.98	4.24	0.54
Cheddar cheese	1 ounce	30.00	6.00	2.68	0.27
Chicken breast	One	157.00	2.22	2.96	1.84
Salad dressing—ranch style	1 tablespoon	3.90	0.74	1.35	2.70
Salad dressing—oil and vinegar	1 tablespoon	0	1.42	2.31	3.76
Salad dressing—Italian	1 tablespoon	0	1.03	1.65	4.12
Salad dressing—French	1 tablespoon	9.05	1.48	1.25	3.38
Salad dressing—blue cheese	1 tablespoon	2.60	1.51	1.88	4.25
Salad dressing—thousand island	1 tablespoon	4.06	0.94	1.29	3.09
Egg	1 large	212.00	1.55	1.91	0.68
Hamburger	1 large	14.69	1.74	2.05	0.44
Fried chicken	2 ounces	51.76	0.73	0.98	0.61
Beef taco	1 serving	63.00	8.68	8.76	2.86
Roast beef sandwich	1 serving	43.10	7.00	8.00	3.50
Cheeseburger	1 serving	65.00	9.00	7.02	1.17

Phospholipids

Phospholipids, as their name indicates, are a combination of phosphorus and lipids. These compounds resemble triglycerides except that a phosphorus-containing unit is a substitute for one of the fatty acids. Phospholipids facilitate digestion, absorption, and transportation of lipids in the body. They help retain moisture in the body, particularly in the skin. A common phospholipid is **lecithin,** which is found in cell membranes. It mixes well with both watery and oily substances, a property that classifies it as an **emulsifier.** Lecithin is added to foods such as margarine to give them a smooth, uniformly blended quality. It is also used for emulsification in salad dressings, whipped toppings, and many processed foods.

Sterols

Sterols are structurally different from triglycerides in their arrangement of carbon, hydrogen, and oxygen. They are insoluble in water and soluble in ether. The best-known sterol is a compound that has received wide publicity: **cholesterol.** So important is cholesterol that the body manufactures its own supply, much more than is normally taken in through the diet. In the presence of ultraviolet rays from

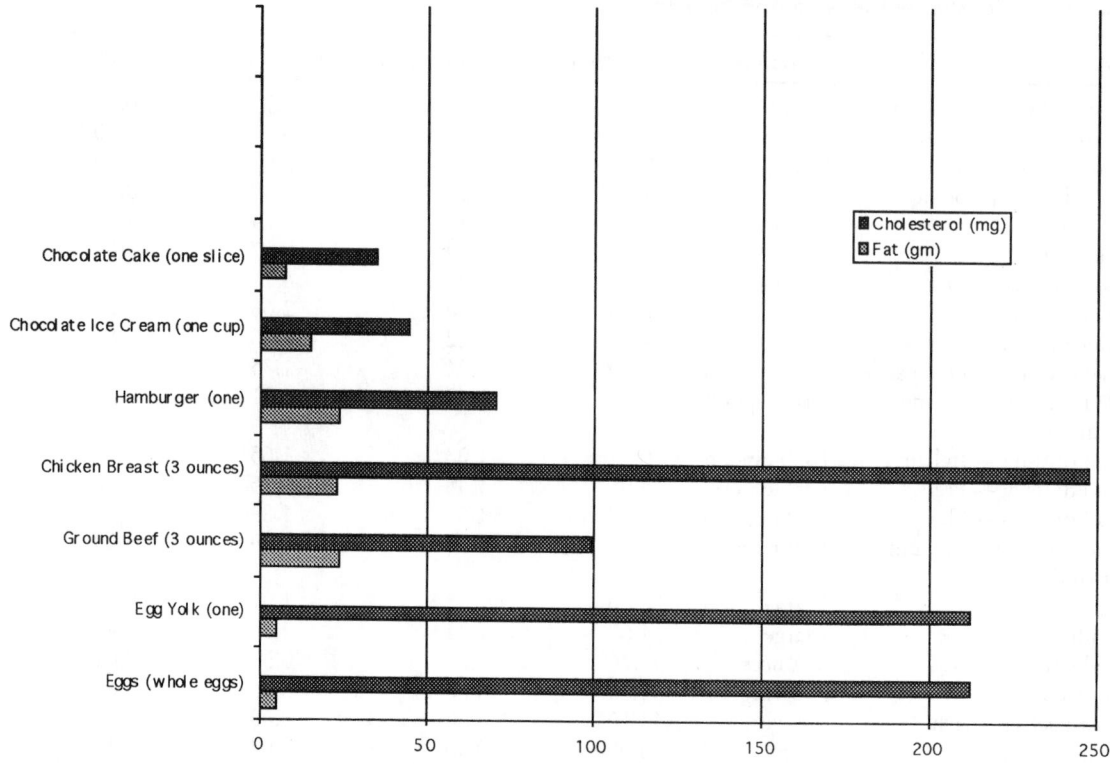

Figure 4.3   Fat and Cholesterol Content of Selected Foods

the sun, cholesterol in the skin forms vitamin D. Cholesterol is found in eggs, dairy products, meat, poultry, fish, shellfish, and organ meats such as liver. Rich sources of cholesterol in foods are egg yolks and organ meats, including liver, kidney, sweetbread, and brain. Plants do not make cholesterol or store it, so fruits, vegetables, and grains do not contain it. In short, cholesterol and saturated fats are lipids typically found in animal products. Figures 4.3 and 4.4 show the fat content and cholesterol content of selected foods.

Lipids in Food Processing

Due to the widespread use of lipids in foodservice, various processes are utilized to increase their application. When processes such as refining, bleaching, and deodorization are used, the shelf life of lipids can be prolonged. Mono- and diglycerides are commonly used as emulsifiers. They are also used as food additives to prevent the separation of water from fatty substances in commonly used food products such as margarine, salad dressings, and pastes. Lecithin is used for the same purpose. One of the most useful technological changes in lipid modification is called **hydrogenation.** In this process, hydrogen is forced into PUFAs, thereby increasing their

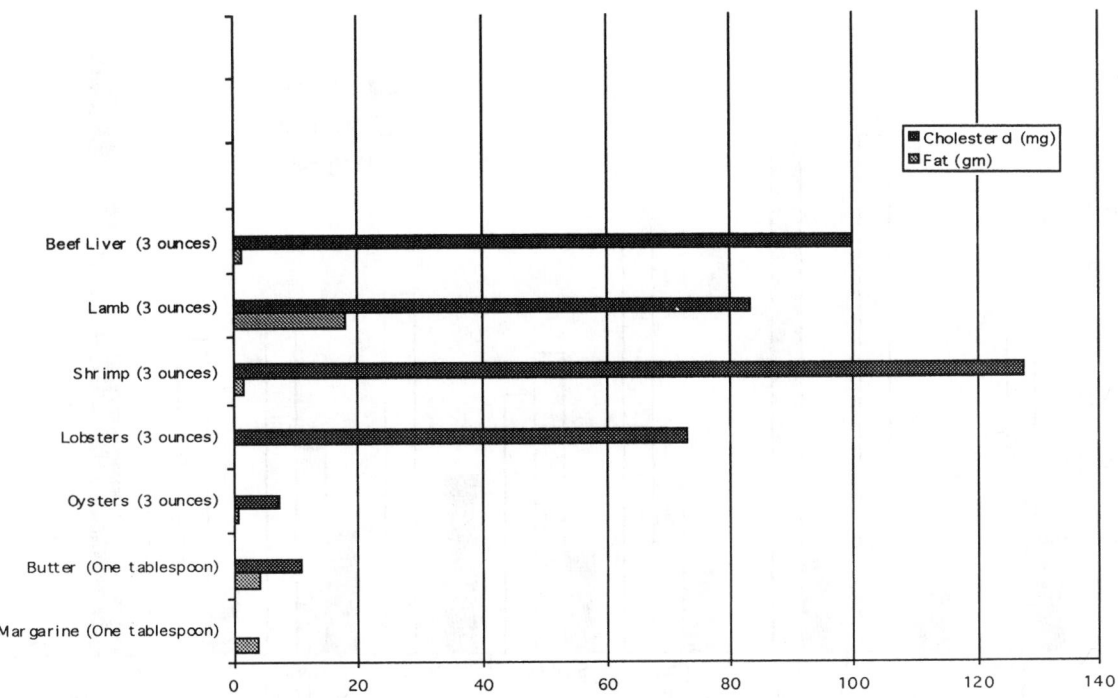

Figure 4.4   Fat and Cholesterol Content of Selected Foods

degree of saturation; making them solid, thereby increasing their shelf life; making them spreadable; increasing the smoke point of frying; and providing ease in packaging. It is the double or unsaturated bonds easily taken over by oxygen that cause rancidity in fats. Hydrogenation thus increases the shelf life of lipids by reducing the chances of rancidity. Margarine and shortenings are hydrogenated lipids that are hardened to different degrees of solidification. Products that are subjected to hydrogenation are called *hydrogenated*. Oils that are unsaturated can be hydrogenated, providing different degrees of solidification: spread, semisolid, buttery, and so on. These hydrogenated oils can be used as a substitute for saturated fats. The major drawback of hydrogenation is that it turns unsaturated fats into saturated fats. Generally, the harder or more solid the fat, the more saturated it is. The saturation levels of different oils commonly used in foodservice are shown in Figure 4.5.

LIPIDS IN FOODS

Lipids are found in different foods in a variety of forms. Naturally, plant foods such as fruits, vegetables, and grains have little fat. However, they contain lipids when these foods are cooked with fats and oils during preparation. A good example is potatoes, which naturally contain only a trace of fat, whereas potato chips may

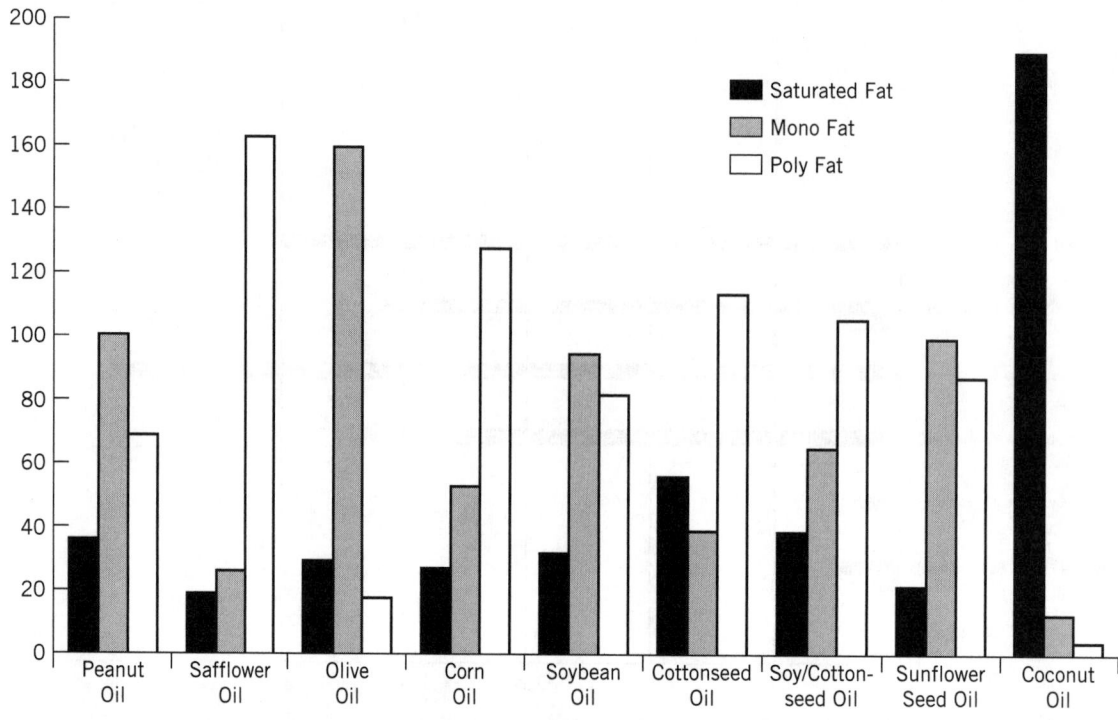

Figure 4.5   Saturation Levels of Selected Oils (1 cup)

contain up to 10 grams of lipids in 1 ounce. Similarly, flour contains only a trace of fat, but it can become very rich in lipids when fats and oils are added in cakes and pastries. All food fats, whether derived from animal or plant sources, contain a mixture of saturated and unsaturated fatty acids; however, animal fats are generally more saturated than vegetable oils.

Foods that are naturally high in fat are meat and meat products, some dairy products, and nuts. Saturated fat is present in the fat that surrounds red meat. It is also present in poultry, fish, and shellfish, although to a lesser extent. Dairy products such as whole milk, cheese, ice cream, butter, and cream all have high amounts of saturated fat. Today fats are being removed from many products. They can be easily removed from dairy products, resulting in skim milk, low-fat milk, and low-fat or nonfat yogurt. Products made from skim milk also contain less fat, such as mozzarella, parmesan, and cottage cheeses. Although saturated fats are present mainly in animal foods, some plant foods contain saturated fats in large quantities, including most of the tropical oils, such as coconut, palm kernel, and palm oils. These oils are commonly used in baked products such as cookies and crackers. They may also be present in nondairy substitutes such as whipped toppings, coffee creamers, cake mixes, potato chips, popcorn, candies, and some frozen dinners. They are preferred since they impart special flavors to foods. Tropical oils are also commonly present in foods from Asian countries.

Compared to saturated fats, polyunsaturated fats are found primarily in oils of plant origin, such as safflower, corn, soybean, cottonseed, and sunflower oils. These oils are used in cooking, salad dressings, and many manufactured foods. A type of polyunsaturated fat, omega-3 fatty acids, is found in the oils derived from fish and shellfish, which have certain beneficial health properties. Olive and peanut oils are high in monounsaturated fats.

From a foodservice point of view, fats are extremely useful, adding richness, flavor, and appeal to foods. Many types of fats are available for food preparation, such as vegetable oil, butter, and shortening. Depending on their use, fats can act as moisturizers, emulsifiers, aerators, tenderizers, flavor enhancers, or texturizers. For example, in batters, fats trap air and form pockets that facilitate the expansion of leavening agents, thereby providing the desirable volume and texture to the finished product. Fats also provide shortening or tenderizing effects in many pastries, cookies, and biscuits. Puff pastries contain layers of fat. In the presence of heat and steam these layers are separated, creating desirable texture and flavor. Butter or solid fats are needed in these pastries, since oil can get absorbed into the flour rather than providing layers that cause the desired flakiness. Whether providing greasiness to pans or aromas to finished foods, lipids play an important role in food preparation. Because fats are insoluble in water, they interfere with the development of firm masses or strands formed by flour protein gluten, thereby shortening these strands and providing tenderness. They provide texture to baked goods, flakiness to pies, tenderness to cakes, crumbs to biscuits, dressings to salads, and accompaniment to breads. Fats also influence the texture of foods by inhibiting crystal formation, thereby resulting in a much smoother product. In meats it is fat that provides juiciness, taste, marbling, and flavor. In fact, meats are graded based on the extent of marbling and the fat content. Fat helps in roasting, barbecuing, broiling, or grilling of meats. The smoked flavor in some foods is caused by the burning of fat as it drips on the hot plate. Hydrogenated oils and fats are used as substitutes for saturated fats. Fats can be combined with other binders such as crumbs or flours. Proteins and carbohydrates can also be combined with fats, utilizing the desirable qualities and complementing each other. Fats are commonly used in fried foods. The heated oil cooks the outside of the food, while the pressure of steam escaping from within the food prevents the fat from penetrating. Fat eventually enters if the food is allowed to fry for a longer period of time.

Rancidity is the deterioration of fats, resulting in undesirable flavors and odors described as rancid. Rancidity reduces the quality of the fat and of the foods that contain it. This problem can occur in any type of food containing fat, even if it is present in small quantities. Fats become rancid upon oxidation, which results in the breakdown of fatty acid chains. This produces free radicals, which are unstable molecules and potential carcinogens. Foods commonly susceptible to rancidity include salad dressings, mayonnaise, cheese, cookies, ready-to-eat cereals, wholegrain flours, fish, potato chips, and nuts. Rancidity occurs when fats lose a hydrogen atom and take on an oxygen atom in the presence of air. To reduce rancidity and increase the shelf life of oils and fats, certain antioxidants are added, such as butylated hydroxyanisole (BHA) and butylated hydroxytolulene (BHT). To prevent rancidity, fats and oils should be kept tightly covered, with as little exposure to air as possible. Oils are also winterized to counteract their tendency to solidify, such as when refrigerated. Winterization consists of centrifuging the oils to reduce the heavy saturated molecules, which are drained off.

A sucrose polyester (SPE) commonly known as *olestra* is used as a synthetic fat substitute. It smells, looks, and tastes like fat. Sucrose polyesters are manufactured by linking sucrose with fatty acids. Since SPE cannot be broken by any enzyme, they are neither digested nor absorbed by the body. They are being tested for use in preparing foods, since they can impart desirable tastes without providing calories.

FATS AND OILS IN FOODSERVICE

Fats and oils are extensively used in foodservice operations. They are used with different methods of food preparation because of their properties, as well as the distinct flavors they impart to foods. They act as a cooking medium, emulsifier, tenderizer, aerator, flavor enhancer, and texturizer. Fats are usually selected on the basis of their plant or animal origin. They help shorten the gluten strands in batters and doughs, thus softening the texture as well as tenderizing the product. They also help waterproof the gluten in flour, providing a tender product. In products where layers of fat and flour (such as in puff pastries) are alternated and baked, the heat results in the production of steam, which forces the separation of the layers, creating a flakier, more tender product. The tenderizing effect of fats on baked foods results in flakiness, as seen in pastries. Fats provide or enhance the special flavors of foods, as well as retaining the moisture of baked foods. They also act as leavening agents by releasing steam. They are used in salad dressings. Fats can be emulsified and used in different types of food preparation. An **emulsion** is a mixture of two (usually nonmixable liquids) in which one is evenly dispersed in the other and held in suspension. A good example of an emulsion is mayonnaise, a flavored emulsion of egg yolks and oil. Emulsions have three basic components: (1) a dispersed liquid, which is primarily in the form of small oil droplets uniformly dispersed; (2) the liquid into which these oil droplets are dispersed; and (3) an emulsifying agent that helps to produce this suspension. Emulsifiers have both water-soluble and fat-soluble molecules. A good example is lecithin, a phospholipid, which is present in egg yolk and used in the preparation of mayonnaise. Care should be taken to avoid breaking an emulsion, resulting in separation of the suspended ingredients. Fats also help to inhibit crystal formation, resulting in a smoother product, as seen in ice creams and frozen desserts.

Fats and oils that are used in foodservice do not occur free in nature; they are usually extracted from plant or animal sources. Many oils come from seeds or fruits, while many fats, such as lard and butter, are derived from animal sources. Some commonly used fats and oils and their uses in foodservice are described below.

Butter

Butter, used in food preparation for centuries, is fat separated from cream by churning or agitation. The protein film around fat globules is ruptured by agitation, breaking the oil-in-water emulsion. The resulting emulsion is butter, which is actually a water-in-oil emulsion. Butter can be made from sweet or sour cream. Pasteurization is done to destroy any pathogenic bacteria present. Pure butter is white, and yellow coloring is added. Butter is graded on the basis of flavor, odor, freshness, plasticity, and texture. It provides special qualities and flavors that are very desirable in desserts and pastries. It also contains moisture, which helps to leaven the foods to which it is added. It has a relatively low melting point and is used exclusively for making some pastries. However, due to its high caloric density, other types of fat that simulate or provide the same qualities as those of butter are often used.

Margarine

Margarine is a butter substitute made from hydrogenated animal or vegetable fats. It contains water and provides most of the properties of butter. In fact, it is also a water-in-oil emulsion. It is manufactured with pasteurized skim milk combined with other ingredients. Soybean and cottonseed oils, which are refined and partially hydrogenated, are commonly used in the manufacture of margarines. Whipped margarines, which contain gas that increases their volume and decreases their density, are also available.

Lard

Lard is one of the oldest forms of fat used in food preparation. Its use has diminished greatly because it is an animal fat and because other substitutes are available.

Oils

Oils are mostly extracted from different plant seeds and are liquid at room temperature. Winterized oils remain liquid at room temperature and are more suitable for salads than for frying. The most commonly used oils are corn, cottonseed, sesame, soy, olive, canola, and peanut oils. Oils are also used in salads in combination with other ingredients.

Hydrogenated Shortenings

Liquid oils are transformed into solid fats by the process of hydrogenation, in which hydrogen is added to the carbons joined by double bonds, thus saturating them. Oils such as margarine can also be partially hydrogenated. Hydrogenated vegetable oils have the same plasticity as other animal fats, such as butter; however, they have the distinct advantage of containing no cholesterol, which is not found in plant products. Hydrogenation also protects fats from spoilage and rancidity. Hydrogenated shortenings are still saturated fats, regardless of their plant origin, and are therefore likely to raise the blood cholesterol level.

FATS AND OILS IN FOOD PREPARATION

Fats and oils are good cooking media since they can reach high temperatures in a short period of time. In addition, they impart special flavors and textures to foods. Different kinds of fat are used in food preparation. The functions of fats and oils in food preparation are summarized in Table 4.2. Since fats provide far more calories per gram than other nutrients, their use needs to be carefully controlled. For foodservice use, fats and oils should be selected on the basis of their plant or animal origin, degree of saturation, eating quality, cooking quality, smoke point, resistance to spoilage, and, most important, their effect on health.

Upon heating, fats undergo chemical and physical changes. Repeated use leads to degradation of desired characteristics due to exposure to heat, oxygen, water, and food particles. High heat can result in the hydrolysis of triglycerides and can also cause the free fatty acids formed by hydrolysis to form polymers or chains of fatty acids, making the fats more viscous. These fatty acids may cause discoloration of prepared foods, stickiness, smoke, and foam formation during frying and may form residues on cooking equipment.

Foods absorb different amounts of fats based on the quality of the fats. It is desirable that fried foods cook from the inside out, have in most cases a golden brown color, and absorb a minimum amount of fat. Fat should be used primarily as a cooking medium secondary to imparting flavor while frying foods. The temperature of the cooking medium determines the end product, as well as the amount of fat absorbed. If the temperature is too low, cooking will take longer, increasing fat absorption. If the temperature is too high, the outside of the food will be cooked quickly but the inside may not be properly cooked. The size, shape, surface area, contents, and fresh or frozen state of food determine the optimum temperature for its cooking. The content of doughs or batters used to coat fried foods also determines the absorption of fats. High proportions of ingredients such as sugar, eggs, and milk products may increase the proportion of fats absorbed by foods.

When fats and oils are heated to high temperatures, they disintegrate, forming

Table 4.2   Functions of Lipids in Food Preparation

Functions	Examples
Inhibiting crystallization	Ice cream
Tenderization	Biscuits
Aeration	Puff pastries
Emulsification	Mayonnaise
Providing texture	Pastries
Enhancing flavor	French fries
Leavening	Breads
Providing smoothness and rich texture	Custard
Cooking media and heat transfer	Deep-fat frying

smoke. The temperature at which smoke rises from heated fats or oils is referred to as the **smoking point.** Smoke is formed due to the conversion of glycerol to acrolein. Fats with high smoking points should be used, particularly when high-temperature cooking is desired, such as in deep-fat frying. The higher the concentration of free fatty acids, monoglycerides, and diglycerides in fats, the lower the temperature at which fat smokes. Optimum temperatures should be used to preserve the frying quality of fats. Each time the same fat is used, its smoking point is lowered. Smoking points of at least 400°F are preferred for frying foods. Oils with such smoking points include safflower, corn, peanut, and sesame oils. Most animal fats smoke at lower temperatures.

For deep-fat frying, the oil should be odorless and tasteless, in addition to being able to withstand high temperatures without smoking or breaking down. Most animal fats are not suitable for deep-fat frying since they smoke at low temperatures. Untreated vegetable fats are also unstable. Specially processed oils with high stability should be used for frying. Care should be taken to avoid the breakdown of oils even if they are of high quality and stability. Common causes of breakdown are overheating and exposure to salt, water, crumbs, and certain fatty acids. If care is taken, fats can be reused. Precautions include heating the fat gradually to the cooking temperature; removing crumbs and restricting the use of salt and water; straining fat daily; and cleaning the equipment used for frying. Also, fats and oils should be stored in a cool, dark place in closed containers.

Chapter 5

FAT-SOLUBLE VITAMINS

INTRODUCTION

Vitamins derive their name from "vital amines" since they are considered vital for metabolic processes. **Vitamins** are organic substances that are needed in minute amounts and that regulate metabolic functions within the body. They occur naturally in small quantities in foods, but they can also be prepared synthetically and added to foods. Compared to fats, proteins, and carbohydrates, vitamins are structurally unrelated. There is no sequential arrangement of the carbon, hydrogen, and oxygen in a vitamin molecule. There are 13 known vitamins. They have different characteristics—solubilities, absorption efficiencies, and storage capacities—which makes them different but still classifiable as vitamins. Vitamins are needed in minute quantities; their excess intake is either wasted or results in harmful consequences. Thus, it is imperative to understand fully the role and nature of vitamins.

CLASSIFICATION OF VITAMINS

Vitamins are subdivided based on whether they are soluble in **water** or fat. The fat-soluble vitamins are **A, D, E,** and **K.** The water-soluble vitamins are **thiamin, riboflavin, niacin, vitamin B_6, folacin, vitamin B_{12}, pantothenic acid, biotin,** and **vitamin C.** The solubility of vitamins in water or fat influences how they are consumed in food and utilized within the body. Normally, the body maintains a certain amount of vitamins in the tissues, referred to as the **saturation level.** Fat-soluble vitamins can be stored, whereas water-soluble vitamins cannot be stored and are excreted. From the foodservice point of view, the property of being water-soluble or fat-soluble is extremely important. Vitamin retention in and losses from foods are related to their solubility. Vitamins can be found in their final form in foods or certain compounds can be converted into vitamins within the body. The compounds that can be converted into vitamins are called **provitamins.** For example, carotene is a provitamin for vitamin A, and the amino acid tryptophan is a provitamin of niacin. Vitamins and provitamins occur in nature in different forms. The potency of a vitamin depends on the form in which it occurs because various forms have different absorption rates. Synthetic vitamins function similarly to those obtained from natural sources.

Vitamins are useful in small quantities; if taken in large quantities, some vitamins can result in toxicity. This is primarily true of fat-soluble vitamins, which can be stored in the body and can exceed safe levels. Although it is commonly believed that water-soluble vitamins are excreted if taken in large quantities, there is evidence that some of them can also reach toxic levels within the body. Large doses of vitamins taken for long periods of time may result in toxicity.

Different vitamins have different chemical and physical characteristics. Some vitamins are stable, others less so. Vitamins can be degraded by light, exposure to oxygen, various pH conditions, heat, time, water, and processing. The vitamin content of foods is affected by a number of factors, such as the maturity of fruits and vegetables, transportation, storage, prepreparation, preparation, processing, cooking methods and temperatures, serving temperatures, and storage of leftovers. Water-soluble vitamins are more easily destroyed than fat-soluble vitamins. The loss of both water-soluble and fat-soluble vitamins during food processing will be discussed in detail in Chapter 13. It is paradoxical that the role and importance of vitamins are determined by their absence rather than their presence. Deficiency symptoms indicate the lack of vitamins within the body. Also, vitamins do not contain calories and thus do not directly provide energy. No one food can provide all the vitamins required by the body.

Vitamins are measured in different units based on their type and potency. They are normally quantified in milligrams or micrograms. For some vitamins, International Units (IUs) are used. Since some vitamins and their precursors have varying potencies, they are expressed as *equivalents.* These equivalents are used to reflect as accurately as possible the amount of vitamin activity. Normally, vitamins A, E, and niacin are expressed in equivalents. For example, vitamin A is expressed in retinal equivalents (RE) and niacin in niacin equivalents (NE). These units are used interchangeably in different food tables and in some food labels.

All vitamins will be discussed individually, outlining their functions, typical intakes, food sources, impact of deficiency and excess, and ways in which they can be stored or lost in foods or in the body. These vitamins are not listed in any priority order, and most of them function in conjunction with other nutrients. Also, their labels—A, B, C, and so on—are not grades, and no order of preference is assigned to them. Vitamins work and interact with other vitamins as well as with nutrients. For example, vitamin C increases iron absorption. Thus there is a connection between vitamins and other nutrients.

VITAMIN A

Vitamin A is found preformed in food in the form of retinol. Other forms are retinal, retinaldehyde, and retinoic acid. Carotene is a provitamin for vitamin A that is found in orange and deep green produce. Several compounds are classified as carotenoids; 30 of them can be converted to retinol by the body. These are provitamins of vitamin A. The most important of these provitamin A compounds is *beta-carotene (β-carotene)*.

Functions and Deficiency

Vitamin A keeps the skin and mucous membranes healthy and helps the eyes adjust to dim lights, such as at night or in a movie theater. Vitamin A is essential for vision, growth, cellular differentiation and proliferation, reproduction, and the integrity of the immune system. It is important for cell development, since it affects the nuclei of cells. It maintains membrane structure and functions. It is also important for the growth and health of cartilage, bone, and body coverings and linings (known as *epithelial tissues*). One such epithelial tissue with which vitamin A is often linked is the cornea of the eye. Other epithelial tissues are the mucous membranes, linings of nasal passages, GI tract, genitourinary tract, and the skin. Vitamin A deficiency is found most commonly in children under five years of age and is usually due to an insufficient dietary intake. Its deficiency can also be due to chronic malabsorption of fat. Lack of vitamin A is seen in the abnormality of epithelial tissues. *Keratinization*, or hardening of the epithelial tissues, occurs in the absence of this vitamin. Dryness of skin, with roughness and cracking of mucous membranes, is another sign of vitamin A deficiency. It is often accompanied by hemorrhage. This hardening becomes critical when vital tissues such as the cornea of the eye are affected. With prolonged deficiency of vitamin A, keratinization of the cornea can result in blindness, which is seen in malnourished children. *Xerophthalmia* is the technical name of the condition that results from vitamin A deficiency.

Vitamin A plays a significant role in the eye in addition to its impact on the cornea. This vitamin is a component of *rhodopsin* and *iodopsin,* colored, light-sensitive substances found in the retina of the eye. When light falls on these compounds, they undergo changes that are translated as messages about what is within the field of vision. This is a very important function of the eye. If vitamin A is deficient, these conversions are hindered or perform slowly, and there is a time lag between what is seen and what is translated as an image. This slow transformation causes a condition referred to as **night blindness.** It is seen commonly in children deficient in vitamin A.

Although research is in progress, evidence already exists that vitamin A (both the vitamin and carotene) intake from diets may protect against certain forms of cancer of the lung, bladder, and larynx. However, routine overconsumption of vitamin A may result in toxicity. Symptoms of such toxicity include skin lesions, hair loss, and, in advanced stages, liver, kidney, and bone damage. Normally, the overdose occurs when one consumes more than 50,000 IU daily for extended periods of time.

Table 5.1   Good Sources of Vitamin A

Food	Selected Serving Size	Percent of U.S. RDA[a]
Breads, Cereals, and Other Grain Products		
Fortified oatmeal, instant	⅔ cup	+++
Ready-to-eat cereals (fortified)	1 ounce	++
Fruits		
Apricot nectar	½ cup	+
Apricots, dried, cooked, unsweetened	½ cup	++
Cantaloupe, raw	½ cup diced	++
Mandarin orange sections	½ cup	+
Mango, raw	½ medium	+++
Melon balls (cantaloupe and honeydew)	½ cup	+
Nectarine, raw	1 medium	+
Plums, canned, juice-pack	½ cup	+
Watermelon, raw, diced	1¾ cups	+
Vegetables		
Broccoli, cooked	½ cup	+
Carrots		
Cooked	½ cup	+++
Raw	Four 3-inch strips	+++
Chard (cooked)	½ cup	+
Collards (cooked)	½ cup	+
Endive, chicory, romaine, or escarole (raw)	1 cup	+
Kale (cooked)	½ cup	+++
Mustard greens (cooked)	½ cup	+
Peas and carrots (cooked)	½ cup	+++
Pepper		
Sweet, red (cooked)	½ cup	++
Sweet, red (raw)	1 small	+++
Plantain, green or ripe, boiled	1 medium	+
Pumpkin, (cooked)	½ cup	+
Spinach		
Cooked	½ cup	+++
Raw	1 cup	+
Squash, winter, mashed (cooked)	½ cup	+++
Sweet potato		
Baked or boiled	1 medium	+++
Canned	½ cup	+++
Tomatoes		
Cooked	½ cup	+
Raw	1 medium	+
Tomato juice, canned	¾ cup	+
Tomato-vegetable juice cocktail	¾ cup	+
Turnip greens or turnip greens with turnip (cooked)	½ cup	+++

Table 5.1   *(Continued)*

Food	Selected Serving Size	Percent of U.S. RDA[a]
Meat, Poultry, Fish, and Alternatives		
Beef or calf liver, braised	3 ounces	+++
Chicken or turkey liver, braised	½ cup diced	+++
Mackerel, canned, drained	3 ounces	+
Milk, Cheese, and Yogurt		
Milk, low-fat or skim	1 cup	+

[a] A selected serving size contains:
+ 10–24 percent of the U.S. RDA.
++ 25–39 percent of the U.S. RDA.
+++ 40 percent or more of the U.S. RDA.
Source: USDA/Human Nutrition Information Service.

Requirements and Food Sources

The RDA for adult males is 1000 micrograms (or 5000 IUs) RE, and for adult females it is 800 micrograms RE. The amount of vitamin A recommended during lactation is about 1200 micrograms RE.

A good source of vitamin A is one that contains a substantial amount of vitamin A and/or carotenes in relation to its calorie content, as well as contributing at least 10 percent of the RDA for vitamin A in a selected serving size or a unit of measure. Vitamin A activity in foods is expressed as *retinol equivalents (RE):* 1 RE is defined as 1 microgram of all-*trans* retinol, 6 micrograms of all-*trans* beta-carotene, or 12 micrograms of other provitamin A carotenoids. Vitamin A can be obtained as either preformed retinol or beta-carotene. Retinol is found in animal foods such as liver, egg yolk, and dairy products, and beta-carotene is found in the orange pigment of deep yellow, orange, and dark green leafy vegetables and fruits. Foods that have the highest amount of vitamin A are the carotene-containing deep orange and dark green varieties. Thus, the fruit and vegetable groups have the most sources of vitamin A. Foods containing significant amounts of vitamin A are carrots, apricots, broccoli, cantaloupe, pumpkin, squash, sweet potatoes, spinach, and other dark leafy vegetables. Formerly, there was a misconception that the intensity of color indicates the amount of carotenoid or provitamin content. However, since other yellow and orange carotenoids and other pigments are present in plants, this conclusion is unjustifiable. Among animal sources, vitamin A is found in large amounts in liver, the major source of retinol. In fact, the richest sources of preformed retinol are liver and fish liver oils; considerable quantities are also present in whole and fortified milk and in eggs. Dairy products and eggs contain significant amounts of both retinol and carotenoids. Most of the vitamin A in dairy products comes from fortification. In the United States, the major contributors of dietary vitamin A or provitamin A are liver, carrots, eggs, vegetable-based soups, and whole-milk products. Other major sources are fortified food products. In addition to food sources, this vitamin is provided by vitamin supplements. Table 5.1 gives the amount of vitamin A in selected foods.

Foodservice Applications

Vitamin A can be lost from foods during preparation, cooking, or storage. To retain this vitamin, it is important to serve fruits and vegetables raw whenever possible. Most vegetables and fruits should be covered and refrigerated during storage (except sweet potatoes and winter squash). Also, vegetables should be steamed and meats should be braised, baked, or boiled instead of fried. Some vitamin A is lost in the fat during frying. Low-fat and skim milks are often fortified with vitamin A since this vitamin is removed from milk with fat. Margarine is fortified with vitamin A to make its contents similar to those of butter. Most ready-to-eat and instant-prepared cereals are also fortified with vitamin A.

VITAMIN D

Vitamin D (calciferol) is essential for proper formation of the skeleton. It is one of the vitamins that can be produced by the body. It is referred to as the "sunshine vitamin" because ultraviolet light from the sun changes a compound in the skin called *7-dehydrocholesterol* into vitamin D. In foods vitamin D occurs as *calciferol* and *ergosterol*. It acts as both a vitamin and a hormone. It is stored in liver, skin, and bones.

Functions and Deficiency

Vitamin D is essential for the absorption and use of calcium, thereby maintaining strong bones and teeth. The primary roles of vitamin D are to enhance the intestinal absorption of calcium and phosphorus and to increase the retention of calcium. These activities help the body maintain desired levels of calcium and phosphorus in the blood, which are necessary for normal nerve and muscle activity. The deficiency of vitamin D results in calcium deficiency and soft, weak bones. In children, severe deficiency results in deformation of the skeleton, a condition referred to as *rickets*. Rickets is characterized by abnormal bone development that results in bowed legs and other deformities. It is rarely prevalent in countries where milk and other foods are fortified with vitamin D. When vitamin D deficiency occurs in adults, the condition is referred to as *osteomalacia*. Vitamin D is potentially toxic, particularly for children if taken in excessive quantities. Effects of excessive intake include hypercalcemia and hypercalciuria, which lead to deposition of calcium in soft tissues and irreversible renal and cardiovascular damage. Symptoms of vitamin D toxicity include vomiting, diarrhea, weight loss, intense thirst, lack of appetite, high blood calcium level, and deposition of calcium in muscles. Vitamin D is regarded as the most toxic vitamin, so its dosage, particularly in children, should be monitored very carefully.

Requirements and Food Sources

In the United States, the usual dietary intake of vitamin D is from fortified milk for both children and adults. There are limited food sources of vitamin D. Rich food sources of vitamin D include fish liver oil, egg yolks, liver, and butterfat.

Table 5.2   Vitamin D Content of Selected Foods

Foods	Measure	Vitamin D Content (μg)
Milk (regular), whole	1 cup	2.550
Milk (skim)	1 cup	2.630
Egg, raw, whole	1 large	0.613
Corn pudding	1 serving (3 ounces)	0.436
Macaroni and cheese	1 serving	0.979
Margarine	1 tablespoon	0.376
Butter	1 tablespoon	0.037
Beef burrito	One	0.931
Cottage cheese	1 cup	0.125
Cereal (corn flakes)	1 cup	1.250

Since this vitamin is linked to bone growth and maintenance, it is required in relatively large quantities during the growth period. The RDA for vitamin D is 10 micrograms per day. This allowance is similar for males and females. The allowance is reduced to 5 micrograms in the later stages of life when skeletal formation is complete. The requirement for this vitamin is lower than that of other vitamins since the body has the capacity to produce it. The amounts of vitamin D provided by different food sources are listed in Table 5.2.

VITAMIN E

Vitamin E occurs in food as *tocopherol* and *tocotrienol* compounds, the most active form being *alpha-tocopherol.* The word *tocopherol* is derived from the Greek words *tokos* and *pherin,* which mean "to bear a child" since it was once thought to be associated with fertility.

Functions and Deficiency

Tocopherols are **antioxidants,** preventing oxygen from combining with other substances. Vitamin E protects PUFAs from oxidation, which occurs in foods as well as in the body, where PUFAs are part of cell membranes. Vitamin E is also thought to protect vitamin A from oxidation. Thus, vitamin E is the primary defense against potentially harmful oxidation. It maintains cell membranes (such as those of red blood cells and the lining of the lungs), which are constantly exposed to oxidation. It has also been suggested that vitamin E may help protect against certain types of cancer.

Vitamin E deficiency is extremely rare since this vitamin is widespread in foods. Most of the deficiency symptoms are reported in infants. In rare cases, deficiency occurs in persons who are unable to absorb fat and fat-soluble vitamins for a long period of time.

Table 5.3   Good Sources of Vitamin E

Food	Selected Serving Size	Percent of U.S. RDA[a]
Breads, Cereals, and Other Grain Products		
Multigrain cereal (cooked)	⅔ cup	+
Wheat germ, plain	2 tablespoons	++
Ready-to-eat cereals (fortified)	1 ounce	+++
Fruits		
Apple, baked, unsweetened	1 medium	+
Apricots, canned, juice-pack	½ cup	+
Nectarine, raw	1 medium	+
Peaches, canned, juice-pack	½ cup	+
Vegetables		
Chard (cooked)	½ cup	+
Collards (cooked)	½ cup	+
Dandelion greens (cooked)	½ cup	+
Kohlrabi (cooked)	½ cup	+
Mustard greens (cooked)	½ cup	+
Pumpkin, (cooked)	½ cup	+
Turnip greens (cooked)	½ cup	+
Meat, Poultry, Fish, and Alternatives		
Liver, braised	½ cup diced	+
Chicken or turkey liver, braised	½ cup diced	+
Mackerel, canned, drained	3 ounces	+
Clams, steamed, boiled, or canned, drained	3 ounces	+
Croaker, mackerel, mullet, or ocean perch, baked or broiled	3 ounces	+
Salmon		
Baked, broiled, steamed, poached	3 ounces	+
Canned, drained	3 ounces	+
Scallops, baked, or broiled	3 ounces	+
Shrimp		
Broiled, steamed, or poached	3 ounces	++
Canned, drained	3 ounces	+
Nuts and Seeds		
Almonds, unroasted	2 tablespoons	+++
Brazil nuts	2 tablespoons	+
Hazelnuts	2 tablespoons	+++
Peanuts, roasted or dry-roasted	2 tablespoons	+
Peanut butter	2 tablespoons	++
Sunflower seeds, hulled, roasted, or dry-roasted	2 tablespoons	+++
Milk, Cheese, and Yogurt		
Milk, low-fat or skim	1 cup	+

[a] A selected serving size contains:

+ 10–24 percent of the U.S. RDA.

++ 25–39 percent of the U.S. RDA.

+++ 40 percent or more of the U.S. RDA.

Source: USDA/Human Nutrition Information Service.

Requirements and Food Sources

A good source of vitamin E contains a substantial amount of the vitamin in relation to its calorie content and contributes at least 10 percent of the U.S. RDA. The recommended intake of vitamin E is expressed in equivalents. A vitamin E equivalent has activity equal to that of 1 milligram of alpha-tocopherol. The RDAS are 10 vitamin E equivalents (10 milligrams of alpha-tocopherol) for adult males and 8 milligrams for adult females. During pregnancy, larger amounts of vitamin E must be consumed for the growth of the fetus. An additional 2 milligrams during pregnancy is recommended, increasing the RDA to 10 milligrams per day. The body's need depends on the degree of unsaturation of fats in the diet. Since vitamin E protects the unsaturated bonds from oxidation, persons who consume diets high in PUFAs need more vitamin E than those with lower intakes. Eating a variety of foods that contain vitamin E is the best way to get an adequate amount. Compared to other fat-soluble vitamins, vitamin E is relatively nontoxic. However, excessive supplementation of this vitamin is not recommended.

The tocopherol content of foods varies greatly, depending on processing, storage, and preparation procedures, during which large losses normally occur. The richest sources are the common vegetable oils, such as soybean, corn, cottonseed, and safflower oils, as well as the products (margarine, mayonnaise, salad dressings, and shortenings) made from them. Wheat germ and nuts are high in vitamin E. Meats, fish, animal fats, butter, liver, fish, whole-grain cereals, eggs, and some fruits and vegetables (particularly green leafy vegetables) contain vitamin E. The vitamin E content of diets also varies widely, depending on the type (animal or vegetable) and amount of fat present. The amounts of vitamin E present in common foods are listed in Table 5.3. Vitamin E can be lost from foods during cooking, processing, and storage. Using whole-grain flours, storing foods in air-tight containers, and avoiding exposure to light are recommended to avoid losses. Most ready-to-eat cereals are fortified with vitamin E. They usually contain at least 40 percent of the U.S. RDA.

VITAMIN K

Vitamin K is known mostly for its role in the clotting of blood. This vitamin can be synthesized within the body by some bacteria. It occurs in nature in the forms of *phylloquinone* (synthesized by green plants) and *menaquinones* (synthesized by bacteria).

Functions and Deficiency

Vitamin K is essential for the formation of several proteins that are necessary for blood clotting, as well as other proteins that have different purposes. Compounds with vitamin K activity are essential for the formation of *prothrombin,* which is involved in the regulation of blood clotting. Prothrombin, after undergoing a series of chemical reactions, forms **fibrin,** which is primarily responsible for the clotting of blood. Defective blood clotting is therefore the major sign of vitamin K deficiency.

Table 5.4   Good Food Sources of Vitamin K

Food	Serving Size	Vitamin K Content (μg)
Beef burrito	1 serving	16.5
Beef liver	3 ounces	88.0
Macaroni and cheese	1 serving	21.9
Corn pudding	1 serving	8.1
Whole milk	1 cup	9.8
Carrots	1 cup	27.5
Spinach (raw), chopped	1 cup	149.0
Egg yolk	1 large	25.0
Cheddar cheese	3 ounces	29.3
Celery (raw)	1 cup	10.7
Green peas	1 cup	44.8

Table 5.5   Food Sources of Fat-Soluble Vitamins

Good Food Sources	Better Food Sources
Vitamin A	
Tomatoes	Liver
Butter	Dark green vegetables (broccoli, spinach)
Margarine	Dark orange vegetables (squash, carrots)
Whole milk cheeses	Cantaloupe
Egg yolk	Apricots
Peaches	Fish liver oils
Vitamin D	
Egg yolk	Fortified dairy products
Fish (herring, sardines, tuna, salmon)	Fish liver oils
Butter	
Vitamin E	
Liver	Vegetable oil
Codfish	Margarine
Whole grains	Shortenings
Legumes	Sunflower seeds
Leafy green vegetables	Wheat germ
	Nuts
Vitamin K	
Egg yolk	Leafy green vegetables
Organ meats	Cauliflower
Cheese	Cabbage
	Tomatoes
	Wheat bran
	Soybeans

Requirements and Food Sources

Since this vitamin is available from different sources and can be synthesized within the body, no specific daily requirement has been established. Also, the required dosage of this vitamin is not fully understood.

Vitamin K is found in large amounts in green leafy vegetables, tea, egg yolks, liver, and alfalfa sprouts. Even one serving of these foods is believed to provide the recommended safe dietary level. Green leafy vegetables, which provide 50 to 800 micrograms of vitamin K per 100 grams of food, are the best dietary sources of this vitamin. Vitamin K is also manufactured by the microorganisms within the intestines. Small amounts of the vitamin are present in milk and dairy products, meats, eggs, cereals, and fruits. The vitamin K content of commonly consumed foods is not known precisely; therefore, this vitamin is not included in the food composition tables. Babies and mothers may need vitamin K to prevent hemorrhage during birth. Vitamin K taken in large quantities can be toxic, due mainly to its interaction with other compounds. Table 5.4 lists good food sources of vitamin K. Food sources of fat-soluble vitamins are summarized in Table 5.5.

Chapter 6

WATER-SOLUBLE VITAMINS

Water-soluble vitamins act primarily as *coenzymes,* substances that unite with specific protein precursors to form active enzymes. They also take part in reactions that are essential for the breakdown of three energy nutrients discussed earlier—carbohydrates, fats, and proteins. Water-soluble vitamins can be directly absorbed from the digestive tract and, if not needed, are usually excreted; unlike fat-soluble vitamins, they are not stored. Since these vitamins are not stored, they should be provided on a daily basis. Fortunately, they are available in a variety of foods. Also, since these vitamins are water soluble, they can be easily lost during delivery, storage, processing, and serving of foods.

THIAMIN

Thiamin is also known as vitamin B_1. (Numbers were given to some of the earlier-discovered factors that were commonly grouped as B vitamins.) Thiamin is needed to supply constant energy to cells. It is found in muscles, where it works with other nutrients, enzymes, and coenzymes to provide fuel and oxygen to cells. Thiamin helps in the production of ribose, a five-carbon sugar needed to make RNA and DNA.

Functions and Deficiency

Thiamin serves as a coenzyme. It has a role in energy-producing biochemical reactions involving carbohydrates, fats, proteins or amino acids, and alcohol. At the usual level in the diet, thiamin is rapidly absorbed, mostly in the small intestine.

Thiamin deficiency is associated with abnormalities of carbohydrate metabolism. Prolonged thiamin deficiency results in a disease referred to as *beriberi,* which means "I cannot" and involves the nervous and cardiovascular systems. This disease is characterized by neuromuscular changes that may result in paralysis of the legs or heart failure; sometimes these conditions are accompanied by edema. Characteristic symptoms of beriberi include mental confusion, anorexia, muscular weakness, paralysis, edema, muscle wasting, tachycardia, and enlarged heart. In beriberi there is a loss of energy and vitality. Persons who are alcoholics tend to develop thiamin deficiency.

Requirements and Food Sources

Since thiamin is responsible for energy metabolism, the recommended intake is directly proportional to the energy intake. In other words, the more kcalories a person consumes, the higher the intake of thiamin. In general, it is not difficult to meet the dietary requirement for this vitamin since foods that provide a lot of energy are also likely to contain it; in addition, enriched products contain thiamin. The requirement for adults is 1 to 2 milligrams per day of thiamin or 0.5 milligram for every 1000 kcalories. A minimum of 1 milligram per day is recommended even for persons consuming fewer than 2000 kcalories daily. The thiamin requirement increases during pregnancy and lactation. Excessive thiamin intake is easily cleared by the kidneys. There is no evidence of toxicity if this vitamin is taken in excess.

A good source of thiamin contains a substantial amount of the vitamin in relation to its calorie content and contributes at least 10 percent of the U.S. RDA. Dietary sources of thiamin include cereal grains (unrefined), brewer's yeast, organ meats (liver, heart, kidney), lean meats, legumes, seeds, and nuts. Grain products, fruits, and vegetables provide approximately 40 to 60 percent of the thiamin requirement. Whole grains, particularly the enriched and fortified ones, provide a significant amount. Milk and milk products and meats and meat alternatives are also excellent sources. Pasta and most breads made from refined flours are enriched with thiamin because this is one of the nutrients lost in processing. Other nutrients added to refined flours and pasta are iron, niacin, and riboflavin. Enriched products or products made from enriched flour are labeled as such. Most ready-to-eat and instant-prepared cereals are fortified with thiamin. Fortified ready-to-eat cereals usually contain at least 25 percent of the U.S. RDA. Since cereals vary in the amounts of enriched nutrients, packaging labels should be checked for contents. The thiamin contents of most common foods are given in Table 6.1.

Table 6.1　Good Sources of Thiamin

Food	Selected Serving Size	Percent of U.S. RDA[a]
Breads, Cereals, and Other Grain Products		
Bagel, plain, pumpernickel, or whole-wheat	1 medium	+
Bread, raisin, rye, or white	2 slices	+
Cornbread	1 piece (2.5-inch square)	+
Farina, regular or quick, cooked	⅔ cup	+
English muffin, plain, plain with raisins, or whole-wheat	1	+
Grits, corn or hominy, regular or instant, cooked	⅔ cup	+
Macaroni, noodles, or spaghetti, cooked	1 cup	+
Oatmeal		
Instant, prepared	⅔ cup	+ +
Regular or quick, cooked	⅔ cup	+
Pita bread, plain or whole-wheat	1 small	+
Pretzel, soft	1	+
Ready-to-eat cereals (fortified)	1 ounce	+ +
Rice, white, cooked	⅔ cup	+
Rolls		
Hamburger or frankfurter	1	+
White, hard	1 medium	+
Waffles, plain	2 4-inch square	+
Wheat germ, plain	2 tablespoons	+
Fruits		
Melon balls (cantaloupe and honeydew), frozen, unsweetened	½ cup	+
Orange juice, fresh	¾ cup	+
Watermelon, raw, diced	¾ cup	+
Vegetables		
Corn, cooked	½ cup	+
Jerusalem artichoke, raw	½ cup	+
Peas, green (cooked)	½ cup	+
Peas and carrots (cooked)	½ cup	+
Meat, Poultry, Fish, and Alternatives		
Ham, roasted, lean only	3 ounces	+ +
Liver, braised	½ cup diced	+
Pork chop, baked or broiled	1 chop	+ + +
Mackerel or salmon, baked or broiled	3 ounces	+
Mussels, steamed, boiled, poached	3 ounces	+
Oysters, steamed or canned, undrained	3 ounces	+
Pompano, baked or broiled	3 ounces	+
Peas, split, green, or yellow, cooked	½ cup	+
Brazil nuts	2 tablespoons	+
Pine nuts (pignolias)	2 tablespoons	+
Sunflower seeds, hulled, unroasted	2 tablespoons	+ +

[a] A selected serving size contains:
　+ 10–24 percent of the U.S. RDA.
　+ + 25–39 percent of the U.S. RDA.
　+ + + 40 percent or more of the U.S. RDA.

Source: USDA/Human Nutrition Information Service.

RIBOFLAVIN

Riboflavin, also known as vitamin B_2, like thiamin, serves as a coenzyme. It functions primarily as a component of two flavin coenzymes—flavin mononucleotide (FMN) and flavin adenine dinucleotide (FAD). Both of these compounds take an active part in oxidation-reduction reactions. Riboflavin is water soluble and easily absorbed in the intestine; the excess vitamin is excreted in urine. Some riboflavin can be made by intestinal bacteria.

Functions and Deficiency

Riboflavin joins with other vitamins in providing energy. Riboflavin deficiency results in skin lesions. Deficiency symptoms include oral-buccal cavity lesions, dermatitis, skin changes, and normocytic anemia. These symptoms are sometimes associated with deficiencies of other B vitamins.

Requirements and Food Sources

A good source of riboflavin contains a substantial amount of the vitamin in relation to its calorie content and contributes at least 10 percent of the U.S. RDA. The RDA for riboflavin is 1.5 milligrams for adult males and 1.3 milligrams for adult females. The allowances are higher for pregnant and lactating women, adolescents, and infants. No toxicity from ingestion of riboflavin in large quantities has been reported.

In general, animal proteins are good sources of riboflavin. Milk and milk products, meat and eggs, fish, poultry, and organ meats contain a large amount of this vitamin. Leafy deep green vegetables are also fair sources. Enriched products such as rice, cereals, pasta products, flours, crackers, and bread products provide large quantities. Pasta and most breads made from refined flours are enriched with riboflavin because this is one of the nutrients lost in processing. Other nutrients added to refined flours and pasta are iron, niacin, and thiamin. Enriched products or products made from enriched flour are labeled as such. Most ready-to-eat and instant-prepared cereals are fortified with riboflavin. Fortified ready-to-eat cereals usually contain at least 25 percent of the U.S. RDA for riboflavin. Since cereals vary in the amounts of enriched nutrients, packaging labels should be checked for contents. Some breakfast cereals are enriched to provide almost 100 percent of the RDA for riboflavin. Table 6.2 lists good food sources of riboflavin.

NIACIN

Niacin is a vitamin whose requirement can be met normally in part by the conversion of dietary tryptophan to niacin. To make 1 milligram of niacin, 60 milligrams of tryptophan is needed. As noted earlier, tryptophan is one of the essential amino acids. Once it is converted to niacin, it is not available to function as an amino acid. *Niacin* is a generic term for *nicotinic acid,* and *nicotinamide*

Table 6.2　Good Sources of Riboflavin

Food	Selected Serving Size	Percent of U.S. RDA[a]
Breads, Cereals, and Other Grain Products		
Bagel, plain, pumpernickel, or whole-wheat	1 medium	+
English muffin, plain	1	+
Multigrain cereal, cooked	⅔ cup	+
Oatmeal, instant, fortified, prepared	⅔ cup	+
Pancakes, plain	Two 4-inch square	+
Pita bread, plain	1 small	+
Pretzel, soft	1	+
Ready-to-eat cereals (fortified)	1 ounce	+ +
Waffles, plain or bran	Two 4-inch square	+
Vegetables		
Broccoli, cooked	½ cup	+
Mushrooms, cooked	½ cup	+
Spinach (cooked)	½ cup	+
Sweet potato, boiled	1 medium	+
Meat, Poultry, Fish, and Alternatives		
Beef		
⠀⠀⠀Ground, extra lean or lean, baked or broiled	1 patty	+
⠀⠀⠀Steak, baked or broiled, lean only	3 ounces	+
⠀⠀⠀Stew meat, simmered, lean only	3 ounces	+
Chicken leg (thigh and drumstick), broiled or roasted without skin	1 leg	+
Cornish hen, roasted, without skin	Half hen	+
Ham, fresh, roasted, lean only	3 ounces	+
Lamb, lean only		
⠀⠀⠀Chop, shoulder, braised, broiled, or baked	1 chop	+
⠀⠀⠀Roast, shoulder, roasted	3 ounces	+
Liver		
⠀⠀⠀Braised, beef or calf	3 ounces	+ + +
⠀⠀⠀Braised, chicken or turkey	½ cup diced	+ + +
Pork chop, baked or broiled	1 chop	+
Tongue, braised	3 ounces	+
Turkey, dark meat, roasted without skin	3 ounces	+
Veal, roast, leg, roasted, lean only	3 ounces	+
Clams, steamed, boiled, or canned, drained	3 ounces	+
Mackerel, canned and drained	3 ounces	+
Mackerel or trout, baked or broiled	3 ounces	+
Mussels, steamed, boiled, or poached	3 ounces	+
Oysters, canned, undrained	3 ounces	+
Almonds, roasted	2 tablespoons	+

Table 6.2 *(Continued)*

Food	Selected Serving Size	Percent of U.S. RDA[a]
Milk, Cheese, and Yogurt		
Cottage cheese, regular and low-fat	½ cup	+
Feta cheese	1 ounce	+
Ice milk, soft-serve, not chocolate	½ cup	+
Milk		
Buttermilk	1 cup	+
Chocolate	1 cup	+
Evaporated, whole or skim, diluted	1 cup	+
Whole, low-fat, or skim	1 cup	+
Yogurt		
Frozen	8 ounces	+
Plain, made with whole milk	8 ounces	+
Plain, made with low-fat or nonfat milk	8 ounces	+ +

[a] A selected serving size contains:

    + 10–24 percent of the U.S. RDA.

    ++ 25–39 percent of the U.S. RDA.

    +++ 40 percent or more of the U.S. RDA.

Source: USDA/Human Nutrition Information Service.

(niacinamide). Nicotinamide is the active form of the vitamin. Nicotinic acid is readily converted to active form by the body. There is no relation with these compounds to nicotine that is found in tobacco.

Functions and Deficiency

Nicotinamide functions in the body as a component of nicotinamide adenine dinucleotide (NAD) and nicotinamide adenine dinucleotide phosphate (NADP), two coenzymes present in all cells. They participate in metabolic processes including glycolysis, fatty acid metabolism, and tissue respiration. Thus, they are necessary for releasing energy. Niacin is therefore present in three forms: niacin, niacinamide, and nicotinic acid.

Since niacin, thiamin, and riboflavin all often occur in the same foods, the low intake of one vitamin influences the intake of the others. *Pellagra* is a condition resulting from the deficiency of niacin. The symptoms include diarrhea, dermatitis (inflammation of the skin), and dementia (mental illness), which can result in death. When niacin is deficient, the overall amino acid level will probably be low, which adds to the complications of symptoms. In the absence of niacin, body cells do not receive adequate energy for daily functions. Pellagra is common in persons whose diet lacks lean meat, milk, and eggs.

Requirements and Food Sources

Niacin, which is found in large amounts in meats, is very stable and can withstand reasonable periods of heating, cooking, and storage with little loss. However, the level of niacin in certain foods may be low. As mentioned, 60 milligrams of tryptophan is equivalent to 1 milligram of niacin and is regarded as 1 NE for calculating both the dietary contribution and the RDA. The extent of conversion is affected by hormones and appears to increase during pregnancy or when contraceptive pills are used. Some foods may have very little niacin, such as eggs and milk, but contain a sufficient amount of tryptophan, which can be converted into niacin. Meats contain high levels of both preformed niacin and tryptophan.

The RDA for niacin is 17 to 20 NE daily for adults. The need for niacin is directly related to the production of energy. It is estimated that 6.6 milligrams of niacin is needed for every 1000 kcalories expended. Even though niacin is water soluble, overdoses can result in toxic effects, including transient flushing, widespread itching, headaches, cramps and nausea, high blood sugar level, irregular heartbeat, peptic ulcers, and liver damage.

A good source of riboflavin contains a substantial amount of the vitamin in relation to its calorie content and contributes at least 10 percent of the U.S. RDA. Pasta and most breads made from refined flours are enriched with niacin because this is one of the nutrients lost in processing. Other nutrients added to refined flours and pasta are iron, riboflavin, and thiamin. Enriched products or products made from enriched flour are labeled as such. Most ready-to-eat and instant-prepared cereals are fortified with niacin. Fortified ready-to-eat cereals usually contain at least 25 percent of the U.S. RDA for niacin. Since cereals vary in the amounts of enriched nutrients, packaging labels should be checked for contents. Good sources of niacin include organ meats, tuna, poultry, peanuts, and enriched and whole-grain products. Fresh and dry legumes also contain tryptophan. Table 6.3 lists good sources of niacin.

VITAMIN B$_6$

Vitamin B$_6$ is found in foods in three forms: *pyridoxine, pyridoxamine,* and *pyridoxal.* They are closely related chemically, structurally, metabolically, and functionally, providing equivalent vitamin activity. These forms are converted into pyridoxal phosphate and pyridoxamine phosphate, which serve primarily as coenzymes. Vitamin B$_6$ is sensitive to light, alkalis, and oxygen.

Functions and Deficiency

Like other B vitamins discussed earlier, vitamin B$_6$ serves as a coenzyme and acts in many important forms of metabolism, primarily protein metabolism. The conversion of essential to nonessential amino acids requires vitamin B$_6$. This vitamin also participates in the production and transformation of tryptophan to niacin, as well as other important body reactions. Vitamin B$_6$ deficiency involves nervous system

Table 6.3 Good Sources of Niacin

Food	Selected Serving Size	Percent of U.S. RDA[a]
Breads, Cereals, and Other Grain Products		
Bagel, plain, or whole-wheat	1 medium	+
Bulgar, cooked or canned	⅔ cup	+
English muffin, plain or whole-wheat	1	+
Muffin, bran	1 medium	+
Oatmeal, instant, fortified, prepared	⅔ cup	+
Pita bread, plain or whole-wheat	1 small	+
Pretzel, soft	1	+
Ready-to-eat cereals (fortified)	1 ounce	+ +
Roll, hoagie or submarine	1 medium	+
Vegetables		
Mushrooms, cooked	½ cup	+
Potato, boiled, with skin	1 medium	+
Meat, Poultry, Fish, and Alternatives		
Beef		
Brisket, braised, lean only	3 ounces	+
Ground, extra lean or lean, baked or broiled	1 patty	+
Roast, rib, roasted, lean only	3 ounces	+
Steak, baked or broiled, lean only	3 ounces	+
Stew meat, simmered, lean only	3 ounces	+
Chicken, without skin (breast), broiled or roasted	½ breast	+ + +
Chicken leg (thigh and drumstick), broiled or roasted without skin	1 leg	+ +
Chicken, without skin: light or dark meat, broiled, roasted, or stewed	3 ounces	+ +
Cornish hen, roasted, without skin	Half hen	+ + +
Ham, fresh, roasted, lean only	3 ounces	+
Lamb, lean only		
Chop, shoulder, braised, broiled, or baked	1 chop	+ +
Roast, shoulder, roasted	3 ounces	+
Liver		
Braised, beef or calf	3 ounces	+ +
Braised, chicken	½ cup diced	+
Liverwurst	1 ounce	+
Pork chop, baked or broiled	1 chop	+
Turkey, dark meat, roasted without skin, ground	3 ounces	+
Veal		
Chop, braised, lean only	1 chop	+ + +
Lean only, roast, leg, roasted	3 ounces	+ +
Catfish, flounder, haddock, pompano, or pike, baked or broiled	3 ounces	+
Crabmeat, steamed	3 ounces	+

Table 6.3   *(Continued)*

Food	Selected Serving Size	Percent of U.S. RDA[a]
Meat, Poultry, Fish and Alternatives (cont.)		
Croaker, porgy, or trout, baked or broiled	3 ounces	+
Mackerel		
Baked or broiled	3 ounces	+++
Canned and drained	3 ounces	++
Mullet, baked or broiled	3 ounces	++
Salmon		
Baked, broiled, poached, or steamed	3 ounces	+
Canned, drained	3 ounces	+
Shrimp; boiled, broiled, steamed, or canned; drained	3 ounces	+
Swordfish steak, baked or broiled	3 ounces	+++
Tuna, canned, drained	3 ounces	+
Peanuts, roasted or dry-roasted	2 tablespoons	+
Peanut butter	2 tablespoons	+

[a] A selected serving size contains:

    + 10–24 percent of the U.S. RDA.

    ++ 25–39 percent of the U.S. RDA.

    +++ 40 percent or more of the U.S. RDA.

Source: USDA/Human Nutrition Information Service.

manifestations such as depression, confusion, and convulsions. Dermatitis, and anemia are the most common symptoms. This deficiency rarely occurs alone; it is most commonly seen in conjunction with the deficiency of other B-complex vitamins. Vitamin B$_6$ deficiency is sometimes mistaken for niacin deficiency since the symptoms are very similar. With an increase in protein intake, the onset of deficiency becomes more rapid.

Requirements and Food Sources

Since vitamin B$_6$ plays a significant role in protein metabolism, the requirement for this vitamin is linked to protein intake. The requirement for vitamin B$_6$ increases with the intake of protein. The RDA for adults is 2.0 milligrams per day for men and 1.6 milligrams per day for women based on average intake of protein. During pregnancy this requirement is increased to 2.2 milligrams per day.

A good source of vitamin B$_6$ contains a substantial amount of the vitamin in relation to its calorie content and contributes at least 10 percent of the U.S. RDA. Most ready-to-eat and instant-prepared cereals are fortified with vitamin B$_6$. Fortified ready-to-eat cereals usually contain at least 25 percent of the U.S. RDA of this vitamin. Since cereals vary in the amount of enriched nutrients, packaging labels

Table 6.4　Good Sources of Vitamin B$_6$

Food	Selected Serving Size	Percent of U.S. RDA[a]
Breads, Cereals, and Other Grain Products		
Oatmeal, instant, fortified, prepared	⅔ cup	++
Ready-to-eat cereals (fortified)	1 ounce	++
Fruits		
Banana, raw	1 medium	++
Prunes, dried, cooked, unsweetened	½ cup	+
Prune juice, unsweetened	½ cup	+
Watermelon, raw, diced	About 1¾ cups	+
Vegetables		
Plaintain, green or ripe, boiled	1 medium	++
Potato, baked or boiled, with skin	1 medium	+
Spinach, cooked	½ cup	+
Sweet potato, baked or boiled	1 medium	+
Tomato juice, tomato juice cocktail, or tomato-vegetable juice cocktail, canned	¾ cup	+
Meat, Poultry, Fish, and Alternatives		
Beef		
Brisket, braised, lean only	3 ounces	+
Ground, extra lean, lean, or regular baked or broiled	1 patty	+
Pot roast, braised, lean only	3 ounces	+
Roast, rib, roasted, lean only	3 ounces	+
Shortribs, braised, lean only	3 ounces	+
Steak, baked, braised, or broiled, lean only	3 ounces	+
Stew meat, simmered, lean only	3 ounces	+
Chicken		
Without skin (breast), broiled	½ breast	+
Without skin (breast), roasted	½ breast	++
Chicken leg (thigh and drumstick), broiled or roasted	1 leg	+
Cornish hen, roasted, without skin	Half hen	++
Ham, fresh, roasted, lean only	3 ounces	+
Liver		
Braised, beef	3 ounces	++
Braised, calf	3 ounces	+
Braised, chicken	½ cup	+
Pork chop, baked or broiled	1 chop	+
Turkey, light or dark meat, roasted without skin	3 ounces	+
Veal, chop, braised, lean only	1 chop	+
Cod, croaker, haddock, mackerel, ocean perch, porgy, or sea bass, baked or broiled	3 ounces	+

Table 6.4 *(Continued)*

Food	Selected Serving Size	Percent of U.S. RDA[a]
Meat, Poultry, Fish, and Alternatives (cont.)		
Mackerel, canned and drained	3 ounces	+
Mullet or trout, baked or broiled	3 ounces	+
Salmon, canned, drained	3 ounces	+
Shrimp, boiled, broiled, steamed, or canned, drained	3 ounces	+
Swordfish steak, baked or broiled	3 ounces	+++

[a] A selected serving size contains:

+ 10–24 percent of the U.S. RDA.

++ 25–39 percent of the U.S. RDA.

+++ 40 percent or more of the U.S. RDA.

Source: USDA/Human Nutrition Information Service.

should be checked for contents. Meats and meat products are generally good sources of vitamin B$_6$. Table 6.4 lists good sources of this vitamin. The richest sources include chicken, fish, kidney, liver, pork, avocados, and eggs, each providing about 0.4 milligram in every 100-gram serving. Other good sources are unmilled rice, soybeans, oats, whole-wheat products, peanuts, and walnuts. Fruits and vegetables, milk products, and red meats are relatively poor sources of the vitamin. Among fruits, bananas are rich in vitamin B$_6$. Since the vitamin is sensitive to light, alkali, and oxygen, considerable losses can occur during food processing and preparation. It is estimated that 15 to 70 percent of the vitamin can be lost in freezing fruits and vegetables, 50 to 70 percent in the processing of luncheon meats, and 50 to 90 percent in the milling of cereals. Large doses of vitamin B$_6$ produce toxic effects, although the acute toxicity of this vitamin is low.

FOLACIN

Folacin is also called *folate,* which refers to compounds that are similar in structure to *folic acid* (also known as *pteroylglutamic acid*). Folate and folacin are general descriptors for compounds that are structurally and functionally similar to folic acid.

Functions and Deficiency

Folates function as coenzymes and help to transport single-carbon fragments from one compound to another in amino acid metabolism and nucleic acid synthesis. Since DNA and RNA are responsible for cell division, this vitamin is especially important during growth periods. Deficiency of this vitamin leads to impaired cell division and affects protein synthesis. Pregnancy increases the incidence of folate deficiency among populations with a low or marginal intake of this vitamin. Deficiency of this vitamin results in a form of anemia referred to as *megaloblastic anemia,* which is characterized by the presence of large, immature red blood cells.

This vitamin is affected by heat, oxidation, and ultraviolet light, and care should be taken during preparation and processing. As much as 50 percent of folate can be destroyed in food processing and storage.

Requirements and Food Sources

A good source of folate contains a substantial amount of the vitamin in relation to its calorie content and contributes at least 10 percent of the U.S. RDA. Most ready-to-eat and instant-prepared cereals are fortified with folate. Fortified ready-to-eat cereals usually contain at least 25 percent of the U.S. RDA for folate. Since cereals vary in the amounts of enriched nutrients, packaging labels should be checked for contents. The RDA for folate is approximately 3 micrograms per kilogram of body weight for men, nonpregnant, nonlactating women, and adolescents. The allowance is 200 micrograms for adult males and 180 micrograms for adult females. The required amount is increased to 400 micrograms during pregnancy. Folacin is usually supplemented during pregnancy. Folate is present in a variety of foods. Rich sources of this vitamin include liver, yeast, green leafy vegetables, legumes, and some fruits. The word *folacin* is linked to foliage since most fruits and vegetables contain folacin. Fair amounts are included in starchy vegetables such as potatoes and lima beans, milk products, eggs, and whole-wheat breads. It is present in smaller amounts in grains, legumes, nuts, and dairy products. Table 6.5 lists good sources of folate. Since considerable amounts of folic acid can be destroyed by heat, raw vegetables are recommended for optimum intake of this vitamin.

A high intake of folic acid can mask the symptoms of pernicious anemia caused by the deficiency or malabsorption of vitamin B_{12} or its cofactor. For strict vegetarians, this can be a problem, since a large amount of folic acid is provided by vegetables and there is no intake of vitamin B_{12}, which is derived from animal products.

VITAMIN B_{12}

Vitamin B_{12} (*cobalamin*) refers to all members of a large group of cobalt-containing substances that can be converted into two important coenzymes that are very active in human metabolism. Cobalamin refers to "cobalt" and "amine," which are both present in vitamin B_{12}. *Cyanocobalamin* is the commercially available form of vitamin B_{12} that is used in vitamin pills and other supplements. This form of the vitamin is water soluble and heat stable.

Functions and Deficiency

Like folacin, vitamin B_{12} is especially important during the growth period since DNA and RNA are substances that direct cell division. Like folacin, vitamin B_{12} is

Table 6.5 Good Sources of Folate

Food	Selected Serving Size	Percent of U.S. RDA[a]
Breads, Cereals, and Other Grain Products		
English muffin, whole-wheat	One	+
Pita bread, whole-wheat	1 small	+
Ready-to-eat cereals (fortified)	1 ounce	+ +
Wheat germ, plain	2 tablespoons	+
Fruits		
Grapefruit and orange juice, frozen, reconstituted	¾ cup	+
Orange juice, fresh, frozen, reconstituted	¾ cup	+
Vegetables		
Artichoke, globe (french), cooked	1 medium	+
Asparagus, cooked	½ cup	+
Beets, cooked	½ cup	+
Broccoli, cooked	½ cup	+
Brussel sprouts, cooked	½ cup	+
Cauliflower, cooked	½ cup	+
Chinese cabbage, cooked	½ cup	+
Corn, cream style, cooked	½ cup	+
Endive, chicory, escarole, or romaine, raw	1 cup	+
Mustard greens, cooked	½ cup	+
Okra, cooked	½ cup	+
Parsnips, cooked	½ cup	+
Peas, green, cooked	½ cup	+
Spinach		
Cooked	½ cup	+ +
Raw	1 cup	+
Turnip greens, cooked	½ cup	+
Meat, Poultry, Fish, and Alternatives		
Liver		
Braised, beef	3 ounces	+ + +
Braised, calf	3 ounces	+ +
Braised, chicken or turkey (diced)	½ cup	+ + +
Crabmeat, steamed	3 ounces	+
Beans, cooked	½ cup	+
Bayo, black, brown, calico, chickpeas (garbanzo beans), lima, mexican, pinto, or white		
Beans		
Black-eyed peas (cowpeas)	½ cup	+ + +
Red kidney	½ cup	+ +
Lentils, cooked	½ cup	+ + +
Peas, split, green or yellow, cooked	½ cup	+

[a] A selected serving size contains:

    + 10–24 percent of the U.S. RDA.

    + + 25–39 percent of the U.S. RDA.

    + + + 40 percent or more of the U.S. RDA.

Source: USDA/Human Nutrition Information Service.

the part of coenzymes involved in DNA and RNA metabolism. It is also important in the metabolism of certain amino acids. Body stores of vitamin B_{12} last longer than those of any other vitamin.

Vitamin B_{12} deficiency results in *macrocytic megaloblastic* anemia. It also causes neurological symptoms affecting the spinal cord, brain, and optic and peripheral nerves. Other symptoms include sore tongue and weakness. Dietary deficiency of vitamin B_{12} is rare and is generally due to lack of intake of meat products or inadequate absorption. Since it is not found in plants, vegans are at risk of developing vitamin B_{12} deficiency.

The presence of vitamin B_{12} in the diet does not guarantee that it will be absorbed. Absorption of this vitamin depends on the presence of a substance referred to as *intrinsic factor* (*IF*), which is produced by the lining of the stomach. If it is lacking, very little vitamin B_{12} is absorbed. IF sometimes decreases, mostly in the elderly, causing a deficiency disease referred to as *pernicious anemia*. In such cases, since vitamin B_{12} cannot be absorbed when taken in foods, it has to be provided in the form of injections.

Requirements and Food Sources

Animal products are the primary dietary source of vitamin B_{12}. The dominant forms of this vitamin in meat are adenosyl- and hydroxocobalamin, whereas dairy products contain mainly methyl- and hydroxocobalamin. In the human diet, vitamin B_{12} is provided primarily by animal products, in which it is accumulated by bacterial synthesis. Plant foods are essentially devoid of vitamin B_{12}; in a very few cases, it can be formed microbially in soil or water. Bacteria, fungi, and algae can synthesize vitamin B_{12}; yeasts, higher plants, and animals cannot. Although folacin and vitamin B_{12} have similar functions within the body, their food sources are entirely different. It should also be noted that folacin cannot substitute for vitamin B_{12} in many ways. In fact, it is not advisable to take folacin if it is possible that vitamin B_{12} is the problem since folacin will mask the vitamin B_{12} deficiency. Therefore, the cause of the megaloblastic anemia (the common deficiency symptom for both folacin and vitamin B_{12}) must be accurately determined and the appropriate vitamin used to treat the deficiency.

A good source of vitamin B_{12} contains a substantial amount of the vitamin in relation to its calorie content and contributes at least 10 percent of the U.S. RDA. Most ready-to-eat and instant-prepared cereals are fortified with folate. Good sources of vitamin B_{12} are meats, eggs, and milk and milk products. Some fermented foods, including yeast, brewer's yeast, and soy products, provide vitamin B_{12}. Table 6.6 lists good source of this vitamin.

Dietary intake of 1 microgram daily of vitamin B_{12} is considered optimal for average normal adults. The RDA for adults, both males and females, is 2 micrograms. During pregnancy this level is increased to 2.2 micrograms. No clear toxic effects from overdosage of vitamin B_{12} have been reported.

Table 6.6 Good Sources of Vitamin B$_{12}$

Food	Selected Serving Size	Percent of U.S. RDA[a]
Meat, Poultry, Fish, and Alternatives		
Beef	3 ounces	++
Brisket, braised, lean only		
Ground, extra lean, baked or broiled	1 patty	+++
Ground, lean or regular, baked or broiled	1 patty	++
Pot roast, braised, lean only	3 ounces	++
Roast, rib, roasted, lean only	3 ounces	++
Shortribs, braised, lean only	3 ounces	++
Steak, baked or broiled, lean only	3 ounces	+++
Steak, braised, lean only	3 ounces	++
Stew meat, simmered, lean only	3 ounces	++
Frankfurter, beef	1	+
Lamb, lean only		
Chop, shoulder, braised, broiled, or baked	1 chop	+++
Roast, shoulder, roasted	3 ounces	++
Ground, cooked	1 patty	++
Liver		
Braised, beef or calf	3 ounces	+++
Braised, chicken or turkey	½ cup diced	+++
Liverwurst	1 ounce	+++
Pork chop, baked or broiled, lean only	1 chop	+
Tongue, braised	3 ounces	+++
Veal, roast, leg, roasted, lean only	3 ounces	++
Carp, cod, flounder, haddock, ocean perch, pompano, or porgy, baked or broiled	3 ounces	+
Catfish, perch, pike, or whitling, baked or broiled	3 ounces	++
Clams, steamed, boiled, or canned, drained	3 ounces	+++
Crabmeat, steamed	3 ounces	+++
Croaker, baked or broiled	3 ounces	+++
Lobster, steamed or boiled	3 ounces	+++
Mackerel, baked, broiled, or canned, drained	3 ounces	+++
Mussels, steamed, boiled, or poached	3 ounces	+++
Oysters		
Baked, broiled, or steamed	3 ounces	+++
Canned, undrained	3 ounces	+++
Salmon		
Baked or broiled	3 ounces	++
Steamed, poached, or canned, drained	3 ounces	+++
Scallops		
Baked or broiled	3 ounces	+
Boiled or steamed	3 ounces	+
Shrimp, broiled, steamed, boiled, or canned, drained	3 ounces	+
Swordfish steak, baked or broiled	3 ounces	++
Trout, baked or broiled	3 ounces	+++
Tuna, canned, drained	3 ounces	++
Egg, whole, cooked	1 large egg	+

Table 6.6   *(Continued)*

Food	Selected Serving Size	Percent of U.S. RDA[a]
Milk, Cheese, and Yogurt		
Cottage cheese, regular or low-fat	½ cup	+
Ice milk, soft-serve, not chocolate	½ cup	+
Milk, whole, low-fat, or skim	1 cup	+
Yogurt		
Flavored or fruit, made with whole or low-fat milk	8 ounces	+
Frozen	8 ounces	+
Plain, made with whole milk	8 ounces	+
Plain, made with low-fat or nonfat milk	8 ounces	+ +

[a] A selected serving size contains:

    + 10–24 percent of the U.S. RDA.

    + + 25–39 percent of the U.S RDA.

    + + + 40 percent or more of the U.S. RDA.

Source: USDA/Human Nutrition Information Service.

BIOTIN

Biotin is a sulfur-containing vitamin that is essential for humans. It is a component of various foods and can also be synthesized in the lower GI tract by microorganisms and some fungi. There are two chemically related compounds, *oxybiotin* and *biocytin,* which are also biologically active.

Functions and Deficiency

Biotin is an integral part of enzymes that fix carbon dioxide in animal tissue. The conversion of biotin to the active coenzyme depends on magnesium and adenosine triphosphate (ATP). In adult humans, biotin deficiency can be produced by the ingestion of large amounts of *avidin,* a biotin-binding glycoprotein found in raw egg white.

Deficiency symptoms of biotin include anorexia, nausea, vomiting, glossitis, pallor, mental depression, alopecia, and a dry, scaly dermatitis. Dermatitis and neuromuscular disorders are common deficiency symptoms. An increase in serum cholesterol and bile pigments is also present.

Requirements and Food Sources

Biotin is found in several foods. The best dietary sources include liver (100 to 200 micrograms per 100 grams); egg yolk (16 micrograms per 100 grams); soy flour (60 to 70 micrograms per 100 grams); cereals (3 to 30 micrograms per 100 grams);

and yeast (100 to 200 micrograms per 100 grams). Other sources include kidney, legumes, nuts, egg yolk, milk, yeast, and tomatoes. Fruits and meats are usually poor sources of biotin. The bioavailability of biotin varies considerably, depending on whether it is present in a biologically available or bound form. In most foods it is available in unbound form, whereas in wheat it is present in bound form. Due to the lack of definite studies on the need for biotin, it is hard to recommend a dietary requirement. A daily dose of 30 to 100 micrograms is provisionally recommended for adults. There are no reports of toxicity due to overdosage.

PANTOTHENIC ACID

Pantothenic acid (*pantothenate*) is a B-complex vitamin that plays a significant role as a component of the coenzyme A molecule and is involved in the synthesis of vital body substances. The word *pantothenic* is derived from a Greek word meaning "from all sides," which refers to its abundant availability in a variety of food sources, as well as its wide usefulness as a nutrient. It takes part in a series of reactions that are important in the release of energy from carbohydrates; in gluconeogenesis; in the synthesis and degradation of fatty acids; in the synthesis of such vital compounds as sterols and steroid hormones; and in acylation reactions.

Functions and Deficiency

Evidence of a dietary deficiency of pantothenic acid has not been established. The lack of deficiency symptoms may be attributed to the abundant availability of pantothenic acid in a variety of foods and most likely due to the difficulty of estimating the contributions by intestinal microflora. This vitamin has been implicated in the "burning feet" syndrome. Pantothenic acid is needed for growth, normal skin, normal tissues, and efficient functioning of the nervous system.

Requirements and Food Sources

Pantothenic acid is widely distributed in foods and is found abundantly in animal tissues, organ meats, egg yolk, whole-grain cereals, yeast, and legumes. Smaller amounts are found in milk, vegetables, and fruits. Almost 50 percent of pantothenic acid in grains is lost during the milling process. Since the vitamin is heat sensitive, losses can be expected during freezing and canning. It is suggested that an intake of 4 to 7 milligrams per day is safe and adequate for adults. Pantothenic acid has been found to be relatively nontoxic.

VITAMIN C

Vitamin C, also referred to as *ascorbic acid* and *ascorbate,* is a water-soluble vitamin that is also an antioxidant. It can be synthesized by many mammals but not by humans. The disease resulting from the deficiency of vitamin C is referred to as *scurvy,* which led to the discovery of the vitamin. In recent years, vitamin C has been implicated in the cure of the common cold, as well as in reduction of the incidence of some forms of cancer. These claims are not firmly established, and published studies show contradictory results.

Functions and Deficiency

The functions of vitamin C are different from those of the B vitamins. It is needed for the formation of collagen, the protein that serves as a connective agent in many parts of the body. Collagen-containing materials and structures in the body include the gingivae (gums) and the binding materials in skin, muscle, and scar tissue. Vitamin C is also necessary for the production of certain hormones and neurotransmitters, as well as in the metabolism of some amino acids and vitamins. It also helps blood cells fight infection; aids the liver in detoxifying harmful substances; and helps the gut absorb iron from foods. Vitamin C also activates folic acid.

Just as the functions of vitamin C are diverse, so are its deficiency symptoms. These range from a generalized feeling of weakness, bleeding gums, loosened teeth, easy bruising, and small hemorrhages in the skin to impaired immune function.

Requirements and Food Sources

The adult RDA for vitamin C is 60 milligrams per day. This amount can easily be taken in from foods since this vitamin is widely available. A good source of vitamin C contains a substantial amount of the vitamin in relation to its calorie content and contributes at least 10 percent of the U.S. RDA in a selected serving size. Some juices not normally a source of vitamin C, such as grape and apple juices, have vitamin C added. Vitamin C is also added to frozen peaches to prevent discoloration. Most ready-to-eat cereals are fortified with this vitamin. Fortified ready-to-eat cereals usually contain at least 25 percent of the U.S. RDA for vitamin C. Labels should be checked since cereals vary widely in nutrient contents. Table 6.7 lists good sources of vitamin C.

Common fruits and vegetables have a high content of this vitamin. Citrus fruits are especially rich in this vitamin, but other fruits and vegetables also contain large quantities. These include broccoli, cabbage, cantaloupe, cauliflower, green and red peppers, collard greens, spinach, tomatoes, potatoes, and strawberries. Meat, fish, poultry, eggs, and dairy products contain smaller amounts; grains contain none. Vitamin C can be lost during processing since it is water soluble, sensitive to heat and oxygen, and easily lost in cooking water. It is added to a variety of processed foods and drinks. Many kinds of beverages, such as fruit juices, carbonated beverages, and fruit-flavored drinks, are supplemented with it. Vitamin C functions as an antioxidant and is used as a coating for cut fruits to prevent them from browning due to oxidation. For example, lemon juice is used over cut apple or banana slices. Although excess vitamin C is excreted since it is water soluble, if taken in excess amounts it may cause adverse effects.

Table 6.7   Good Sources of Vitamin C

Food	Selected Serving Size	Percent of U.S. RDA[a]
Breads, Cereals, and Other Grain Products		
Ready-to-eat cereals, fortified	1 ounce	++
Fruits		
Apples, baked, unsweetened, raw	1 medium	+
Apple juice	¾ cup	+++
Banana, raw	1 medium	+
Blackberries, raw	½ cup	++
Bluberries, raw	½ cup	+
Cantaloupe, frozen balls, unsweetened	½ cup	+++
raw	About ½ cup diced	+++
Cranberry juice cocktail	1 cup	+++
Grapefruit, raw	½ medium	+++
Grapefruit juice, fresh, canned, or reconstituted frozen, unsweetened	¾ cup	+++
Grapefruit and orange juices, unsweetened	½ cup	+++
Grapefruit and orange sections, canned, unsweetened	½ cup	+++
Grape juice, unsweetened	¾ cup	+++
Honeydew melon, raw	About ¾ cup diced	+++
Kiwifruit, raw	1 medium	+++
Mandarin orange sections, canned or frozen, juice-pack	½ cup	+++
Mango, raw	½ medium	+++
Nectarine, raw	1 medium	+
Orange, raw	1 medium	+++
Orange juice, fresh, canned, or reconstituted frozen; unsweetened	¾ cup	+++
Papaya, raw	¼ medium	+++
Peaches		
Frozen, unsweetened	½ cup	+++
Raw	1 medium	+
Pear, raw	1 medium	+
Pineapple		
Canned, chunks, juice-pack	½ cup	+
Raw	½ cup	+
Pineapple juice, canned, unsweetened	¾ cup	++
Pineapple-grapefruit juice, canned or reconstituted frozen, unsweetened	¾ cup	+++
Pineapple-orange juice, canned or reconstituted frozen, unsweetened	¾ cup	+++
Plum, raw	1 medium	+
Pomegranate, raw	1 medium	+

Table 6.7 *(Continued)*

Food	Selected Serving Size	Percent of U.S. RDA[a]
Fruits (cont.)		
Apples, baked, unsweetened, raw	1 medium	+
Raspberries, frozen, unsweetened; raw	½ cup	++
Strawberries, raw, frozen, or canned, unsweetened	½ cup	+++
Tangelo, raw	1 medium	+++
Tangerine, raw	1 medium	+++
Watermelon, raw	About 1¾ cups diced	+++
Vegetables		
Artichoke, globe (french), cooked	1 medium	+
Asparagus, cooked	½ cup	+++
Beans, green or yellow, lima, cooked	½ cup	+
Bean sprouts, raw or cooked	½ cup	+
Broccoli, raw or cooked	½ cup	+++
Brussels sprouts, cooked	½ cup	+++
Cabbage		
Chinese, cooked	½ cup	++
Green, raw or cooked	½ cup	++
Red, raw or cooked	½ cup	+++
Cauliflower, raw or cooked	½ cup	+++
Chard, cooked	½ cup	+
Collards, cooked	½ cup	+
Endive, chicory, escarole, or romaine, raw	1 cup	+
Dandelion greens, raw	½ cup	+
Kale, cooked	½ cup	+++
Kohlrabi, cooked	½ cup	+++
Mustard greens, cooked	½ cup	++
Okra, cooked	½ cup	+
Onion, spring		
Cooked	1 large	+
Raw	1 medium	+
Parsnips, cooked	½ cup	+
Peas, green, cooked	½ cup	+
Pepper, sweet, green or red, raw or cooked	½ cup	+++
Plantain, green or ripe, boiled	1 medium	+++
Poke greens, cooked	½ cup	+++
Potato with skin, baked or boiled	1 medium	++
Pumpkin, cooked	½ cup	+
Radishes, raw	6 large	+
Rutabagas, cooked	½ cup	++
Snow peas, raw or cooked	½ cup	+++
Spinach		
Cooked	½ cup	+
Raw	1 cup	+

Table 6.7 *(Continued)*

Food	Selected Serving Size	Percent of U.S. RDA[a]
Vegetables (cont.)		
Squash		
Summer, yellow, raw	½ cup	+
Winter, cooked, mashed	½ cup	+
Sweet potato		
Baked or boiled	1 medium	+++
Canned	½ cup	+++
Tomatoes		
Cooked	½ cup	++
Raw	1 medium	++
Tomato juice or tomato-vegetable juice cocktail, canned	¾ cup	+++
Turnip greens with turnips, cooked	½ cup	+
Turnips, cooked	½ cup	+
Watercress, raw	½ cup	+
Meat, Poultry, Fish, and Alternatives		
Liver		
Beef, braised	3 ounces	++
Chicken, braised	½ cup diced	+
Clams, steamed, boiled, or canned, drained	3 ounces	+
Mussels, steamed, boiled, or poached	3 ounces	+

[a] A selected serving size contains:

    + 10–24 percent of the U.S. RDA.

    ++ 25–39 percent of the U.S. RDA.

    +++ 40 percent or more of the U.S. RDA.

Source: USDA/Human Nutrition Information Service.

NONVITAMINS

There are several products that are not categorized as vitamins since they are produced in sufficient amounts in the body. However, they are involved in metabolic reactions similar to those of vitamins. These substances include rutin, inositol, carnitine, para-aminobenzoic acid (PABA), bioflavinoids, lipoic acid, choline, and ubiquinone. Although some of them are marketed as supplements, a healthy body does not need them. Other vitamins are under study at this time; little is known about their functional significance.

Table 6.8 provides a complete summary of the sources of water-soluble vitamins.

Table 6.8   Summary of Food Sources of Water-Soluble Vitamins

Good Food Sources	Better Food Sources
Vitamin B$_1$ (thiamin)	
Enriched cereals, pasta, and rice	Sunflower seeds
Whole grains	Sesame seeds
Oatmeal	Wheat germs
Eggs	Peanuts
Poultry	Liver
Dried beans	Kidney
	Pork
	Peas
	Brewer's yeast
Vitamin B$_2$ (riboflavin)	
Meat, poultry, fish	Milk
Eggs	Cheese
Dark green leafy vegetables	Wheat germ
Dry beans and peas	Yeast
Enriched breads and cereals	Liver
Nuts	Kidney
Vitamin B$_6$ (pyridoxine)	
Meat, poultry, fish	Wheat germs
Whole grains	Wheat bran
Nuts	Yeast
	Sunflower seeds
	Avocado
	Banana
	Organ meats (liver)
Vitamin B$_{12}$ (cyanocobalamin)	
	Clams
	Oysters
	Shrimp
	Organ meats
	Eggs
	Chicken
	Pork
	Milk
	Cheeses
Niacin	
Legumes	Beef, poultry, fish
Nuts	Organ meats
Wheat germ	Yeast
Enriched cereals, breads, and pasta	Sunflower seeds
	Sesame seeds
	Peanut butter

Table 6.8 *(Continued)*

Good Food Sources	Better Food Sources
Folic acid	
Melons	Liver, kidney
Sweet potato	Yeast
Pumpkin	Wheat germ
Beef	Oranges
Fish	Asparagus
Eggs	Green leafy vegetables
Pantothenic acid	
All plant and animal foods	Liver
	Kidney
	Yeast
	Whole grains
	Eggs
	Legumes
	Vegetables
Biotin	
Found in almost all foods	Liver
	Kidney
	Egg yolk
	Milk
	Yeast
Vitamin C	
Tomatoes	Citrus fruits and juices
Potatoes (white and sweet)	Brussel sprouts
Honeydew melon	Broccoli
Berries (raspberries, blackberries, blueberries)	Peppers
	Parsley
	Greens
	Cabbage
	Strawberries
	Cantaloupe
	Kiwi
	Papaya
	Guava
	Starfruit
	Watermelon

Chapter 7

MINERALS

Minerals are the chemical elements other than carbon, hydrogen, oxygen, and nitrogen, which usually make up the body. They are present in minute quantities compared to the other elements. For example, carbon, hydrogen, oxygen, and nitrogen account for 96 percent of body weight, whereas minerals account for only 4 percent. At least 20 minerals are commonly found in the human body. Minerals are also described as the part of food that remains as ash or residue after the food is digested and burned.

Minerals are divided into two categories based on the amount found in the body. **Macrominerals** or **major minerals** are those minerals present in amounts greater than 0.01 percent of body weight or needed in the diet in amounts of 100 milligrams or more per day. They include calcium, phosphorus, sulfur, potassium, sodium, chloride, and magnesium. Calcium is present in the largest amount in the body, followed by phosphorus. Minerals present in the body in quantities less than 0.01 percent of body weight are called **trace minerals, trace elements,** or **microminerals.** They include iron, iodine, fluoride, zinc, selenium, copper, chromium, manganese, molybdenum, cobalt, silicon, arsenic, nickel, and vanadium. Among the trace minerals, iron and zinc are mostly prevalent in the human body. Although some of these minerals are needed in only small quantities, this does not reduce their importance in body functions. Furthermore, the consequences of an essential trace mineral deficiency are just as severe as those of a macromineral deficiency. Although minerals are needed by the body in minute quantities, they play a very important role in human health and are needed for growth, reproduction, and other functions. As with proteins, it is not possible to distinguish essential from nonessential minerals. RDAs have been established for three of the macrominerals (calcium, phosphorus, and magnesium) and for four of the microminerals (iron, zinc, iodine, and selenium). As with other nutrients, excess intake of minerals can result in toxicity. More than for other nutrients, the bioavailability of minerals is critical. **Bioavailability** refers to the degree to which the body is able to use a substance in the form or amount present. Several factors affect the bioavailability of minerals. Minerals are not as readily absorbed as proteins, carbohydrates, or fats from the diet. Also, different minerals have different absorption capabilities. Although minerals cannot be lost as easily as some of the sensitive vitamins, they can be lost during prepreparation or preparation of foods, such as by disposing of cooking water, trimming, or carving of foods.

FACTORS THAT INCREASE THE BIOAVAILABILITY OF MINERALS

Dietary Factors

Some dietary factors increase the bioavailability of minerals. A good example is iron, which occurs in two forms. *Heme iron* is found in the hemoglobin of blood and in the myoglobin of animal meats. This type of iron accounts for about 40 to 50 percent of the iron found in meat, fish, and poultry. *Nonheme iron* accounts for the remainder of the iron found in foods. It occurs in eggs, milk, and plant foods. It has been found that humans absorb about 15 to 35 percent of heme iron but only 1 to 20 percent of nonheme iron from the diet. Apparently, the body absorbs more iron from meats than from meals containing eggs or milk. This different in absorption is critical for those who do not eat meat or meat products. Adding meats containing heme iron to foods containing nonheme iron can increase the absorption of iron from non-heme-containing foods. For example, adding meat to a macaroni and cheese casserole will increase the efficiency of iron absorption from both the heme and nonheme iron portions.

Vitamin C

It has been found that vitamin C helps the absorption of nonheme iron. For example, adding orange juice to a meal containing eggs can considerably increase the absorption of iron in those foods. Similarly, recipes that contain tomato sauce can improve the availability of iron from pasta products or rice. Vitamin C–rich foods should be consumed with the meal to influence the absorption of nonheme iron. For example, orange juice at breakfast is more useful in iron absorption when taken with scrambled eggs, whereas drinking orange juice alone for breakfast and eating eggs for lunch may have no effect on the absorption of iron.

Other Nutrients

Vitamin D, either from the diet or synthesized by the body, increases the absorption of calcium and phosphorus. The lactose in foods also facilitates the absorption of calcium and magnesium. Dietary proteins promote increased absorption of zinc.

FACTORS THAT DECREASE THE BIOAVAILABILITY OF MINERALS

Dietary Fiber

Dietary fiber and some compounds associated with it can decrease the absorption of minerals. One such substance is phytate. Phytate and fiber are commonly present in whole grains, bran, and soy products. They can decrease the absorption of zinc, calcium, magnesium, and iron. Phytate can be broken down by an enzyme in yeast. Thus, yeast-leavened bread has higher bioavailability than a whole-grain unleavened bread. This should be considered in preparing menus for individuals who may be lacking some of the minerals that are susceptible to phytates.

Organic Components of Diets

Other organic components in diets can reduce the bioavailability of certain minerals. Tannins found in tea and grains such as sorghum can decrease the bioavailability of iron. Oxalates, organic compounds found in spinach, rhubarb, and chocolate decrease the bioavailability of calcium. Large amounts of ascorbic acid decrease the utilization of copper. Dietary phosphorus affects the intake of calcium.

Competition Among Minerals

Minerals can compete with each other, affecting their bioavailability and absorption rate. When diets are supplemented with calcium, the absorption of magnesium, zinc, and iron is reduced. When zinc is added as a supplement, it reduces the absorption of copper. Zinc and iron compete with each other, as do magnesium and iron.

Other factors that affect the bioavailability of minerals include certain medications and the physiological status of the individual.

FUNCTIONS OF MINERALS

Building Tissue

Minerals form part of the tissue structure and take part in building body cells. They are involved in the formation of both hard and soft tissues. Calcium and phosphorus promote the formation of bones and teeth. Soft tissues such as blood, muscles, organs, and glands contain several minerals. Minerals are also stored in bones, eyes, muscles, and other organs.

Acting as Components of Organic Molecules

Minerals are components of different enzymes, cartilages, tendons, hemoglobin, thyroid hormones, and vitamins. Thus, minerals are responsible for regulating important body functions. The mineral iodine is a component of the hormone thyroxin, which regulates the speed of different body processes. Phosphorus, magnesium, iron, iodine, zinc, selenium, copper, manganese, and molybdenum are examples of minerals that are components of enzymes.

Facilitating Nerve Impulse Transmission and Muscle Contraction

Minerals facilitate nerve impulse transmission and muscle contraction. Calcium helps to release the energy needed for muscle contraction; sodium signals muscle responses, and other minerals control body fluid levels and help nutrient absorption and oxygen transportation. Calcium, sodium, and potassium promote nerve impulse transmission.

Maintaining Water, Acid-Base, and Electrolyte Balance

Minerals help maintain the water balance and the acid-base balance of body fluids. They also help maintain the fluid-electrolyte balance—for example, by osmosis, diffusion, and absorption. Sodium and chloride play important roles in water balance and acid-base balance, as well as in the formation of gastric juice. Mineral elements like sodium and chloride have electrical charges, which are used to maintain a proper acid-base balance in the body. Sodium chloride is made up of a sodium atom with a positive charge and a chloride atom with a negative charge. The positive and negative charges attract each other, and sodium chloride is formed. This electrolytic function is used by minerals in controlling the acid-base balance. If body forms have more acidity than desired, alkaline electrolytes are used to neutralize them, and vice versa. Proteins are described as amphoteric; because of their structure, they act both as an acid or as a base.

Electrolytes also help maintain the water balance inside and outside the cells; this process is conducted by osmosis. The functions of different minerals and food sources, and the role they play in human nutrition, are discussed in detail as follows.

MACROMINERALS

Calcium

Almost 99 percent of calcium is present in the skeleton; the other 1 percent is found in extracellular fluids, intracellular structures, and cell membranes. Extraskeletal calcium plays an important role in vital functions such as nerve conduction, muscle contraction, blood clotting, and membrane permeability. Several hormones play a critical role in maintaining the blood calcium concentration. Calcium is lost from the body in feces, urine, and sweat.

Functions   Calcium helps to build bones and teeth. It is stored in bones and is used when needed by the blood and soft tissues. By osmosis, it promotes the movement of fluids. Another important function of calcium is in the contraction of muscles. It teams up with potassium, magnesium, and sodium to stimulate the nerve impulses that facilitate muscle relaxation. Heart muscles need calcium for contraction; in the absence of calcium, the heart may beat irregularly and develop other malfunctions. Calcium is also helpful in the conversion of milk into curds in the stomach with the help of the enzyme rennin. This action facilitates the digestion of milk.

Requirements and Food Sources   Dairy products contribute more than 55 percent of the calcium intake in the U.S. population. A good food source of calcium contains a substantial amount of calcium in relation to its calorie content and provides at least 10 percent of the U.S. RDA. Some foods, such as orange juice, bread, and ready-to-eat cereals, are not normally good sources of calcium but may have had calcium added. The food fact label is a good source of information since cereals come in a variety of forms. Some good food sources of calcium are listed in Table 7.1. Milk products such as cheese, yogurt, and ice cream are good sources. Other sources include some green leafy vegetables (such as broccoli, kale, and collards), citrus fruits, legumes, meats and whole or enriched grains, lime-processed tortillas, calcium-precipitated tofu, and calcium-fortified foods. Bones, especially soft bones of fish like sardines and salmon, are good sources. Calcium from dairy products tends to be highly bioavailable. The levels of protein and phosphorus in the diet can affect the metabolism of calcium and its requirements. The recommended calcium allowance for adults is 1200 milligrams per day for both men and women. This amount can easily be obtained from dairy products. Calcium deficiency may be seen in persons who do not or cannot take dairy products due to lactose intolerance. However, there are other sources of calcium that can be substituted. Persons who have osteoporosis, a condition in which bones become porous and fragile, must take higher amounts of calcium under medical supervision. Calcium deficiency in children causes poor growth and poor bone and tooth formation. It may also result in reduced absorption of some other minerals. High intake of calcium for a prolonged period of time may result in constipation, the development of urinary stones, and malfunctioning of the kidneys.

Calcium is used as a supplement in orange juice and other fruit juices. It is also used as a food additives in conjunction with other nutrients. A commonly used food additive is calcium propionate, which acts as a leavening agents and a dough conditioner. Calcium chloride and calcium hydroxide are also used as food additives.

Table 7.1   Good Sources of Calcium

Food	Selected Serving Size	Percent of U.S. RDA[a]
Breads, Cereals, and Other Grain Products		
English muffin, plain, plain with raisins	1	+
Muffin, bran	1 medium	+
Oatmeal, instant, fortified, prepared	⅔ cup	+
Pancakes, plain, fruit, buckwheat, or whole-wheat	Two 4-inch pancakes	+
Waffles		
Bran, cornmeal, or fruit	Two 4-inch squares	+
Plain	Two 4-inch squares	+ +
Vegetables		
Broccoli, cooked	½ cup	+
Spinach, cooked	½ cup	+
Turnip greens, cooked	½ cup	+
Meat, Poultry, Fish, and Alternatives		
Mackerel, canned, drained	3 ounces	+
Ocean perch, baked or broiled	3 ounces	+
Salmon, canned, drained	3 ounces	+
Tofu (bean curd)	½ cup cubed	+ +
Milk, Cheese, and Yogurt		
Cheese, natural		
Blue, brick, camembert, feta, gouda, monterey, mozzarella, muenster, provolone, or roquefort	1 ounce	+
Gruyere or Swiss	1 ounce	+ +
Parmesan (hard) or romano	1 ounce	+ +
Cheese		
Processed, cheddar or Swiss	¾ ounce	+
Ricotta	½ cup	+ +
Ice cream or ice milk, soft-serve	½ cup	+
Milk		
Buttermilk	1 cup	+ +
Chocolate	1 cup	+ +
Dry, nonfat, reconstituted	1 cup	+ +
Evaporated, whole or skim, diluted	1 cup	+ +
Low-fat or skim	1 cup	+ +
Whole	1 cup	+ +
Yogurt		
Flavored or fruit, made with whole or low-fat milk	8 ounces	+ +
Frozen	8 ounces	+ +
Plain, made with whole milk	8 ounces	+ +
Plain, made with low-fat or nonfat milk	8 ounces	+ + +

[a] A selected serving size contains:

    + 10–24 percent of the U.S. RDA.

    + + 25–39 percent of the U.S. RDA.

    + + + 40 percent or more of the U.S. RDA.

Source: USDA/Human Nutrition Information Service.

Phosphorus

Like calcium, phosphorus is involved in body structure, with 85 percent being present in bones and teeth. A combination of calcium, phosphorus, oxygen, and hydrogen forms the compound *hydroxyapatite,* which is found in bones and teeth.

Functions

Phosphorus, in addition to its role in the formation of bones and teeth, maintains the acid-base balance and is a component of coenzymes. It is an essential component of bone mineral, where it occurs in a mass ratio of 1 phosphorus to 2 calcium. Functionally, therefore, phosphorus and calcium are metabolically related. Phosphorus is also present in soft tissues, lipids, proteins, carbohydrates, and nucleic acid. It combines with lipids to form *phospholipids,* which play an essential role in body metabolism. It is also present as a modulator of activities in enzymes. One important source of energy for metabolic processes is derived largely from the phosphate bonds of adenosine triphosphate (ATP). Phosphorus is the energy storage molecules in adenine diphosphate (ADP) and ATP. The deficiency symptoms of phosphorus include weakness and demineralization of bones. Absorption of other minerals may also be depressed.

Requirements and Food Sources Phosphorus is present in many foods, major contributors being protein-rich foods and cereal grains. A good source of phosphorus contains a substantial amount of this mineral in relation to its calorie content and contributes at least 10 percent of the U.S. RDA. Good food sources of phosphorus are listed in Table 7.2. Milk, meat, poultry, and fish are major sources in the United States. There is twice as much phosphorus as calcium in some foods, such as eggs, grains, nuts, dry beans, peas, and lentils. The ratio of phosphorus to calcium is considered in setting the dietary requirements of both minerals. A 1-to-1 ratio of calcium to phosphorus is considered sufficient for most age groups. The RDA for phosphorus is 800 milligrams for children 1 to 10 years of age and 1200 milligrams for persons 11 to 24 years of age of both sexes. A total allowance of 1200 milligrams per day of phosphorus is considered sufficient during pregnancy and lactation. Common food sources of phosphorus include milk, cheese, meat, poultry, and whole grains. Many foods that are rich sources of calcium also provide phosphorus; however, the reverse is not true. Meat, fish, poultry, and eggs are rich sources of phosphorus, but they usually contain very little calcium. Most fruits and vegetables are not good sources of phophorus, which is present mainly in the seeds. Phosphorus is also found in some of the additives used in processing foods such as carbonated beverages, processed meats, processed cheeses, and dressings.

Magnesium

Magnesium is found in muscles and soft tissues, extracellular fluid and the skeleton. It is essential for all biosynthetic processes, glycolysis, energy-dependent membrane transport, and transmission of the genetic code. Like calcium and phospho-

Table 7.2 Good Sources of Phosphorus

Food	Selected Serving Size	Percent of U.S. RDA[a]
Breads, Cereals, and Other Grain Products		
Bread, whole-wheat	2 slices	+
Bulgar, cooked or canned	⅔ cup	+
Oatmeal, regular or quick, cooked	⅔ cup	+
Pancakes, plain	Two 4-inch square	+
Ready-to-eat cereals, whole-grain	1 ounce	+
Roll, whole-wheat	1 medium	+
Waffles, plain	Two 4-inch square	+ +
Wheat germ, plain	2 tablespoons	+
Vegetables		
Beans, lima, cooked	½ cup	+
Meat, Poultry, Fish, and Alternatives		
Beef		
Brisket, braised, lean only	3 ounces	+
Ground, extra lean, lean, or regular, baked or Broiled	1 patty	+
Pot roast, braised, lean only	3 ounces	+
Roast, rib, roasted, lean only	3 ounces	+
Shortribs, braised, lean only	3 ounces	+
Steak, baked, braised, or broiled, lean only	3 ounces	+
Stew meat, simmered, lean only	3 ounces	+
Chicken, without skin		
Breast, broiled or roasted	½ breast	+
Leg (thigh and drumstick), broiled or roasted	1 leg	+
Ham, fresh, smoked or cured, roasted, lean only	3 ounces	+
Lamb, lean only		
Chop, loin, or shoulder, braised, broiled, or baked	1 chop	+
Ground, cooked	1 patty	+
Roast, shoulder, roasted	3 ounces	+
Liver		
Braised, beef or calf	3 ounces	+ +
Braised, chicken	½ cup diced	+ +
Pork chop, baked or broiled, lean only	1 chop	+
Turkey		
Light or dark meat, roasted without skin	3 ounces	+
Ground cooked	3 ounces	+
Veal		
Cutlet or steak, pan-broiled, lean only	3 ounces	+
Ground cooked	3 ounces	+
Roast, leg, roasted, lean only	3 ounces	+
Carp, baked or broiled	3 ounces	+ + +
Catfish, cod, croaker, mackerel, mullet, ocean perch, pike, pompano, porgy, trout, or whiting, baked or broiled	3 ounces	+

Table 7.2 *(Continued)*

Food	Selected Serving Size	Percent of U.S. RDA[a]
Meat, Poultry, Fish, and Alternatives (cont.)		
Clams, steamed, boiled, or canned, drained	3 ounces	+
Crabmeat, steamed	3 ounces	+
Flounder, haddock, perch, or sea bass, baked or broiled	3 ounces	+
Lobster, steamed or broiled	3 ounces	+
Mackerel, canned and drained	3 ounces	++
Mussels, steamed, boiled, or poached	3 ounces	+
Oysters		
Baked, broiled, or steamed	3 ounces	+
Canned, undrained	3 ounces	+
Salmon		
Baked, broiled, or steamed	3 ounces	+
Canned, drained	3 ounces	++
Scallops, baked, broiled, steamed, or boiled	3 ounces	+
Shrimp, broiled, steamed, boiled, or canned (drained)	3 ounces	+
Swordfish steak, baked or broiled	3 ounces	++
Tuna, canned, drained	3 ounces	+
Beans, calico, chickpeas (garbanzo beans), lima, mexican, mung, pinto, or red kidney, cooked	½ cup	+
Lentils, cooked	½ cup	+
Soy milk (not baby formula)	1 cup	+
Almonds, roasted	2 tablespoons	+
Brazil nuts	2 tablespoons	+
Peanut butter	2 tablespoons	+
Pine nuts (pignolias)	2 tablespoons	+
Sesame seeds	2 tablespoons	+
Sunflower seeds, hulled; roasted, unroasted, or dry-roasted	2 tablespoons	+
Milk, Cheese, and Yogurt		
Cheese, natural: blue, brick, cheddar, colby, edam, gouda, Gruyere, havarti, limburger, monterey, mozzarella, muenster, Parmesan (hard), port du salut, provolone, roquefort, Swiss, tilsit	1 ounce	+
Cheese		
Processed, cheddar or swiss	¾ ounce	+
Ricotta	½ cup	+
Cheese spread, cheddar	1 tablespoon	+
Cottage cheese, regular and low-fat	½ cup	+
Ice milk, soft-serve	½ cup	+
Milk		
Chocolate	1 cup	+
Dry, low-fat, or nonfat; reconstituted	1 cup	+
Evaporated, skim, diluted	1 cup	+
Evaporated, whole, diluted	1 cup	++
Whole, low-fat, or skim	1 cup	+

Table 7.2 *(Continued)*

Food	Selected Serving Size	Percent of U.S. RDA[a]
Milk, Cheese, and Yogurt (cont.)		
Yogurt		
Flavored or fruit, made with whole or low-fat milk	8 ounces	++
Frozen	8 ounces	+
Plain, made with whole milk	8 ounces	+
Plain, made with low-fat or nonfat milk	8 ounces	++

[a] A selected serving size contains:

   + 10–24 percent of the U.S. RDA.

   ++ 25–39 percent of the U.S. RDA.

   +++ 40 percent or more of the U.S. RDA.

Source: USDA/Human Nutrition Information Service.

rus, magnesium has diverse functions and is involved in a variety of metabolic processes. More than 300 enzymes are activated directly or indirectly by magnesium. Along with calcium, it is necessary for the transmission of nerve impulses involved in the contraction and relaxation of muscles. It also helps to stabilize DNA and RNA, which are involved in cell division. Magnesium deficiency has been reported with other diseases, with symptoms including GI tract abnormalities, electrolyte losses, renal dysfunction, and general malnutrition. Other symptoms include nervous disorders, convulsions, and calcification of soft tissues.

Requirements and Food Sources Magnesium is widely distributed in foods, with the highest concentrations found in nuts, legumes, seafood, and unmilled grains. A good source of magnesium contains a substantial amount of this mineral in relation to its calorie content and contributes at least 10 percent of the U.S. RDA for magnesium. The RDA for both sexes is 4.5 milligrams per kilogram of body weight, which means about 280 milligrams for women and 350 milligrams for men aged 19 and above. Slightly higher amounts are recommended during pregnancy and lactation. Processing can remove a considerable amount of magnesium. Almost 80 percent of magnesium is lost when the germ and outer layer of cereal grains are removed. Vegetables are good sources of magnesium since it is found in chlorophyll. It is also found in chocolate and cocoa. Fish, meat, and milk are relatively poor sources of magnesium. Except for bananas, fruits are also poor sources. Diets that are high in vegetables and unrefined grains are much higher in magnesium than diets that have substantial quantities of refined foods, meats, and dairy products. Table 7.3 provides a list of good sources of magnesium.

Table 7.3 Good Sources of Magnesium

Food	Selected Serving Size	Percent of U.S. RDA[a]
Breads, Cereals, and Other Grain Products		
Bread, whole-wheat	2 slices	+
English muffin, whole-wheat	1	+
Muffin, bran	1 medium	+
Multigrain cereal, cooked	⅔ cup	+
Noodles, whole-wheat, cooked	1 cup	+
Pita bread, whole-wheat	1 small	+
Ready-to-eat cereals, whole-grain	1 ounce	+
Rice, brown, cooked	⅔ cup	+
Spaghetti, high-protein	1 cup	+
Wheat germ, plain	2 tablespoons	+
Vegetables		
Artichoke, globe (french), cooked	1 medium	+
Beans, lima, cooked	½ cup	+
Broccoli, cooked	½ cup	+
Chard, cooked	½ cup	+
Okra, cooked	½ cup	+
Plaintain, green or ripe, boiled	1 medium	+
Spinach, cooked	½ cup	+
Meat, Poultry, Fish, and Alternatives		
Croaker, mackerel, or sea bass, baked or broiled	3 ounces	+
Oysters		
Baked, broiled, or steamed	3 ounces	+
Canned, undrained	3 ounces	+
Scallops, baked, broiled, steamed, or boiled	3 ounces	+
Beans: black-eyed peas (cowpeas), chickpeas (garbanzo beans), soybeans, or white, cooked	½ cup	+
Lentils, cooked	½ cup	+
Soy milk (not baby formula)	1 cup	+
Tofu (bean curd)	½ cup cubed	+
Almonds, dry-roasted or unroasted	2 tablespoons	+
Brazil nuts, filberts (hazelnuts)	2 tablespoons	+
Cashews, roasted or dry-roasted	2 tablespoons	+
Mixed nuts, roasted	2 tablespoons	+
Peanut butter	2 tablespoons	+
Pine nuts (pignolias)	2 tablespoons	+
Pumpkin or squash seeds, hulled, unroasted	2 tablespoons	+
Sesame seeds	2 tablespoons	+
Sunflower seeds, hulled; unroasted	2 tablespoons	+
Milk, Cheese, and Yogurt		
Milk, chocolate, made with skim milk	1 cup	+
Yogurt, plain, made with nonfat milk	8 ounces	+

[a] A selected serving size contains:

    + 10–24 percent of the U.S. RDA.

    ++ 25–39 percent of the U.S. RDA.

    +++ 40 percent or more of the U.S. RDA.

Source: USDA/Human Nutrition Information Service, 1990.

TRACE ELEMENTS

Iron

Iron is an essential nutrient for humans since it is a constituent of blood protein (*hemoglobin*), and muscle protein (*myoglobin*), and a number of other enzymes. Although iron accounts for less than 1 percent of hemoglobin and myoglobin, it enables them to perform the essential tasks of moving oxygen and carbon dioxide to and from all body cells. As much as 30 percent of iron is found as *ferritin* and *hemosiderin,* storage forms occurring in spleen, liver, and bone marrow. A small amount of iron is associated with the blood transport protein *transferrin.* Among the trace elements, iron deficiency has probably been studied most thoroughly, and therefore much is written about it in the literature. *Anemia* is a general term used for the condition that results in lowering of the hemoglobin level or when the *hematocrit* (concentration of red blood cells) is lower than normal. When this condition occurs, body cells receive less oxygen and carbon dioxide waste is not removed efficiently. The result is conditions described as stress or fatigue. Iron deficiency is not the only cause of anemia; other factors are also responsible. Three stages of iron deficiency have been identified. In the first stage, iron stores are diminished, with a fall in the level of plasma ferritin. The second stage consists of iron-deficient erythropoiesis, in which the hemoglobin level falls within 95 percent of the desirable level for age and sex. In the third stage, iron deficiency anemia, the total blood hemoglobin level is reduced below normal values for the age and sex of the subject. Severe iron deficiency is identified by small red blood cells (microcytosis) with low hemoglobin concentrations. Iron deficiency is also associated with decreased immune function.

Requirements and Food Sources   A good source of iron contains a substantial amount of this mineral in relation to its calorie content and contributes at least 10 percent of the U.S. RDA. Iron is widely available naturally in foods, as well as in enriched foods. Meat, eggs, vegetables, legumes, organ meats (particularly liver), clams and oysters, and cereals (especially fortified and enriched products) are rich sources. Meat, fish, and poultry are superior sources since they have higher bioavailability. Fruits, vegetables (particularly leafy vegetables), and juices contain varying amounts of iron. Pasta, white rice, and most breads made from refined flours are enriched with iron because iron is one of the nutrients lost during processing. Minimum and maximum levels for enrichment are specified for thiamin, riboflavin, and niacin, but only a minimum level of iron is required for farina. Thus iron enrichment levels for farina may vary from brand to brand. Most ready-to-eat and instant-prepared cereals are fortified with iron. Food facts labels should be checked to determine the amount of iron in packaged foods. Dried fruits contain iron, which is concentrated during the drying process. Molasses contains more iron than does refined sugar. Table 7.4 lists good sources of iron. The use of iron utensils such as cast iron skillets can enhance to a limited extent the availability of iron from foods prepared in them.

Table 7.4   Good Sources of Iron

Food	Selected Serving Size	Percent of U.S. RDA[a]
Breads, Cereals, and Other Grain Products		
Bagel, plain, pumpernickel, or whole-wheat	1 medium	+
Farina, regular or quick, cooked	⅔ cup	++
Muffin, bran	1 medium	+
Noodles, cooked	1 cup	+
Oatmeal, instant, fortified, prepared	⅔ cup	++
Pita bread, plain or whole-wheat	1 small	+
Pretzel, soft	1	+
Ready-to-eat cereals, fortified	1 ounce	++
Rice, white, regular or converted, cooked	⅔ cup	+
Fruits		
Apricots, dried, cooked, unsweetened	½ cup	+
Vegetables		
Beans, lima, cooked	½ cup	+
Spinach, cooked	½ cup	+
Meat, Poultry, Fish, and Alternatives		
Beef		
Brisket, braised, lean only	3 ounces	+
Ground, extra lean, lean, or regular, baked or broiled	1 patty	+
Pot roast, braised, lean only	3 ounces	+
Roast, rib, roasted, lean only	3 ounces	+
Shortribs, braised, lean only	3 ounces	+
Steak, baked, braised or broiled, lean only	3 ounces	+
Stew meat, simmered, lean only	3 ounces	+
Liver		
Braised, beef	3 ounces	++
Braised, chicken or turkey	½ cup diced	++
Braised, pork	3 ounces	+++
Liverwurst	1 ounce	+
Tongue, braised	3 ounces	+
Turkey, dark meat, roasted without skin	3 ounces	+
Clams, steamed, boiled, or canned; drained	3 ounces	+++
Mackerel, canned and drained	3 ounces	+
Mussels, steamed, boiled, or poached	3 ounces	+
Oysters		
Baked, broiled, or steamed	3 ounces	++
Canned, undrained	3 ounces	++
Shrimp, broiled, steamed, boiled, or canned (drained)	3 ounces	+
Trout, baked or broiled	3 ounces	+

Table 7.4 *(Continued)*

Food	Selected Serving Size	Percent of U.S. RDA[a]
Meat, Poultry, Fish, and Alternatives (cont.)		
Beans: black-eyed peas (cowpeas), chickpeas (garbanzo beans), white, or red kidney, cooked	½ cup	+
Lentils, cooked	½ cup	+
Soybeans cooked	½ cup	+ +
Pine nuts (pignolias)	2 tablespoons	+
Pumpkin or squash seeds, hulled, roasted	2 tablespoons	+

[a] A selected serving size contains:
+ 10–24 percent of the U.S. RDA.
+ 25–39 percent of the U.S. RDA.
+++ 40 percent or more of the U.S. RDA.
Source: USDA/Human Nutrition Information Service.

The availability of iron can be increased by consumption of foods containing ascorbic acid. Only about 10 percent of the iron from foods is absorbed. The RDA for iron is 15 milligrams per day for women and 10 milligrams per day for men. The allowance is higher for women to compensate for menstrual losses. During pregnancy, it is doubled to 30 milligrams per day due to the demands of the growing fetal, placental, and maternal tissues. Persons who eat little or no animal protein and whose diets are low in ascorbic acid may require higher amounts of iron. High fiber content can interfere with iron absorption. Vegetarian diets may have less iron, which may also be less absorbable compared to the iron in diets containing meats. Iron absorption is affected by phytates, which are present in whole grains, bran, cellulose in vegetables, and tannic acid in tea. Meats, in addition to providing iron, enhance the absorption of iron from other foods. Since vitamin C promotes iron absorption, it is advisable to include drinks that contain this vitamin with meals containing iron-rich foods.

Zinc

Zinc is an essential nutrient for plants, animals, and humans and is a constituent of enzymes involved in major metabolic pathways. Relatively large amounts are stored in bone and muscle. Zinc is a cofactor for many enzymes that take part in the metabolic processes involving cell production, structuring of bones, utilization of vitamin A, the immune response, and protein synthesis. Zinc is necessary for adequate immune function. The composition of the diet affects the bioavailability of zinc. The symptoms of zinc deficiency include loss of appetite, growth retardation, deformed bones, poor healing, skin changes, decreased taste acuity, and immunological abnormalities. Zinc is toxic when consumed in large quantities.

Highly acidic foods can break down zinc, forming poisonous compounds. This is a problem if zinc-coated utensils (galvanized containers) are used for preparing or storing highly acidic foods or beverages.

Requirements and Food Sources   Most of the zinc consumed in the diet is provided by meats and cereals. Table 7.5 lists good sources of this mineral. The bioavailability of zinc varies considerably. Meat, liver, eggs, and seafoods (particularly oysters) are good sources; whole-grain products contain it in less available form. Other good sources include dairy products and legumes, such as peanuts. Dietary fiber and phytates inhibit the bioavailability of zinc. The RDA is 15 milligrams per day for adult men and 12 milligrams per day for adult women. Much is still unknown about this nutrient.

Iodine

Iodine is an essential micronutrient for humans and is an integral part of the thyroid hormones *thyroxin* and *triiodothyronine.* It is present in water and food as iodide. Iodide is rapidly and almost completely absorbed and transported to the thyroid gland for synthesis. Iodine deficiency can lead to a wide variety of diseases ranging from mental retardation to enlargement of the thyroid gland (goiter). Iodine deficiency disorders, including goiter, can be prevented but not cured by providing adequate iodine intake.

Requirements and Food Sources   Seafood, water, and iodine-containing ocean mist are major sources of iodine. Iodine is also present in soil; thus, crops grown on land near the ocean may contain iodine. Iodized salt is a very reliable source. Iodine also occurs as food additives such as iodates in doughs. The RDA for both sexes is 150 micrograms per day. Increments of 25 and 50 micrograms per day are allowed during pregnancy and lactation, respectively.

Selenium

The significance of selenium in nutrition was discovered recently, and deficiency symptoms were confirmed in animal studies. Selenium is known to be interdependent with vitamin E. It is a component of an important enzyme called *glutathione peroxide,* which is helpful in preventing damage to the cell structure. Recent studies indicate that it may protect against some forms of cancer. Seafoods, kidney, liver, and, to a lesser extent, other meats are good sources. Grains and other seeds may also contain selenium based on the soil types in which they are grown. Fruits and vegetables generally contain little selenium. The RDA is 70 and 55 micrograms per day for adult males and females, respectively. Excess selenium can result in loss of hair, brittle nails, discolored teeth, and swelling of tissues.

Copper

Copper is an essential nutrient that is also present in enzymes and is distributed in blood, grain, liver, kidneys, bone marrow, and hair. It is important in the synthesis

Table 7.5   Good Sources of Zinc

Food	Selected Serving Size	Percent of U.S. RDA[a]
Breads, Cereals, and Other Grain Products		
Ready-to-eat cereals, fortified	1 ounce	+
Wheat germ, plain	2 tablespoons	+
Meat, Poultry, Fish, and Alternatives		
Beef:		
Brisket, braised, lean only	3 ounces	+ +
Ground, extra lean, lean, or regular, baked or Broiled	1 patty	+ +
Pot roast, braised, lean only	3 ounces	+ + +
Roast, rib, roasted, lean only	3 ounces	+ +
Shortribs, braised, lean only	3 ounces	+ + +
Steak, baked or broiled, lean only	3 ounces	+ +
Steak, braised, lean only	3 ounces	+ + +
Stew meat, simmered, lean only	3 ounces	+ + +
Chicken, leg (thigh and drumstick), broiled or roasted, without skin	1 leg	+
Ham, fresh, smoked, or cured, roasted, lean only	3 ounces	+
Lamb		
Chop, shoulder; braised, broiled, or baked; lean only	1 chop	+ +
Ground, cooked	1 patty	+
Roast, shoulder, roasted, lean only	3 ounces	+ +
Liver		
Braised, beef	3 ounces	+ +
Braised, calf	3 ounces	+ + +
Braised, chicken or turkey	½ cup diced	+
Braised, pork	3 ounces	+ +
Liverwurst	1 ounce	+
Pork, ground, roast	3 ounces	+
Tongue, braised	3 ounces	+ +
Turkey, dark or light meat, roasted without skin	3 ounces	+
Turkey, ground, cooked	3 ounces	+
Veal		
Chop, braised, lean only	1 chop	+
Ground, cooked	1 patty	+
Roast, leg, roasted, lean only	3 ounces	+ +
Carp, baked or broiled	3 ounces	+
Crabmeat, steamed	3 ounces	+
Lobster, steamed, or boiled	3 ounces	+
Mussels, steamed, boiled, or poached	3 ounces	+

Table 7.5 *(Continued)*

Food	Selected Serving Size	Percent of U.S. RDA[a]
Meat, Poultry, Fish, and Alternatives (cont.)		
Oysters		
Baked, broiled, or steamed	3 ounces	+++
Canned, undrained	3 ounces	+++
Pumpkin or squash seeds, hulled, roasted	2 tablespoons	+
Milk, Cheese, and Yogurt		
Cheese, ricotta	½ cup	+
Yogurt		
Flavored, made with whole or low-fat milk	8 ounces	+
Plain, made with low-fat or nonfat milk	8 ounces	+

[a] A selected serving size contains:
  + 10–24 percent of the U.S. RDA.
  ++ 25–39 percent of the U.S. RDA.
  +++ 40 percent or more of the U.S. RDA.

Source: USDA/Human Nutrition Information Service.

of collagen, normal cardiovascular function, and normal immune function. Copper deficiency results in anemia since it influences iron metabolism. It may also cause other blood diseases. Organ meats, particularly liver, are the richest sources of copper. It is also available in several other foods, such as seafoods, whole grains, shellfish, legumes, grapes, seeds, and nuts. Other fair sources include vegetables, dried and fresh fruits, egg yolks, and meat. Dairy foods are poor sources of copper. Copper interacts with highly acidic foods and beverages; therefore, copper utensils used in foodservice should be coated before any food is allowed to come in contact with them.

Because the requirement for copper is uncertain, no RDA has been set. However, 1.5 to 3 milligrams per day is recommended as a safe and adequate dietary range for adults.

Manganese

Manganese activates several enzymes that are responsible for energy metabolism and the production of fatty acids, cholesterol, bile, and urea. Rich sources include whole-grain cereals, nuts, organ meats, legumes, coffee, cocoa, and tea. Dairy products, meat, fish, and poultry are poor sources. The recommended safe and adequate dietary manganese level for adults has been set at 2.0 to 5.0 milligrams per day.

Fluorine

Fluorine is present in small quantities in soils, water supplies, plants, and animals. *Fluoride* is the term used for the ionized form of fluorine, and both terms are used interchangeably. Fluoride is incorporated in bones and tooth enamel. It functions in teeth and bones by becoming part of hydroxyapatite crystals and making them larger and less soluble, thereby increasing their strength and durability. There is enough evidence to support the positive effect of fluorine on dental health, particularly in the reduction of dental caries. Food processing influences the fluoride content of foods. It can be increased severalfold by cooking foods in fluoridated water. It has also been reported that cooking in utensils coated with Teflon, a fluoride-containing polymer, can increase the fluoride content of foods. The richest dietary source of fluoride are tea and marine fish that are consumed with bones (such as sardines). The estimated range of safe and adequate intake of fluoride for adults is 1.5 to 4.0 milligrams per day. In view of fluoride's beneficial effects on dental health and its safety at the prescribed intake levels, fluoridation of public water supplies is recommended for communities where the water supply has a low fluoride content. Although small amounts of fluoride can lower the incidence of dental caries, excess intake of fluoride (four or more times the recommended level) can cause *mottling* of teeth, which is characterized by spotty discoloration. Intake of even higher levels of fluoride can cause *fluorosis,* which is characterized by severe mottling of the teeth and degenerative, crippling bone and joint disorders.

Chromium

Chromium promotes normal glucose metabolism, apparently in conjunction with insulin. It has also been suggested that a low chromium intake may be a factor in adult-onset diabetes in some individuals. Common food sources include whole-grain cereals, vegetables and fruits, meats, cheese, and peanuts. Less common sources include molasses and brewer's yeast. During the processing of foods, chromium can be easily lost. Because there are no methods to diagnose the status of chromium, the requirement is difficult to estimate. An intake of 50 to 200 micrograms per day is tentatively recommended for adults.

Molybdenum

Molybdenum is a component of enzymes that are responsible for several biochemical reactions. The concentration of molybdenum in foods varies considerably, depending on the environment in which the food was grown. Rich sources of molybdenum include milk, beans, breads, and cereals. The estimated safe and adequate daily dietary intake is 75 to 250 micrograms for adults and older children. Higher intake can result in toxicity.

8

WATER AND ELECTROLYTES

This chapter focuses on water and electrolytes, which are essential nutrients. These nutrients are treated separately based on their importance. In many textbooks, they are not covered adequately in spite of their enormous significance in nutrition. It should be noted that survival depends more on water than on any other nutrient. Water and the principal electrolytes (sodium, potassium, and chloride) are essential dietary components and have to be acquired from the diet for needs that far exceed the amount that can be produced metabolically. Recent concerns relate to the possible overconsumption of sodium and chloride and underconsumption of potassium. It is also likely that many persons do not consume enough water. Each of these nutrients will be discussed individually, emphasizing the role that they play collectively.

WATER

Water accounts for about 50 to 75 percent of body weight and is the most abundant constituent of the body. It is crucial to the survival of living beings, yet it is often ignored as a significant nutrient. For example, one can survive without essential nutrients for several weeks but die due to shortage of water in few days or hours. Every body cell and tissue contains water in different proportions. The approximate percentages of water in different parts of the body are: muscle tissue, 72 percent; bone, 25 percent; teeth, 10 percent; and fat tissues, 20–35 percent. The amount of water content depends on body fat and other factors, such as age, sex, and health status. Although water is present in large amounts, the body cannot afford to lose as little as 3 percent of its water compared to body weight. Human performance starts to deteriorate if the water loss reaches 3 percent. If this loss continues muscular endurance is reduced, eventually resulting in the collapse of the circulatory system. In extreme cases, death can occur. The symptoms of dehydration start with thirst, progressing to a decrease in blood volume, with fatigue setting in, finally resulting in abnormal blood circulation and associated kidney failure.

Water Losses

There is continuous turnover of water via different routes on a daily basis. The normal daily turnover of water is about 4 percent of total body weight in adults and as high as 15 percent of total body weight in infants. Even in the absence of visible perspiration, approximately one-half of the turnover occurs through what is referred to as **insensible** water losses (losses that occur without being perceived). These losses are due to loss of water from the lungs and skin. These insensible losses are accelerated under certain conditions, such as high temperature, high altitude, and dry air. Even more losses can occur with exertion under the above-mentioned conditions, which can increase the water loss from skin and lungs as much as tenfold.

Water is needed by the kidneys to excrete all waste products. These waste products are the result of metabolism and are composed primarily of the nitrogen-containing breakdown products of protein metabolism (primarily urea), sulfates, phosphates, and other electrolytes. The amounts of these products determine the amount of water that is needed to flush them out. Fortunately, the demand for more water is signaled by the thirst mechanism; however, this may not be triggered until it is too late or it may be inoperative due to sustained exertion or high altitudes. Dehydration becomes life-threatening when more than 10 percent of body weight is lost.

Under normal circumstances, an adult loses 2 to 3 liters of fluid each day, of which more than half is usually lost as urine. Some fluid is lost by evaporation and by insensible water losses. Exertion and sweating also result in water losses. Small amounts of water are lost in breathing, as well as in feces. Losses from sweat can be considerable, depending on the physical activity. Certain substances described as *diuretics*, such as alcohol, caffeine, and certain drugs, increase water loss by promoting greater urine production. Diuretic drugs are sometimes prescribed, such as for high blood pressure to reduce the volume of blood. Athletes who are involved in strenuous activities can easily lose 2 to 10 pounds of water, primarily by sweating. Such water losses have to be replenished as quickly as possible to avoid any damage.

Sources of Water

Drinking water and beverages are the most common sources of water. Other than soft drinks, water is found in milk, tea, coffee, and fruit juices. The percentage of water present in some foods is shown in Table 8.1. Less obvious sources of water include fruits and vegetables, meats and meat alternatives, and even cereals. The

Table 8.1   Percentage of Water in Selected Foods (Based on Percentage of Weight)

Foods	Percentage
Apple	84
Apricots (dried)	31
Lettuce	95
Orange	86
Potato, baked	72
Peas, cooked	81
Bread	34
Cakes	24
Crackers	4
Cheddar cheese	46
Milk	88
Nuts	3
Soda	90
Cheese pizza	48
Chocolate chip cookie	6
Corn chips	1
Ice cream	56
Chicken breast (fried)	60
Beef burrito	27
Bean burrito	47
French fries	40
Hamburger	45
Spaghetti	66

water content of foods can be lost during storage, preparation, or cooking. The physical characteristics of food are also affected by loss of water. Precautions should be taken to cover foods or store them at the desired humidity levels. In some foods, like meats, it is important to keep the moisture level that is responsible for juiciness. Ice crystals in foods formed during freezing can rupture cell walls, causing loss of moisture, texture, and flavor. Usually beverages account for only half of the daily intake of water. A smaller amount comes from internal sources as a by-product of fat, carbohydrate, and protein metabolism.

Soft water contains sodium, whereas hard water contains higher levels of calcium and magnesium. Washing with soft water requires less soap or detergent. Hard water can give products a bad taste, result in poor cleaning, and damage equipment. Hard water can be softened by adding sodium.

Water Requirements

The water requirement is based primarily on metabolism. It is also based on the amount necessary to balance insensible losses and maintain a tolerable solute load for the kidneys. Both of these factors can vary considerably based on body metabolism and dietary intake. For practical purposes, 1 milligram per kcalorie of energy expenditure is recommended as the water requirement for adults under average conditions of energy expenditure and environmental exposure. Children and elderly persons need more water, especially during hot summer months. Significantly more water is needed during lactation for milk production and supply. In general, the requirements should be based on the replenishment of fluid losses.

Functions of Water

Water is always found in combination and never in the form it takes within the body. It is an essential component of all body tissues, as mentioned earlier. In each tissue cell, water in the cytoplasm fills the structure and provides firmness and shape. It is also a component of enzymes and other body fluids. In addition, water acts as a solvent for the many biochemical compounds that take part in metabolic activities. Certain chemicals, when dissolved in water, dissociate into ions or *electrolytes,* which are electrically charged particles. These electrolytes help maintain the water balance of the body. The role these electrolytes play in maintaining water balance is discussed later.

Water also takes part in *hydrolysis,* in which nutrients are broken into smaller units for further action. For example, carbohydrates, fats, and proteins are broken down into smaller units for digestion and absorption. Water also acts as a medium of transport for body fluids. Blood, lymph, and urine are examples of such nutrients or wastes whose transportation is facilitated by water. Water also serves as a lubricant, helping to move materials. Saliva and tears are examples of such lubricants, helping to move solid foods particles or keep the eyeballs rotating smoothly. There are other parts of the body, such as joints, where water also serves as a lubricant.

Another important function of water is to control body temperature. The body maintains its temperature by constricting or dilating the capillaries near the skin in cold or hot temperatures, respectively. This water-involved mechanism helps to maintain body temperature as close to normal as possible. Perspiration is another mechanism by which cooling is effected. Perspiration results in sweat, which evaporates, cooling the body's surface and thereby controlling body temperature. Water is needed in different parts of the body in different amounts. When ingested, water enters the body through the digestive system and, once absorbed, becomes part of either the intracellular or the extracellular compartment. Water moves between the two compartments across cell membranes. An equal concentration on both sides of the compartment is maintained by the process of osmosis.

ELECTROLYTES

Potassium, sodium, and chloride are referred to as electrolytes since they perform similar functions. **Electrolytes** are substances that carry an electrical charge when dissolved in water. These electrical charges cause minerals to bond to others, forming compounds. Sodium and chloride have a sodium atom (Na^+) with a positive charge and a chloride (Cl^-) ion with a negative charge. The positive and negative charges attract each other, and sodium chloride, or table salt, is formed. When dissolved in water, sodium and chloride ions split apart, retaining their positive or negative **ions.** These ions are free to join with other ions to form new compounds. For example, a hydrogen ion (H^+) can join with a chloride ion (Cl^-) to form hydrochloric acid. **Solutes** are substances dissolved in solvents such as water. When the dissociation of a solute results in an excess of positively charged hydrogen ions (H^+), the solution is called an **acid;** when it produces more negatively charged hydroxyl ions (OH^-) than H^+ ions, the solution is called a **base** or an **alkali.** When equal numbers of H^+ and OH^- ions are present, the solution is referred to as **neutral.** The concentration of hydrogen ions in a solution is measured by a **pH scale,** on which 7 is the neutral value; values below 7 are acidic, and values above 7 are alkaline. The body is very sensitive to pH, which is affected by various metabolic activities and dietary intakes. Blood and lymph are maintained at around 7.4 pH. The maintence of a constant pH requires a sophisticated balancing mechanism. This balance is maintained by a buffer system, in which several nutrients participate. Proteins are helpful as buffers, since they are *amphoteric,* acting as both an acid and a base.

Minerals use their electrical charges to maintain the acid-base balance within the body and the balance between water inside and outside body cells. Electrolytes can also pull substances with the opposite charge into or out of a cell. In addition, they help to transmit nerve impulses to the brain, as well as facilitate the relaxation and movement of muscles. In the presence of too much acid, the body uses alkaline electrolytes to neutralize the acid, and vice versa. Important electrolytes needed by the body are sodium, potassium, and chloride; these are discussed individually in the following sections.

SODIUM

Sodium is the principal cation of extracellular fluids and controls their volume. Sodium is important in the regulation of osmolarity, acid-base balance, and the membrane potential of cells. It is also involved in active transport across cell membranes. Foods and beverages containing sodium chloride are the main sources of sodium. Table 8.2 lists the sodium content of selected foods. Sodium is also present as an additive in many substances, such as sodium bicarbonate or monosodium glutamate (MSG). It has been estimated that about 10 percent of the salt in the body comes from natural content in foods, about 15 percent from salt added during cooking or at the table, and the rest from salt added during the processing and manufacture of foods. However, this may be true only in cases where most of the foods consumed are processed. This salt is in the form of additives that are added as a preservative, for flavor, or to enhance special functions. Sodium additives are present in MSG, baking soda and baking powder, carbonated beverages, and salts and seasonings. Canned products such as soups, TV dinners, pickles, sauces, crackers, processed cheese, potato chips, salted nuts, pretzels, and other

Table 8.2   Sodium Content of Selected Foods

Foods	Serving Size	Sodium (mg)
Table salt	1 teaspoon	2325
Soy sauce	1 tablespoon	1029
Yogurt (plain)	1 cup	190
Baked potato	One	16
Banana	One	1
Cheese spread (processed)	1 ounce	382
Dill pickle	One	833
Chili with beans (canned)	1 cup	1331
Baked beans (canned)	1 cup	1008
Chicken noodle soup	1 cup	1106
Orange juice	1 cup	5
Coke (regular)	6 fl ounces	3
Cracker (saltine)	One	39
Potato chips (salt added)	1 ounce	169
Corn chips	1 ounce	179
Pretzel	1 cup	756
Cheese pizza	1 slice	500
Chocolate chip cookie	One	55
Milk (whole)	1 cup	14
Ice cream	1 cup	100
Cheddar cheese	1 ounce	180
Chicken breast (fried)	One	136
Beef burrito	One	1303
Bean burrito	One	1140
French fries (medium)	One	150
French fries (large)	One	290
Hamburger	One	530
Fish fillet	One	710
Pizza (beef)	1 slice	797
Taco (beef)	One	338
Egg (whole)	One	63
Salad dressing (thousand island)	1 tablespoon	109
Salad dressing (French)	1 tablespoon	214
Salad dressing (Italian)	1 tablespoon	118
Salad dressing (blue cheese)	1 tablespoon	167

snacks contain a considerable amount of sodium. Several low-sodium products are also available. It is advisable to read the ingredient and nutrient label to ascertain the sodium level in foods. Table salt is the most common form of sodium in the diet; it is 40 percent sodium and 60 percent chlorine. A tablespoon of salt, which is 5 grams, has about 2 grams of sodium. Excess sodium intake has been associated with high blood pressure and edema. A daily intake for sodium chloride of 6 grams (2.4 grams of sodium) or less is recommended.

POTASSIUM

Potassium is the electrolyte found in the highest concentration within body cells and is therefore the principal intracellular cation. It functions as potassium chloride inside cells to exert osmotic pressure and balance the sodium chloride outside the cells. It is also helpful in neuromuscular transmission, in the control of skeletal muscle contractibility, and in the maintenance of normal blood pressure. It is found in a broad range of foods since it is an essential constituent of all living cells. Good sources are legumes, fruits, bananas, dried fruits, avocado, meats, peanuts, bran, and whole-grain cereals. Tea, cocoa, coffee, and molasses also contain fair amounts of potassium. The minimum requirement of potassium in diet is estimated to be 1600 to 2000 milligrams per day. Good food sources of potassium are listed in Table 8.3.

Table 8.3 Good Sources of Potassium

Food	Selected Serving Size	Percent of U.S. RDA[a]
Breads, Cereals, and Other Grain Products		
Ready-to-eat cereals:		
Oat flakes, fortified with soy flour	1 ounce	+
100 percent-bran cereals	1 ounce	+ +
Fruits		
Apricots		
Dried, cooked, unsweetened	½ cup	+ + +
Dried, uncooked	¼ cup	+ +
Banana, raw	1 medium	+ +
Cantaloupe, raw	About ½ cup diced	+
Grapefruit juice, fresh; canned or reconstituted, frozen, unsweetened	¾ cup	+
Honeydew melon, raw	About ¾ cup diced	+
Melon balls (cantaloupe and honeydew), frozen, unsweetened	½ cup	+
Nectarine, raw	1 medium	+
Orange juice, canned	¾ cup	+
Orange juice, fresh or reconstituted frozen, unsweetened	¾ cup	+ +
Peaches		
Dried, cooked, unsweetened	½ cup	+ +
Dried, uncooked	¼ cup	+ +
Pears, dried, cooked, unsweetened	½ cup	+
Pomegranate, raw	1 medium	+ +
Prunes, dried, cooked, unsweetened	½ cup	+ +
Prune juice, unsweetened	½ cup	+ +
Raisins	¼ cup	+
Watermelon, raw	About 1¾ cups diced	+

Table 8.3 *(Continued)*

Food	Selected Serving Size	Percent of U.S. RDA[a]
Vegetables		
Artichoke, globe (french), cooked	1 medium	+
Asparagus, cooked	½ cup	+
Beans		
Green, cooked	½ cup	+
Lima, cooked	½ cup	+ + +
Cauliflower, cooked	½ cup	+
Chard, cooked	½ cup	+ +
Corn, cooked	½ cup	+
Jerusalem artichoke, raw	½ cup	+
Mushrooms, cooked	½ cup	+
Parsnips, cooked	½ cup	+
Peas, green, cooked	½ cup	+
Plantain, green or ripe, boiled	1 medium	+ + +
Potato		
Baked or boiled, with skin	1 medium	+ + +
Baked or boiled, without skin	1 medium	+ +
Pumpkin, cooked	½ cup	+ +
Rutabaga	½ cup	+
Spinach, cooked	½ cup	+ +
Squash, winter, cooked, mashed	½ cup	+ + +
Sweet potato		
Baked	1 medium	+ +
Boiled	1 medium	+
Tomatoes		
Raw	1 medium	+
Stewed	½ cup	+ +
Tomato juice, canned	¾ cup	+ +
Tomato-vegetable juice or tomato juice cocktail, canned	¾ cup	+ +
Meat, Poultry, Fish, and Alternatives		
Beef		
Brisket, braised, lean only	3 ounces	+
Ground, extra lean, lean, or regular, baked or broiled	3 ounces	+
Pot roast, braised, lean only	3 ounces	+
Roast, rib, roasted, lean only	3 ounces	+
Shortribs, braised, lean only	3 ounces	+
Steak, baked, braised, or broiled, lean only	3 ounces	+
Stew meat, simmered, lean only	3 ounces	+
Chicken, without skin		
Breast, broiled or roasted	½ breast	+
Leg (thigh and drumstick), broiled or roasted	1 leg	+
Cornish hen, roasted, without skin	½ hen	+

Table 8.3 *(Continued)*

Food	*Selected Serving Size*	*Percent of U.S. RDA[a]*
Meat, Poultry, Fish, and Alternatives (cont.)		
Ham, fresh, smoked or cured, roasted, lean only	3 ounces	+
Lamb, lean only		
Chop, shoulder; braised, broiled, or baked	1 chop	+
Roast, leg or shoulder, roasted	3 ounces	+
Liver		
Braised, beef or calf	3 ounces	+ +
Braised, chicken	½ cup diced	+ +
Pork chop, baked or broiled, lean only	1 chop	+
Turkey		
Light or dark meat, roasted without skin	3 ounces	+
Ground cooked	3 ounces	+
Veal		
Cutlet or steak, pan-broiled, lean only	1 cutlet	+ +
Chop, braised	1 chop	+
Roast, leg, roasted, lean only	3 ounces	+
Carp, catfish, flounder, or mullet, baked or broiled	3 ounces	+ +
Haddock, mackerel, or porgy, baked or broiled	3 ounces	+
Clams, steamed, boiled, or canned, drained	3 ounces	+
Cod, croaker, pompano, or trout, baked or broiled	3 ounces	+ +
Crabmeat, steamed	3 ounces	+
Lobster, steamed or broiled	3 ounces	+
Mussels, steamed, boiled, or poached	3 ounces	+
Ocean perch, perch, pike, sea bass, or whiting, baked or broiled	3 ounces	+
Oysters, canned, undrained	3 ounces	+
Salmon		
Baked or broiled	3 ounces	+
Steamed, poached, or canned, drained	3 ounces	+
Scallops, baked, broiled, steamed, or boiled	3 ounces	+
Swordfish steak, baked or broiled	3 ounces	+
Tuna, canned, drained	3 ounces	+
Beans		
Bayo, black, brown, or red kidney, cooked	½ cup	+ +
Calico, chickpeas (garbanzo beans), mungo or pinto, cooked	½ cup	+
Lima, soybeans, or white; cooked	½ cup	+ +
Lentils, cooked	½ cup	+ +
Soy milk (not baby formula)	1 cup	+
Milk, Cheese, and Yogurt		
Milk		
Buttermilk	1 cup	+ +
Chocolate, made with whole or skim milk	1 cup	+ +
Skim	1 cup	+ +
Whole or lowfat	1 cup	+ +

Table 8.3 *(Continued)*

Food	Selected Serving Size	Percent of U.S. RDA[a]
Milk, Cheese, and Yogurt (cont.)		
Milk-based fruit drinks	1 cup	+++
Yogurt		
Flavored, made with low-fat milk	8 ounces	++
Frozen	8 ounces	++
Fruit, made with low-fat or nonfat milk	8 ounces	++
Plain, made with whole milk	8 ounces	++
Plain, made with low-fat milk	8 ounces	+++

[a] A selected serving size contains at least:

    + 200–349 milligrams.

    ++ 350–499 milligrams.

    +++ 500 or more milligrams.

Souce: USDA/Human Nutrition Information Service.

CHLORIDE

Chloride is the principal inorganic anion in the extracellular fluid compartment. It is essential in maintaining fluid and electrolyte balance and is a necessary component of gastric juice. Chloride also functions in a buffering system that compensates for excess acid or alkali and maintains the acid-base balance. Dietary chloride comes almost entirely from sodium chloride or table salt. Meat, milk, and eggs also supply chloride. Small amounts come from potassium chloride. Processed foods have considerable amounts of sodium chloride. The level of intake parallels that of sodium. Ingestion of high levels of sodium chloride tends to increase the urinary loss of calcium. The suggested intake of chloride is 1700 to 5100 milligrams per day. Sodium and chloride are the two primary electrolytes that are lost in sweat with water.

Chapter 9

NUTRITIONAL RECIPE DEVELOPMENT

O ne of the most common nutritional assessments of recipes involves the caloric content of foods. This requires a thorough understanding of the energy components and energy requirements of the body. Recipes are also evaluated on the basis of their caloric content. Thus, it is imperative to understand how energy is used and how it can be obtained from different food components in a recipe and finally in menus.

ENERGY NEEDS OF THE HUMAN BODY

It is a general misconception that energy is used by the body only during physical activity. In fact, the body uses energy whether it is active or passive. A person who is resting is also consuming energy, which is continuously used to carry out the basic processes that keep the body alive. The beating of the heart, the movements of the lungs, the functioning of kidneys, and all other actions of the organs are using the body's energy. Most body energy is converted into heat, expressed as **thermal energy.** In addition, the movements of the body are expressed as **mechanical energy;** energy powering metabolic reactions is called **chemical energy;** and electrical impulses generated by nerve cells is represented by **electrical energy.** Thus, energy is expressed in several forms in the body.

Energy is provided by different foods in varying amounts. This energy is measured in kcalories. It is a misconception that all nutrients, including vitamins, provide energy. The amount of energy provided by foods directly depends on the amount of energy available from macronutrients—proteins, fats, and carbohydrates. These are the primary sources of energy, and therefore they are extensively and exclusively used in the caloric calculations of recipes. Since different foods consist of varying amounts of these nutrients, the caloric contents of foods vary widely.

Prior to any discussion of the energy contents of foods, it is important to understand the ways in which the body expends energy. The body uses energy for (1) supporting life-sustaining functions, (2) performing physical activity, and (3) processing foods after consumption. These functions will now be discussed.

Life-Sustaining Functions

There are general functions, such as breathing, and maintaining body temperature and muscle tone; functioning of organs; activities of the nervous system; and other similar internal functions, for which the body expends energy. These are all life-sustaining processes that are basic to survival and are therefore referred to as **basal metabolism.** The amount of energy required to maintain basal metabolism is called the **basal metabolic rate (BMR),** which accounts for almost 60 to 70 percent of the total daily energy expenditure. BMR is expressed as the number of kcalories required to maintain life-sustaining activities for a specified period of time. Energy can be measured during activity or while resting. The latter, referred to as the **resting metabolic rate (RMR),** is the number of kcalories used during a specified amount of time at rest. The BMR is affected by the following factors:

1. *Body size:* the height and weight of a person. A tall, large person requires a higher BMR than a short, small one.

2. *Age:* the number of kcalories required for basal processes is considerable during growth phases.

3. *Sex:* compared to females of the same age, males generally have a higher BMR, due mostly to the fact that males usually have more lean body tissue than females. Hormones produced at various stages of life also affect the BMR.

4. *Health status:* a physically fit person generally has a higher BMR, due largely to greater muscle mass. Fever raises the BMR considerably.

5. *Thyroid hormone level:* when there is an overproduction of thyroxin in the body, the BMR increases, and vice versa.

6. *Special conditions:* individual variations in BMR may be due to a combination of most of the factors mentioned earlier. Also, during pregnancy and lactation, the BMR increases significantly due to increased metabolism.

Physical Activity

Physical activity requires the use of energy, and the energy level varies greatly based on the type of activity. The energy used for physical activity varies from day to day compared to the relatively constant use of energy for basal metabolism. The use of energy depends on the type, intensity, and duration of the activity, as well as the body weight. For example, running requires more energy than walking per unit of time. Even small actions such as eating, typing, or scratching requires energy. The energy required also varies with body weight; heavy persons need more energy for the same activities than thin persons.

Processing of Food

During the processes of digestion, absorption, transport, and storage of food, energy is required. This energy is needed for conducting different physiological processes that are essential to the use of food by the body.

ESTIMATING THE USE OF ENERGY BY THE BODY

If one knows the energy needs for different types of functions, it is relatively easy to estimate the energy needed by the body. This will only be an estimation since it is extremely difficult to calculate the exact amount of energy needed by the body. The following steps can be used to calculate energy:

Step 1: *Estimating BMR:* convert body weight into kilograms by dividing it by 2.2 (2.2 pounds = 1 kilogram). Multiply the body weight in kilograms by 24 (based on typical usage of 1 kcalorie per kilogram per day). This will provide a rough estimate of the BMR.

Step 2: *Estimating energy expenditure for activities:* this can be based on the percentage of BMR used for activities. For example, a relatively inactive level will use 30–40 percent of the BMR; moderately active level will use 40–50 percent, and a very active level will use 50–100 percent.

Step 3: *Estimating energy expenditure for the body's processing of food:* this calculation can be based on 10 percent of the total kcalories required in Step 2 and 3.

Step 4: *Estimating total energy expenditure:* total daily expenditure is the sum of the values in Steps 1 to 3. Additional calories are needed during pregnancy, lactation, sickness, and other conditions. The above steps are illustrated by the following example.

Assume that a person weighs 150 pounds and is moderately active (50 percent of the BMR) on a daily basis. The following calculations can be derived based on the steps mentioned earlier. This example assumes that there are no special needs, such as those during pregnancy or lactation.

$$\text{BMR} = \frac{\text{Body weight in lb}}{2.2 \text{ lb/kg}} \times 24 \text{ kcal/kg/day}$$

$$= \frac{150}{2.2} \times 24 = 1636 \text{ kcal/day (A)}$$

$$\text{Energy use for activities} = \text{BMR} \times \text{factor for activity}$$
$$= 1636 \times 0.5 = 818 \text{ kcal/day (B)}$$
$$\text{Energy use for processing of food} = (\text{A} + \text{B}) \times 10\%$$
$$= (1636 + 818) \times 0.1 = 245 \text{ kcal/day (C)}$$
$$\text{Total day's energy needs} = \text{A} + \text{B} + \text{C}$$
$$= 1636 + 818 + 245 = 2699 \text{ kcal/day}$$

CALCULATING THE ENERGY VALUE OF FOODS

In the above example, the calculation of the body's energy needs is shown. The next step is to find out how much energy each food item (the primary source of energy) provides to the body. This is a very important factor that should be clearly understood since it is involved in food labeling, as well as in developing healthy recipes. Although the number of nutrients discussed in the earlier chapters are numerous, it is relatively easy to calculate energy, since there are only a few of them that provide energy. The amount of energy provided by food can be calculated if the grams of protein, fat, carhobydrate, and/or alcohol contents are known. Vitamins, minerals, and water do not provide energy, although they are involved in many vital bodily functions. Thus, the focus should be on the content of proteins, fats, and carbohydrates, although it may be necessary to note the alcohol contents of some foods. Once the amounts are known, the energy provided can be calculated from the number of grams of these nutrients included in foods, as shown in Table 9.1

These are the common values used in the calculation of energy provided by foods. These values are based on average amounts of energy provided by these nutrients when present in foods. These values can be substituted for each nutrient provided by a food. Each ingredient in the recipe has to be examined individually to determine how many grams it provides of all of the above nutrients, if present. The energy value of whole food in the recipe will then be the sum of the caloric values of its ingredients. A recipe is shown in Table 9.2, and the calculation of energy provided by this recipe is shown in Table 9.3.

For nutritional analysis of the recipe shown in Table 9.2, the steps described in Table 9.3 should be followed. The stepwise approach will lead to the calculation of

Table 9.1   Calories Provided by Nutrients

Nutrient	*Kcalories per Gram*
Proteins	4
Carbohydrates	4
Fats	9
Alcohol	7

Table 9.2 Lemon Chicken Recipe

Ingredient	Amount	Procedure
Chicken breast	4 (6-ounce pieces)	Place the chicken on a baking pan
Lemon	one	Use lemon to marinate the chicken
Corn flake crumbs	½ cup	Mix with yogurt
Yogurt	¼ cup	Spread yogurt mix on the marinated chicken
Black pepper	¼ teaspoon	Sprinkle uniformly over chicken
Salt	¼ teaspoon	Sprinkle lightly over chicken
		Broil marinated chicken at 400°F for 35 minutes
Parsley sprigs	8 pieces	Garnish chicken with parsley sprigs before serving

Table 9.3 Energy Calculation of a Recipe

Steps	Ingredients	Amounts	Proteins (g)	Protein kcal = g × 4	Fat (g)	Fat kcal = g × 9	Carbo-hydrates (g)	Carbo-hydrate kcal = g × 4	Total Ingredient kcal
1. Enter the ingredients in a recipe	Chicken breast	4 (6 ounce pieces)	214	856	25	225	0	0	1081
2. Number of kcal/g provided by nutrients are multiplied by grams of the nutrients in each ingredient	Lemon	1	1	4	0.3	3	12	48	55
3. Total kcal are computed by kcal provided by proteins, fats, and carbohydrates	Corn flake crumbs	½ cup	4	16	0	0	36	144	160
4. Divide the total kcal by the number of servings. (Since this recipe serves four, the total kcal has to be divided by four.)	Yogurt	¼ cup	3	12	0.1	1	4	16	29
	Black pepper	¼ teaspoon	0.1	0	0	0	0.3	1	1
	Salt	¼ teaspoon	0	0	0	0	0	0	0
	Parsley	8 pieces	0.2	1	0.5	5	0.6	2	8
Total kcal provided by the recipe				889		234		211	1334
Total kcal provided by each serving of the recipe				222		59		53	334

Table 9.4 Summary of Nutrient Analysis of the Lemon Chicken Recipe

A. Macronutrients

Kilocalories	1334
Protein	222.3 grams
Carbohydrate	52.9 grams
Fat	25.9 grams
Alcohol	0 grams
Cholesterol	585 milligrams
Saturated fat	7.089 grams
Mono fat	8.613 grams
Poly fat	5.401 grams
Dietary fat	0.667 grams
Sugar	9.6 grams

B. Percent of Calories

Protein	66.5 percent
Carbohydrate	15.9 percent
Fat	17.6 percent
Alcohol	0 percent

C. Vitamins

Vitamin A	128.9 RE
Beta-carotene	3.518 micrograms
Thiamin (B_1)	1.042 milligrams
Riboflavin (B_2)	1.521 milligrams
Niacin (B_3)	101.3 milligrams
Pyridoxine (B_6)	4.908 milligrams
Folate:	186.8 micrograms
Cobalamin (B_{12})	2.688 micrograms
Vitamin E	—
A-tocopherol	—
Pantothenic acid	7.32 milligrams
Biotin	1.215 micrograms
Vitamin C	125 milligrams
Vitamin D	0 micrograms
Vitamin K	0.068 micrograms

D. Minerals

Sodium	1625 milligrams
Potassium	2157 milligrams
Iron	19.92 milligrams
Calcium	306.8 milligrams
Magnesium	232.5 milligrams
Phosphorus	1683 milligrams
Zinc	7.707 milligrams
Copper	0.648 milligrams
Manganese	0.166 milligrams
Selenium	1.188 milligrams
Fluoride	—
Chromium	0.182 milligrams
Iodine	—
Molybdenum	2.6 micrograms

Table 9.5 Chocolate Chip Cookies (Yield: 10 Dozens)

Amount	Ingredient	Procedure
12 ounces	Margarine	Cream margarine and sugar until sugars are
8 ounces	Sugar, granulated	dissolved
8 ounces	Sugar, brown	
4	Eggs	Beat egg and vanilla gently until light and fluffy
2 teaspoons	Vanilla	
1 pound 4 ounces	Flour, all-purpose	Add all ingredients to creamed mixture
2 teaspoons	Salt	
2 teaspoons	Baking soda	
1 pound	Nuts	Add nuts and chocolate chips and mix until
1 pound 8 ounces	Chocolate chips	well blended
		Drop on greased baking sheets
		Bake at 375°F for 10 to 12 minutes

the number of kcalories provided by each serving of the recipe. In Step 1, all the ingredients in the recipe should be entered, followed by Step 2, in which the number of kcalories per gram of each ingredient is calculated by multiplying by the number of grams of nutrients provided by the ingredient. Total kcalories can then be calculated by computing the number of kcalories provided by each nutrient (Step 3), that is, 4 kcalories per gram provided by proteins and carbohydrates and 9 kcalories per gram provided by fats. Finally, in Step 4, the total kcalories are divided by the number of servings. The energy of large-quantity recipes can be calculated similarly. The values given in Table 9.3 refer only to energy, but this recipe also provides vitamins and minerals. The complete nutrient analysis of the recipe will show its energy, vitamin, and mineral contents. These values for the same recipe are given in Table 9.4. In addition, values for individual amino acids can be derived. In the same manner as illustrated above, the energy provided by a quantity recipe (Table 9.5) can be calculated as shown in Table 9.6. The chocolate chip cookie recipe shown in this table can be analyzed for nutrients and then divided by 120 to get the nutrient values per cookie. These nutrient values are presented in Table 9.6.

COMPUTERIZED NUTRIENT ANALYSIS

It would be extremely tedious and time-consuming to calculate all the nutrients by hand. Several software programs are available that can provide nutrient analysis in a short period of time. Several thousand ingredients and their nutrient information are added to the program's data bank. Each ingredient is given a code number. In addition to nutrient information, the amounts in different measures are filled in for each ingredient. Recipes can be calculated by inputting the code number or the name of the ingredient in the amount required in a specific recipe. The nutrient values are automatically computed, and different reports can be printed. Some of

Table 9.6 Chocolate Chip Cookies: Nutrient Values per Cookie

Kilocalories

	105 kcalories

Macronutrients

Protein	1.842 grams
Carbohydrate	11.84 grams
Fat	5.87 grams
Alcohol	0 grams

Fats

Cholesterol	8.250 milligrams
Saturated fat	1.329 grams
Mono fat	1.453 grams
Poly fat	2.365 grams

Carbohydrates

Dietary fiber	0.444 gram
Soluble fiber	0.051 gram
Insoluble fiber	0.230 gram
Crude fiber	0.280 gram
Sugar	7.283 gram

Vitamins

Vitamin A	33.85 RE
Beta-carotene	0.454 microgram
Vitamin E	1.206 milligrams
Alpha-Tocopherol	0.319 milligram
Thiamin (B_1)	0.033 milligram
Riboflavin (B_2)	0.036 milligram
Niacin (B_3)	0.259 milligram
Pyridoxine (B_6)	0.029 milligram
Folate	5.011 micrograms
Cobalamin (B_{12})	0.019 microgram
Pantothenic acid	0.109 milligram
Biotin	1.733 microgram
Vitamin C	0.196 milligram
Vitamin D	0.247 microgram
Vitamin K	0.857 microgram

Minerals

Sodium	97.45 milligrams
Potassium	56.68 milligrams
Iron	0.408 milligram
Calcium	10.85 milligrams
Magnesium	13.23 milligrams
Phosphorus	37.76 milligrams
Zinc	0.257 milligram

these programs can also produce a food fact label, as well as a list of ingredients and serving sizes. These softwares should definitely be utilized for nutritional assessment of all recipes served in a foodservice operation. It is also very easy to input additional information about ingredients and nutrients. Some of the software packages are extremely user friendly. In addition, they perform other functions, such as recipe costing, menu analysis, menu engineering, food labelling, and recipe printing. A computer printout of the chocolate chip cookie recipe is shown in Figure 9.1.

Healthy Recipe Development

Based on the earlier discussion, it should be easy to select healthy ingredients for a healthy recipe. You cannot prepare a healthy recipe by using unhealthy ingredients. It is important to evaluate every recipe ingredient to see if it fits into the health-conscious menus being planned. The frequency of use of the recipe in an establishment should also be examined. While reviewing and reevaluating the recipe, the guidelines/goals for good nutrition, as well as the Food Guide Pyramid, should be kept in mind. It is not surprising to find that most traditional recipes have some ingredients that are unnecessary, that occur in excessive amounts, and/ or that can be easily replaced by relatively healthy ingredients. Most often the ingredients are high in calories, fat, cholesterol, sugar, salt, or alcohol. Equally surprising, these ingredients can be easily replaced without sacrificing quality, flavor, or taste. In fact, these attributes are sometimes enhanced by changing to healthy ingredients. The following attributes should determine if the recipe is based on health conscious principles:

1. *The recipe should contain ingredients that have high nutrient/caloric density.* The nutrients in ingredients should have high value compared to the ingredients' caloric content. Some ingredients provide "empty calories," or more calories than nutrients. This measure is also referred to as the *Index of Nutritional Quality (INQ)* or *Nutrient Density.* If you substitute ingredients that provide more nutrients in relation to calories, the recipes will automatically become healthy. For example, chocolate provides more calories than nutrients, whereas fruits provide more nutrients than calories.

2. *The recipe should not contain ingredients that are not desirable or not recommended for health reasons and/or that may involve health risks.* Ingredients containing large amounts of nutrients that are not recommended for health reasons, such as salt, sugar, saturated fat, cholesterol, and alcohol, should be avoided or reduced as much as possible. Many ingredients can be substituted to reduce the use of these nutrients, as shown in the following paragraphs and tables.

3. *The recipe should yield adequate portion sizes, which will reduce the chance of serving excessive calories.* As noted earlier, the grams of protein, fat, carbohydrates, and alcohol determine the total caloric content of the final recipe. Reducing portion sizes or the yield of the recipe is one way of reducing calories, as well as the amount of undesirable nutrients they may contain.

Chocolate Chip Cookies (1 serving)

Cookbook Entry	Code	Description	Amount	Portion	Wt.
Margarine	929	Margarine, corn, regular, soft	12.000	Ounce	12.53%
Sugar	561	Sugar, white, granulated	8.000	Ounce	8.35%
Sugar	559	Sugar, brown, packed	8.000	Ounce	8.35%
Eggs	96	Egg, raw, whole, large, chicken	4.000	Item	7.36%
All-purpose flour	6088	Flour, wheat, white, all-purpose	20.000	Ounce	20.88%
Salt	822	Salt, table salt	2.000	Tsp	0.44%
Baking soda	1611	Baking soda	2.000	Tsp	0.34%
Walnuts	529	Nut, walnut, black, dried, chopped	1.000	Pound	16.7%
Candy	1781	Candy, M&M, plain, package, M&M/Mars	24.000	Ounce	25.05%

Macronutrients

Kilocalories	104.6	Kc
Protein	1.852	Gm
Carbohydrate	11.84	Gm
Fat	5.827	Gm
Alcohol	0.000	Gm

Fats

Cholesterol	8.250	mg
Saturated fat	1.329	Gm
Mono fat	1.453	Gm
Poly fat	2.365	Gm

Carbohydrates

Dietary fiber	0.444	Gm
Soluble fiber	0.051	Gm
Insol. fiber	0.230	Gm
Crude fiber	0.280	Gm
Sugar	7.283	Gm

Vitamins

Vitamin A	33.85	RE
Beta-carotene	0.454	μg
Vitamine E	1.206	mg
A-tocopherol	0.319	mg
Thiamin (B_1)	0.033	mg
Riboflavin (B_2)	0.036	mg
Niacin (B_3)	0.259	mg

Vitamins (cont.)

Pyridoxine (B_6)	0.029	mg
Folate	5.011	μg
Cobalamin (B_{12})	0.019	μg
Pant. acid	0.109	mg
Biotin	1.733	μg
Vitamin C	0.196	mg
Vitamin D	0.247	μg
Vitamin K	0.857	μg

Amino Acids

Misc.

Weight	22.63	Gm
Moisture	2.581	Gm
Ash-	0.437	Gm
Cost	0.066	$

Minerals

Sodium	97.45	mg
Potassium	56.68	mg
Iron	0.408	mg
Calcium	10.85	mg
Magnesium	13.23	mg
Phosphorus	37.76	mg
Zinc	0.257	mg

Components: Pro: 7% Carb: 44% Fat: 49%

Figure 9.1 Chocolate Chip Cookies—Single-Serving Nutrient Values

Chocolate Chip Cookies
Number: 0
Serving size:
Category: Recipes

Nutrient	1 Serv	Goal	Goal%	Miss	Nutrient	1 Serv	Goal	Goal%	Miss
Kilocalories	12552	2000	627%	(0)	Biotin (μg)	207.9	300.0	69%	(6)
Protein (g)	222.2	50.00	444%	(0)	Vitamin C (mg)	23.54	60.00	39%	(0)
Carbohydrate (g)	1420	300.0	473%	(0)	Vitamin D (μg)	29.6	10.00	295%	(5)
Fat (g)	699.2	65.00	1075%	(0)	Vitamin K (μg)	102.8	80.00	128%	(6)
Cholesterol (mg)	990	300.0	330%	(0)	Dietary Fiber (g)	53.3	25.00	213%	(0)
Saturated Fat (g)	159.5	20.00	797%	(0)	Soluble Fiber (g)	6.124	None	—%	(1)
Mono fat (g)	174.4	None	—%	(1)	Insol. Fiber (g)	27.56	None	—%	(1)
Poly fat (g)	283.8	None	—%	(1)	Crude Fiber (g)	33.58	None	—%	(0)
Oleic fat (g)	169.2	None	—%	(2)	Sugar (g)	874	None	—%	(1)
Linoleic fat (g)	257.5	None	—%	(1)	Glucose (g)	11.75	None	—%	(3)
Linolenic fat (g)	15.05	None	—%	(2)	Galactose (g)	0	None	—%	(2)
EPA-omega 3 (g)	0.008	None	—%	(3)	Fructose (g)	0.907	None	—%	(4)
DHA-omega 3	0.072	None	—%	(3)	Sucrose (g)	420.1	None	—%	(2)
Sodium (mg)	11693	2400	487%	(0)	Lactose (g)	0	None	—%	(2)
Potassium (mg)	6801	3500	194%	(0)	Maltose (g)	0	None	—%	(5)
Iron (mg)	48.93	18.00	271%	(0)	Tryptophan (mg)	2484	None	—%	(1)
Calcium (mg)	1302	1000	130%	(0)	Threonine (mg)	6101	None	—%	(1)
Magnesium (mg)	1587	400.0	396%	(0)	Isoleucine (mg)	7821	None	—%	(1)
Phosphorus (mg)	4531	1000	453%	(0)	Leucine (mg)	13888	None	—%	(1)
Zinc (mg)	30.85	15.00	205%	(0)	Lysine (mg)	6354	None	—%	(1)
Copper (mg)	8.688	2.000	434%	(1)	Methionine (mg)	3963	None	—%	(1)
Manganese (mg)	26.91	2.000	1345%	(1)	Cystine (mg)	3945	None	—%	(1)
Selenium (mg)	0.366	0.070	522%	(5)	Phenylalanine (mg)	9298	None	—%	(1)
Fluoride (μg)	220	None	—%	(6)	Tyrosine (mg)	6185	None	—%	(1)
Chromium (mg)	0.157	0.120	130%	(6)	Valine (mg)	9709	None	—%	(1)
Iodine (μg)	—	150.0	—%	(9)	Arginine (mg)	18101	None	—%	(2)
Molybdenum (μg)	98	75.00	130%	(8)	Histidine (mg)	4978	None	—%	(1)
Vitamin A (RE)	4062	1000	406%	(0)	Alanine (mg)	6203	None	—%	(2)
Beta-carotene (μg)	54.43	None	—%	(3)	Aspartic acid (mg)	13681	None	—%	(2)
Vitamin E (mg)	144.8	30.00	482%	(8)	Glutamic acid (mg)	26909	None	—%	(2)
A-Tocopherol (mg)	38.29	None	—%	(7)	Glycine (mg)	6297	None	—%	(2)
Thiamin (B_1) (mg)	3.947	1.500	263%	(0)	Proline (mg)	5245	None	—%	(2)
Riboflavin (B_2) (mg)	4.38	1.700	257%	(0)	Serine (mg)	7480	None	—%	(2)
Niacin (B_3) (mg)	31.05	20.00	155%	(0)	Alcohol (g)	0	None	—%	(5)
Pyridoxine (B_6) (mg)	3.468	2.000	173%	(0)	Moisture (g)	309.7	None	—%	(0)
Folte (μg)	601.3	400.0	150%	(0)	Ash (g)	52.4	None	—%	(0)
Cobalamin (B_{12}) (μg)	2.29	6.000	38%	(1)	Caffeine (mg)	17.9	None	—%	(6)
Pant. acid (mg)	13.03	10.00	130%	(1)					

Figure 9.1   *(Continued)*

4. *The recipe should provide some nutrients that are important for health and well-being.* Eating cannot be done for pleasure alone. It should provide necessary nutrients to carry out daily activities. Thus, the purpose of recipes should be to provide nutrition in addition to fulfilling the physiological needs of the body.

5. *The recipe should have sufficient amounts of ingredients that are healthy, as well as contributing to the flavor and preservation quality of foods.* Certain ingredients, such as vinegar and lemon juice, not only provide natural flavors but also add to the flavor and keeping quality of foods. A careful selection of ingredients will achieve this multipurpose goal.

Keeping the above-mentioned criteria in mind, the recipes can be evaluated. It may be necessary to modify and standarize the recipes to meet the nutritional requirements. Prior to making modifications, it is necessary to understand some of the substitution of ingredients that can be done from the nutritional point of view without sacrificing the taste of the final product. Tips for reducing fat and cholesterol in recipes are presented in Table 9.7, and tips for reducing sodium in recipes are listed in Table 9.8. Other suggested ingredient substitutions for healthy recipes are given in Table 9.9. Examples of traditional and modified recipes are provided in Tables 9.10, 9.11, and 9.12.

Table 9.7 Tips for Reducing Fat and Cholesterol in Recipes

Instead of	*Use*
Frying vegetables	Steam, boil, bake, or microwave vegetables
Using fatty sauces, butter, or margarine	Season vegetables with herbs and spices
Using fatty salad dressings on salads	Flavored vinegars, lemon juice, or low-fat dressings
Using solid shortening, margarine, or butter	Vegetable oils
Using regular flours for all kinds of baking	Whole-grain flours
Using whole milk or half and half in puddings, soups, and other baked products	Low-fat or skim milk
Using sour cream or mayonnaise	Low-fat yogurt or blender-whipped low-fat cottage cheese
Using meat and poultry with fat and skin	Lean cuts of meat; trim fat from meat and poultry before cooking; remove skin from poultry before or after cooking
Frying meat, poultry, or fish	Roast, bake, broil, or simmer
Using regular pans and cooking methods	Cook meat or poultry on a rack so that the fat will drain off. Use a nonstick utensil for cooking so that added fat is unnecessary
Using fat-containing broth	Chill meat and poultry broth until the fat becomes solid; then remove the fat before using the broth
Using egg yolks and whites in scrambled eggs	Limit egg yolks to a minimum and use egg whites for larger servings
Using whole egg in muffins, cookies, and puddings	Substitute egg whites in recipes calling for whole eggs; use two egg whites in place of one whole egg for larger servings

Table 9.8   Tips for Reducing Sodium in Recipes

Instead of	*Use*
Salted, smoked, cured, and canned meat, fish, and poultry	Unsalted fresh or frozen beef, lamb, fish, or poultry
Regular hard and processed cheeses	Low-sodium cheeses
Saltine crackers	Unsalted crackers
Regular canned or dehydrated soups, broths, and bouillons	Low-sodium canned soups, broths, and bouillons
Regular canned vegetables	Fresh or frozen vegetables and low-sodium canned vegetables
MSG	Natural flavorings from fruits and vegetables
Salt-containing snacks such as potato chips, pretzels, tortilla chips, and popcorn	Unsalted potato chips, pretzels, tortilla chips, popcorn, and other similar items

Recipe Modification

A careful review of the recipe is necessary before any modification is attempted. It should be understood that changing one ingredient may lead to a complete change in the receipe in order to get the specified yield. While reviewing the receipe, keep in mind the tips listed in this chapter, as well as the general principles of nutrition. It is always better to provide more nutrients than calories. The percentage of fat from calories should also be taken into account. Table 9.10 shows some of the changes that can be made in a traditional recipe to make it more nutritious as well as appealing. A little creativity can go a long way. The changes noted below are only examples; modifications can be incorporated based on the type of the recipe as well as the serving instructions. For example, apple sauce may be added to replace fat. The focus should be on recipes that are high in undesirable ingredients or nutrients.

As seen in this recipe, pastry flour was changed to whole-wheat flour and butter was replaced by margarine. The number of whole eggs was reduced from five to two. The table salt was eliminated, and whole milk was replaced with skim milk. Vanilla extract was added for extra flavoring. Now consider the extent of the changes in calories and nutrients that resulted from the modification of the recipe. The caloric content was reduced by almost half, and the proportion of calories from carbohydrates increased by 31 percent. A dramatic change occurred in the fat content, which was reduced by 84 percent. With the modification, the calories from fat were decreased from 33 to 9 percent, a 73 percent reduction. This could be further reduced by using applesauce in place of fat. Similar drastic changes occurred in the saturated fat and cholesterol contents. The sugar content decreased, and the fiber content increased. This recipe is shown only as an example to illustrate the extent of possible modifications that can be done to make a recipe nutritionally wholesome.

Table 9.9 Suggested Ingredient Substitutions for Healthy Recipes

Category	Ingredient	Substitute
Meat, Fish, and Poultry		
	Hamburger (all meat)	85 to 90 percent lean ground beef or ground turkey
	Bacon (pork)	Turkey ham
	Beef or meat frankfurters	Chicken frankfurters
	Red meats	White meats
	Tuna packed in oil	Tuna packed in water
	Chicken with skin	Chicken without skin
	Whole eggs	Egg whites (two egg whites for one whole egg)
	Organ meats	Use small portions only when necessary
	Salted, smoked, cured, and canned meat, fish, and poultry	Use unsalted fresh or frozen beef, lamb, fish, or poultry
Dairy Products		
	Whole milk	Skim milk or low-fat milk; reconstituted nonfat dry milk
	Evaporated whole milk, half and half, whipped cream	Evaporated skim milk, 2 percent low-fat milk
	Sour cream, mayonnaise	Low-fat or nonfat yogurt, low-fat cottage cheese, buttermilk
	Whole-milk cheese	Skim milk or imitation cheese
	Margarine or butter	Vegetable oil
	Cream cheese	Low-fat cream cheese, yogurt cheese, neufchatel
	Ice cream	Frozen yogurt, sherbet, sorbet, ice fruit
	Milk shakes	Natural fruit drinks, sherbet
	Regular hard and processed cheese	Low-sodium cheese
Fruits and Vegetables		
	High-fat salad dressings	Low-fat dressings, flavored vinegars, lemon juice, low-fat cottage cheese
	Regular canned vegetables	Fresh or frozen vegetables, low-sodium canned vegetables, vegetables canned in water
	Regular canned fruits	Fresh or frozen fruits, fruits canned in water rather than syrup
Fats and Seasonings		
	Lard, animal shortenings	Vegetable oils
	MSG	Spices, herbs, natural flavorings, lemon juice
	Sugar	Artifical sweeteners, maple syrup, fresh fruits, honey, molasses
	Salt	Lemon juice, spices, herbs, spice extracts, citrus peels
	High-fat sauces	Seasonings, herbs and spices
	Oil and soy sauce marinades	Fruit juice marinades, flavored vinegars, worcestershire sauce, other spices

Table 9.9 *(Continued)*

Category	Ingredient	Substitute
Grains		
	All-purpose flour	Whole-wheat flour, cornstarch
	White rice	Brown rice
	Saltine crackers and salt-containing snack foods	Low-salt crackers and snack foods
Sauces, Dressings, and Soups		
	Regular canned or dehydrated soups	Low-sodium canned soups
	Broth	Use after removing fat
	Roux	Cornstarch, tapioca, arrowroot
	Cream sauces	Yogurt, evaporated skim milk, nonfat dry milk
	Oil in salad dressings	Vegetable oils, vegetable and fruit juices, low-calorie dressings

Table 9.10 Banana Nut Bread
(64 Servings: ½-Inch Slices)

Traditional Recipe	*Modified Recipe*
2 pounds Pastry flour	2 pounds Whole-wheat flour
10 ounces Butter	10 ounces Margarine
26 ounces White sugar, granulated	13 ounces White sugar, granulated
5 Whole eggs	2 Whole eggs
26 ounces Banana, mashed	20 ounces Banana, mashed
4 teaspoons Baking powder	4 teaspoons Baking powder
2 teaspoons Table salt	
0.5 teaspoon Baking soda	0.5 teaspoon Baking soda
0.75 cup Whole milk	0.75 cup Skim milk
8 ounces Walnut	2 ounces Walnuts
	2 teaspoons Vanilla extract

Nutrients/Calories	*Traditional Recipe*	*Modified Recipe*	*Percent Change*
Kcalories	168	88	−48%
Protein	2.8 grams	2.5 grams	−11%
Percent of calories from protein	6	11	+83%
Carbohydrates	26 grams	18 grams	−30%
Percent of calories from carbohydrates	61	80	+31%
Fat	6.3 grams	1.0 grams	−84%
Percent of calories from fat	33	9	−73%
Saturated fat	2.6 grams	0.1 gram	−96%
Dietary fiber	0.7 gram	1.9 grams	+171%
Sugar	13.4 grams	7.1 grams	−47%
Cholesterol	26.7 grams	6.7 grams	−75%

Table 9.11 Pepper Steak
50 servings

Traditional Recipe	Modified Recipe
13 pounds Ground beef	8 pounds Ground beef, lean
8 ounces Shortening	2 ounces Shortening
100 grams Beef stock base	50 grams Beef stock base
6 pounds Tomatoes, whole	10 pounds Tomatoes, whole
3 cloves Garlic, raw	4 cloves Garlic, raw
2 teaspoons Table salt	1 teaspoon Table salt
12 cups Sweet peppers	20 cups Sweet peppers
3 ounces Cornstarch	2 ounces Cornstarch
6.75 cups Water	6.75 cups Water
⅔ cup Soy sauce	1 cup Soy sauce
56 ounces Rice, white	56 ounces Rice, brown
2 teaspoons Table salt	1 cup Lemon juice
2 teaspoons Corn oil	2 teaspoons Corn oil

Nutrients/Calories	Traditional Recipe	Modified Recipe	Percent Change
Kcalories	450	251	−44%
Protein	31.1 grams	23.8 grams	−23%
Percent of calories from proteins	28	39	+35%
Carbohydrates	17 grams	19 grams	+12%
Percent of calories from carbohydrates	16	31	+94%
Fat	27.6 grams	8.2 grams	−70%
Percent of calories from fat	56	30	−46%
Saturated fat	10.2 grams	2.6 grams	−75%
Dietary fiber	1.8 grams	3.1 grams	+72%
Cholesterol	99.1 grams	55.7 grams	−44%

In the example shown in Table 9.11, ground beef was replaced by lean ground beef, and the amount of beef was reduced. Vegetables such as sweet peppers and tomatoes were increased in volume to make up for the weight of the reduced beef, as well as to keep the yield of the recipe constant. Soy sauce was increased to add flavor. Brown rice was substituted for white rice, which added fiber to the recipe. Table salt was reduced and replaced by lemon juice to provide flavor.

As with the recipe in Table 9.10, drastic changes can be seen in the reduction of calories, fat, and the percentage of calories from fat. Similar changes involve the reduction in cholesterol. Further changes can be made by using light soy sauce, which will further reduce the sodium content of the recipe.

Modifications were also made to the recipe shown in Table 9.12. The amount of flour was reduced to decrease the serving size, thereby reducing the calories to start with. Lemon juice was substituted for salt, and butter was replaced by

Table 9.12　Mushroom Quiche
48 servings

Traditional Recipe	Modified Recipe
29 ounces Wheat flour, all-purpose	20 ounces Wheat flour, all-purpose
1 teaspoon Table salt	0.5 cup Lemon juice
32 ounces Butter	1 pound Vegetable shortening
1.25 cups Water	1.25 cups Water
30 Whole eggs	30 Egg whites
2 quarts Half and half	2 quarts Evaporated skim milk
2 quarts Whole milk	2 quarts Skim milk
1.5 teaspoon Table salt	1.5 teaspoon Table salt
0.5 teaspoon White pepper	0.5 teaspoon White pepper
36 ounces Swiss cheese	20 ounces Swiss cheese
8 ounces Parmesan cheese	4 ounces Parmesan cheese
1 pound Mushrooms, raw	2 pounds Mushrooms, raw

Nutrients/Calories	Traditional Recipe	Modified Recipe	Percent Change
Kcalories	423	245	−42%
Protein	16.4 grams	12.8 grams	−22%
Percent of calories from protein	15	21	+40%
Carbohydrates	18 grams	18 grams	0%
Percent of calories from carbohydrates	17	29	+71%
Fat	31.9 grams	13.8 grams	−57%
Percent of calories from fat	68	50	−26%
Saturated fat	19 grams	5 grams	−74%
Cholesterol	217.5 grams	15.0 grams	−93%

vegetable shortening. Whole eggs were replaced by egg whites, although the number of eggs was not increased. Half and half, which contains considerable fat and calories, was replaced by evaporated skim milk. The amount of Swiss and Parmesan cheeses was reduced. The amount of mushrooms was increased to maintain the yield. Again, as seen in the other two recipes, a drastic change was observed in the number of calories and the amount of saturated fat. The cholesterol content was reduced by about 93 percent.

After making necessary modifications, all recipes should be standardized and new recipe files maintained. A blank form (Figure 9.2) is provided that can be used for recipe modification. This will help to create recipes that are nutritious as well as appealing to the clientele. There are many other innovative ideas that can be implemented in recipes. From portion sizes to ingredient contents, changes can be made to provide healthy choices. Thus, recipe modifications may make it unnecessary to change all or part of the menu in order to make it nutritionally wholesome.

Number of servings:
Serving size:

Traditional Recipe	Modified Recipe
Nutrients/Calories	Percent change
Kcalories	
Protein	
Percent of calories from proteins	
Carbohydrate	
Percent of calories from carbohydrate	
Fat	
Percent of calories from fat	
Saturated fat	
Cholesterol	

Instructions:

Comments:

Date:

Figure 9.2   Form for Use in Recipe Modification

Chapter 10

NUTRITIONAL MENU PLANNING

M enu planning is one of the most important tasks in any type of foodservice operation. This task becomes more complicated if nutritional menu planning is desired. Simply stated, a **menu** is a list of food items served by any foodservice operation. In more complex terms, it is a statement of the food and beverage items provided by a foodservice establishment, based primarily on consumers' needs and/or demands and designed to achieve organizational objectives. **Menu planning** is the process by which menus are planned, taking into consideration all aspects of a foodservice system. Extending this definition, **nutritional menu planning** involves planning menus that provide the nutrients, ingredients, and calories required for healthy living, based on consumers' needs and/or demands, and to achieve organizational objectives. In planning nutritional menus, it is important to take into account the nutrition goals for healthy living, as well as the Food Guide Pyramid. Menus represent the focal point of any foodservice operation. In fact, the success or failure of a foodservice operation depends on the menu and how the foods on it are selected and served. This can also determine the degree of profit or success of an operation. From the management point of view, all efforts should be directed to menu planning, taking into consideration all nutritional aspects as well as other operational factors. It is a misconception that nutritionally rich menus are expensive, unpopular, and/or difficult to plan. It is not easy, but neither is it impossible to plan such menus. Although the principles discussed in this chapter are applicable to menu planning in general, they are described in order to provide fundamental knowledge.

BASIC CONSIDERATIONS IN NUTRITIONAL MENU PLANNING

Careful menu planning will result in consumer satisfaction, employee motivation, and management success. The basic principles of menu planning are the same whether the menu is nutritious or not. The many factors that should be considered in planning menus are shown in Figure 10.1. These factors may be considered from two points of view, management's and consumers', as shown in the figure.

From Management's Viewpoint

Organizational Goals and Objectives For nutritional menu planning, there should be a thorough commitment from the organization so that the goals and objectives reflect clearly the nutritional importance of the menus. This commitment is essential for any menu plan to be successful. The primary consideration in menu planning is whether the menu conforms to the organization's goals and objectives.

Figure 10.1   Factors to be Considered in Menu Planning for a Foodservice Operation

These vary greatly, depending on the type of foodservice operation, such as commercial or institutional. This factor is very important in menu planning. For example, the menu planned for a health club will be different from that of a restaurant.

Budget Once the organization's goals and objectives are set, a budget allocation is essential. The amount of money that can be spent depends on several factors, such as the income from food sales and the relative food cost percentage. In turn, the income from food sales depends on consumers' available disposable income (ADI), the location of the facility, the type of service, and several other factors. Nutritional menu planning requires careful consideration of the relative costs of food, labor, and equipment. There are several economic constraints, such as inflation and availability of ingredients, that have a considerable impact on the amount of money available at specific times. There is seasonal availability of products such as fruits and vegetables used in nutritional menus. Commercial foodservices experience more fluctuations in sales/income than institutional foodservices, where budgets are based primarily on consumer counts for a longer period of time. Institutional foodservices are usually on a tight budget; therefore, menu planning is critical for this type of operation. This is not to imply that variety and nutritional appeal in menus cannot be planned under tight budgets. Careful planning with a blend of innovativeness, efficiency, and creativity is important for success. Efficient utilization of all resources is essential.

The food cost percentage is a valuable tool in determining budgets. Precosted standardized recipes, when updated periodically, facilitate the calculation of costs to be used in budgeting. This information can easily be inputted into the computer and the forecast done very easily. Menu planning becomes complex when both high- and low-cost items aer included in a menu and when one or more of these items are offered as choices. Careful screening and selection of wholesome items are necessary to arrive at the desired combination that will result in a consistent average consumer check.

Market Conditions Nutritional menus require considerable amounts of raw or unfrozen products, particularly fruits and vegetables. These products are subject to seasonal fluctuations that have an enormous impact on demand and supply. Good weather conditions may result in an overabundance of a product and lower prices. Conversely, bad weather may cause severe shortages of food products and higher prices. This factor is of primary importance in planning menus, particularly for long time periods. To be on the safe side, it is advisable to have alternative equivalent items on menus or recipes that can be easily substituted when necessary. Menus should be planned to take maximum advantage of the seasonal availability of various foods. The location of the foodservice operation and its accessibility to the market were once factors in menu planning. However, due to technological advances in shipment by air or surface transportation, they are no longer important. For example, it is easy to obtain live lobsters or other seafood from Maine in the Midwest by overnight shipment.

Physical Facilities and Equipment   Generally, the physical facilities and equipment available in a foodservice operation dictate the types of menus that may be planned. Not only the availability of certain pieces of equipment but also their number plays an important role. With given facilities and equipment, it may be difficult to include a menu item or a variety of menu items within a desired period of time. However, a major modification of the kitchen equipment or layout may not be necessary; only a modification or a change in the parameters may be necessary. For example, a deep-fat fryer can be replaced by a rotary oven, tilting skillet, or combi-ovens. These provide versatility and choices in recipe preparation methods. However, if the entire kitchen is being planned, consideration should be given to the menu. Conventional equipment may not be desirable when including nutritional menu items. For example, deep-fat fryers, which were once considered a must in conventional foodservice operations, may not be necessary or may have only limited use. More versatile equipment such as tilting skillets, steam kettles, braising pans, steamers, and broilers, is more useful. The availability and sequential arrangement of this equipment is also important as are labor-saving devices such as food processors, vegetable slicers, peelers, and corers, which facilitate menu planning by providing various choices. Efficient menu planning requires a well-balanced approach to the utilization of materials, equipment, and employees. The simultaneous use of a variety of equipment facilitates smooth food production and service operations. For example, steam ovens, grills, tilting skillets, braising pans, and broilers may be used simultaneously to provide a variety of menu items. Trunnions may be used to prepare soups or steamed vegetables, while an adjustable and tilting skillet may be used for another menu item. Thus, prior menu planning is necessary so that there is optimum use of all types of equipment available at the foodservice operation.

The other important factor is the size and capacity of the equipment. As mentioned earlier, the equipment required for nutritional menus is different from that needed for conventional menus. If possible, the entire layout and design may have to be changed. However, it may not be feasible or necessary to plan from scratch. A minor change may be all that is required. Other conventional equipment, such as deep-fat fryers, may still be used for certain menu items. In addition, the availability and type of storage space is critical. Nutritional menu items require more freezer, refrigerator, and dry storage space than conventional items. Also, to utilize the kitchen facilities fully, work and production schedules should be carefully planned.

Personnel Skills   For nutritional planning and performance, the staff must be aware of the nutritional significance of the menu items. Nutritional attributes of menu items can easily be lost by improper handling, processing, or serving of food. As noted earlier, many nutrients are sensitive to light, heat, and moisture. Nutritionally prepared meals can lose their healthy quality in minutes. Employees must therefore understand the significance of preserving nutritional quality. Frequent training programs, workshops, and meetings may be helpful. When planning menus, it is desirable to consider the time and labor required for various processes at different stages of production and service. It may be necessary to have more prepreparation of menu items, as well as careful control of time and the temperature to which food items can be exposed. For example, raising the temperature even a few degrees may destroy essential nutrients. Improper coring and peeling may result in the loss of fiber content or nutrients naturally present in foods. This problem increases when temporary and untrained employees are used. Selection of menu items that efficiently utilize employees' time and skills is therefore necessary. The menu items selected should be those that can be produced easily, utilizing the average level of skills of the available workers within a reasonable length of time. Providing assistance to skilled employees, like chefs, will free their time for use in the preparation of other menu items or for supervision. Many nutritious menu items cannot be prepared and stored well before the time of service, and many items may need last-minute preparation. This should be considered when planning menus. Since the cost of food may be a major consideration in planning nutritional menus, all these factors deserve careful thought.

Types of Production and Service Systems   Production types have a strong impact on the choice of menu items. Further, the time lag between production and service is critical. In a conventional food production and delivery system, where foods are prepared, held at serving temperature, and served on the same day, many choices may be included on the menu. By contrast, in systems where food is cooked and chilled or frozen, there are strong limitations. The amount of time required for service is also important. For example, in a large multiwinged hospital, the time lapse between tray assembly and service may be so long that certain foods cannot be used. Another example involves home delivery of food by a commercial or noncommercial operation.

From the Consumer's Viewpoint

Nutritional Requirements   This is the most important factor in menu planning. At some foodservice operations, it may be mandated by regulatory agencies. Meeting nutritional needs in such institutions as hospitals, nursing homes, and schools must be given top priority when planning menus. More and more commercial operations are giving nutrition serious thought. Food and nutrient labeling laws are also bringing pressure on establishments to consider serving nutritionally wholesome foods. Growing nutritional concerns among many consumers have resulted in careful assessment of menu items and portion sizes by many institutional and commercial foodservice operations. In general, a variety of foods, when properly used, will provide most of the necessary nutrients. Equally related to the nutritional content of foods in menu planning are *consumers' food habits and preferences* and *food characteristics and attributes*. Factors affecting consumers' food habits and preferences are discussed in Chapter 1; all of them should be considered in planning menus. Food characteristics and attributes are also mentioned in Chapter 1 and described below; all of them are important. Certain foods, such as liver and organ meats, may be rich in nutrients but may not be liked by the average consumer. One must always remember that nutritional content alone does not make a menu item popular. When planning menus based on nutritional requirements, consumers' needs and wants should be considered. Menus for children are different from those of elderly persons since their nutritional needs are different. Careful planning of menus for long-term clients, such as those in elder-care centers, is important since long-term planning is necessary and monotony can result in disapproval of menu items.

Food Characteristics   After nutritional attributes, the most important factor to consider in menu planning is the food itself. Characteristics of food, including their organoleptic (sensory) properties, play an important role in their acceptance. The most important characteristics are described below.

Color: Color can be a good indicator of the nutritional content of menus— rich green spinach, red tomatoes, yellow oranges, and red carrots. Interesting color combinations and coordination not only help stimulate appetite but also ensure the nutritional variety of menus. Choosing and arranging foods so that there is a good color combination on a plate, tray, counter, or salad bar is an important aspect of menu planning. Even a small garnish, like a parsley sprig or a cherry, can make an enormous difference in the appearance of food and contribute to its nutritional content. It is much easier to come up with a colorful combination of foods when the menu is nutritionally planned. Colorful foods have eye appeal, which can lead to their selection. Color also emphasizes the variety available for selection. When planning menus, items of different colors should be included and too many items with a similar color should be avoided. In some printed menus, the visual aspects of the foods can be enhanced by providing colored pictures. Bright, desirable food combinations add to a menu's attractiveness, while dull colors convey a sense of blandness in the food. Since a consumer will often select food first by its eye appeal, color is important to consider in menu planning.

Colors also have a psychological impact on consumers. Red, orange, peach, pink, brown, yellow, and light green are considered desirable colors for foods; purple, violet, dark green, gray, and olive are less inviting. The intent should be to use the natural color of foods; however, artificial coloring may be added to enhance goods so long as it is safe and does not impart bitterness or any other undesirable taste. Fruits and vegetables, in all their variety of forms, add to the colors of menu items. Garnishing, plate decorations, and attractive counter displays add color and should be considered in planning menus.

Texture and Shape: In planning menus, the textures and shapes of foods should be considered. A combination of soft- and hard-textured items is essential. Impressions of the texture and shape of a particular food are formed even before it is tasted. Texture of foods are described in various ways, such as "soft," "hard," "crispy," "crunchy," "chewy," "smooth," "brittle," and "grainy." Certain combinations of food items with different textures go well together. Soups are preferred with crispy crackers, soft-textured potatoes go well with chewy steaks, and casseroles are desirable with crisp vegetables. Foods in different shapes also add to the attraction and appeal of the menu items. For example, vegetable and fruit carvings provide interesting shapes and add to food appeal. Special equipment is needed for dicing, cutting, or carving products into various shapes and sizes. Vegetables can be cut into squares, strips, circles, balls, screws, and other interesting shapes. Since vegetables and fruits are likely to be included most often in nutritionally wholesome foods, it is desirable to provide different textures and shapes for menu items. Mixed vegetables in interesting shapes provide color and texture, enhancing the attractiveness of food on the plate. Different textures and shapes also break the monotony of food items.

Consistency: Consistency refers to the degree of viscosity or density of a product. Like texture, consistency adds variety to menu items. The most common adjectives used to describe consistency are "runny," "gelatinous," "pasty," "thin," "thick," "sticky," and "gummy." These terms are most often used to describe semisolid foods such as sauces and gravies. It is desirable to have menu items with differing consistencies. Too many runny items may not only be unacceptable but will make it difficult to keep them separated on the plate. As a rule, items that have a hard texture should be complemented by items with a thin consistency. Relatively hard-textured items such as meats go well with thin gravies, while nuts in thin items create a desirable combination of texture and consistency.

Flavor: The flavor of foods is an important consideration when planning menus. Foods can have sweet, sour, bitter, or salty flavors, which can be present alone or in combination. In addition, there are various off-flavors or undesirable flavors specific to certain foods. A desirable blend of flavors is essential for acceptance of menu items. Reduction of portion sizes and caloric content increases the importance of flavor. The predominance of any one flavor is usually undesirable. Contrasts in flavor and intensity increase the acceptability of menu items. Bland foods may be made more appetizing by adding pungent sauces, or a blend of sweet and sour flavors may be added to a menu. The reduction or elimination of salt can be compensated for by lemon juice or vinegar. Spices and herbs can also be added to increase the flavor of foods. The right combinations of spices and herbs can make a big difference. Sometimes, adding two contrasting flavors is also desirable, such as in sweet-and-sour meatballs. Fats normally provide special flavors, as in the case of fried foods. Since adding fat is not desirable, additional flavors, preferably from natural ingredients, can be used. Examples of foods with desirable combinations of flavor are curried chicken and rice, lamb with mint sauce, sauerkraut and lean sausage, chicken with orange sauce or honey, and broccoli with hollandaise sauce. Flavors can be masked or enhanced by adding contrasting items to the menu—for example, liver and onions, curried eggplant, and vanilla pudding. Some recipes call for the addition of certain natural or artificial flavor enhancers, which, as their name implies, increase the flavors of foods rather than provide their own flavors. Some flavor enhancers, such as MSG, contain sodium and have other side effects; therefore, they should be used with caution when necessary. A combination of strong- and mild-flavored vegetables is desirable. Broccoli, cabbage, and onions provide strong flavors and therefore should be complemented by mild-flavored vegetables. On the other hand, strong-flavored sauces and gravies go well with bland items like rice or mashed potatoes. Such bland items can be used to provide a "bed" to which other flavored foods can be added.

Method of Food Preparation: Food preparation methods also deserve careful attention in planning nutritious menus. Food can be prepared in many ways, and variety is essential. Some restaurants are limited to or known for a certain types of food preparation, but most foodservices have the option of preparing foods in different ways. These methods include baking, broiling, boiling, frying, steaming, grilling, braising, or a combination thereof. They may be variations in these methods as well. It is advisable to group by method of preparation all the recipes of a foodservice operation. This makes it easier to select items for preparation and to avoid items that are similar in preparation. From the management point of view, there must be a uniform distribution of food preparation methods to facilitate optimal use of employee skills and equipment. Predominant use of a single preparation method is not desirable for many reasons. For example, too many fried or steamed items on the menu—even with variability in the types of foods—are undesirable and unappetizing. Balance in the methods of food preparation is required.

Serving Temperature: Temperature is probably the most easily controlled and least complex component in planning menus based on food characteristics and nutrition. Serving temperatures preferred by individuals vary with age and other personal factors. Both hot and cold foods should appear on the menu. A chilled gazpacho appetizer is desirable with hot entreés, a cold salad may go well with hot bread, or a cold sandwich may be desirable with hot soup. Similarly, cold desserts are preferred after hot entreés. There is no strong evidence that season or weather has an impact on the selection of particular temperatures of food, but it may be desirable to include lemonade or sherbet on a hot day and hot chocolate on a cold day. Seasonal availability of foods will also affect their inclusion on menus. Strawberry shakes, watermelon, and peach desserts can be added in warm or hot seasons. One factor that should be considered is the loss of nutrients on exposure to heat, light, and moisture. When foods are on display on a heated counter or under a lamp, their nutrient contents may be degraded.

Presentation: The final appearance of food—whether on a plate, serving tray, cafeteria counter, buffet table, or salad bar or in a display case, delivery package, or takeout package—is an important factor in the selection and consumption of food. Consumers, particularly those who prefer nutritionally wholesome foods, are looking for eye appeal. Three-dimensional, nicely presented food adds to its attractiveness and appeal, whether on paper or in actuality. Consumers buy with their eyes and taste foods afterward. For example, a plate of all-flat food items, regardless of their taste, is unappealing and, to a great extent, undesirable. Similarly, all-tall food items on the plate are unappetizing and do not contribute to contrast and sequence in the arrangement of menu items. A large meat chop, a baked potato, a dressed whole tomato, a rectangular piece of cornbread, and cut celery stalks presented together are unappealing, regardless of their color, flavor, or nutritional value. Thus, when planning menus, the height of foods and the overall appearance of different items should be considered. A combination of tall, flat, and variously shaped items, arranged in a symmetrical pattern, is eye-catching and should be kept in mind when planning menus.

Nutritional requirements can also be based on the RDAs discussed earlier. These are the intake levels of essential nutrients that, based on scientific knowledge, are judged to be adequate to meet the known nutrient needs of practically all healthy persons. These values are based on age, sex, and condition. RDAs are also helpful in planning nutritional menus.

The other important factor that should be considered is the Dietary Guidelines for Americans, which were also discussed in Chapter 1. These guidelines, developed by USDA and HHS, are based on seven principles, which are also embodied in the Food Guide Pyramid. These guidelines, which are summarized below, are extremely important in planning nutritionally wholesome menus.

1. Eat a variety of foods.

2. Maintain a healthy weight.

3. Choose a diet that's low in total fat, saturated fat, and cholesterol.

4. Choose a diet with plenty of vegetables, fruits, and grain products.

5. Use sugars only in moderation.

6. Use salt and sodium only in moderation.

7. If you drink alcoholic beverages, do so in moderation.

Although the guidelines, serving instructions, and steps described in this chapter concern the setting in which all three meals are consumed, such as an institution, most of them can be used by any commercial establishment, such as a restaurant. The recommended daily serving sizes are:

- Grain and grain products: 6 to 11 servings
- Vegetables: 3 to 5 servings
- Fruits: 2 to 4 servings
- Dairy products: 2 to 3 servings
- Meats and meat alternatives: 2 to 3 servings

The recommended daily servings for different age groups are shown in Table 10.1. These recommendations are based on the Food Guide Pyramid. Examples of what constitutes a serving are shown in Table 10.2.

Table 10.1   Daily Servings Needed by Different Groups

Calorie Level*	Women and Some Older Adults — About 1600	Children, Teen Girls, Active Women, Most Men — About 2200	Teen Boys and Active Men — About 2800
Bread group	6	9	11
Vegetable group	3	4	5
Fruit group	2	3	4
Milk group	2–3**	2–3**	2–3**
Meat group	2	2	3
	(for a total of 5 ounces)	(for a total of 6 ounces)	(for a total of 7 ounces)

* These are the calorie levels if low-fat, lean foods from the five major groups are chosen and foods from the fats, oils, and sweets group are used sparingly.

**Women who are pregnant or breast-feeding, teenagers, and young adults to age 24 need three servings.

Source: U.S.D.A.

Table 10.2   Examples of What Counts as a Serving

Bread, Cereal, and Pasta Group	Vegetable Group	Fruit Group	Milk, Yogurt, and Cheese Group	Meat, Poultry, Fish, Dry Beans, Eggs, and Nuts Group	Fats, Oils, and Sweets Group
1 slice of bread 1 tortilla ½ cup cooked rice, or cereal 1 ounce ready-to-eat cereal ½ hamburger roll, bagel, or English muffin 3–4 plain crackers (small) 1 pancake (4-inch) ½ croissant (large) ½ doughnut or danish (medium) 1/16 cake (average) 2 cookies (medium) 1/12 pie (2-crust, 8″)	½ cup chopped raw or cooked vegetables 1 cup raw, leafy vegetables ¾ cup vegetable juice ½ cup scalloped potatoes ½ cup potato salad 10 French fries	1 piece fruit or melon wedge ¾ cup fruit juice ½ cup chopped, cooked, or canned fruit ¼ cup dried fruit	1 cup milk or yogurt 1½ ounces natural cheese 2 ounces process cheese 1½ cups ice cream or ice milk 1 cup frozen yogurt	2½–3 ounces cooked lean beef, pork, lamb, veal, poultry, or fish ½ cup cooked beans or 1 egg or 2 tablespoons peanut butter or ⅓ cup nuts count as 1 ounce of meat Lean beef choices include round tip, top round, eye of round, top loin, tenderloin, and sirloin	Use sparingly

Source: Adapted from the Food Guide Pyramid information provided by the U.S.D.A, Human Information Service.

THE FOOD GUIDE PYRAMID AND MENU PLANNING

The Food Guide Pyramid can be used in planning nutritionally wholesome meals; methods of doing so are described in the following paragraphs. The Pyramid can be used as a dietary management and menu-planning tool that, by virtue of its graphic simplicity and its variety of applications, promises to be indispensable. As discussed in Chapter 1, the Food Guide Pyramid divides food groups into different sections. At the tip of the pyramid are fats, oils, and sugars, indicating limited consumption, whereas bread, cereals, and pastas are at the bottom, indicating the maximum number of servings. Thus, in a very simple way, the Food Guide Pyramid provides considerable latitude in the selection of food items. It illustrates with graphic simplicity three important components or attributes of a healthy diet:

1. *Variety:* the need to include all food groups and to vary menu items.

2. *Serving sizes:* the relative proportions of foods that can be chosen from each food group.

3. *Moderation:* the consumption of fats, oils, and sugars in very limited amounts.

This stepwise approach based on the Food Guide Pyramid can also be used in planning menus. It provides foodservice operators with a basis to plan healthy menus that give customers great freedom of choice. It offers a selection of desired nutrients in menu-planning strategies, including innovative and modified versions of traditional dishes. Both commercial and institutional foodservice managers recognize the Food Guide Pyramid as a tool that can be used to provide foods that are nutritious and flavorful, as well as offering a wide variety of choices.

As shown in Chapter 1, the Food Guide Pyramid consists of the following five major food groups: breads, vegetables, fruit, milk, and meat. The Pyramid itself represents variety and selection from different food groups. However, it should be remembered that (1) no one food group is more important than any other, regardless of the quantities or servings recommended, and that (2) foods from one group cannot be substituted for foods from another group. Food items are selected on the basis of nutritional requirements and thus are not substitutable. For example, the meat group provides proteins and the milk group provides calcium.

THE MECHANICS OF MENU PLANNING USING THE FOOD GUIDE PYRAMID

As noted previously, menu planning is one of the most important tasks of management, and persons with this responsibility should be aware of all aspects of production, service, and nutrition. It is advisable to have a meeting involving all those concerned so that different ideas can be explored. The persons in charge of purchasing and production could also be included in this meeting, which should take place at a convenient time and location, with no distractions or interruptions. Sufficient lead time should be allowed for food ordering, production planning, and employee scheduling. Some reference materials that should be readily available for menu planning include:

1. Standardized recipe files, showing detailed methods of preparation, portion sizes, portion costs, and nutrient content

2. Copies of previous menus, if available

3. Cookbooks

4. Pictures of prepared foods, if available

5. Food preference data, if available

6. Market statements

7. Consumer comments, if available

8. Food delivery schedules

9. A comprehensive list of menu items, preferably with nutrient contents and prices

10. Food sales record

11. Production records

12. Professional and trade journals

13. Organizational manuals

14. Other pertinent publications

To start the process of menu planning, it is important to have several blank menu forms for use, since planning may involve much trial and error. These forms should be based on the menu patterns and the number of choices planned for each meal. Careful planning of forms will avoid much inconvenience. These forms may be printed on regular-size paper or incorporated on a large chalkboard or flip chart. Erasable ink, chalk, pens, and pencils are needed. An example of a menu-planning form used on a weekly basis is shown in Figure 10.2. Meal types are listed on the left-hand side, with the number of choices available under each (entrees, vegetables, salads, hot breads, and desserts) for each meal. This is the simplest type of menu form that can be used in any foodservice operation. Similar forms with modifications may be prepared for all three meals, as shown in Figure 10.3. These forms may be modified to suit individual needs. Planning of weekly or monthly menus requires consideration of menu items offered on preceding days or other days of the week. A menu form should include meal pattern(s), number of meals, days of the week, and types of food items. When planning menus, care should be taken to avoid leftovers. It is advisable to keep a record of leftover items and consider those items in planning menus. Leftovers are also indicative of the popularity or dislike of certain menu items. An early decision in menu planning concerns which meal or type of food to consider first. Certain meals and food items have

Breakfast/Lunch/Dinner (circle one)	*Dates: From* _____		*Through* _____		
Food Items	*Monday*	*Tuesday*	*Wednesday*	*Thursday*	*Friday*
Soups					

Entrees
  1.
  2.
  3.
  4.					

Vegetables
  1.
  2.
  3.					

Salads
  1.
  2.					

Hot Breads					

Desserts
  1.
  2.					

Figure 10.2   A Typical Blank Form for Planning Menus

priority. It is advisable to follow the same sequence every time a menu is planned. Steps that have proven successful in menu planning are summarized on the following pages. These steps are not very different from those used in most menu-planning publications. Nevertheless, since the nutritional content of menus is of paramount importance, and since these steps are based on the Food Guide Pyramid, there are certain variations that should be considered. The following steps are recommended for menu planning from a nutritional point of view.

Step 1. Select Pasta, Starch, and Bread Items for the Entire Menu Period

---

Six to 11 Servings of Grains and Grain Products Daily

In traditional methods of menu planning, the first item to be selected is normally the entrees. However, since the Food Guide Pyramid recommends 6 to

Operation: Dates: From _____ Through _____					
Meal/Items	*Monday*	*Tuesday*	*Wednesday*	*Thursday*	*Friday*
Breakfast					
Cereal					
1.					
2.					
Meat or meat alternative(s)					
1.					
2.					
Breads					
1.					
2.					
Beverages/ fruit					
1.					
2.					
Lunch					
Appetizer					
1.					
2.					
Entrees/salads					
1.					
2.					
3.					
Vegetables					
1.					
2.					
3.					
Breads					
1.					
2.					
Desserts					
1.					
2.					
Beverages					
1.					

Figure 10.3   Blank Form for Use in Planning a Menu for a Week

Operation:					
Dates: From _____ Through _____					
Meal/Items	Monday	Tuesday	Wednesday	Thursday	Friday
Dinner					
Appetizer					
1.					
2.					
Entrees					
1.					
2.					
3.					
4.					
Vegetables					
1.					
2.					
3.					
Breads					
1.					
2.					
Salads					
1.					
2.					
Desserts					
1.					
2.					
Beverages					
1.					
2.					

Figure 10.3 *(Continued)*

11 servings of grain products per day, priority is given to pasta items, which can be used for entrees as well as different types of bread. Menu items from these categories should be selected for both main and secondary meals of the day, which are generally dinner and lunch, respectively. As the foundation of the Food Guide Pyramid, grains and pastas provide complex carbohydrates (starches), which are important sources of energy. These products are good sources of iron, zinc, vitamin B_6, thiamin, niacin, and riboflavin. Most cereals and grains are also enriched or fortified, ensuring their nutrient contents.

In addition to selecting the required number of servings from this group, these items should be chosen first (1) to select other menu items that will complement them; (2) because these items are relatively less costly unless meats are added; (3) there are many varieties; (4) they are relatively easy to prepare; and (5) they provide the bulk of the meal items and influence the satiety value of other foods.

In planning, one should make sure that the same types of items are not offered on the preceding or succeeding day, even if the preparation methods are different. If several choices are provided for the same meal, combinations may be selected on the basis of preference ratings. Even among choices, duplication should be avoided. Variety can easily be provided by changing the types of meats used in combination, the preparation method(s), or the garnishings and gravies. Texture, preparation method, color, and other physical attributes of the menu items should be taken into consideration. Choices should include highly seasoned and blander items to provide variety.

Starchy food such as grains, pasta, rice, yams, and white potatoes provide variety in color, texture, consistency, shape, and flavor. If the entrees are relatively dry, moist and creamed dishes should be selected; if the items have drippings or juice, bland foods such as mashed potatoes should be included to complement their flavor. The caloric contents of starchy foods should be checked and carefully monitored, since they may differ significantly. Starchy foods can also be used as fill-ins when the meal items are low in calories. One advantage of starchy foods, mainly pasta, is that they are preferred by both young and old people; they are also versatile, inexpensive, and easy to prepare. Among the most nutritious choices available in the grains category are *whole-grain breads and rolls, bagels, pita bread, tortillas, english muffins, rice, pasta, bulgur, couscous, bread sticks, low-fat cereals, low-fat whole-grain crackers, and low-salt pretzels.* Breads and pastas also come in different shapes and sizes and provide variety inexpensively, in addition to meeting health requirements. Other items that can be included on the menu are rice (plain and seasoned, white and brown, basmati or another specialty), low-fat cereals, and several varieties of whole-grain breads and rolls. Among the many varieties of bread are yeast, quick, sweet-dough, sourdough, flat, and several specialty types. Since most breads are eaten with butter or margarine, greasy items should be limited when breads are provided. Bland breads may be included when spicy and/or juicy items are on the menu. Breads may also be used in entrees, such as cheese rarebit on rye bread or a pita sandwich.

Similar criteria should be used for the second most important meal of the day, which is normally lunch. All of the above-mentioned guidelines should be followed except the one concerning portion sizes, which can be reduced if lunch is not the primary meal of the day. Most people prefer salads or pasta for lunch. If choices are provided, there should be a balance among these items. Costs should also be balanced by selecting expensive and inexpensive items. For example, if a costly entree was selected for dinner, an inexpensive one may be chosen for lunch, and vice versa. The item selected should complement the one previously chosen for the most important meal of the day.

Step 2. **Select Meat and Meat Alternatives Serving in Conjunction with Step 1**

Two to 3 Servings of Meats and Meat Alternatives Daily

After selecting the items from the grains category, it is advisable to choose items from the meat and meat alternative groups. These groups must be considered at this time since the entree is the main meal of the day. Since the foundation of a nutritional menu is plant-based foods, these products should be added in conjunction with the items selected earlier. For example, meatballs and spaghetti is a good combination. Meats and meat alternatives continue to be very important sources of protein and other nutrients. Alternatives to meats, such as dried beans, eggs, nuts, and tofu, are also included in this group and provide similar nutrients.

Since the primary concern with meat groups is the saturated fat and cholesterol content, these items should be included very carefully. In addition, controlling portion sizes will automatically reduce some of these undesirable nutrients. Lower-fat items, lean meats, and cholesterol-free items should be selected. Chicken and turkey, legumes, lean meats, and tofu, served in small portion sizes (2 to 3 ounces), are recommended. Pastas can also be served with low-fat meat sauces.

When planning entrees, the guideline on providing less than 30 percent of calories from fat should be followed. There are items other than meats that can contribute to the fat content. Some dairy products may contain saturated fats and sugars, which should be checked. There are many fat-free and low-fat items that can be easily substituted for fat-containing foods without sacrificing flavor. For example, "light" deli cheese, 1 percent milk, and frozen yogurt can be used as foods, as well as ingredients for various types of preparation. Plain low-fat or nonfat yogurt can replace sour cream and/or mayonnaise in dressings, dips, and sauces.

Despite the importance given to other items, meats will continue to be preferred by consumers and the foodservice manager should consider this fact in menu planning. Although it will be a challenge, the foodservice manager should follow the dietary guidelines, as well as give customers satisfying and creative entrees. Using skinless, baked, or broiled chicken and seafoods; using smaller portions of high-quality lean cuts; and removing as much fat as possible are some measures that can be adopted. Other options are blending ground beef and ground turkey, mixing vegetables and grains with meats, and using water-packed rather than oil-packed tuna. Regarding the method of preparation, broiling, stir-frying, roasting, grilling, or poaching should be used rather than deep-fat frying. Several meatless entrees can be prepared using dried beans, peas, and other legumes, thereby providing proteins from plant sources.

Step 3. Add Vegetables

Three to 5 Servings of Vegetables Daily

The vegetables selected should complement the entree items and should be chosen on the basis of color, shape, size, texture, preparation method, and flavor. The food characterics discussed earlier in this chapter should all be taken into consideration. In addition to contributing nutrient value, vegetables play an important role in making the total meal appealing. The variety and versatility of vegetables add to their desirability. Vegetable colors, textures, and preparation methods provide many possibilites and alternatives for the menu. They may be served whole, halved, quartered, sliced, diced, cubed, julienned, or carved into attractive shapes. They may be combined to give a variety of colors. Carrots, broccoli, peas, cauliflower, beans, and other vegetables provide rich colors and interesting combinations. They may be prepared by steaming, boiling, or sautéing. They may be creamed or prepared with gravies. Many sauces and seasonings go well with vegetables. When more than one vegetable is provided, texture should be considered, and both soft- and hard-textured vegetables should be provided. Contrast in color, shape, and preparation methods is essential when choices are provided or when more than one vegetable is included in the menu. Flavors should also be considered since some vegetables are pungent and have stronger flavors than others. For example, onions and vegetables belonging to the cabbage group are strongly flavored and should be used with vegetables that are relatively bland. Vegetables should complement the entrees of the day—highly seasoned entrees with mild-flavored vegetables and vice versa. Minimal amounts of salt and fat should be added while preparing vegetables. Vegetables can be provided fresh or frozen. Selecting high-quality frozen vegetables can reduce labor costs. Vegetables can also be purchased canned, such as tomato products, which can be used in sauces and other dishes. For canned vegetable products, the sodium content should be checked. Vegetables can also be used as entrees in combination with other items, such as stir-fried vegetables with pasta or with small amounts of meat. Vegetable burgers and stuffed pita sandwiches, vegetable soups and stews, and stuffed potatoes with low-fat topping options are also gaining popularity. In addition, salad bars can provide a variety of vegetables and fruits, which can serve as main entrees for the day.

Nutritionally, vegetables are an important food group, and more than one type of vegetable should be included each day. A menu that provides dark green and deep yellow vegetables daily ensures a high content of certain required vitamins. Vegetables should be served raw or cooked as little as possible to preserve their nutritional contents. Various types of garnishes may be provided by careful selection and carving of vegetables. Vegetables add visual appeal in addition to complementing entrees in other ways. They are naturally low in fat, good sources of fiber, and provide vitamins A and C, beta-carotene, iron, potassium, calcium, folate, and magnesium. Although all vegetables are included in the Food Guide Pyramid, care should be taken to offer a variety based on their nutritional contents. For example, dark green leafy vegetables such as spinach, greens, romaine lettuce, and broccoli are especially good sources of vitamins and minerals. Legumes such as beans or lentils are good sources of protein and can be used as meat substitutes. Deep yellow vegetables (carrots, sweet potatoes, and many hard-shelled squashes) are rich in beta-carotene, vitamin C, niacin, phosphorus, and potassium. Vegetables are also low in calories, low in sodium, and high in fiber. Some suggested low-calorie entrees are:

- Grilled poultry or seafood served on brown rice
- Chicken breast with celery, carrot, and pepper filling
- Turkey slices rolled with broccoli
- Lean meat slices rolled with fruit or vegetable fillings
- Poached fish with vegetables

Step 4. Add Salads in Complementation with Step 3

Salads may consist of one or more combinations of the vegetables mentioned earlier or of fruits, meats, fish, cheese, gelatin mold, and a variety of condiments, garnishing, and dressings. Salads add color, flavor, and texture to the meal. When selecting salads, the entrees and vegetables chosen earlier should be considered to avoid repetition. All factors discussed earlier for menu planning should be taken into consideration; for example, the vegetables, meats, or pastas used in the salad should be different from those selected for other menu items. Salad temperature should also be selected based on the entrees. Chilled salads complement hot entrees, and this variation in serving temperature adds to the variety and appeal of the menu. Salads may also be selected as entrees. If choices are included, there should be at least one large salad and possibly a variety of other salads in smaller sizes. A small salad may be preferred with a filling entree or a large salad may be desirable with a sandwich. Salads such as tuna fish, meats, vegetables, or cheese can become popular attractions or specialties of an operation. In general, if salads complement the entrees, smaller sizes are appropriate. Salads contribute greatly to the nutritional value of a meal, and this fact should be considered when planning menus. Although salads may not require elaborate equipment, a good deal of labor is involved in their preparation and arrangement. Salads require relatively large amounts of storage space, as well as careful handling during preparation and holding, primarily to save their nutritional quality. Many of the calories in salads come from dressings, which at times may provide more calories than the salads alone. There are many low-calorie dressings that can be used with the same desirable results. Also, dressings can be replaced by low-calorie substances such as lemon juice, other fruit juices, low-fat cottage cheese, and yogurt.

Step 5. Select Soups and Appetizers

As with salads, there are numerous types of appetizers and soups from which to choose. These precede entrees or the main item of the meal. As their name indicates, appetizers stimulate the appetite. Soups, to a great extent, serve the same function. Since these foods are included to whet the appetite, it is essential to select appropriate recipes. Soups and appetizers can be light or heavy, depending on their ingredients. A light appetizer should be planned when heavy, filling entrees are offered and vice versa. Light entrees or sandwiches may be complemented by heavier soups. Leftover vegetables, juices, and drained syrups from canned foods may be utilized effectively in soups. Soups for the succeeding meal should be planned to incorporate possible leftovers. However, costs should be considered in using leftover items. It is necessary to determine whether leftover vegetables would be more profitable as an accompaniment to entrees or as ingredients in soups. Various spices, condiments, and garnishes are used to complement appetizers and soups in such a way that there is no repetition of other items on the menu. Creamed soups should not be served with creamed entrees. Fish chowders should not be included when other fish dishes are on the menu. The temperature at which soups are served is important, since temperature preferences dictate equipment and labor, which must be considered in menu planning. It is essential to keep soups at desirable temperatures until they reach the consumers. Soups and appetizers, although used in small quantities, can be good sources of nutrients. Care should be taken to restrict sodium and fat, particularly when canned soups are used.

Step 6. Plan Nutritious Desserts

Two to 4 Servings of Fruits Daily

Since most of the items have already been selected, it is relatively easy to plan desserts. However, these become the most calorically dense items if not properly planned. Desserts are very important menu items since they are preferred by consumers. They not only add a final touch to the menu but also provide a lasting impression of the meal. Careful menu planning is essential, as a well-planned meal may be spoiled by a disappointing dessert. It is the taste of the dessert that is important, not the quantity. A tasty, small serving is sufficient to leave a lasting impression of the meal.

Fruits can serve, individually or in combination, as nutritious desserts. Fruits and fruit juices provide important amounts of vitamins A and C, as well as potassium. They are also low in fat and sodium. They add variety as well as fiber. Vitamin A–containing fruits include apricots, cantaloupe, mango, and papaya. There are several fruits that are rich in vitamin C, such as all citrus fruits, kiwi, cantaloupe, honeydew, pineapple, papaya, mango, raspberries, strawberries, and watermelons. Bananas are good sources of potassium. Apples, oranges, bananas, and strawberries are commonly used. In addition, some exotic and less familiar fruits should be included. In addition, fruit purees, low-fat dressings and sauces, and fruit smoothies blended with nonfat yogurt and ice can add to the dessert offerings. Fruits are also used as displays on salad bars and banquets. Low-fat ice creams and yogurts are popular desserts.

When planning desserts, the color, consistency/texture, and shape should be considered, as well as the intensity of the sweetness. A hot, spicy entree may be followed by an intensely sweet dessert, or a hot meal item may be followed by ice cream. Sweet and soft desserts go well with filling entrees. Like entrees, desserts should be carefully selected since these two items are of particular importance to consumers. When a variety of desserts are considered, analyze the type of dessert as well as its consistency, texture, color, and flavor. Pie, cake, and pudding are good combinations. The ingredients that provide sweetness or fat in desserts need to be checked and controlled. Natural sweeteners and low-fat items should be considered. It is relatively easy to provide low-calorie desserts with little creativity. The appearance of desserts is very important when they are presented on a dessert cart or in display cases. Nuts, condiments, liqueurs, chocolate drinks, and syrups should be added only when necessary since they can increase the calories. A well-planned, nutritious meal can be ruined by improper desserts.

Step 7. Add Beverages

Two to 3 Servings of Dairy Products Daily

Selecting beverages is probably the easiest step in menu planning, as several hot and cold beverages are usually included. Most beverages can be made relatively easily and frequently, or are readily available for serving, so little effort is needed in planning. At many operations, the list of beverages is standardized. Seasonal availability and variations should be taken into consideration. Consumers may select from among alcoholic or nonalcoholic beverages, carbonated beverages, fruit juices, lemonade, coffee, milk shakes, hot tea, iced tea, and various types of milk products. Herbal teas are becoming increasingly popular. Selection of alcoholic drinks is complex because of the wide variety of beverages available and the many possible combinations that may be requested.

Beverages can be used to fulfill the dairy requirement by including milk, yogurt, cheese, and other dairy products. These products are the best sources of calcium in the diets of most Americans. They also provide protein, vitamins B_{12} and A, thiamin, riboflavin, and, in fortified products, vitamin D. Calcium is critical for growing children, as well as for helping to maintain strong bones in adults. Some of these products are naturally high in saturated fat, so their inclusion in the menu should be carefully monitored. There are several new dairy products that provide reduced-fat and fat-free choices in different flavors. Some products that should be included are low-fat or nonfat yogurt (frozen and regular, but check for sugar content), skim or 1 percent milk (one serving of whole milk has 8 grams of fat versus less than 1 gram of fat in a serving of skim milk), part-skim or low-fat cheese, and ice milk.

Step 8. Plan Breakfast Menus

Compared to other items, breakfast items are relatively easy to plan. Normally, there are certain items that need to be included on the menu, although variations in the method of preparation are desirable. Breakfast items should be prepared easily on short notice. Several choices may be included, since preferences vary, and there are standard foods desired by many consumers. Juices, cereals, toasts, eggs, sausage, and biscuits are among the most popular breakfast items. Duplication and repetition should be avoided as much as possible.

Some suggestions for a low-calorie breakfast are:

- Poached or soft boiled eggs
- Omelets with egg whites and vegetable filling
- High-fiber, low-sugar cereals with skim milk
- Fresh fruits
- Low-fat yogurt
- Whole-grain/bran muffins
- Part skim milk cheese
- Exotic fruits such as papaya, mango, kiwi, or guava
- Whole wheat toast with light fruit spreads

POSSIBLE SUBSTITUTIONS OF MENU ITEMS TO MEET DIETARY GUIDELINES

The steps outlined above are recommended for menu planning; possible variations are based on individual operations. Since fat is a key target of the Dietary Guidelines and the Food Guide Pyramid, the challenge of any foodservice manager is to reduce it to meet the 30 percent fat requirement with 10 percent from saturated fats. To accomplish this, a revision of the preparation methods to reduce the amount of oil, mayonnaise, and other fats traditionally used in preparing foods may be necessary. Also, new innovative foods and food products that are low in fat but high in calories, fiber, and nutrients must be developed. At the same time, there may be a demand for the reduction of sodium, cholesterol, and sugar in meals. To reduce fat, whole milk can be replaced by 1 percent milk or mayonnaise can be reduced by 50 percent and blended with plain nonfat yogurt in items such as tuna salad. The use of table butter or margarine can be reduced. To compensate for the loss of calories, it may be necessary to add a considerable amount of fresh produce. More rice, beans, baked potatoes, bean tacos, pasta with meatless sauce, and vegetable pizza may be used.

Draining and rinsing reduce the fat and cholesterol in items such as beef and sausage after browning and result in a crumbly, nongreasy product. The taste can be made acceptable by adding selected seasonings and sauces. Steam cooking 80 percent lean ground beef and thoroughly draining, rinsing, and redraining results in a 65 percent fat reduction. One method of doing this is by cooking and stirring ground beef in a steam-jacketed kettle. After cooking, the fat is drained. Hot water is added to the kettle (about 1 gallon per 10 pounds of meat). The meat is stirred thoroughly, and fat and liquid are drained while keeping the meat away from the drain.

Fat and cholesterol can also be reduced by using a 50/50 blend of ground beef and ground turkey. Beef can also be blended with soy vegetable protein for hamburgers. Using skinless chicken, preparing pizza with reduced-sodium sauce and part-skim mozzarella cheese, and using low-fat or fat-free salad dressing are other means of reducing fat and cholesterol.

The tip of the Food Guide Pyramid, composed of fats, oils, and sweets, although small, presents the biggest dietary challenge to any foodservice manager. The role fat plays in providing flavor, aroma, texture, and satiety should be considered before any replacements or substitutions are planned. Fat is used in the form of cooking oil and butter in frying. There are also hidden sources of fats such as nuts, crackers, breads, whole milk, and meats. In addition to total fat, the focus should be on the amount of saturated fat. Saturated fat is found in largest amounts in fats from meat and dairy products, as well as in some vegetable fats such as palm, coconut, and palm kernel oils.

The restriction of dietary fat has led to consumption of vegetarian meals. Although work is still in progress, there are now many menu items that can meet the needs of those who desire vegetarian meals. There are also different types of vegetarian menus, such as **semivegetarian** menus including poultry, fish, eggs, and dairy foods; **pesco-vegetarian** menus including fish, eggs, and dairy foods; **lacto-ovo vegetarian** menus including eggs; and **vegan** menus, which exclude animal-derived foods of all types. Vegetarian diets are healthy and nutritionally adequate when appropriately planned. Consuming adequate amounts of protein, iron, and calcium is especially important. Nonmeat sources of these nutrients should be used. Other factors to consider include using steam for cooking vegetables, raw fruits and vegetables as much as possible, salad and fruit bars, vegetable lasagna, chicken fajita with nonfat sour cream, grilled marinated turkey fillet, stir-fried vegetables, carrots and celery sticks in place of french fries or chips, poaching shrimp and other seafoods, grilled fruits, and blackened chicken and fish.

The sugar content of foods also needs careful scrutiny. Added sugars can be found in items such as donuts, cakes, pies, fruit canned in light or heavy syrup, chocolate milk, yogurt, chocolate shakes, ice cream, jams, jellies, and fruit and cola drinks. The salt content should also be checked—both added to foods and present in foods or ingredients used.

After the menu is finalized, a check should be made to see if all the requirements have been met. The horizontal and vertical lines on the menus should be checked and rechecked. Menu planning is like putting the pieces of a puzzle together; moving one piece may alter another. The menu should be planned in two different sessions, one for active planning and one for finalization. A trial menu may be offered for the first two weeks, particularly if the foodservice operation is new. Modifications and changes may be necessary. Enough flexibility must be built into the menu to accommodate future changes and/or unexpected conditions. A check should be made to see if all the servings are available. A final checklist is desirable for every type of foodservice operation. Examples of such checklists are provided in Figures 10.4, 10.5, and 10.6. Either one of these check-

---

[ ] Is the menu consistent with management's goals and objectives?
[ ] Does the menu include all choices planned in the menu pattern?
[ ] Does the menu have a balance between the low- and high-priced items?
[ ] Are all the equipment and facilities adequately utilized?
[ ] Are all the personnel skills effectively utilized?
[ ] Are seasonal foods effectively used in the menu?
[ ] Will there be sufficient time for production of all the menu items planned?
[ ] Are the workloads balanced?
[ ] Does the menu conform to the desired nutritional requirements?
[ ] Is the menu well balanced from the nutritional point of view?
[ ] Are the color combinations of the menu well planned and attractive?
[ ] Does the menu include items with varying consistencies and textures, thereby providing well-balanced meals?
[ ] Are all the flavors selected to provide a well-balanced menu?
[ ] Do the items selected have different shapes and sizes?
[ ] Is there a balanced distribution of food items based on their preparation methods?
[ ] Does the menu include hot and cold items distributed evenly?
[ ] Are choices provided according to food preferences or popularity?
[ ] Is the menu free of duplication, repetition, and blanks as to the food items included in the menu for the same day as well as the same week?
[ ] Does the overall menu represent high-quality, wholesome, appealing, and manageable food and beverage items?

Comments:

Date:

Checked by:

Figure 10.4   Checklist for Use in Planning Menus

Considerations	*Mon*	*Tue*	*Wed*	*Thu*	*Fri*	*Sat*	*Sun*
1. Management's point of view							
a. Conforms to the menu pattern							
b. Provides balance in the cost of menu items							
c. Meets nutritional requirements							
d. Is based on seasonal fluctuations							
e. Provides optimum workload							
f. Provides optimum equipment load							
g. Utilizes personnel skills							
h. Facilitates production							
i. Facilitates fast and efficient service							
j. Appears promising and profitable							
2. Consumer's point of view							

Variety is present in:

- Color
- Texture
- Shape
- Flavor
- Consistency
- Preparation
- Other _____

Conforms to food habits
Overall acceptability
Other aspects _____

Remarks:

Yes: √   No: X   Needs Improvement: NI

Figure 10.5   Final Checklist of Weekly Menus

Considerations	Mon	Tue	Wed	Thu	Fri	Sat	Sun
• Does the menu provide variety among all items?							
• Does the menu contribute less than 30% of calories from fat?							
• Does the menu have less than 10% of calories from saturated fats?							
• Does the menu provide enough dietary fiber?							
• Is the sugar content of all menu items moderate?							
• Is the salt/sodium content of all menu items moderate?							
• Is the cholesterol content within the desired limit?							
• Are there enough servings per day of:							
1. grain and grain products?							
2. vegetables?							
3. fruits?							
4. dairy products?							
5. meats and meat alternatives?							

Other aspects _____

Remarks:

Yes: √   No.   X   Needs Improvement: NI

Figure 10.6   Final Checklist of Weekly Menus for Nutritional Contents

lists or one planned along these lines should be used to ensure that everything essential for the success of the menu has been considered.

The above-mentioned general guidelines should be followed whether the menu is planned for an institutional or commercial foodservice operation. For resturants the menu should include a variety of choices based on the principles discussed earlier.

NUTRITIONAL ANALYSIS OF MENUS

Nutritional analysis of menus can be conducted using one of the methods described in earlier chapters. A dependable nutritional analysis software program can do this easily and quickly. It can also provide graphic illustrations, as well as print a report of the nutritional contents, highlighting the amounts necessary. As a rule, low-calorie items should contain about 350 to 400 calories and appetizers, soups, and side dishes no more than 100 to 200 calories. It is also desirable to have no more than 12 grams of fat in entrees and 5 grams of fat per appetizer, soup, or other side dish. In any case, the overall fat content derived from calories should be below 30 percent. Other nutrients, such as proteins and carbohyrates, should then be checked, as well as the amounts of saturated fat, cholesterol, sodium, sugar, and dietary fiber.

MENU FORMAT

After the menus are written, revised, refined, and finally approved, they are ready to be implemented. The menus have to be rewritten in two different formats, although the items themselves will remain unchanged. These two formats are written (1) for foodservice personnel and (2) for consumers. Menus written for foodservice personnel are supplemented by such pertinent technical information as recipe file number, name of the recipe, production schedule, equipment usage, preparation schedule, and so on. Simple names of the menu items, with which all foodservice personnel are familiar, are included in this format. From the consumers' point of view, menus are designed to sell, and therefore foods are described to attract consumers' attention. The descriptions are planned to create a desire for the items offered.

Since the purpose of the menu is to communicate with the consumer, a good menu is one that presents its message well. Careful selection is required. Nutrition-rich menu items should be highlighted. Many foodservice operations are now using a heart, apple, or pyramid as symbols to indicate the nutritional significance of menu items. Care should be taken to ensure that food and nutrition labeling requirements are met or are not violated. Any items that may be responsible for an allergy or a sensitivity should be so labeled. Every effort should be made to describe the contents of the menu items as accurately as possible. In general, menus should be simple and easy to read, informative, attractive, self-explanatory, and complete. They should portray accurately the nutritional quality and richness of the items that were carefully planned and executed by the foodservice staff. The menus can be displayed as hard copy, bulletin boards, neon signs, table tents, menu boards, electronic monitors, or any other display device.

Chapter 11

FOOD AND NUTRITION LABELING

The food label, referred to as the *food fact label,* has become an important source of nutrition information for the public as well as foodservice managers. The Food and Drug Administration (FDA) of HHS and the Food Safety and Inspection Service of USDA require the food label to offer useful and accurate nutrient information. Its purpose is to provide consumers with nutrition information and to help them choose healthy diets, as well as offer an incentive to food companies to improve the nutritional qualities of their products.

Key features of the food label are the following:

- Almost all foods contain a label, so consumers can learn about the nutritional qualities of almost all products.
- The format is consumer-friendly, distinctive, and easy to read, enabling consumers to quickly find the information they need to choose healthy foods.
- The label includes information on the amount per serving of saturated fat, cholesterol, dietary fiber, and other nutrients of major health concern to consumers.
- Nutrient reference values are expressed as the percentage of Daily Values, helping consumers see how a food fits into an overall daily diet.
- Uniform definitions for terms such as *light, low-fat,* and *high-fiber* are used to ensure that they have the same meaning for any product on which they

appear. These descriptors are particularly important for consumers who are trying to cut calories, fat, or other nutrients or for those trying to increase their intake of certain nutrients.

- The label describes claims about the relationship between a nutrient or food and a disease or health-related condition, such as calcium and osteoporosis or fat and cancer. This is helpful information for people who are concerned about eating foods that may help keep them healthier longer.

- Standardized serving sizes are used, making nutritional comparisons of similar products much easier.

- Declarations of the total percentages of materials such as juice in juice drinks are given, enabling consumers to know exactly how much exists in a product.

- Voluntary information on many raw foods is included.

All of these features are added to the new label, which has much more useful nutritional information than the old label. These requirements are published in the *Federal Register.* FDA rules implement the provisions of the Nutrition Labeling and Education Act of 1990 (NLEA), which requires nutrient labeling for most foods (except meat and poultry) and authorizes the use of nutrient content claims and appropriate FDA-approved health claims. Meat and poultry products regulated by USDA are not covered by NLEA; however, USDA's regulations closely parallel FDA's rules.

The regulations, most of which went into effect in 1994, require nutritional labeling for most foods. In addition, they set up voluntary programs for nutrition information for raw foods: the 20 most frequently eaten raw fruits, vegetables, and fish under FDA's voluntary point-of-purchase nutrient information program and the 45 best-selling cuts of meat under USDA's program. Although voluntary, FDA's program for raw produce and fish carries a strong incentive for retailers to participate. This voluntary requirement may change in the future.

Most of the labeling requirements are restricted to packaged products and some raw foods, although nutrition information will also be provided for some restaurant foods in the future. The current regulations require nutrient information for foods about which health or nutrient-content claims are made on restaurant signs or placards.

Under NLEA certain foods are exempt from nutrition labeling, including the following:

- Foods served for immediate consumption, such as those in cafeterias and on airplanes, and foods sold by vendors such as mall cookie counters, sidewalk vendors, and vending machines.

- Ready-to-eat food that is not for immediate consumption but is prepared primarily on site, such as bakery, deli, and candy store items.

- Food shipped in bulk, as long as it is not for sale in that form to consumers.

- Medical foods, such as those used to address the nutritional needs of patients with certain diseases.

- Plain coffee and tea, some spices, and other foods that contain no significant amounts of any nutrients.

Food produced by small businesses also is exempt under 1993 amendments to NLEA. Under these amendments, exemptions are based on the number of people a company employs and the number of units within a product line made yearly. Although these foods are exempt, their manufacturers are free to provide nutrient information when appropriate—as long as it complies with the regulations.

Game meats such as deer, bison, rabbit, quail, wild turkey, and ostrich do not require nutrition information on individual packages; instead, this information can be given on counter cards, signs, or other point-of-purchase materials. This option is primarily due to the fact that too few nutrient data exist for these types of foods.

Examples of food labels are shown in Figures 11.1 and 11.2. Food labels can clearly be identified by their uniform appearance. The title "Nutrition Facts" is easily identifiable, and there are requirements for the type size, style, spacing, and contrast to ensure a distinctive, easy-to-read label. A typical **Nutrition Fact label** on packaged foods contains six parts, as shown in Figures 11.1 and 11.2. Part one, which follows the name of the product, contains the **serving size** and **number of servings** per package or container. Part two consists of the number of calories as consumed, singly or in addition to other products, and the number of calories derived from fat. Part three consists of total fat, broken down into saturated and unsaturated fats, cholesterol, sodium, potassium, and different types of carbohydrates. All of these are given as percentages of **Daily Values.** Part four consists of vitamins and minerals, also expressed as percentages of Daily Values. Part five lists Daily Values for selected nutrients based on a 2000- or 2500-calorie diet. The last portion of the label consists of a list of ingredients present in the food product.

SERVING SIZE

The first information below the title is the serving size, which is the basis for reporting each food's nutrient content. These serving sizes are uniform and reflect the amounts people actually eat. For example, on the Ritz cracker Nutrition Fact label, 5 crackers (15 g) is given as a serving size, which is easily understood by a consumer since it is expressed in both common household and metric measures.

FDA allows the following household measures: cup, tablespoon, teaspoon, piece, slice, fraction (such as ¼ pizza), and common household containers used to package food products (such as a jar or tray). Ounces may be used, but only if a common household unit is not applicable and an appropriate visual unit is given, for example, 1 ounce (28 grams, about ½ pickle). Grams (g) and milliliters (ml) are the metric units used in serving size statements. Other definitions and appropriate serving sizes are also specified by NLEA.

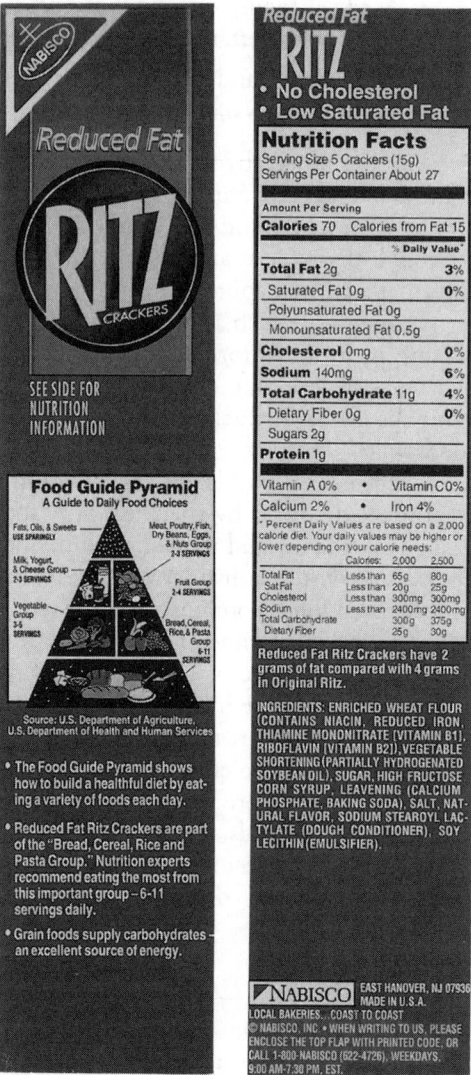

Figure 11.1 An Example of a Nutrition Fact Label

NUTRITION PANEL COMPONENTS

Immediately following the serving size is the number of servings per container. This is followed by dietary components on the nutrient panel based on the amount per serving. The mandatory (**boldface**) and voluntary (lightface) components and the order in which they must appear on the nutrition facts label are as follows:

- **Total calories**
- **Calories from fat**

Figure 11.2   A Different Example of a Nutrition Fact Label

- **Calories from saturated fat**
- **Total fat**
- **Saturated fat**
- Polyunsaturated fat
- Monounsaturated fat
- **Cholesterol**
- **Sodium**
- Potassium
- **Total carbohydrate**
- **Dietary fiber**
- Soluble fiber
- Insoluble fiber
- **Sugars**
- Sugar alcohol (e.g., the sugar substitutes xylitol, mannitol, and sorbitol)
- Other carbohydrates (the difference between total carbohydrate and the sum of dietary fiber, sugars, and sugar alcohol if desired)
- **Protein**
- **Vitamin A**
- Percent vitamin A present as beta-carotene
- **Vitamin C**
- **Calcium**
- **Iron**
- Other essential vitamins and minerals

If a claim is made about any of the optional components, or if a food is fortified or enriched with any of them, nutrient information for these components becomes mandatory. The required nutrients were selected because they address today's health concerns, and the order in which they appear reflects the priority of current dietary recommendations.

NUTRITION PANEL FORMAT

On the nutrition panel, all nutrients must be declared as percentages of the Daily Values. The amount, in grams or milligrams, of macronutrients (such as fat, cholesterol, sodium, carbohydrates, and protein) must be listed to the immediate right of the name of each nutrient. A column headed as "% Daily Values" is included above the listed macronutrients. Requiring nutrients to be provided as a percentage of the Daily Values prevents misinterpretations that arise with quantitative values. For example, a food with 140 milligrams of sodium could be mistaken for a high-sodium food because 140 is relatively large number; however, that amount represent less than 6 percent of the Daily Value for sodium, which is 2400 milligrams. On the other hand, a food with 5 grams of saturated fat could be construed as being low in that nutrient; in fact, however, it provides one-fourth of the total Daily Value because 20 grams is the Daily Value for saturated fat based on a 2000-calorie diet.

NUTRITION PANEL FOOTNOTE

As seen in Figure 11.1 the "% Daily Value" listing carries the footnote "Percent Daily Values are based on a 2,000 calorie diet. Your daily values may be higher or lower depending on your calorie needs." This footnote may include:

- A sentence noting that individual goals are based on the person's calorie needs
- Lists of the Daily Values for selected nutrients for a 2000- and a 2500-calorie diet
- An optional footnote for packages of any size giving the number of calories per gram of fat (9), carbohydrate (4), and protein (4)

The size and format specifications for different kinds of packages are also specified in the regulations.

DAILY VALUES—DRVs

Daily Values consist of two sets of dietary standards: Daily Reference Values (DRVs) and Reference Daily Intakes (RDIs). Only DRVs appears on the label to make the label less confusing. DRVs have been established for macronutrients that are sources of energy—fat, carbohydrates (including fiber), and protein—and for cholesterol, sodium, and potassium, which do not contribute calories. DRVs for the energy-producing nutrients are based on the number of calories consumed per day. A daily intake of 2000 calories has been established as the reference. This level was chosen, in part, because it approximates the caloric requirements of post-menopausal women. This group has the highest risk of excessive intake of calories and fat.

DRVs for energy-producing nutrients are calculated as follows:

- Fat based on 30 percent of calories
- Saturated fat based on 10 percent of calories
- Carbohydrate based on 60 percent of calories
- Protein based on 10 percent of calories (the DRV for protein applies only to adults and children over the age of four. RDIs for protein are established for special groups).
- Fiber based on 11.5 grams of fiber per 1000 calories.

Under current public health recommendations, DRVs for some nutrients represent the upper limit that is considered desirable. The DRVs for fats and sodium are:

- Total fat: less than 65 grams
- Saturated fat: less than 20 grams
- Cholesterol: less than 300 milligrams
- Sodium: less than 2400 milligrams

DAILY VALUES—RDIs

RDI replaces the term *U.S. RDA,* which was introduced earlier as a label reference value for vitamins, minerals, and protein in voluntary nutrition labeling. This change was made because of confusion that existed over *U.S. RDAs,* the values determined by FDA and used on food labels, and *RDAs* (Recommended Dietary Allowances), the values determined by the National Academy of Sciences for various population groups and used by FDA to determine the U.S. RDAs. However, the values for the new RDIs remain the same as the old U.S. RDAs for the time being.

NUTRIENT CONTENT DESCRIPTORS

Terms that may be used to describe the level of a nutrient in a food and how these terms can be used are also spelled out by the regulations. The core terms are as follows:

- *Free:* this term means that a product contains none or only trivial or "physiologically inconsequential" amounts of one or more of these components: fat, saturated fat, cholesterol, sodium, sugars, and calories. For example, *calorie-free* means fewer than 5 calories per serving, and *sugar-free* and *fat-free* both mean less than 0.5 gram per serving. Synonyms for *free* include *without, no,* and *zero.*

- *Low:* this term can be used on foods that can be eaten frequently without exceeding dietary guidelines for one or more of these components: fat, saturated fat, cholesterol, sodium, and calories. Thus, descriptors are defined as follows:

  Low-fat: 3 grams or less per serving

  Low-saturated fat: 1 gram or less per serving

  Low-sodium: 140 milligrams or less per serving

  Very low sodium: 35 milligrams or less per serving

  Low-cholesterol: 20 milligrams or less and 2 grams or less of saturated fat per serving

  Low-calorie: 40 calories or less per serving

  Synonyms for *low* include *little, few,* and *low source of.*

- *Lean and extra lean:* these terms can be used to describe the fat content of meat, poultry, seafood, and game meats.

  Lean: less than 10 grams of fat, 4.5 grams or less of saturated fat, and less than 95 milligrams of cholesterol per serving and per 100 grams.

  Extra lean: less than 5 grams of fat, less than 2 grams of saturated fat, and less than 95 milligrams of cholesterol per serving and per 100 grams.

- *High:* this term can be used if the food contains 20 percent or more of the Daily Value for a particular nutrient in a serving.

- *Good source:* this term means that one serving of a food contains 10 to 19 percent of the Daily Value for a particular nutrient.

- *Reduced:* this term means that a nutritionally altered product contains at least 25 percent less of a nutrient or of calories than the regular, or reference, product. However, a "reduced" claim cannot be made for a product if its reference food already meets the requirement for a "low" claim.

- *Less:* this term means that a food, whether altered or not, contains 25 percent less of a nutrient or of calories than the reference food. For example, pretzels that have 25 percent less fat than potato chips can carry a "less" claim. *Fewer* is an acceptable synonym.

- *Light:* this descriptor can mean two things: First, it can mean that a nutritionally altered product contains one-third fewer calories or half the fat of the reference food. If the food derives 50 percent or more of its calories from fat, the reduction must be 50 percent of the fat. Second, it can mean that the sodium content of a low-calorie, low-fat food has been reduced by 50 percent. In addition, "light in sodium" may be used on food in which the sodium content has been reduced by at least 50 percent.

- The term *light* still can be used to describe such properties as texture and color, as long as the label explains the intent, for example, "light brown sugar" or "light and fluffy."
- *More:* this term means that a serving of food, whether altered or not, contains a nutrient that is at least 10 percent of the Daily Value more than the reference food. The 10 percent of Daily Value also applies to "fortified," "enriched," and "added" claims, but in those cases the food must be altered.

Alternative spelling of these descriptive terms and their synonyms are allowed—for example, "hi" and "lo"—as long as the alternatives are not misleading.

OTHER DEFINITIONS

- *Percent fat free:* a product bearing this claim must be low in fat or fat free. In addition, the claim must accurately reflect the amount of fat present in 100 grams of the food. Thus, if a food contains 2.5 grams of fat per 50 grams, the claim must be "95 percent fat free."
- *Implied:* these types of claims are prohibited when they wrongfully imply that a food contains or does not contain a meaningful level of a nutrient. For example, the claim that a product is made with an ingredient known to be a source of fiber (such as "made with oat bran") is not allowed unless the product contains enough of that ingredient (e.g., oat bran) to meet the definition for a "good source" of fiber. As another example, a claim that a product contains "no tropical oils" is allowed—but only on foods that are low in saturated fat because consumers have come to equate tropical oils with high saturated fat.
- *Meals and main dishes:* claims that a meal or main dish is "free" of a nutrient, such as sodium or cholesterol, must meet the same requirements as those for individual foods. Other claims can be used under special circumstances. For example, *low-calorie* means that the meal or main dish contains 120 calories or less per 100 grams. *Low-sodium* means that the food has 140 milligrams or less per 100 grams. *Low cholesterol* means that the food contains 20 milligrams of cholesterol or less per 100 grams and no more than 2 grams of saturated fat. *Light* means the meal or main dish is low-fat or low-calorie.
- *Standardized foods:* any nutrient content claim, such as *reduced fat, low calorie,* or *light,* may be used in conjunction with a standardized term if the new product has been specifically formulated to meet FDA's criteria for that claim, if the product is not nutritionally inferior to the traditional standardized food, and if the new product complies with certain compositional requirements of the referenced traditional standardized food. If the product does not, and if the differences materially limit the product's use, its label must state the difference (e.g., "not recommended for baking") to inform consumers.

- *Healthy:* a food so labeled must be low in fat and saturated fat and contain limited amounts of cholesterol and sodium. In addition, if it is a single-item food, it must provide at least 10 percent of one or more of vitamins A or C, iron, calcium, protein, or fiber. If it is a meal-type product, such as a frozen entree or multicourse frozen dinner, it must provide 10 percent of two or three of these vitamins or minerals, or 10 percent of protein or fiber, in addition to meeting the other criteria. Limits on sodium content in these products are to be implemented by FDA regulations.

- *Fresh:* although not mandated by NLEA, FDA has issued a regulation for this term. The agency took this step because of concern over the term's possible misuse on some food labels. The regulation defines *fresh* when it is used to suggest that a food is raw or unprocessed. In this context, *fresh* can be used only on a food that is raw, has never been frozen or heated, and contains no preservatives. (Irradiation at low levels is allowed). *Fresh frozen, frozen fresh,* and *freshly frozen* can be used for foods that are quickly frozen while still fresh. Blanching (brief scalding before freezing to prevent nutrient breakdown) is allowed. Other uses of the term *fresh,* such as in "fresh milk" or "freshly baked bread," are not affected.

HEALTH CLAIMS

The allowed nutrient-disease relationship claims and rules for their use are as follows:

- *Calcium and osteoporosis:* to carry this claim, a food must contain 20 percent or more of the Daily Value for calcium (200 milligrams) per serving, have a calcium content that equals or exceeds the food's content of phosphorus, and contain a form of calcium that can be readily absorbed and used by the body. The claim must name the target group most in need of adequate calcium intake (i.e., teens and young adults; white and Asian women) and state the need for exercise and a healthy diet. A product that contains 40 percent or more of the Daily Value for calcium must carry a statement on the label that a total dietary intake greater than 200 percent of the Daily Value for calcium (i.e., 2000 milligrams or more) has no further known benefit.

- *Fat and cancer:* to carry this claim, a food must meet the descriptor requirements for *low fat* or, if fish and game meats, for *extra lean.*

- *Saturated fat and cholesterol and coronary heart disease (CHD):* this claim may be used if the food meets the definitions for the descriptors *low saturated fat, low-cholesterol,* and *low-fat* or, if fish and game meats, for *extra lean.* It may mention the link between the reduced risk of CHD and lower saturated fat and cholesterol intakes to lower blood cholesterol levels.

- *Fiber-containing grain products, fruits, vegetables, and cancer:* to carry this claim, a food must be or must contain a grain product, fruit, or vegetable and meet the descriptor requirements for *low-fat;* in addition, without fortification, it must be a "good source" of dietary fiber.

- *Fruits, vegetables, and grain products that contain fiber and risk of CHD:* to carry this claim, a food must be or must contain fruits, vegetables, and grain products. It also must meet the descriptor requirements for *low saturated fat, low cholesterol,* and *low fat* and contain, without fortification, at least 0.6 gram of soluble fiber per serving.

- *Sodium and hypertension (high blood pressure):* to carry this claim, a food must meet the descriptor requirements for *low sodium.*

- *Fruits and vegetables and cancer:* this claim may be made for fruits and vegetables that meet the descriptor requirements for *low fat* and that, without fortification, for *good source* of at least one of the following: dietary fiber or vitamins A or C. This claim relates to diets low in fat and rich in fruits and vegetables (and thus in vitamins A and C and dietary fiber) in regard to a reduced cancer risk. FDA authorized this claim in place of an antioxidant vitamin and cancer claim.

INGREDIENT LABELING

An ingredient declaration is required on all foods that have more than one ingredient. The list of ingredients requires full ingredient labeling of standardized foods. The ingredient list includes, when appropriate:

- FDA-certified color additives, such as FD&C Blue No. 1, by name
- Sources of protein hydrolysates, which are used in many foods as flavors and flavor enhancers
- A declaration of caseinate as a milk derivative in the ingredient list of foods that claim to be nondairy foods, such as coffee whiteners

These new requirements were designed to help persons who may be allergic to such additives. As required by NLEA, beverages that claim to contain juice now must declare the total percentage of juice on the information panel. In addition, FDA's regulation establishes criteria for naming juice beverages. For example, when the label of a multijuice beverage states one or more—but not all—of the juices present, and the predominantly named juice is present in minor amounts, the product's name must state that the beverage is flavored with that juice or declare the amount of the juice in a 5 percent range—for example, "raspberry-flavored juice blend" or "juice blend, 2 to 7 percent raspberry juice."

THE FOOD LABEL AND THE FOOD GUIDE PYRAMID

As noticed in earlier chapters, the Food Guide Pyramid was developed by USDA and is supported by HHS. It is based on the foods American eat, the nutrients in these foods, and how to make the best food choices to promote good health. The food label is helpful in identifying good sources of nutrients among the foods listed in the Pyramid. Examples of such help are as follows:

- The descriptors listed on the label, such as "free," "low," or "reduced," indicate that a food is low in a certain dietary component, such as calories, fat, saturated fat, or sodium. Similarly, descriptors such as "good source" and "high" can help identify foods that have significant amounts of components such as dietary fiber, vitamins, and minerals.

- Claims about the relationship between a nutrient or food and the risk of a health-related condition also may be included on the label, as mentioned earlier. This can help identify foods with certain nutritional and health-related qualities.

- The nutrition fact label lists all significant nutrients, particularly calories, which are a very important health consideration.

- In addition to being listed, nutrient contents are expressed as a percentage of the Daily Values, which can very easily be understood. These Daily Values are based on a 2000-calorie diet.

- Based on the Daily Values, the amount of fat, saturated fat, sugar, sodium, and cholesterol can be checked and controlled.

EXEMPTIONS AND SPECIAL LABELING REQUIREMENTS

There are certain exemptions from the labeling requirements, including (1) small businesses based on gross sales; (2) low-volume food products based on the average number of full-time equivalent employees and the approximate units of food products sold in the United States; (3) foods served or sold in establishments that provide food for immediate consumption (such as restaurants, schools, cafeterias, trains, airplanes, and retail stores such as bakeries and delicatessens that have facilities for immediate consumption) or that are sold for use only in such establishments; (4) ready-to-eat foods not for immediate consumption (e.g., restaurant-type foods sold by delicatessens and bakeries that do not have facilities for immediate consumption) that are processed primarily at the retail location or are portioned and packaged to the consumer's specifications; (5) foods of no nutritional significance (e.g., plain coffee or tea); (6) bulk foods for further manufacturing; (7) raw fruits, vegetables, and seafood; (8) custom-processed fish and game meat; (9) small packages with less than 12 square inches of available label space (e.g., a pack of gum), provided that the label gives consumers a way to obtain nutrient information for the food (e.g., address, phone number); and (10) foods sold from bulk containers, provided that nutrient information is given at the point of sale.

Most of these exemptions are contingent on the food's bearing no nutrient content claim, health claim, or other nutrition-related information on its label or labeling. Like other regulations, they are subject to change; also, there are other related consequences. For further detailed information, explanation, and changes in these regulations appropriate government agencies and/or the *Federal Register* should be consulted.

FOOD LABELING AND RESTAURANTS

Restaurants, as defined by FDA, include conventional full-service restaurants and other establishments that offer restaurant-type services. The term *restaurant* applies broadly to establishments where food is served or sold for immediate, on-site consumption (e.g., institutional food service establishments, such as those in schools and hospitals; cafeterias; transportation carriers such as trains and airplanes; and delicatessens and catering establishments where there are facilities for immediate consumption on the premises). The definition of a restaurant extends to estabishments where foods are generally consumed immediately where purchased or while walking away (e.g., lunch wagons, cookie counters in a mall, and vending machines, including similar convenience stores that sell food), and food delivery systems or establishments from which ready-to-eat foods are delivered to homes or offices for immediate consumption.

Food in a restaurant or another retail establishment (e.g., a bakery or delicatessen) that is sold from behind a counter and placed in a wrapper, carry-out box, or other nondurable container whose sole purpose is to facilitate handling is not considered packaged food and does not need to bear a net weight statement, ingredient declaration, or other labeling required of packaged foods. However, if consumers choose food based on its packaged form (e.g., if the food is wrapped or boxed by the retailer and sold from a self-service case in a corner of a restaurant or across aisle from an in-store delicatessen), the food must bear all required information.

Food that is served in a restaurant or similar establishment is exempt from nutrition labeling provided that it does not bear a claim. Foods sold in restaurants that are exempted from labeling include (1) ready-to-eat foods served in restaurants and other establishments in which food is sold for immediate consumption and (2) foods sold for sale or use *only* in such establishments. Condiments in individual packages placed in a bowl on a table in a full-service restaurant or in a container on a lunch counter or vending facility for consumers to use at their discretion are exempt. Condiments served in larger, multiserving containers are also eligible for the exemption provided that they do not bear a claim. Commercially packaged foods such as soft drinks in cans, bags of potato chips, and candy bars that may be sold in restaurants and vending machines but that are sold through other retail outlets (e.g., grocery stores) must bear nutrient labeling, regardless of whether they bear a claim (subject to the low-volume product and small-business exemptions). If a restaurant makes a claim for one food item, the nutrition information supporting that claim should be provided. The restaurant may voluntarily provide nutrient information for restaurant foods that do not bear a claim.

Restaurant foods that bear a claim must comply with the same definitions for nutrient content claims or qualify to bear health claims under the same authorizing regulations as foods from other sources. Once a food bears a claim, nutrient information must be readily accessible to consumers (e.g., on the label attached to the food or in labeling at the point of purchase). A *nutrient content claim* is any statement about a food product that directly or by implication characterizes the level of a nutrient in the food. Thus, nutrient content claims include direct statements about the level (or range) of a nutrient in a food (e.g., "low sodium," "reduced fat," or "contains 100 calories"). An implied nutrient content claim is any claim that (1) describes the food, or an ingredient in the food, in a manner that suggests that a nutrient is absent from or present in a certain amount (e.g., "no tropical oils") or (2) suggests that the food, because of its nutrient content, may be useful in maintaining healthy dietary practices when the claim is made in conjunction with an explicit nutrient content claim (e.g., "healthy, contains 3 grams of fat"). A statement that is not presented in a nutrient context, such as statements to facilitate avoidance (e.g., "contains no dairy ingredients"), information characterizing ingredients perceived to add value (e.g., "contains real butter"), and information on ingredients that do not serve nutritive purposes (e.g., "no preservatives") would not be considered an implied nutrient content claim. The statement would be an implied nutrient content claim if it highlights a preparation method that affects the nutrient content of a food. For example, "made only with vegetable oil" implies that, because vegetable oil was used instead of animal fat, the food is "low in saturated fat" or "cholesterol free." On the other hand, a statement about a preparation method that affects the character of a food but that does not characterize its nutrient content (e.g., "made with fresh fruit" or "prepared fresh daily") would not be an implied claim. Terms such as *broiled, fried,* or *steamed* do not subject a food to the nutrient content claims requirements if they are part of a food's identity statement (e.g., "baked potato," "steamed shrimp," or "fried zucchini") or are used solely to identify different categories of food. However, a statement such as "doughnuts, baked not fried," which highlights the preparation method in a way that implies that the food, because of the way it was prepared, has less or more of a nutrient, would be an implied claim.

A heart symbol may be considered an implied health claim if the nutrient content claim could imply that the food, because of its nutrient content, may be useful in reducing the risk of developing a disease or health-related condition, specifically heart disease. However, if it is used to indicate, for example, that "You'll love our home-made pies and cakes," it would not be considered an implied claim. Generally, a health claim must (1) be complete, truthful, and not misleading; (2) contain "may" or "might" to express the relationship between a substance and a disease; and (3) indicate that the risk of disease depends on many factors.

Nutrition information may be presented in a variety of formats, although percent Daily Values are considered very important information. If a restaurant chooses to use the Nutrition Facts format, labeling must contain all information, including percent Daily Values, required for the chosen format. Generally, nutrition information should be presented on a per serving basis. It is especially important that the basis be declared when a food is available in more than one size serving—for example, pizza that is available whole and by the slice or soup that is available by the cup or by the bowl. The restaurant may provide additional information, such as "8 slices per medium 16-inch pizza, 1 slice contains . . ." to help consumers put nutrition information in context. Full nutrition labeling is not required for restaurant foods, nor is it required that nutrient information be presented in Nutrition Facts format, since restaurant foods tend to be prepared and sold differently from foods from other sources.

Chapter 12

FOOD PURCHASING AND STORAGE: THE NUTRITIONAL POINT OF VIEW

F ood purchasing is an important function in any type of foodservice operation. The success of a business depends to a great extent on its purchasing policies. The basic principles of purchasing are the same in any type of business; however, in this chapter, the emphasis is on purchasing foods from a nutritional point of view. The primary function of any foodservice operation is to convert raw food products into cooked or edible products. Thus, the success of an operation depends on how efficiently and profitably raw ingredients are converted into edible products and subsequently served to consumers. Food quality, particularly nutritional quality, depends directly on the quality of the raw ingredients. It has been rightly said that one can produce a low-quality food from high-quality ingredients but not the reverse. Thus, it is essential for a foodservice manager to give prime importance to food purchasing. Food purchasing for quantity food preparation and for preserving its nutritional quality is a very difficult task. This is due in part to the fact that foods are perishable items and need extra care at all stages of purchasing, selection, and storage. Expensive food losses may occur overnight due to improper purchasing and/or handling. Foodservice purchasing requires knowledge of terminology, specifications, and processing requirements, as well as a thorough objective and subjective assessment of quality. Foodservice purchasing has been described as an *art* since it requires talent and sophistication in judging the right combinations of color, shape, size, and consistency of food. It has also been decribed as a *science* since it requires understanding of scientific principles, as well as skill in the utilization of resources. Food purchasing from a nutritional point of view requires a good working knowledge of nutrition, as well as skill and experience.

Once a menu is established, the next step is to decide how many servings of each item on the menu are needed for a particular meal. The quantity of each ingredient to be ordered depends on the *number of servings*. Once this is determined, the next step is to prepare a complete list of items to be purchased. For this, a number of information sources are necessary. Several types of records and forms make the task easier. It is also important to know and understand certain terms used in purchasing. Food **as purchased (AP)** refers to food as it is purchased, without peeling, coring, or cutting. By contrast, an **edible portion (EP)** refers to food as it will be finally available for direct use, in edible form after processing. Thus, EP represents the actual usable portion of AP foods. Relative percentages of AP and EP should be calculated before placing a food purchasing order. This is a very important consideration for foods rich in nutritional value, such as vegetables and fruits. The EP may be considerably less than the AP portion of foods, and that should be taken into account in placing food orders. Tested and standardized recipes normally indicate the amount to be used in preparing a fixed number of servings. **Waste** and **shrinkage** losses are also calculated and included in some recipes. It is necessary to know these losses to determine the final yield of the recipe. The final yield may be calculated as follows:

$$\text{Percentage of yield} = \frac{\text{weight after cooking}}{\text{weight before cooking}} \times 100$$

For example, if 70 pounds of cooked ground beef can be prepared from 100 pounds of raw beef, the **percentage of yield** for the ground beef in this type of preparation will be $70 \div 90 \times 100 = 70$ percent. Thus, 30 percent additional ground beef is needed to get the desired cooked ground-beef servings. In the case of meats, the loss of weight upon cooking is referred to as *shrinkage*. Similarly, waste losses of fruits and vegetables can be calculated. Yield percentages depend on various factors, such as cooking temperatures, types of ovens, and time, which vary with the type of foodservice operation. Serious shortages in prepared food will result if this factor is not considered when planning purchasing or production. When purchasing, sufficient margins should be allowed to compensate for losses. The fat content of meats also affects the percentage of yield. It is advisable to include the yield percentages in the recipe so that the final EP can be calculated. This can be derived as follows:

$$\text{EP} = \text{AP} - \text{shrinkage (or preparation) losses} = \text{percentage shrinkage or prepreparation losses}$$

$$= \frac{\text{losses due to shrinkage or prepreparation (weight)}}{\text{AP (weight)}} \times 100 = \frac{\text{AP (weight)} - \text{EP (weight)}}{\text{AP (weight)}}$$

Several procedures are used to determine the amount of food to be purchased. A recommended standard procedure is outlined in the following list.

1. From the recipe, determine the factor to be used in calculating the desired number of servings. For example, if the recipe is for 100 servings and the desired servings total 400, the factor will be 400 divided by 100, which is 4. If only 50 servings are desired, the factor will be 50 divided by 100, or 0.5. This factor is very important in further calculations.

2. Multiply all the ingredients in the recipe by the factor derived in Step 1. For example, the recipe for 50 servings requires 15 pounds ($30 \times 0.5 = 15$) of chicken; the amount to be purchased for 300 servings will be $6 \times 15 = 90$ pounds (EP) of chicken. The AP amount for chicken can be calculated by dividing the EP by the percentage of yield or the amount of EP provided by 1 pound, or a standard unit of the commodity. Such calculations should be done for all the ingredients in the recipe.

3. The AP value should be converted into the nearest possible wholesale purchase unit (such as carton, case, box, lug, basket, crate, flat, dozen, bushel, or sack). The quantity selected should be such that the remainder of the commodity is easily utilizable and is not wasted. Often ordering in bulk is economical and desirable in foodservice purchasing. Items included in the menu for the following day or for that week should be taken into consideration. On the other hand, when items are for one-time use only, the nearest possible unit size should be used or alternative uses for the remainder of the commodity should be planned in advance.

4. Once the amounts are determined for one menu item, the same procedure should be followed for all other items on the menu, and daily totals for each item should be calculated.

5. Finally, totals for the week, month, or any other fixed period of time may be calculated and used for ordering. This period should be decided by management based on the purchasing methods selected by an operation. Convenience should be given top priority when making this decision.

The above-mentioned steps may be facilitated by the use of several types of forms.

PURCHASING DECISIONS

Management should decide, on the basis of previous experience, how frequently foods and supplies should be purchased. Too frequent food purchasing may add to the total cost, whereas a long delay in purchasing may result in shortages and other problems. An optimum buying schedule should be established for each operation. Some factors that should be considered in deciding the frequency of purchasing are discussed below.

Inventory on Hand

Complete, continuous turnover of inventory is highly desirable based on the type of facility. Some facilities want to maintain a week's inventory on hand, while others prefer to have a month's supply. Since much of the food purchased may be fresh or kept for a minimum period of time, to provide the nutritional value it may be desirable to keep as little inventory as needed. This will avoid losses due to the perishability of items or the danger of nutrient degradation upon long standing. In any case, this is an important decision and should be made after considering all factors, including the fact that tying up money in inventory may reduce needed cash flow.

Storage Capacity

The capacity of dry, refrigerated, and frozen storage areas primarily dictates the quantities to be purchased. Again, since most of the foods will need careful handling to preserve their nutritional value, it is important to assess the storage capacity ahead of time. With limited storage capabilities, frequent buying may be necessary.

Seasonal Fluctuations

Since produce and other perishable items are most likely to be used, seasonal availability is an important factor. It may be economical to buy certain items when there is an abundant supply. Price fluctuations and storage capacity should also be considered.

Type of Market and Proximity

The type of market and its location with respect to the foodservice operation are important factors. For foodservices close to a larger market, such as a seaport or livestock market, large inventories may not be necessary, whereas for foodservices that have access only to smaller markets, such as farmers' markets, only small inventories may be possible. Seasonal items often may be purchased at bargain prices during peak periods. On the other hand, items that are hard to find due to seasonal availablity should not be included in the menu.

SPECIFICATIONS

Specifications may be defined as the description of a particular commodity in terms of its size, quality, or condition. Specifications, which are very important in purchasing any product, especially foods, represent the technical language in which the buyer communicates with the seller in describing what is needed. Since there are numerous products and different types within each product, it is essential to use distinct, specific terminology. Specifications should be complete in all respects to be understood and implemented by everyone involved.

Specifications, commonly referred to as *specs,* are pieces of information that should be readily understood by most foodservice personnel. Specs have to be written and selected very carefully since they determine the quality of food to be purchased and served. They have an impact on food costs and, consequently, on the operation's profits. Specs also identify products and verify them upon receipt. They help eliminate misunderstanding and friction throughout the process of foodservice management. Since they are specific to the particular operation, it is desirable to have them in writing. They should also be easily accessible and placed at convenient locations for ready reference. It is imperative to plan and select specifications very carefully and to consider them as statements of management policy. They should be planned for the operation and, in fact, should be custom-made for a specific facility. It is not adequate to follow specifications written for another operation. Some of the attributes and factors that should be considered in writing specifications are as follows:

- They should be clear, concise, complete, and simple.
- They should be based on management's policy, taking into account all requirements, including nutritional ones.
- They should be based on tests and objective measurements that are recognized and are relatively easy to perform.
- They should be accurate and specific, with no room for misinterpretation.
- They must comply with all standards, including nutritional standards, set by local, state, and/or federal regulatory agencies.
- They must be used and revised to increase their usefulness.
- They must be based on technical advances and improvements (such as new and innovative packaging methods).
- They must conform to the goal of healthy eating.

In addition, specifications should include the following information wherever applicable:

- Common, trade, or brand name of the product
- Amount to be purchased in the most commonly used unit, such as a case, crate, pound, carton or lug
- Recognized trade, federal, or local grade
- Name and size of the basic container
- Count and size of the items or units within the basic container such as 12/2's, 6/#10 cans, 12/3-pound packages, or number of dozens
- Ranges in weight, thickness, or size, wherever applicable, such as 8 to 10 pounds or ¼ to ½ inch thick.
- Minimum and maximum trims or fat content/percentages/ratios, wherever applicable
- Degree of maturity or stage of ripening
- Type of processing required, such as freeze-dried, cooked, or peeled
- Type of packaging desired
- Food and nutrition fact label requirements

- Any additional information pertaining to nutrients or any modifications to the common specifications and additional clarifications to describe the exact item(s) desired

Specific factors to be considered when ordering various types of food products are discussed in this chapter. The specifications should describe the item to the fullest extent.

Since buying is one of the most important and most specialized functions, the person in charge of it should understand the various systems within the foodservice operation, as well as their interrelationship. The food purchaser should possess the following skills and experience:

- Awareness of the markets and market procedures
- Ability to forecast needs and to respond to fluctuating market situations
- Knowledge of items to be purchased and how they will be used
- Ability to understand and set specifications, understand test data, and use specifications properly
- Knowledge of food processing, food labeling, nutrition, and other related information
- Knowledge of different food grades and food qualities
- Comprehension of the laws and regulations governing all aspects of purchasing
- Ability to judge quality by objective and subjective evaluations
- Good decision-making ability
- Adequate fundamental and applied nutritional knowledge

REGULATORY AGENCIES

Several regulatory agencies have as their primary responsibility the assurance of food quality. They set standards and regulations designed to provide wholesome food and safe food processing. These regulations are very useful to a food buyer in setting specifications and ensuring that the products are safe and of desired quality. Federal agencies establish standards on a national basis and provide regulatory control for these standards. They also set regulations for foods intended for interstate commerce. Regulations established by these agencies are instrumental in controlling food quality, food sanitation, and overall food marketing. Some of the agencies, as well as their regulations that affect food purchasing, are described below.

U.S. Department of Agriculture (USDA)

The Agricultural Marketing Services Act of 1953 (revised in 1957), implemented by USDA, is probably the most important law with a direct impact on food purchasing. It provides for grading and inspection of agricultural commodities.

Since there are numerous agricultural commodities, they are categorized for inspection purposes and are handled by different departments. For most commodities, grading is voluntary. However, inspection is mandatory for meats, poultry, and other processed foods distributed through interstate commerce. Inspection agencies are located at several points, particularly shipping centers, markets, ports, and other marketing terminals. A stamp is placed on the product (as in the case of meat), container, tape, invoice, or another easily identifiable place. An approval stamp indicates that the product meets the federal standard(s) set by the agency and/or the buyer. Thus, the products can be verified by the agency for quality. Individual specifications, which meet or exceed the federal standards, may be set by any operation, and a representative of the agency will certify when those specifications are met. An inspection certificate may also be requested. Fees for this service may be paid by the buyer or the seller. This is a very useful service for the buyer since quality is assured. Specific standards may be set by the organization to meet its requirements when the regulations are considered too general.

The Agricultural Marketing Service also helps to stabilize prices based on supply, demand, and fluctuations in prices. The Wholesome Meat Act of 1967, an amended form of the Meat Inspection Act of 1906, requires inspection, at least as stringent as federal inspection, of all meat, whether it moves within or between states. This act also provides technical and financial assistance for meat-inspection programs. The Wholesome Poultry Products Act of 1968 requires inspection of all poultry and provides assistance to states to improve their inspection procedures. Tests are conducted to check for contamination of poultry products. The Egg Products Inspection Act of 1970 requires mandatory inspection of egg-processing plants and pasteurization during the freezing and drying of liquid eggs.

Food and Drug Administration (FDA)

FDA, as part of the Department of Health and Human Services, has regulations that pertain to various practices in the food industry and have considerable impact on the foodservice industry. One of the pioneer laws enacted by this agency is the well-known Food, Drug, and Cosmetic Act of 1906, which was later revised to become the Food, Drug, and Cosmetic Act of 1938. It was designed to provide "safe and wholesome," honestly labeled, and properly packaged products. Further revisions were made to this act, the significant one being the one in 1958, commonly referred to as the *Delaney Clause,* which states that "producers may not use any additives found to induce cancer in man or animals." This clause has been the cause of controversy from time to time and is often debated. The FDA regulations have a profound influence on the market, and a foodservice manager should be aware of them and any changes in them. Introduction of new analytical methods and technological advances may require future changes in these laws.

Another important regulation under this act deals with the food and nutrition labeling of food products. The Food, Drug, and Cosmetic Act also defines "adulteration and misbranding" and, in so doing, provides important standards for processed foods. Three standards are checked by food inspectors: (1) standards of quality, (2) standards of identity, and (3) standards of fill. A detailed description of these standards can be obtained from the respective agencies and must be reviewed by food purchasing managers.

Standards of Quality   *Standards of quality* refer to the quality of the food products, which may be measured by objective as well as subjective methods. Various instrumental, chemical, and other methods are used for assessing the quality of foods. Grades are based on different factors, so the grading system varies from one food to another. Some of the attributes considered in grading include color, texture, tenderness, and freedom from defects. Grades for processed food items are different from those for fresh foods. For most processed foods, a scale ranging from 1 to 100 is used, with a product scoring 90 and above being designated as A, 80 to 89 as B, 70 to 79 as C, and below 70 as below standard. This grading system also varies from product to product. It should be noted that "below standard" does not mean "unwholesome." Reasons for such grading are normally given, and as long as nutritional quality is not affected, these products may be used; usually it is economically beneficial to do so. For example, broken foods that may be perfectly wholesome are graded as below standard. They may be used in prepared foods where appearance is not significant, such as fruits in puddings. Grades also depend on types for fruits or vegetables, marbling for meats, bacterial counts for milk, and color for apples.

Standards of Identity   *Standards of identity* have been set mainly to describe or distinguish a product. They are means of identifying a product and differentiating it from other products. These standards prevent misrepresentation and misbranding. Exact descriptions of the products and their contents are required. USDA sets standards of identity for meat, poultry, and egg products, while FDA sets standards for other foods. Certain products may have several common names, but these standards identify the products by one specific name. For example, "fruit cocktail" may mean different things to different producers, and the contents may vary widely. These standards precisely describe the contents required before a product can be labeled and identified as fruit cocktail. Thus, products such as salad dressings, ice cream, preserves, jams, and jellies are all identified and must meet specific standards. The word *artificial* is used when additives fitting into this category are used. A product is designated as misbranded if the identity names are used without meeting the standards.

Standards of Fill   *Standards of fill* refer to the quantity required in packaged foods or how full a container must be to prevent deceptive filling practices. As with the standards of quality, containers that do not meet the standards are labeled as "below standards of fill." Use of federal grades for quality is voluntary, but standards of fill are mandatory. Criminal actions, convictions, fines, and other penalties are imposed on food manufacturers when these standards are violated. Precise weights and volumes are specified for different containers. The approved label ensures that the container is legally full to the quantity stated on the label.

In addition to fill standards, FDA has other regulations that deal with the food processing and nutritional labeling of products. FDA has introduced a set of regulations grouped under *Good Manufacturing Practices (GMPs)*. These guidelines list practices for the maintenance of sanitary conditions involving food plants, grounds, equipment, utensils, facilities, controls, processes, and personnel.

U.S. Department of Commerce (USDC)

A voluntary grading system is maintained by USDC, mainly for fish and fish products. The grades ensure that there is in-plant inspection during processing. For seafood, the inspection is conducted by the National Marine Fisheries Service. FDA and the U.S. Public Health Service are indirectly involved in the inspection of certain types of fish and shellfish. Since grading is voluntary, a product that is not graded is not necessarily unwholesome or unfit for consumption. Various grades and technical terms are used for grading and defining seafood products. These foods are handled by the USDC since they are largely imported from other countries.

Other regulatory agencies and regulations govern many of the state and local areas. The milk, shellfish, and other foods served by foodservice operations are frequently inspected by local public health agencies. Regulations and inspections are designed to ensure the quality and quantity of products, encourage good marketing practices, promote good practices related to advertisements and promotions, establish fair trade practices and prices, ensure the safety and health of consumers and workers, and promote healthy competition. A foodservice manager or a person in charge of food purchasing should know and utilize these regulations advantageously.

THE PURCHASE OF SPECIFIC COMMODITIES

Fresh Fruits and Vegetables

Fresh fruits and vegetables are full of nutrients but are also perishable. This poses a problem not only in purchasing but also in setting specifications. In addition, since there are numerous variations among different types of fresh fruits and vegetables, it is impossible to have one set standard of specifications. The grading system, the terminology used, and other specifications are different for individual types of fresh fruits and vegetables. In general, the following factors need to be considered.

Grade Different sets of standards are specific for each fruit and vegetable. The quality varies within each set of grades. These **U.S. grades** may be listed by numbers, such as No. 1, or No. 2, or by such terms as *U.S. Fancy* or *U.S. Extra Fancy*. Since perishable items are involved and quality is subject to deterioration in transport, it is essential to specify that the grade desired is at the time of delivery rather than at the time of shipping. This will also help in purchasing fruits and vegetables with approximate nutrients that can be ensured. U.S. grades are handy tools and reference sources for buyers since they avoid the use of lengthy specifications and eliminate misunderstandings. Any special requirements of a foodservice operation can always be obtained from USDA.

Quality Additional factors of quality that are not specified in the food grades should be included in food orders. Grades may be supplemented by an explanation of what is desired, and often it is helpful if the intended use is given. Examples of such explanations are "lettuce for salads," "tomato for relishes," and "spinach for entrees." It is important to specify and insist on freshness. Similarly, the need for nutritional quality should be spelled out. Although it is difficult to predict nutritional quality and other quality parameters, general desirable characteristics include bright attractive colors, good shape and appearance, good proportion of weight and size, and absence of any mechanical damage or signs of decay. Lack of freshness may also be a sign of poor handling and transportation, which also can be an indication of poor nutritional quality. Consequently, this may result in shortened storage capability and reduced useful life of the fruits and vegetables, even though they may be suitable for immediate use. Most fresh fruits and vegetables may have undesirable attributes at the beginning and end of the growing season. These attributes may include sourness, lack of juiciness, lack of flavor, lack of texture, unripeness, or overripeness. Quality should be compared with the price to be paid, and the decision should be based on overall considerations.

Variety The variety and type of fruits and vegetables are important indications of nutritional quality. Variety helps in selecting specific products. For example, "Golden Delicious" or "McIntosh" specifies the exact type of apples desired, with no misunderstanding. Variety and type are also helpful in selecting the best fruits and vegetables for a particular purpose. A good example is Russet or Katahdin potatoes, which are different in appearance, specific gravity, and cooking qualities. Although the varietal names of most fruits, particularly vegetables, are seldom used, type is commonly used and is helpful in setting specifications.

Size Size is one of the most important aspects of specification, particularly for fruits. The optimum size desired for the purpose should be selected since the cost of many commodities depends on size. Normally, smaller sizes are preferable when appearance is not significant, whereas larger sizes are recommended when whole or large portions of fruits and vegetables are used. In addition, wastage, nutritional advantage, and labor should be taken into consideration in selecting the size. Larger fruits and vegetables may be necessary for artistic displays and plate presentations.

Sizes also determine the count that is packaged in a container. For example, apple sizes may vary from 56 to 252 per western apple box. Similarly, many fruits are sized by count per box or by diameter. The diameter is measured not around the girth but transversely from stem end to blossom end. Some vegetables, especially greens, may be shipped in large bunches and may be specified in dozens of bunches per container. The terms used for specification should be carefully selected from the prevalent terminology. Care should be taken to avoid terms that are not included in the standards for that product. *Small* or *large* should be used only if they fit into the definition of a standard grade.

Packaging   Fruits and vegetables are available in different types of packages. Buyers should specify the type of packaging or the container desired. An item may be available in more than one kind of package, such as bushel baskets, boxes, lugs, sacks, crates, and cardboard containers. Specifications should clearly state what kind of packaging is desired, such as apples by counts per box, cantaloupes in counts per crate, or broccoli in bunches per basket. In some cases, the type of packaging selected indirectly indicates the quantities desired. Special packaging, such as ventilated containers or containers for hydro-cooled vegetables, may also be requested and specified. Packaging selected should be based on the quality and quantity of the products desired. Storage space should also be considered; for example, smaller packages may be easier to shelve than large containers.

Other Information   Other pertinent information, when applicable, should be included to enhance the specifications, such as the brand name or the growing area of the product. Produce from one area may have better nutritional quality than the same produce from other areas. For example, fruits from California may be different from the same types of fruits grown in Florida. As an example, a list of specifications for purchasing fruits and vegetables is given in Table 12.1.

Table 12.1   Guidelines for Specifications of Fresh and Packaged Fruits and Vegetables

Description	*Example*
Geographical area of production	California peaches, Florida oranges
Variety	Valencia, Golden Delicious
Type	Long-cut or short-cut
Style	Slices or pineapple tidbits
Size	Large, small, medium
Count	Number per gallon; 80-count apples
Syrup density	Light, medium heavy, extra-heavy Water packed; Brix
Specific gravity	For tomatoes and potatoes
Mix percentage	Types of fruits in fruit cocktail
Container/package	Can, case, package, or lug
Weight tolerance	Struck full or rounded full
Cut	Diced, julienne
Condition upon receipt	Fresh, frozen, or ice-packed
Type of flavor	Sweetened, unsweetened, salt-free
Federal or other grades	U.S. No. 1 or U.S. Fancy
Other specific factors	Pitted, sun-dried

Processed Fruits and Vegetables

Standards for processed fruits and vegetables have been well developed. Minimum quality standards, set by the federal Food, Drug, and Cosmetic Act, are the standards of identity, fill, and quality. In addition to these standards, grades used to classify processed fruits and vegetables based on their quality have been developed by USDA.

Fruits

U.S. Grade A or U.S. Fancy

U.S. Grade B or U.S. Choice

U.S. Grade C or U.S. Standard

Vegetables

U.S. Grade A or U.S. Fancy

U.S. Grade B or U.S. Extra-Standard

U.S. Grade C or U.S. Standard

Processed fruits and vegetables that do not meet the minimum requirements are graded as substandard. Labeling a product as substandard does not mean it is inferior in nutritional quality or is unfit for consumption. Grades are based on a number of factors used in scoring, which may vary according to the fruit or vegetable. Major factors include color, size, consistency, symmetry, finish, maturity, absence of defects, character, flavor, uniformity of size, type of liquor, cut, and wholesomeness. Some of these factors may have a direct impact on the nutritional quality and therefore should be considered before purchasing. A description of important factors follows.

Fill of Container   Unless defined by the Food and Drug regulations, USDA grades generally recommend that cans be filled as full as possible without impairing the quality and that the product and the packaging medium occupy no less than 90 percent of the water capacity of the container. For objective assessment and for all practical purposes, this percentage of fill is determined by measuring the headspace inside the can. **Headspace** is the space between the top of the container and the packaging medium. Containers that fail to meet this requirement are designated as "below standard fill." Maximum gross headspaces for various can sizes are specified—for example, $^{27}/_{32}$ inch for No. 10 cans and $^{19}/_{32}$ inch for No. 2 cans.

Drained Weight   Drained weight is generally not considered in the evaluation of grade since it is not a factor related to the quality of the product as sold. However, it is important from the viewpoint of nutritional quality and product yield. Thus, recommended drained weight should be included in the specifications. **Drained weight** refers to the weight of the canned products after the liquid is allowed to drain for 2 minutes on a standard sieve under specified conditions. The test is done after the product has been allowed to equalize for 30 or more days after canning.

Drained weights are important since the actual yield for a canned product can be determined, and this helps in the calculation of portion sizes.

Syrup Density   *Syrup density* is also not considered in grading a canned product since syrup, or any other liquid medium, is not a factor in quality. The type and density of syrup or the packaging medium, which are specified on the label, are important from two major points of view. First, from the nutritional point of view, it is extremely important to know the sugar content. This is also important when special meals are being planned. Second, the final quality of the canned product, when opened at a foodservice operation, depends on the density of the syrup. The heavier the syrup, the less the chance of the products' breaking up, particularly in the case of fruits.

The scale used to measure the density of syrup is **Brix,** which relates the specific gravity of a solution to an equivalent concentration of pure sucrose. Roughly, for every degree Brix, a fruit has 1 percent sugar. Brix tables should be used for the accurate determination of Brix and sugar content. The taste or tartness of fruits or fruit juices may be described in terms of Brix or the Brix-to-acid ratio. The higher the Brix, the greater the sugar concentration in the juice; the higher the Brix-to-acid ratio, the sweeter and less tart the juice. Although canned fruits are not graded on the basis of syrup density, they are certified as meeting the declared syrup designation. The density of the syrup may be measured by a refractometer or a Brix hydrometer.

Frozen Fruits and Vegetables

Frozen fruits and vegetables are graded in practically the same way as canned products, with minor exceptions. Frozen products are packed in a variety of packages and are available in different weights. Frozen fruits may be packaged in sugar or syrup. It is important to know the medium in which they are packaged, if any. They may also be treated with an antioxidant to avoid browning on the surfaces. Vegetables may have added salt as a preservative.

Meats and Meat Products

Meat and meat products play a very important role in any type of menu in all foodservice operations. It is essential to have well-planned and well-controlled methods of purchasing, receiving, preparing, and serving meat items. Clear, well-defined standards and regulations are helpful in purchasing wholesome and safe meats and their by-products. From a nutritional point of view, these products are important since they are perishable and require preprocessing and processing, which may subject different nutrients to deterioration. It is also important to understand the processing of meats from the slaughterhouse to the processing plant.

All animals intended for food are inspected and approved for normal slaughter. Antemortem and postmortem inspections are conducted to certify the wholesomeness of the meat. The main meat structures responsible for tenderness are the connective tissues and the muscle myofibrils. The connective tissues found in muscle are composed of the proteins collagen, elastin, and reticulin. Collagen is a tough, fibrous protein that upon hydrolysis yields hydroxyproline. Specific plant enzymes, such as papain (found in papaya), ficin (found in figs), and bromelin (found in pineapples), attack tissue collagen and render it soft and tender. Elastin is a yellow protein that is very elastic and practically unaffected by normal heat during cooking. The amount of elastin present, therefore, affects the tenderness of the meat. Reticulin fibers are similar to elastin fibers and are very tough. Muscle tissues normally present in meats contain the muscle proteins actin, myosin, and tropomyosin. The number and size of muscle fibers compared to connective tissues are responsible for the tenderness of meats. In other words, large fibers have less connective tissues than small fibers. Thus, both muscle and connective tissues play an important role in determining the tenderness of meats. Different types of retail cuts are obtained from beef, lamb, or pork carcasses. The main cuts of beef are:

Hindquarter: round, rump, sirloin or loin end, short loin, flank

Forequarter: rib, chuck, plate, brisket, shank

In general, meats are graded on two important bases: *quality,* mainly indicative of palatability, and *yield,* mainly indicative of the cutability for major retail cuts. When writing specifications for meats, either a quality grade or a combination of quality and yield grades is required. The overall grades for meats and their descriptions are:

U.S. Prime: Highest grade; meats have fine texture and firm muscles.

U.S. Choice: High in eating quality; less fat than prime.

U.S. Good: Greater proportion of lean to fat; lacks juiciness but relatively tender.

U.S. Standard: Thin fat covering; high proportion of lean to fat; tender.

U.S. Commercial: From mature animals; lacks tenderness; relatively more wastage.

U.S. Utility: From animals that are advanced in age; lacks tenderness and juiciness.

U.S. Cutter and U.S. Canner: Useful for processed meat products.

It is required that the beef carcass be ribbed for at least 10 minutes before it is graded, allowing some of the grade-determining factors the time to become evident. **Ribbing** involves splitting the carcass down the center of the backbone and cutting between the 12th and 13th rib bones to expose the longissimus dorsi muscle. The longissimus dorsi, or rib-eye, muscle is the longest muscle, extending from the neck to the end of the animal body (rump).

Quality grades are based on:

- *Classes of animals*

    Heifer or steer: Prime, Choice, Good, Standard, Commercial, Utility, Cutter, Canner

Cow: Choice, Good, Standard, Commercial, Utility, Cutter, Canner

Bullock: Prime, Choice, Good, Standard, Utility

Calf or veal: Prime, Choice, Good, Standard, Utility, Cull

Lamb: Prime, Choice, Good, Utility, Cull

Pork: U.S. No. 1, 2, 3, 4, Utility

Mutton: Choice, Good, Utility, Cull

- *Maturity:* Maturity is indicated by bone size, shape, and ossification. Maturity grades are given from A to E, with A being the youngest and E the oldest.
- *Flesh color and texture:* White fat and cherry-colored lean are considered top quality. Lean flesh has fine texture and a light gray color.
- *Marbling:* Streaks of fat running through lean meat are referred to as *marbling.* Good marbling is indicative of well-fed animals and of meats that will be tender, juicy, and flavorful when cooked. Although marbling is desirable to an extent, overabundant marbling imparts an oily taste and has a high fat content. The degrees of marbling for grading are abundant, moderately abundant, slightly abundant, moderate, modest, small, slight, traces, and practically devoid.

Yield grades are based on the amount of external fat; amount of kidney, pelvic, and heart fat; area of the rib eye; and hot carcass weight. Yield grades, which are applicable for all quality grades, are rated from 1 to 5.

When writing the specifications for meats, the following factors should be considered:

Class of animal

USDA grade and the division of grade

USDA yield grade

Acceptance weight range

Fat limitations

Condition upon delivery

Temperature and packaging upon delivery

Weight

Institutional Meat Purchase Specifications number

Other delivery instructions

Poultry and Eggs

Grading of poultry is based on class, quality, quantity, condition, or any combination of these factors. The U.S. consumer grades for poultry are as follows:

U.S. Grade A: A lot of ready-to-cook poultry or parts consisting of one or more ready-to-cook carcasses, or parts of the same kind and class, each of which conforms to the requirements for A Quality, may be designated as U.S. Grade A.

U.S. Grade B: A lot of ready-to-cook poultry or parts consisting of one or more ready-to-cook carcasses, or parts of the same kind and class, each of which conforms to the requirements for B Quality or better, may be designated as U.S. Grade B.

U.S. Grade C: A lot of ready-to-cook poultry or parts consisting of one or more ready-to-cook carcasses, or parts of the same kind and class, each of which conforms to the requirements for C Quality or better, may be designated as U.S. Grade C.

There are two procurement grades: U.S. Procurement Grade I and U.S. Procurement Grade II. There is a voluntary USDA grading and inspection service for poultry. Poultry should be specified by part as follows: breasts, breast with ribs, wishbones, legs, wings, drumsticks, thighs, halves, quarters, and backs. The specifications for poultry should, therefore, include (1) name of the part, (2) quantity, (3) weight, (4) detailed description, (5) required inspection, (6) condition upon delivery, and (7) type of packaging.

The grading of eggs is based upon size, which is determined by weight per dozen. Large and medium-sized eggs are the sizes most frequently used in foodservice operations. They are suitable for frying, poaching, hard or soft cooking, and for dishes where appearance is of primary importance. If eggs are to be used in mixed salads or for baking, size is less important.

The quality of eggs, including the nutritional quality, depends on their exterior as well as their interior condition. The shell should be sound, clean, and unbroken. Eggs lose carbon dioxide and moisture upon storage. The air cell, which is visible under light, enlarges as moisture and carbon dioxide are lost. The white becomes thin and watery, and the yolk flattens out. As a result of these storage changes, an old egg covers a wide area when broken compared to a fresh egg. The yolk also become weak and may break easily. A test known as the *Haugh Unit Breakout Test* is based on the height of the white at the yolk, which is measured using a micrometer. All of these factors should be considered when buying. The grading of eggs depends on some of these factors, which are included in the consumer grades and procurement grades designations. The consumer grades are:

U.S. Grade AA: Clean, unbroken, and practically normal shells; air cell almost regular in shape and no more than ⅛ inch deep; clear, firm white; yolk practically free from defects, with outline slightly defined. The grade is no less than 85 percent U.S. Grade AA at the point of origin and no less than 80 percent U.S. Grade AA at the destination. Individual cases are no less than 75 percent U.S. Grade AA no more than 15 percent U.S. Grade A and 10 percent U.S. Grade B at the point of origin, and no less than 70 percent U.S. Grade AA but no more than 20 percent U.S. Grade A and 10% U.S. Grade B at the destination.

U.S. Grade A: Clean, unbroken, practically normal shells; practically regular air cell, 3⁄16 inch deep or less; clear, reasonably firm white; yolk outline fairly well defined and practically free from defects. The grade is no less than 85 percent U.S. Grade A at the point of origin and no less than 80 percent U.S. Grade A at the destination. Individual cases are no less than 75 percent U.S. Grade A and no more than 25 percent U.S. Grade B at the point of origin, and no less than 70 percent U.S. Grade A and no more than 30 percent U.S. Grade B at the destination.

U.S. Grade B: Clean to slightly stained shells, which may be slightly abnormal in shape; the air cell may be free or bubbly, but no more than 3⁄8 inch deep; the white may be clear but slightly weak; the yolk may be slightly enlarged and have a well-defined outline. The grade should be no less than 85 percent U.S. Grade B at the point of origin and no less than 80 percent U.S. Grade B at the destination. Individual cases are no less than 75 percent U.S. Grade B at the point of origin and no less than 70 percent U.S. Grade B at the destination. No eggs that are less than Grade B can be included.

There are two procurement grades that are mainly used by large processors and rarely by foodservice operations. Thus, for writing specifications for eggs, the factors to be included are (1) size of the eggs, (2) grade of the eggs, (3) type of packaging, (4) condition upon delivery, (5) inspection requirement, and (6) detailed description.

Whole eggs contain cholesterol, so their purchase should be carefully monitored. Since cholesterol is present mainly in egg yolk, frozen or preserved egg whites can be purchased. These can be effectively used in baking, as well as for other cooking needs. From the nutritional point of view, eggs play an important role since they contain significant amounts of different nutrients. A balance should be maintained so that eggs are added to the menu wisely. Since eggs are also rich in proteins, care should be taken to see that they are not cracked upon delivery. It is also important to check the cooking time and temperature of foods in which eggs or egg products are used.

Milk and Milk Products

There are various USDA grades for milk and milk products, which should be considered in purchasing these products. Many areas restrict the sale of milk lower than U.S. Grade A. Thus, grades should be checked before purchasing milk and milk products. Grading is particularly important for such products as butter, margarine, and cheese. State and local authorities have different grading systems, as well as different regulations pertaining to dairy products. In addition to the grade, the processing method is specified on milk packages. Further, milk is pasteurized and homogenized.

From the nutritional point of view, a foodservice manager should be familiar with the types and description of different milk and milk products, some of which are as follows:

Whole milk: In most areas, this consists of milk that contains no less than 3.25 percent milk fat and no less than 8.25 percent milk solids-not-fat.

Skim milk: Milk from which fat has been removed by centrifugation. Ordinarily, skim milk contains 0.1 percent fat.

Two percent milk: Contains 2 percent milk fat.

Certified milk: Special milk with a very low bacterial count, used specifically for patients after surgery or in nursing homes.

Low-sodium milk: Milk from which sodium is removed by the process of ion exchange.

Fortified milk: Milk to which nutrients that are naturally present in milk are added to increase the overall nutrient contents.

Vitamin D milk: Milk to which vitamin D is added.

Concentrated milks: Milks that are concentrated to different proportions. These may be fresh, frozen, evaporated, condensed, or dried.

Cream: Cream is separated from milk and contains a significant amount of milk fat ranging from 16 to 18 percent.

Half-and-half: Equal parts of whole milk fat (3.25 percent) and cream fat (18 percent). This milk product therefore ends up with about 10.5 percent milk fat.

Evaporated milk: Milk from which slightly more than half of the water is removed. The milk fat content is therefore higher in evaporated milk than in whole milk.

Condensed milk: Milk to which sugar is added before it is evaporated.

Cultured milk: Certain desirable bacterial cultures are allowed to grow in pasteurized milk under controlled conditions.

Buttermilk: Cultured milk containing chiefly *Streptococcus lactis.* This milk has a tangy, smooth flavor.

Acidophilus milk: Cultured milk with *Lactobacillus acidophilus.* It is used for its therapeutic value in patients who have been treated with antibiotics.

Yogurt: Manufactured from fresh, partially skimmed milk enriched with added milk solids-not-fat. It has a smooth texture and is available in many flavors.

Chocolate milk: A chocolate-flavored milk.

Filled milk: Milk in which milk fats are replaced by other fats, mostly of vegetable origin.

Dry whole milk: Milk from which the water has been removed.

Instant nonfat dry milk: Prepared by removing fat and water from the milk.

In writing specifications for milk, the type of product, grade, milk fat content desired, and type of packaging should be included. Since milk and milk products contain nutrients that are susceptible to light and heat, packaging and storage are important considerations.

Fish and Shellfish

Seafoods are among the most popular items in most foodservice operations; however, their quality deteriorates very rapidly. The nutritional quality of seafoods is also affected by its deterioration. The quality also depends on the species, which varies greatly. The grading system is not as well defined for seafoods as for other types of meat products. Grading and inspection of seafood products are entirely voluntary. Grading is based on several factors, depending on the product. General factors used in evaluations are odor, flavor, packing, bones, color, appearance, size, broken pieces, texture, and skin. The U.S. grades for seafoods and their descriptions are as follows:

U.S. Grade A: Top or best quality. The products are uniform in size, practically free of blemishes and defects, in excellent condition, and possess good flavor for the species.

U.S. Grade B: Good quality. The products are uniform in size or as free from blemishes and defects as Grade A products. Grade B may be termed a general commercial grade; it is quite suitable for most purposes.

U.S. Grade C: Fairly good quality. Products are just as wholesome as those of higher grades. They are graded lower because of a minor factor, such as breakage. Where appearance is not important, these may be good buys.

Fish, the most common form of seafood, may be bought in any one of the following forms:

Whole fish: Sold just as they come from the water. They have to be dressed before cooking. This involves scaling, eviscerating, and removal of the head, tail, and/or fins. The smaller fish are pan-dressed, and the heads are not removed.

Drawn fish: Have entrails removed, which are the cause of rapid deterioration.

Dressed fish: Are completely cleaned, with the head on and ready for stuffing, if desired.

Chunks: Cross sections of large dressed fish, having the cross section of the backbone as the only bone.

Steaks: Cross-sectional slices from large dressed fish, which are ⅝ to 1 inch thick.

Butterfly fillets: The two sides of the fish cut lengthwise away from the backbone and held together by the uncut flesh and skin of the belly. These steaks have no bone.

Fish sticks: Pieces of fish flesh cut into uniform width and length, usually 3 inches by 1 inch.

Fillets: Sides of the fish cut away from the backbone. They are practically boneless.

Fish portions: Larger than fish sticks but uniform in size and weight.

Breaded fish: Available in a number of cooked, frozen, and other pan-ready forms.

In writing specifications for seafoods, the following factors should be considered: (1) name of the product; (2) species; (3) size and thickness; (4) grade; (5) style (skinless or with the skin on); (6) type (fresh, chilled, or frozen); (7) form; (8) packaging; (9) conditions upon delivery; and (10) inspection requirements.

Other Products

Procedures similar to those described for other food items should be used, providing detailed specifications. These products can include groceries, beverages, cereals, fats, oils, and nonfood supplies. Information about most products is available from vendors, food suppliers, manufacturers, and commodity organizations. The intent is to buy wholesome food products by preserving and maintaining the nutritional quality.

RECEIVING AND STORAGE

Once food products are ordered, it is imperative to have good receiving practices. Those related to preserving the nutritional quality of food products are as follows:

- When shipments are received, they should be promptly checked in and stored at proper temperatures. Many nutrients are heat and light sensitive and can be lost instantly. Even a few minutes' delay can result in nutrient losses.
- Factors to be checked include verification of the exactness of the products ordered, as well as their quality and quantity.
- All merchandise should be carefully checked for the following factors pertaining to quality and quantity:

    Each container should be checked carefully for any signs of external damage. Any signs of damage, leakage, improper packaging, or breakage are indications of poor packaging and delivery practices, and all such packages should be opened carefully and checked to ensure the quality of the merchandise. Nutrients such as water-soluble vitamins can easily be leached out, particularly from fresh produce if not properly stored.

    Each item should be weighed and/or counted, particularly from packages that are open.

    Food and nutrition labels should be checked for the accuracy of the nutritional contents of the products delivered.

When items are received in bulk, all packaging materials, such as paper, ice, or foam, should be removed and inspected. If several items are packaged in one large container, they should be sorted out and inspected separately.

The quality and wholesomeness of the delivered goods should be ascertained. This may be done by random inspection of selected representative samples of the goods and may be undertaken as follows:

The goods should be verified for quality against specifications. Some factors that should be considered include USDA stamps, USDA certification, the USDA shield, brand names, ingredient labels, nutrition labels, and other information provided on the label.

In the case of fresh fruits and vegetables, the color, freshness, freedom from damage, and overall quality of the products should be checked. Representative samples may be cut, peeled, cored, or sliced to examine freshness, maturity, juiciness, and apparent spoilage indicators. For some products, such as potatoes, specific gravity or density may be measured to assess the quality. Size, thickness, and diameter may also be indicators of quality and should be checked.

For canned products, the packaging date, expiration date, batch number, and labels should be checked. Any signs of discoloration, undesirable odor, frothiness, and mold or spore growth should be noted. All labels should be carefully checked to determine the contents. Based on the ultimate use of the products, other factors should be subjectively or objectively evaluated. There are several tests as well as testing equipment that can be used for such evaluations. These test may include drained weights, syrup concentration, and acidity.

All products should be dated on the date received to faciliate a **FIFO (first in, first out)** procedure.

For meats, all barriers, such as ice, plastic wraps, and papers, should be removed before inspection. Packages should be carefully checked for ingredients, particularly in the case of processed meats such as sausages and hamburgers. Representative samples should be checked randomly for meat trim, fat content, fat cover, weight, thickness, and lean percentage. Checks should be made for any signs of discoloration, odor, sliminess, mold growth, and freezer burn. For special kinds or cuts of meats, checks should be made for special characteristics, such as the color of the eyes for whole fish and skin tears in the case of chicken. It is advisable to use a procedure that automatically or conveniently facilitates the FIFO procedure. Computerized methods and optical scanning can be used to check on-time use of such products.

For dairy products, fat percentages, density, and acidity may be checked based on the product(s). It is essential to check the dates on milk and milk-product containers and place them accordingly. Checks should be conducted randomly for any signs of spoilage. Rancid odors in butter, margarine, or other fatty products should be noted.

Random cartons of eggs should be opened and checked for any signs of cracking, soiling, or oiling. Grades and sizes need to be checked in addition to weights. Eggs should be broken at random and checked for quality and blood spots.

Quality checks should be made for other merchandise and nonfood items based on the desirable attributes and the specifications used when placing orders. Ideally, dates should be placed on all items to faciliate stock rotation.

Since most deliveries to foodservice operations include frozen or refrigerated items, it is imperative to check the temperatures at the time of delivery. It is also advisable to have these temperatures listed on the purchase order or the invoice to facilitate checking. Temperature charts in the receiving units are very helpful in checking the required temperatures for various products. Spot checks should be made for temperature since nutritional quality is dependent on the conditions in which the items are handled at various stages of delivery. For certain products, the shape and size of ice crystals are indicative of thawing and refreezing that may have occurred during transportation. Desirable temperatures for some products are: meat and poultry, 33°F to 38°F; fish and shellfish, 23°F to 30°F.

- All items received and checked should immediately be sent to their respective storage areas. Deliveries should be scheduled at convenient times since deliveries received late in the day or during mealtimes may be held longer prior to checking and storage.

STORAGE AREAS

Foodservice operations place raw or cooked ingredients in storage areas before production or service. To preserve the nutritional quality of foods, it is imperative that all items are properly stored and issued in a definite sequence. Loss or waste of food or nonfood items may occur due to improper storage, theft, insect infestation, and nonaccessibility. Storage areas should have easy access from the receiving area and from the prepreparation and production areas. Storage areas should be clean and neatly arranged. They should be able to store all goods ordered; conversely, the quantities ordered should be based on the amount of storage space available. Temperature, humidity, and sanitation guidelines should be followed, with effective controls. Normally, in most type of foodservice operations there are three types of storage areas: (1) dry, (2) refrigerated, and (3) frozen.

Dry Storage

Dry storage is important since many items, such as fresh fruits and vegetables, will be added to menus to enrich their nutritional value. Dry storage areas should be adequately ventilated and clean, with sufficient air circulation and the desired humidity. Shelves should be placed at proper distances from the floor, walls, and ceilings. The items on the shelves should be well organized to facilitate air circulation. Nonfood items, particularly detergents, laundry supplies, and cleaning solutions, should be kept away from food supplies. Foods normally stored in dry storage areas include canned goods, flour, sugar, shortenings, spices, cereals, fruits such as bananas, and certain vegetables like onions and potatoes. Ensure that there is enough air circulation and that food products are not damaged by being placed near heating, drainage, or other utility pipes. These areas should also be safe from insect and pest infestation. Proper labeling of shelves is helpful in organizing as well as in proper storage.

Temperature in dry storage areas should range from 40°F to 75°F. Some perishable foods, such as potatoes and onions, should be stored at slightly lower temperatures (40°F to 55°F) to prevent spoilage. Circulation of air is necessary to maintain the freshness of perishable goods. Air circulation also helps to eliminate odors and remove moisture. Large containers or packages that might hinder the flow of air should be replaced or removed. Sufficient space should be allowed in storage areas for free movement of carts, pallets, and motorized lifts, particularly in the center of the aisles. Spills, leakages, and breakages should be cleaned promptly. Containers with lids that can be closed easily should be used for items such as sugar, flour, shortenings, and cereals. Lids should be closed tightly after every use. Slidable lids, self-closing lids, or half-opening lids are desirable for items not stored in their original containers. As with any item in the storage areas, these containers should always be labeled properly.

Refrigerated Storage

Refrigerated storage areas may be used to store cooked or partially cooked foods, in addition to thawing meats. Care should be taken at every step to maintain the nutritional quality of the fresh and cooked foods. These areas may contain reach-in and/or walk-in refrigerators. It is wise to have an automatic mechanism to alert the staff to any refrigerator failure. A convenient and logical arrangement of items on shelves helps reduce time spent in the storage area. Automatic temperature-recording devices or thermometers should be conveniently and permanently located in these areas. Since the temperature may vary in different parts of the refrigerator space, items placed near doors should be checked for maintenance of the desired temperature. To reduce moisture or ice deposits, it is necessary to keep refrigerated areas as clean as possible. For optimum operation, regular defrosting and/or avoiding overcrowding are vital. As in dry storage areas, no items should be placed on the floor or in contact with the ceiling or walls. There should be no leakage from or on the containers in which food items are placed.

Cooked foods should be placed so that there is no chance of contact with raw food products or ingredients. Raw food items should not be stored above cooked foods. Cooked or leftover cooked foods should be covered and labeled immediately. It is not advisable to place hot items directly in the refrigerated storage unit because it may take a long time for them to reach safe temperatures, and the surrounding temperatures will be affected by the hot food. Depending on the temperature, the nutritional quality of food may be affected. Rapid cooling techniques and the use of shallow, wide containers are recommended for cooling hot foods. Certain products easily pick up odors; such items should be segregated. An example is dairy products, which absorb odors from apples very easily. Fish and fish products impart strong odors and should be stored separately. Separate refrigerators may be desirable for dairy products or frozen desserts.

Frozen Storage

The number of foods that require frozen storage is increasing rapidly. It is important to consider the physical and chemical properties of a product before deciding to place it in the freezer. Frozen storage areas normally have temperatures ranging from 0°F to 20°F. Whenever possible, frozen food items should be ordered in containers or packages of optimum size to avoid the risk of thawing large quantities of food. Individual packages may be desirable to faciliate thawing and rethermalizing. Individually quick frozen (IQF) items should be purchased whenever possible. These include such items as fish that are frozen individually rather than in bulk, the advantage being that they do not stick to each other. Some foods are available in portion-controlled sizes. Thawed food items should not be refrozen since their appearance, flavor, nutritive value, and cooking quality may be adversely affected. If any products must be frozen, they should be placed in their original container or in another clean, clearly labeled utensil. FIFO procedures should be strictly enforced in frozen storage area. Many menu items are suitable for frozen storage soon after cooking. Cooked foods should be placed away from raw food items and should be adequately protected from contamination. A planned system should be used to remove products from the freezer so that there is adequate rotation of food items. Dating and labeling of containers are imperative. One common problem observed in freezer-stored foods is *freezer burn,* which occurs when fat under the surface becomes rancid, causing a brown discoloration or patches. Freezer temperatures should be recorded periodically and maintained at the desirable level. Freezer storage, if properly maintained, can help preserve the nutritional value of many frozen foods.

Chapter 13

FOOD PREPARATION AND NUTRIENT RETENTION

T he primary function of a foodservice operation is to convert raw ingredients into prepared edible foods and to serve them in a way that satisfies consumers' needs. This requires a blend of science and art at various stages of the process. The process may involve heat, light, moisture, contact with ingredients, and physical and chemical reactions. No matter how food is prepared, there are implications that should be considered from the nutrient retention point of view. The best-planned menu and the most efficient purchasing and receiving methods may all be negated (from the nutritional point of view) if adequate precautions are not taken during food preparation. Different types of food products, common method(s) of preparation, and precautions are discussed below.

GENERAL GUIDELINES

Food preparation in any type of foodservice operation is based on recipes. So, the first checkpoint is the contents of a recipe. It is advisable to have a nutritional analysis of the recipes. Standardization of recipes does not refer to their nutritional contents. Serving or portion sizes also dictate the amount of nutrients present in a particular selection. For example, a serving of lasagna in one recipe may have an entirely different nutritional content from that in another recipe. In the same way, the nutrient value of fresh lasagna is different from that of frozen lasagna. Each ingredient should be examined singly and can be (1) reduced in quantity, (2) replaced by a comparable ingredient, or (3) eliminated entirely. This decision should be based on the role of the particular ingredient in that recipe. For example, sugar is used in many baked goods recipes; it can be reduced in quantity or replaced by other low-calorie sweeteners without reducing the palatability of the baked goods. Another example is oils, which can be easily replaced. Taste, texture, and appearance dictate the sensory quality of foods and should not be unduly sacrificed. There are many herbs and seasonings that can not only replace certain ingredients but, in some cases, can enhance the nutritional value of a particular product. For example, lemon juice can be used to replace salt or low-fat yogurt can be used to provide flavor. Another way of modifying the nutritional quality of foods is to change the method of preparation. For example, frying can be replaced by baking or fats can be skimmed from stews. Instead of coating cooking pans with oils and fats, one can use special pans or low/no-calorie fats, or the fats/oils in recipes can be used as a coating. If deep-fat frying is essential, then as much fat as possible should be drained or cooked products placed on absorbent papers so that a considerable amount of fat is absorbed. Also, some high-fat, high-sugar, and high-salt ingredients can be stretched. For example, grated cheese rather than slices can be used to increase the volume while reducing the amount used. Similarly, smaller amounts of spreads, peanut butter, jams, or jellies can be used on toast.

MEAT COOKERY

Meat is the most important menu item in any type of foodservice operation and often the most expensive. Meat also contributes significantly to the nutritive value of the menu since it provides important nutrients, including protein, vitamins, and minerals. Adequate care in the selection of preparation methods is necessary to maintain the flavor, tenderness, color, palatability, and nutritive value of meat items. For the best results when cooking, it is necessary to understand the chemistry of meats. Meats are approximately 75 percent water. The muscle fibers consist of bundles and form the structural units of lean tissue. Connective tissues surround the muscle fibers and help to support the muscle structure. There are primarily two types of connective tissue: collagen and elastin; both are important in cooking. Collagen, which is yellowish-white in color, gelatinizes in the presence of moisture and softens under heat, increasing the tenderness and flavor of the meat. In contrast, elastin is yellow and is very tough; it is not affected by heat and cannot be softened easily. Various tenderization methods, primarily mechanical, are often needed to break and soften these tissues. The amount and distribution of elastin tissues vary with the age of the animal. Due to the presence of water, nutrients can easily be lost during thawing and preparation. Also, mechanical tenderization may result in loss of some nutrients.

Fat is present in meats at various points, including the exterior portions, within the abdominal cavity in rolls, between muscles, and within cells. Like connective tissue, the fat content is dependent on the age of the animal and the type of diet it was fed. To a certain extent, the distribution of fat within the muscle is used in the grading of meats. The intermingling of fat and muscle is referred to as *marbling.* An optimum distribution of fats is responsible for flavor and juiciness. To reduce the fat content of meats, fat can be trimmed on the outside or wherever it is visible. However, it may be difficult to remove the fat ingrained within muscle tissues. Fat melts and adds to the flavor of the meat. Thus, it is important that time and temperature be optimum for retention of the desirable qualities of meats. An appropriate cooking method should be used to enhance their flavor, color, tenderness, juiciness, and nutritive value. Above all, it is the quality of cooked meat when it reaches the consumer that is most important. Thus, service and delivery methods should ensure that all the desirable attributes of meats are intact when they are served. **Shrinkage** occurs when meats are cooked. Since meats consist mostly of water, the loss of water during cooking causes them to shrink. All meats will shrink to some degree with any type of cooking; it is the extent of shrinkage that matters. Various factors are responsible for shrinkage; the most important are cooking time, cooking temperatures, and cooking method.

Tenderization of meat is achieved by the use of enzymes, salt, and vinegar or by mechanical means. The substances act on the collagen and help to tenderize the meats. Such enzymes as papain from raw papaya fruit, bromelin from pineapple, and ficin from figs have a tenderizing effect. These enzymes are sometimes injected into the animal just before slaughter. Commercially available meat tenderizers contain one or more of these enzymes, spices, and flavors such as MSG. In larger portions of meat and where hard connective tissues are present, mechanical means such as pounding, grinding, dicing, chopping, cubing, scoring, or beating help tenderize meats by physically breaking and/or loosening the connective tissues. Whatever means are used, they must be effective since the quality of the finished product depends on its texture. Marinating with oils, acids, tomato juice, vinegar, lemon juice, and sour cream also helps to tenderize meats.

There are several methods for cooking meats, each resulting in a different type of flavor. They are sometimes classified as dry-heat methods (no water is added while cooking) and moist-heat methods (meats are cooked by steam or hot liquids). With dry-heat methods, since no water is added, surface caramelization or browning occurs, resulting in enhanced flavor. Since surface heating is largely unaccompanied by moisture and since there is not enough moisture to soften the collagen, meats cooked by these methods should be either tender or tenderized. With moist-heat methods, meats are exposed to temperatures no higher than the boiling point of water, which ensures slow cooking; this contributes to flavor development and tenderization. The moist-heat process can be hastened by the use of steam or pressure. When meat is cooked in water, care should be taken to ensure that the nutrients are not lost in the juices from the cooked products. The method of cooking selected should be based on the type and grade of meat. The most common methods of cooking various types of meat are described below.

Roasting

Roasting is a dry-heat method in which meats are cooked in various types of ovens, such as conventional, convection, and microwave ovens. Large roasts are usually cooked by placing the meats with the fat side up in an uncovered pan. Moderate to low temperatures and long cooking times are used to develop the flavor. Lower temperatures keep meat shrinkage to a minimum. Roasting meat in an oven overnight, while convenient, poses various safety problems (such as those caused by improper handling or a power failure), in addition to the risk of reducing the meat's nutritive value. If time and temperatures are controlled, the product roasted overnight has superior quality and well-developed flavor. The optimum temperature range for slow roasting is 250°F to 350°F. Tender meat cuts are preferred for roasting, including the less exercised portions of beef and meats attached to the backbone of the carcass. In the case of veal, lamb, and pork, most cuts are suitable for roasting.

It is desirable to start with defrosted meat in foodservice operations to ensure the quality of the finished product, although under certain conditions meats may be roasted without thawing. The internal temperature is the best indicator of degree of doneness. A thermometer should be inserted into the thickest part of the roast without touching fat or bone. A constant low temperature is desirable since the resulting product is evenly done and is more uniform in color when served. The approximate cooking times and temperatures for various cuts of meat are given in Tables 13.1, 13.2, and 13.3. Since roasts will continue to cook even after they are taken out of the oven, they are removed from the oven at an internal temperature slightly lower than desired to allow for the few degrees of increase after removal. Roasts are sliced 15–20 minutes after removal from the oven; this "resting" period permits easier slicing. Roasts have their best flavor right after cooking, so not much time should elapse between roasting and serving. Slicing is done across the grain of the muscle, preferably using a mechanical slicer. For best quality, the slices should be as thin as possible. Sometimes cooked roasts are refrigerated prior to slicing and may be reheated before slicing. Considerable amounts of juice are lost in slicing, and with the juice go the flavor components, and, more important, the nutrients. Care should therefore be taken to utilize as much of the meat juice as possible by adding it back to the meat slices or to the gravy.

Table 13.1 Cooking Times for Beef: For Roasting

		Approximate Total Cooking Time	
Cut	Approximate Thickness	Rare (min)	Medium (min)
Rib, top loin, T-bone,	1 inch	15	20
Porterhouse,	1½ inches	25	35
Tenderloin	2 inches	35	50
Beef sirloin steak	1 inch	20–25	30–35
	1½ inches	30–35	40–45
Ground beef patties	1 in. (4 ounces)	15	20

Table 13.2 Cooking Times for Beef: For Braising and Cooking in Liquid

Cut	Average Weight or Thickness	Approximate Total Cooking Time (hr)
Pot roast	4–6 pounds	3–4
Swiss steak	1–2½ inches	2–3
Short ribs	2 × 2 × 2-inch pieces	1½–2
Corned beef	6–8 pounds	4–6
Beef shank cross-cuts	¾–1 pound	2½–3½
Beef for stew	1- to 2-inch cubes	2–3

Broiling

Broiling is a dry-heat method. The source of energy may be direct or radiant heat from gas flames, charcoal briquettes, or individual electric units. Relatively tender and thicker cuts are most suitable for broiling. Prefabricated or portion-controlled meat cuts can also be broiled and result in uniform serving sizes. The most tender and expensive cuts are usually prepared by broiling. The thickness of the meat plays an important part in the quality and doneness of the finished product; thinner cuts show excessive shrinkage, whereas thicker cuts result in uniform cooking.

In foodservice operations, broiling is done in special broilers (rotary in some cases) or in a salamander. The meat is placed on a rack, with the radiant heat approximately 3 inches away. Turning of the meat ensures cooking on both sides. The temperature, as well as the distance from the heat source, determines the

Table 13.3 Cooking Times for Roast Beef

Cut	Approximate Wt of Single Roast (lb)	Oven Temp (°F)	Interior Temp (°F) of Roast When Removed from Oven	Min per Pound Based on One Roast	Approx Total Cooking Time (hr)
Rib, roast ready	20–25	250	130 (rare)	13–15	4½–5
			140 (medium)	15–17	5–6
			150 (well)	17–19	6–6½
Ribeye roll	4–6	350	140 (rare)	18–20	1⅓–1⅔
			160 (medium)	20–22	1½–2
			170 (well)	22–24	1⅔–2¼
Full tenderloin	4–6	425	140 (rare)		¾–1
Strip loin, boneless	10–12	325	140 (rare)	10	1½–2
Top (inside) round	10	300	140 (rare)	18–19	3–3¼
			150 (medium)	22–23	3½–4
Top (inside) round	15	300	140 (rare)	15	3½–4
			150 (medium)	17	4–4½

cooking time and the degree of doneness. The temperature of the heat source may be as high as 1800°F (982°C). The preferred temperature range for broiling is between 300°F and 350°F (149°C to 177°C). The meat is done at an internal temperature of 140°F (60°C) for rare, 160°F (71°C) for medium, and 170°F (76°C) for well-done orders. *Pan broiling* involves cooking uncovered in a pre-heated, nonstick skillet without added oil or water. Fat can be removed as it accumulates.

Grilling or Griddling

Grilling is a dry-heat method used primarily for cooking steaks or hamburgers. The fat in the meat itself is enough for cooking. Fat and water are not added, although seasonings may be used. Once the meat is browned on one side, it is turned for cooking on the other side. In some griddles or grills, special provision is made for fat drainage. The cooking temperature varies, depending on the ambient temperature, but normally ranges from 325°F to 350°F (163°C to 177°C). The time and cooking temperature also depend on the thickness of the meat.

Braising

In braising, meats are browned in a small quantity of fat. The pan is covered tightly after browning, and cooking continues at a low temperature. Braising may be done in the oven, in a steam-jacketed kettle, in a tilting frying pan, or over the range. The doneness of the meat depends on the required internal temperature and may range from 165°F to 185°F (74°C to 85°C). *Sautéing* involves cooking quickly in a small amount of fat, stirring so that the meat browns evenly. *Stir-frying* refers to cooking small pieces of meat, poultry, fish, and/or vegetables in a very small amount of oil over very high heat, stirring while cooking. Partially frozen meat is easy to slice. Meats are cut into thin, uniform slices and marinated before stir-frying. Meats and vegetables are cooked separately before being combined.

Stewing

Stewing or boiling is done by cooking meat in the presence of moisture. Vegetable or cereals may be added to meat for stewing, and special recipes may be used. The meat may or may not be browned before stewing. The flavor of the stewed meat is enhanced by the cooking juices. Stewing requires cooking meat at a simmering temperature until it is tender. Steam-jacketed or floor-mounted kettles may be used. *Poaching* involves cooking gently in liquid just below the boiling point.

Simmering

Simmering involves the slow cooking of meats in liquid for a long time. This method is especially useful for less tender cuts of meats that require longer cooking times for tenderization. The advantage of simmering is that meats can be cooked longer without shrinkage. *Steaming* is cooking with steam heat.

Table 13.4 lists selected lean cuts of meat and preferred methods of cooking

Table 13.4 Lean Cuts of Selected Meats and Preferred Cooking Methods

	Dry Heat					Moist Heat		
	Roast	*Broil*	*Pan-broil*	*Stir-fry*	*Grill*	*Braise*	*Stew*	*Steam*
Beef								
Top round						X	X	
Eye round						X	X	
Round tip						X	X	
Bottom round						X	X	
Sirloin	X	X	X	X	X			
Top loin	X	X	X	X	X			
Tenderloin	X	X	X	X	X			
Flank		X		X	X			
Ground round	X	X	X		X			
Poultry								
Whole chicken	X				X	X	X	
Breast	X	X	X	X	X			
Drumstick	X	X			X			
Whole turkey	X				X	X		
Fish								
Cod	X	X	X	X	X		X	X
Flounder	X	X	X		X		X	X
Halibut	X	X	X	X	X		X	X
Orange roughy		X	X	X	X		X	X
Shrimp		X	X	X	X		X	X

them. Tips for cooking different meats are presented below. Stewing or boiling meat products results in twice as much vitamin loss as roasting, frying, or grilling.

Tips for Cooking Meats

1. Select methods that are appropriate and provide the fewest calories without sacrificing nutrition. Broiling, grilling, braising, or roasting are preferable to frying—particularly deep-fat frying. Stir-frying is preferable to deep-fat frying.

2. Select lean meats whenever possible, and trim as much visible fat as possible. Trimming fat reduces not only calories but also cholesterol.

3. Use as little processed meat as possible since these meats tend to have more fat. Use fat-free or reduced-fat processed products.

4. Remove the skin from poultry; this cuts the fat content by almost half. If moistness and tenderness are desired, the skin can be removed after cooking.

5. Drain fat from ground meat using a strainer or physical means. Since fat is lighter than water, it rises to the top and can be removed easily by skimming from the top of soups, gravies, broths, stews, and other such preparations. Remember that every tablespoon of fat removed eliminates about 12 grams of fat and 108 calories. Also, soups and stews can be refrigerated; after chilling, the fat can be easily removed.

6. Meats can be cooked in a skillet without any coatings, utilizing the internal fat. Every tablespoon of fat added as a coating can add 120 calories.

7. Marinades used for meat, poultry, or fish should be carefully selected so that they do not contain excessive fat, salt, or sugar. Use of MSG can add considerable sodium. Some herbs, spices, and other ingredients can enhance the quality of marinated meats without decreasing their nutritional value. Examples include buttermilk, low-fat yogurt, lime juice, lemon juice, low-fat broth, and tomato juice.

VEGETABLE AND FRUIT COOKERY

In cooking vegetables and fruits, special care is needed to preserve nutritional values as well as color, texture, flavor, and sensory qualities. The acidity or alkalinity of the liquid in which they are cooked also affects these properties. Most vegetables and fruits contain organic acids that increase the acidity of the medium in which they are cooked. Color and certain nutrients are affected by the pH of the medium. For example, the green color in fruits and vegetables is due to the presence of chlorophyll, which changes in an acid medium to a dull or olive green. By contrast, an alkaline cooking medium may intensify the green color. The presence of slight alkalinity may be desirable to enrich the color, a phenomenon observed on blanching of vegetables. However, an alkaline cooking medium may toughen the texture of the vegetables and destroy such vitamins as thiamin and ascorbic acid. Cooking times and temperatures for vegetables and fruits are important.

To retain their nutrients, vegetables should be cooked for the minimum amount of time. Many water-soluble vitamins can be lost in prepreparation of vegetables and fruits, such as by washing, coring, peeling, cutting, and blanching.

The red color of some vegetables and fruits is commonly due to the presence of the pigment anthocyanin. This pigment is also affected by the pH of the cooking medium. Anthocyanins become bluish-red in acid media and blue-green in alkaline media. Both of these colors are undesirable. Thus, care is needed when cooking red cabbage, beets, and similar vegetables. The yellow color of some fruits and vegetables is due to the presence of carotenoid pigments. Corn, carrots, and sweet potatoes contain carotenoids, which are also precursors of vitamin A. These pigments are fairly stable and are not normally affected by the presence of acid or alkali. The flavonoid pigments provide color to white cabbage, onions, and potatoes. They are not affected by acid media but generally turn yellow in the presence of alkaline media. Normally, syrup with a high sugar content is used in canned fruits so that fruits do not break. Some vegetables are packed in brine- or salt-containing media. The food label should be consulted to examine the caloric content. The most common methods of cooking fruits and vegetables are discussed below.

Steaming

Steaming is the most common as well as the most desirable method for cooking most fruits and vegetables; their texture, color, flavor, and nutrients are better preserved. Steam-jacketed kettles, steamers, or skillets may be used. Perforated pans that allow the steam to circulate around the food product are useful.

Boiling

Boiling is the cooking of fruits and vegetables in water. The main disadvantage is a loss of nutrients, particularly if the water left after cooking is not used. These foods should be boiled in the minimum amount of water at a low temperature. High boiling temperatures may break up the product and destroy heat-sensitive vitamins. Fruits and vegetables may be dipped in hot water in a steam-jacketed kettle attached to the necessary strainers. Recipes used for boiling fruits may require that the fruits be dipped in syrup or sugar-containing water. The number of calories provided by these substances should be taken into consideration.

Baking

The most common fruits and vegetables baked in foodservice operations include potatoes, apples, tomatoes, green peppers, onions, eggplant, and squash. Moist foods are most suitable for baking. Upon heating, their moisture helps to soften the cellulose in the food. Baking may also produce a desirable crust on the outside due to the caramelization of sugars. Baking temperatures may range from 350°F to 450°F (177°C to 232°C), depending on the product.

Sautéing and Braising

Vegetables such as breakfast potatoes are often cooked by sautéing. Celery, onions, cabbage, and lettuce are often braised. For braising, the vegetables are sautéed in a small amount of fat and then quick-stirred. Vegetables can also be cooked with thickening agents or sauces until tender.

Broiling

Broiling is not the most common method of cooking fruits and vegetables since much of the moisture is lost at high temperatures and the foods become charred. Only very tender, moist products broil easily. Bell peppers, tomatoes, and onions are the vegetables most commonly broiled. Maximum loss of heat-sensitive nutrients occur with this method of cooking.

Frying

Vegetables can be deep-fried or stir-fried. Deep-frying provides a crisp, desirable texture, as seen in french fries. It also results in the caramelization of sugar to provide a desirable crust. Vegetables strips may also be dipped in batters before frying. Many vegetables may be parboiled before deep-frying. Vegetables suited for frying include eggplant, onions, potatoes, mushrooms, zucchini, and carrots. Tips for preserving the nutritional value of fruits and vegetables are listed below.

Tips for Cooking Fruits and Vegetables

1. When vegetables are sautéed, as little fat/oil as needed should be used. It is preferable not to use any fats. Other liquids can be used instead.

2. Vegetables should preferably be cooked by steaming for a short period of time. Other desirable methods include stir-frying, simmering, and microwaving.

3. Oven baking of vegetables is preferable to frying. Crisp french fries or onion rings can be prepared by baking.

4. Vegetables of different colors can be mixed to provide a variety of nutrients. Sauces and other ingredients, such as Parmesan or Romano cheese in moderate amounts, can be added to enhance the flavor.

5. The water in which vegetables are cooked should be used in finished products and gravies to utilize any nutrients that may have leached out.

6. As an added source of calcium, shredded cheese can be sprinkled on vegetables, salads, soups, stews, and baked potatoes.

7. Vegetables that have more calcium can be used in the preparation of soups, salads, and stews. Broccoli, collard greens, kale, mustard greens, okra, and turnip greens all provide calcium in varying amounts.

8. Stir-fried dishes can be made using tofu. Tofu, when prepared with calcium sulfate, is a good source of calcium.

9. The best way to boil vegetables is to cook them under steam or boil them until they are crisp-tender. Just enough water to prevent scorching should be used, preferably in a closed container or one with a tight-fitting lid. This will help preserve the maximum amounts of nutrients.

10. Steaming of vegetables reduces the loss of nutrients almost by half compared to boiling.

SALAD PREPARATION

Salads are dishes composed of fruits, vegetables, eggs, and meats, usually topped with salad dressings and/or garnishes, often served cold and placed on an underliner. They consist of a base, a body, garnishes, and dressings. Bases consist of salad greens and are seldom consumed. Ingredients that make up the salad, such as lettuce, raw vegetables, fruits, gelatins, and eggs, are referred to as the *body* of the salad. Garnishes include nuts, croutons, meats, fishes, cheeses, fruits, vegetables, parsley, and condiments. Dressings are of different colors and textures.

Salads are becoming very popular in all types of foodservice operations. They are particularly in demand due to the increasing number of health-conscious consumers. The serving sizes of salads vary widely based on their use as individual entrees or as an accompaniment. Different types of salads include appetizer, side dish, main dish, custom made, salad bar, and dessert salads. Since most salad materials consist of vegetables and fruits, the same principles for preparation and nutrient retention of these items should be observed. More than the salad ingredients, the type of dressing used is significant from the nutritional point of view. Low-fat or reduced-fat dressings should be preferred. Oil and vinegar should be restricted and used carefully.

Salad Dressings

Salad dressings enhance the flavor as well as improve the overall appearance of salads. Most salad dressings are emulsions, primarily of oil and vinegar, which are made by combining two immiscible liquids with the aid of an emulsifying agent. For example, in mayonnaise, eggs act as an emulsifying agent by coating the fat droplets and making them immiscible to form an emulsion of the oil and vinegar. The preparation of salad dressings requires careful, slow blending of the immiscible liquids. Vinegar in emulsions can be replaced by other acidic ingredients, such as lemon or other fruit juices. Bland oils—corn, cottonseed, safflower, and soybean oils, for example—are used to make dressings. To retard rancidity, antioxidants (butylated hydroxyanisole, BHA; butylated hydroxytoluene, BHT; and ethylenediaminetetraacetic acid, EDTA) are added. There are several types of dressings; most of them can be classified on the basis of their method of preparation. Some of the commonly used dressings and their constituents are discussed below.

French Dressings   French dressings are temporary or unstable emulsions made of fixed proportions of oil and acid, blended with different types of seasonings such as paprika, mustard, garlic, sugar, and salt. Salt and seasonings, when blended, form a temporary emulsion with oil and water. Several seasonings can be added to provide special flavors.

Mayonnaise   Mayonnaise is the base for a number of dressings and sauces such as Thousand Island dressing, Russian dressing, and tartar sauce. It is prepared by blending oil, water, egg yolks, and/or whole eggs. Mayonnaise forms a permanent emulsion that does not break down easily. Egg acts as an emulsifier and promote the formation of stable emulsions. Sometimes gelatin or cooked starch is also used as an emulsifying agent.

Cooked or Boiled Dressings   Cooked dressings are oil-vinegar emulsions that contain much less oil than mayonnaise and are thickened by starch and egg yolk. A starch paste made from flour, cornstarch, or other thickeners is added as a thickening agent. Since these thickeners tend to become lumpy, care should be taken to see that they do not coagulate or get scorched while cooking. Thick dressings may be diluted by adding whipping cream or by mixing them with other dressing ingredients.

Cream Dressings   Cream dressings contain sour cream, cream cheese, or whipped sweet cream. They are seasoned with vinegar and other ingredients. Several variations are made possible by adding different types of spices and condiments.

Tips for Salad Preparation

1. Use as little oil and dressing as possible. More vinegar than oil can be used in a mixture.

2. Products such as salsa, tomato ketchup, chili, and onions can be used to flavor salads.

3. Reduced-fat or nonfat dressings should be used in moderation. Dressings can be provided on the side rather than mixing into the salad so that the amount can be controlled by the patrons. Use small utensils for serving salad dressings rather than gravy boats or other larger containers.

4. Use low-fat or nonfat yogurt or mayonnaise in all accompaniments.

5. Add different colored vegetables and fruits to provide a variety of nutrients.

6. Plain yogurt can also be substituted in part for the mayonnaise in salad dressings, sandwich spreads, and dips.

7. For main-dish salads and sandwich spreads, canned salmon with bones can be used. Salmon, sardines, and perch are good sources of calcium and provide distinct flavor.

PREPARATION OF BAKED FOODS, DESSERTS, AND GRAIN PRODUCTS

Baked goods and desserts are important in any type of foodservice operation. It is essential to know the principal ingredients and their properties before attempting any changes from the nutritional point of view. The most important ingredients are discussed below.

Flour

Although many types of flour are used in baking, wheat flour, either alone or in different blends, is the favorite choice. The protein in flour responsible for the baked flavor is gluten, which absorbs moisture and forms an elastic, strong, spongy mass referred to as *batter* or *dough*. Gluten has the unique property of stretching to a considerable degree, which is facilitated by the process of kneading. The network of gluten bands formed by stretching becomes firm on baking. Gluten may be developed to form strong or weak bands. Bread, or hard-wheat, flour forms strong structures, whereas pastry, or soft-wheat, flour forms delicate structures. Pastry flour is also called *weak* flour. Thus, the flour used for baking is selected based on its intended use. All-purpose flour is a blend of 20 percent soft wheat flour and 80 percent bread flour.

Shortening

One of the main requirements of baking is to prevent the sticking of gluten particles, thereby producing tenderness. Hydrogenated fats, oils, butter, and lard are used as shortening in baking. Due to the increased emphasis on low cholesterol, many foodservice operations are using vegetable shortenings only for many baked products.

Sugars

In addition to sweetening products, sugars help to tenderize them. Different types of sugar are used in baking. Powdered sugars, ground sugars to which a small amount of cornstarch is added to prevent clumping, are used for dusting, coating, and icing different types of baked products. Regular coarse sugar can be used to make cakes and meringues. It is also used in baked products for its special flavor.

Leavening Agents

Leavening agents provide texture and volume to baked products. Leavening has to be added carefully and in exact proportions for desired results. Air, incorporated into a product when eggs are whipped to a foam, leavens a batter and when heated swells, causing the product to rise and develop a fine texture. Steam is also used as an automatic leavening agent. For some products a chemical leavening agent, such as baking powder or soda, is added. Cream of tartar is used with soda to form a single-acting baking powder. Several types of baking powder are available. Chemical leavening agents release carbon dioxide, which is responsible for the leavening action. Heat also contributes to the leavening action.

Yeast

Yeast is used to create carbon dioxide gas and alcohol in some yeast baked products. Yeast growth is at an optimum level at 78°F to 90°F (25.5°C to 32°C), and yeast is killed at about 140°F (60°C). It is added to warm water before being stirred with other ingredients.

Eggs

Eggs are used in many baked products and desserts to enhance the baking qualities, as well as provide flavor, color, volume, tenderness, and nutritional value. They also act as a binding ingredient in batters and doughs.

Depending on the type of baked product—yeast bread, muffins, or breads—ingredients are mixed using large blenders and mixers set at different speeds for specific periods of time. Yeast doughs are allowed to ferment. Kneading and mixing of the dough are done by mechanical mixers. During mixing, the temperature of the product may rise and may affect the product's nutritional content. The final conditioning of the bread before baking is called *proofing*. This procedure results in a soft, delicate product of increased volume. Most products are baked at temperatures ranging from 375°F to 450°F (190°C to 232°C). For some bakery products, immediate cooling is required.

Custards are baked desserts prepared from liquids thickened with eggs. Soufflés are desserts thickened and leavened by eggs and baked at lower temperatures than other baked items. Meringues are made using egg whites and sugar with cream of tartar; they are often used for topping pies and desserts. Pies and pastries are baked from various kinds of flour, shortening, salt, and water. The amount of fat, the blending procedure, and the incorporation of shortening into flour result in the formation of a flaky crust. Preparation methods for different baked products vary, although the principles behind the use of certain ingredients are the same.

Most cereal products are cooked by steaming or boiling, which causes starch to gelatinize. Rice can be cooked in a steamer with twice the volume of water. Salt, water, and a little oil may also be added. Macaroni products or pasta are dropped into boiling water and stirred until they are tender.

Tips for Preparing Baked Foods, Desserts, and Grain Products

1. Egg whites can be used in place of whole eggs, reducing the use of yolks. Roughly two egg whites can be used in place of one whole egg in baked products such as breads, pancakes, puddings, french toast, cookies, casseroles, cheesecake, and other recipes. When whole eggs are necessary, such as in puff pastries, the amount used should be reduced. Cholesterol-free liquid egg products can also be used.

2. Recipes for baked products can be adjusted to varying degrees. In cakes, muffins, and brownies, a variety of substitutions are possible. Applesauce, mashed fruits, cottage cheese, and puréed fruits can be mixed.

3. Butter can be replaced or reduced by using margarine and other vegetable oils.

4. Buttermilk, nonfat yogurt, or low-fat yogurt can be used in place of sour cream, butter, and margarine in biscuits, muffins, and other bread products.

5. Flavor as well as volume can be improved by adding dried fruits and nuts. For example, almonds, chopped dates, dried apricots, raisins, cranberries, and prunes can be used effectively in a variety of baked products and desserts. These can be added to ingredients or used as toppings.

6. Skim, low-fat, and nonfat dairy products can be used as a substitute for heavy cream or whole milk products in many recipes.

7. For pastas, oils can be reduced or eliminated from cooking water. Low-fat sauces in reduced quantities should be used. Herbs and spices can be added to increase flavor.

8. Rice and other grain products should be cooked preferably without any oils or fats.

9. Enriched products, particularly rice, should not be washed before cooking since that will drain added water-soluble vitamins (thiamin, niacin, and riboflavin).

10. Baked products should be served with low-fat spreads, fruit jellies, jams, chutney, mustard, nonfat or reduced-fat cream cheese, and spreads.

11. Use whole-grain products as much as possible. These can be in the form of whole-wheat breads, whole-grain pasta—lasagna noodles, macaroni, spaghetti, and so on—as well as wild rice, brown rice, and other varieties, in addition to combinations of these products. These products provide nutrients as well as fiber. Whole-wheat flour can be substituted for white flour or mixed in different proportions.

12. Use other, less familiar grains in different combinations. These include barley, bulgar, millet, buckwheat, sorghum, rye berries, and wheat berries.

13. Bran can be used to provide fiber. It can be mixed into different food products, as well as sprinkled on salads, cereals, yogurt, and sauces. One tablespoon of bran adds slightly more than 1 gram of fiber.

14. Milk can be used in making cooked cereal if calcium is required. Low-fat yogurt is another good source of calcium. Goat cheese is also becoming a popular substitute.

15. The easiest way to reduce calories in desserts and baked goods is to reduce the amount of sugar used. However, the physical or baking quality of the products should not be affected by this modification.

16. Recipes can be sweetened by adding extracts such as vanilla or other spices.

17. Fruits can be used in different combinations as desserts. They can be baked, poached, or chopped.

NUTRIENT LOSSES IN FOODSERVICE OPERATIONS

As the above discussion demonstrates, nutrient losses in cooking and serving foods vary widely based on the methods used. Very little scientific information is available on nutrient losses in different types of foodservice operations. Vitamin losses may occur due to changes in pH; exposure to such factors as oxygen, light, or heat,; with the passage of time; and by the physical separation of vitamins from food. The destruction is due to the change in the chemical structure of the vitamins, rendering them incapable of performing their functions. Nutrients are destroyed when foods are subjected to adverse conditions during processing or preparation. Thiamin is readily degraded in neutral and alkaline solutions even at low temperatures. Sulfite used in food processing can also degrade thiamin. Riboflavin is heat stable in acidic solutions and in the presence of mild oxidizing agents. However, it is very sensitive to light at neutral and alkaline pH. Niacin is one of the most heat-stable and light-stable vitamins found in foods. However, it can be leached out of foods during prepreparation or washing. Pyridoxine is stable to heat in acidic and alkaline solutions but is light sensitive. The stability of folic acid is affected by the conjugate form present in foods. Vitamin B_{12} has moderate to good heat stability. Vitamin A is readily oxidized and is extremely light sensitive. Vitamin D is sensitive to both oxygen and light. All the properties of nutrients therefore need careful consideration to preserve the nutrient quality of foods.

Vitamin losses depends on the *type of food, the stability of the nutrients; the amount of water used in food preparation; the equipment used for food preparation; the cooking time and temperature; the physical and chemical characteristics of foods; and the method used for display/or delivery of service.* Table 13.5 illustrates the stability of vitamins under different conditions. Heating, in particular, affects many vitamins, including the fat-soluble vitamins (especially vitamin A), vitamin C, and thiamin. Water-soluble vitamins can be easily washed away during prepreparation, preparation, holding, and serving. The least stable vitamins are vitamin C and thiamin, both of which are water soluble and can be affected by other conditions. Frozen vegetables have considerably better vitamin retention capacity than those that are canned. Minerals are less affected than vitamins by heat or other factors. They tend to be relatively stable to pH changes, oxidation, light, heat, and time. They are lost primarily by physical separation, such as during the milling of grains or the peeling of fruits. Although mineral losses tend to be lower than vitamin losses, their

Table 13.5 Stability of Vitamins Under Selected Conditions

Vitamins	Acid	Akaline	Neutral	Light	Heat	Air
Vitamin A	0	+	+	0	0	0
Vitamin D		0	+	0	0	0
Vitamin E	+	+	+	0	0	0
Vitamin K	0	0	+	0	+	+
Thiamin	+	0	0	+	0	0
Riboflavin	+	0	+	0	0	+
Niacin	+	+	+	+	+	+
Pyridoxine	+	+	+	0	0	+
Pantothenic acid	0	0	+	+	0	+
Biotin	+	+	+	+	0	+
Carotene	0	+	+	0	0	0
Cobalamin	+	+	+	0	+	0
Folic acid	0	+	0	0	0	0
Ascorbic acid	+	0	0	0	0	0

0 = unstable
+ = stable

bioavailability can be affected. Increases in micronutrients occur primarily when nutrients are added to foods.

Boiling, which requires foods to be cooked in water at a temperature of 212°F, can cause significant nutrient losses. Minerals are lost when large amounts of water are used. Vegetables lose nutrients easily when large amounts of water are used. Since cooking time has an impact, nutrient retention is best when vegetables are cooked for the shortest possible time. Many vegetables are ready to serve after boiling for two to five minutes. Fluid milk can lose riboflavin, which is vulnerable to light. Milk in glass bottles or containers is thus more vulnerable to losses than milk in plastic containers. Vitamin degradation can take place exponentially over time if fruits and vegetables are not consumed immediately after harvesting. Fat-soluble vitamins can be degraded in oxygen-containing environments.

Temperatures in storage areas also affect vitamin losses: the higher the temperature, the greater the loss. Up to 30 to 40 percent of certain water-soluble vitamins, particularly vitamin C, can be lost in one day at room temperature. Nutrient losses are usually proportional to water loss for many fruits and vegetables. Thus, it is advisable to store fresh vegetables in opaque, airtight containers, as well as chilling them immediately after receipt. Trimming, cutting, or peeling vegetables can also have an adverse effect. Some vegetables, like potatoes, have the largest concentration of vitamin C in the layer just below the skin. The outer cabbage leaves, with dark green colors, have more vitamin C, carotene, and vitamin K than the inner ones. The leaves of spinach may contain more vitamins than the stems. Thus, skins, peels, leaves, and so on should be carefully discarded to avoid nutrient losses. As a general rule, any vitamin that is vulnerable to air or oxygen will be partially destroyed if cut or chopped. The smaller the cuts, the larger the surface area and the greater the exposure to oxygen. The media in which fruits and vegetables are stored or prepared also affect nutrient retention. Soaking results in the loss of water-soluble vitamins and minerals, which leach into the water. Thus, peeled vegetables soaked in water can lose vitamins. The drying or dehydration of foods may also result in the loss of vitamins, particularly the water-soluble ones.

Freezing involves lowering the temperatures of stored foods, which control enzyme and microorganism activities. Freezing itself is a nutrient-conserving process; however, nutrients are vulnerable when frozen products are thawed.

Fermentation does not have a drastic effect on nutrient content, and some fermented products have the same amounts of vitamins and minerals as non-fermented products. In some foods, the medium used for fermentation can have an impact; for example, in foods that are fermented in a salt solution or pickled, water-soluble vitamins are lost. Also, brine or a salt solution increases the sodium content of foods. In some fermented or sprouted foods, the vitamin content may increase.

Chemical additives in foods may also have adverse or beneficial effects on nutrient content. MSG adds sodium to foods, and BHA and BHT (antioxidants) protect vitamins vulnerable to oxygen. Baking powder and/or baking soda, which are used as leavening agents in baked goods, can destroy the thiamin in many food products.

In foodservice operations, particularly those in institutions, food is held on steam tables until served. The heat on the steam table or under the lamp can reduce the nutrient content of foods. Considerable loss of water-soluble vitamins can occur in foods left for a long period of time. Up to 40 percent of fat-soluble vitamins and 75 percent of water-soluble vitamins can be lost during preparation and service. It is advisable to serve foods as soon as they are cooked or reheated.

To preserve nutrients in foods as well as to provide nutritious meals, foodservice managers should be aware of the nutrients as well as the conditions that can destroy them. From the back to the front of the house, every step should be evaluated carefully to assess its impact on nutrients. Generally, foods should be prepared properly and cooked at optimum temperatures for as short a period of time as possible. Extra holding during storage, preparation, and service should be reduced to a minimum. Increased nutrient quality of the products will translate into greater profitability for any type of foodservice operation and will result in consumer satisfaction. General guidelines for nutritional preparation of foods are presented in Table 13.6.

Table 13.6   Factors in Food Preparation from Nutritional Point of View

General	Meat and Meat Products	Vegetables and Fruits	Breads and Cereals	Dairy Products
Controlling Caloric Contents				
• Use low-fat products • Avoid deep-fat frying and use baking • Use vegetable oils • Use margarine • Cut portion sizes	• Broil meats rather than frying • Trim visible fat • Remove fat by skimming from soups and sauces • Use lean meats • Remove skin from poultry	• Replace frying by baking • Avoid using fat or fat-containing dressings • Steam vegetables for a short period • Enhance flavors with mixing different vegetables and herbs	• Use less fat in preparation • Use margarine in baking products • Avoid using sugar for baking • Use fruit spreads or low-calorie spreads	• Use low-fat dairy products • Use plain fat-free yogurt • Replace whole milk with skim milk or low-fat milk in recipes
Reducing Fat and Cholesterol				
• Use baking, broiling, steaming, or grilling rather than frying • Avoid animal shortenings • Use margarine or vegetable oils	• Broil or roast meats • Remove fat from stocks, soups, and sauces • Trim visible fat • Use lean meats • Avoid organ meats	• Do not use butter for seasoning vegetables and fruits • Limit the fat used in sauces • Use herbs and fruit juices for seasoning	• Use whole-grain cereals and breads • Avoid pastries and products made with butter • Use vegetable oils instead of animal shortenings • Reduce the amount of fat used in baking	• Replace butter with vegetable oils or margarines • Use low-fat cheese • Use skim or low-fat milk
Increasing Starch and Fiber Contents				
• Use whole-grain cereal products • Add fruits and vegetables (without removing the skin, if possible) • Add beans, peas, and lentils to menus • Add fat-free nuts and legumes	• Combine grain products with meats • Provide fiber-containing vegetables in casseroles • Combine legumes and grains with meats	• Provide salads with fiber-rich vegetables • Serve fruits and vegetables with the skin on, if possible • Steam vegetables for a short period of time just before service • Add bran to salads, soups, and sauces as a topping	• Use whole-wheat flour instead of refined flour • Use bulgar, barley, brown rice, and other high-fiber cereals • Add bran to recipes when possible • Add high-fiber fruits and nuts to baked products	• Add fruits or brans to yogurt • Add nuts to dairy products • Avoid high-fat dairy products

Table 13.6 *(Continued)*

General	Meat and Meat Products	Vegetables and Fruits	Breads and Cereals	Dairy Products
Reducing Sugar Content				
• Reduce the use of sugar in recipes • Use flavorings, spices, and honey for sweetness • Use sugar substitutes wherever feasible	• Use sugar-free accompaniments with meat dishes	• Use fresh fruits • Use sugar-free jams and jellies • Combine diferent types of fruits to provide flavor	• Reduce or eliminate sugar in baked products • Combine fruits with baked products to provide sweetness	• Reduce sugar in desserts made from milk products • Use different flavors and fruits in yogurt, milk shakes, and other dairy products
Reducing Salt Content				
• Offer low-salt options • Reduce the salt in recipes • Use ingredients that contain little or no salt • Use spices, herbs, and fruit juices to enhance flavors	• Use ingredients with a low-salt content • Reduce salt in batters or breading used for meats • Use reduced-sodium soy sauce in recipes • Avoid the use of MSG or marinades high in sodium	• Use low-sodium sauces and dressings with salads or vegetables • Use herbs or sodium in combination with vegetables	• Use little salt with pasta or pasta products • Use little or no salt in preparing rice • Avoid using salt in baked products	• Additives containing sodium should be checked before using dairy products • Use yogurt or sour cream to enhance salty flavor

Chapter 14

SPECIAL DIETS AND NUTRITIONAL NEEDS

Nutritional needs vary with age and other health conditions. It is important for foodservice managers to understand nutritional needs at different stages of life for planning menus and serving foods. In this chapter, essential information is provided to foodservice managers to facilitate menu planning. Nutritional requirements during various phases of the life cycle, and points to consider in planning and serving meals, will be discussed.

NUTRITION DURING PREGNANCY

The RDAs for all nutrients increase during pregnancy. The nutrients that must increase 50 percent or more include protein, vitamin D, iron, folacin, calcium, phosphorus, and magnesium. Energy needs increase by about 15 percent. The increasing amount of body tissue during pregnancy increases the BMR, and therefore more kcalories are required by the body. Extra energy is needed particularly during the last two trimesters. Essential nutrients such as calcium, iron, sodium, potassium, folacin, and vitamin B_{12} are important for the development of bones, blood, and other tissues. These nutrients must be added via foods or provided as supplements. However, caution is necessary because excessive amounts of some of these nutrients can have adverse effects. This factor is especially important when planning vegetarian diets during pregnancy. Enough extra energy, protein, vitamins, and minerals are needed during this stage of the life cycle. Folacin is required for normal cell division in the fetus; iron is needed to produce blood for both the mother and baby and for the development of the placenta and other tissues. The pregnant woman's diet should be well balanced even if nutrient supplements are used. Also, this is not a time for dieting or starving.

Additional milk, meat, vitamin C–containing foods, vegetables, and grain products are recommended. Extra caloric intake, which may be about 300 kcalories per day, is recommended. If a meal is well balanced, most of the nutrients can be included. Pregnant women who are on vegetarian diets should pay special attention to the intake of vitamin B_{12}, which is found in milk, eggs, cheese, and meats. This need can be met by supplementation. The additional nutritional requirements for pregnant women compared to those of nonpregnant women are shown in Table 14.1. Note the increase in all the nutrients, particularly protein, vitamin C, folacin, iron, vitamin B_6, calcium, phosphorus, magnesium, and zinc. Folacin is needed for the growth of cells and because of the increase in blood volume that occurs during pregnancy. Iron is also needed for the formation of blood. Vitamin A promotes the growth and health of cells and tissues. Getting enough folate or folic acid is necessary, especially during the first three months of

Table 14.1   RDAs for Nonpregnant Women (Aged 25 to 50 Years) Compared to Those of Pregnant and Lactating Women

Nutrient	Women Aged 25 to 50 Years	Pregnant	Lactating 1st 6 Months	Lactating 2nd 6 Months
Protein (g)	50	+10	+15	+12
Vitamin A (μg RE)	800	+0	+500	+700
Vitamin D (μg)	5	+5	+5	+5
Vitamin E (mg α-TE)	8	+2	+4	+3
Vitamin K (μg)	65	+0	+0	+0
Vitamin C (mg)	60	+10	+35	+30
Thiamin (mg)	1.1	+0.4	+0.5	+0.5
Riboflavin (mg)	1.3	+0.3	+0.5	+0.4
Niacin (mg NE)	15	+2	+5	+5
Vitamin B_6	1.6	+0.6	+0.5	+0.5
Folate (μg)	180	+220	+100	+80
Vitamin B_{12} (μg)	2	+0.2	+0.6	+0.6
Calcium (mg)	800	+400	+400	+400
Phosphorus (mg)	800	+400	+400	+400
Magnesium (mg)	280	+40	+75	+80
Iron (mg)	15	+15	[a]	[a]
Zinc (mg)	12	+3	+7	+4
Iodine (μg)	150	+25	+50	+50
Selenium (μg)	55	+10	+20	+20

[a] Although additional iron intake may be necessary during this stage, it cannot be acquired through the diet; therefore, supplementation is needed.

pregnancy. The increased need for vitamin C can be met very easily by providing fruits and vegetables that contain this vitamin. Vitamin C also helps the body absorb iron from plant sources. Eating good sources of vitamin C, such as citrus fruits and juices, broccoli, tomatoes, and kiwi, with meals also facilitates the absorption of iron present in these foods. Zinc, another mineral recommended during pregnancy, can be provided by foods of animal origin, such as meat, seafood, whole-grain products, and poultry. Vitamin D helps the absorption of calcium needed during pregnancy. An extra serving of vitamin D–fortified milk can fill this need. Minerals are needed for bones and teeth. They also complement the functions of protein and vitamins. Calcium and iron are the two minerals that require special attention during pregnancy. Consuming enough calcium during pregnancy helps to prevent osteoporosis in later stages of life. Dairy products can provide the extra calcium. Also, calcium-fortified foods such as juices, cereals, and breads can be added to meals. Another nutrient that is essential during pregnancy is water. As part of the body's transportation system, water helps to carry the nutrients that must pass from the mother to the baby. At least 8 to 12 cups of water is recommended. For pregnant teenagers, nutritional requirements are especially important.

Alcoholic beverages, caffeine, and smoking should be avoided. There may be an urge for certain types of foods, such as ice cream and pickles, as well as other food cravings. Conversely, certain foods may become distasteful to some pregnant women. Constipation may also become a problem during this stage; therefore, fiber should be included in the diet. Nausea, changes in taste and smell, constipation, and heartburn are common problems during pregnancy and should be considered while planning diets. The nutrient needs during pregnancy and lactation can be met by a well-balanced diet with enough variety to suit individual tastes.

Due to the increase in the BMR during pregnancy, it takes about 300 extra calories per day for the development of a healthy baby. Carbohydrates should be the main source of energy, saving protein for other bodily functions. Carbohydrate-rich foods include fruits, bread, cereals, pasta, rice, potatoes, legumes, and corn.

Tips for Selecting Healthy Foods During Pregnancy

Healthy food choices during pregnancy are essential, first, for getting adequate nutrition and, second, to control weight gain. Keeping these goals in mind, the following guidelines should be considered in planning meals for consumers during this stage of life.

Protein Foods

- Select poultry and fish often, and avoid breaded and fried methods of preparation.
- In addition to traditional meat entrees, include legumes, grains, and dairy products as sources of protein.
- Choose only the leanest cuts of meats and trim any visible fat.

- Bake, broil, poach, or simmer rather than fry.
- Avoid processed meats.

Milk Products

- Use nonfat or low-fat milk and yogurt.
- Limit the use of cheeses and, if possible, use part-skim milk cheeses.
- Limit the use of sweetened milk products such as fruit-flavored yogurts, chocolate milk, custard, ice cream, and pudding.

Breads, Cereals, Grains

- Use whole-grain breads, cereals, and grains such as whole-wheat bread, oatmeal, brown rice, and whole-grain pasta and crackers.
- Limit the use of sweetened breads and cereals.
- Limit the use of products made with added fat (granola, crackers, croutons, muffins, pancakes, and waffles).

Fruits and Vegetables

- Use raw vegetables and fruits as snacks.
- Choose fruits rather than juices so that fiber can be included.
- Limit the use of sweetened fruits and juices.
- Limit the use of sauces, butter, or margarine products with fruits and vegetables.
- Avoid fried vegetables such as french fries and hashed browns.
- Assorted fruits and vegetables should be used in all areas of menu, including appetizers, salads, entrees, side dishes, and desserts.

Fats and Sweets

- Low-fat diet salad dressings, mayonnaise, and margarines should be used as much as possible.
- Fats such as butter and other saturated fats should be avoided.
- Fried snacks and fast foods should be avoided.
- Sweets such as candy, cakes, cookies, and pies should be avoided or restricted.
- Sweetened beverages should be restricted.

NUTRITION DURING LACTATION

The need for most nutrients increases during breast-feeding. Extra nutrients needed during different stages of lactation are shown in Table 14.1. Calcium and protein intake must be increased. Three to four calcium-rich foods should be added daily. Vegetables and fish also provide calcium. Vitamins B$_{12}$ and D are also necessary.

NUTRITION DURING CHILDHOOD AND ADOLESCENCE

Growing children have extra nutritional needs. Food habits and preferences also become evident at this time and have an impact on children's nutritional intake. Pre-schoolers also become attached to particular foods. All food groups should be included in their meals so that they become used to them. Vegetables and fruits, in particular, should be introduced at this stage. Foods should also be easy to chew, and strongly flavored, although spicy foods should be avoided. Small, bite-sized foods are also preferred, as are finger foods and crackers. As children approach school age, they become ready to accept more varieties of food. Developing or providing good snack choices at this stage is important. Such snacks can include fresh fruits and vegetables, juices, breads, popcorn, muffins, biscuits, milk, yogurt, cheese, sliced meats and poultry, and eggs. All children up to age ten need to eat small amounts of food frequently throughout the day. Snacking may be necessary between meals. Snacks as well as meals should provide all nutrients, especially calcium, iron, and zinc. Fortified milk and dairy products can be added to children's meals as good sources of calcium. This nutrient pattern should be continued until adolescence.

After pregnancy and lactation, nutrient needs increase most during adolescence. Many physiological, sociological, and emotional changes are taking place that have an impact on nutritional status during this period. Eating disorders also create problems at this stage since proper nutrition is needed for growth. Rigorous dieting and overeating can both result in serious health problems and risks from a nutritional point of view. Irregular meals and snacking are common due to changes in social, school, and after-school activities. Ready-to-eat foods and snacks such as cookies, chips, french fries, and soft drinks are commonly consumed. Although minimum recommendations are similar to those for adults, certain nutrients should be given special attention when formulating a healthy meal plan. The nutrients most important for adolescents are iron, folacin, and vitamin A. Meats are particularly important since iron intake is low in this age group, especially in girls. Inadequate milk or other dairy products in the diet may lead to calcium deficiency. Several other products that adolescents like can be added to meals, such as pizza, macaroni and cheese, pasta with cheese, yogurt, ice cream, custards, and milk shakes. In addition to dairy products, meats, poultry, fish, eggs, legumes, and dried fruits should be added to provide iron and vitamin A. Leafy green vegetables and complex carbohydrates have a variety of nutrients. Liver provides vitamin A and folacin. Iron from plant foods can be made more available by serving these foods with a vitamin C source such as orange juice. To control caloric intake, low-fat milk products and other low-fat or fat-free foods should be included. Particular attention should be paid to snacks. Nutritious snack choices include fresh fruits, fresh vegetables, crackers, pita pockets stuffed with cheese/vegetables, low-fat yogurt, cottage cheese, and dried fruits and nuts. The menu should feature foods that are attractive, interesting, filling, and preferably accompanied by special beverages like orange juice, milk, ice cream, and diet carbonated drinks. For adolescents, salads, vegetables, and low-calorie menu items are particularly attractive.

NUTRITION FOR THE ELDERLY

As people grow older, they use less energy or calories than during the younger years. Basic body processes start using less energy at a slower rate, and daily activities decrease. The reduced need for calories, however, does not mean a reduced need for nutrients. Nutrients are still required while reducing the caloric intake. Also to be considered are the physiological, social, and economic needs of the elderly. Among the factors that affect the food habits and preferences of elderly persons are loneliness; diminished taste and olfactory sensitivity; physiological changes; anxiety; depression; dental problems; rigid food habits; lack of mobility; lack of nutritional knowledge; resistance to change; fear of going out; economic status or financial constraints; and health problems. Consideration should be given to these factors when planning menus and foodservice facilities intended for the elderly. Many elderly persons are confined to their homes, nursing homes, convalescence centers, and other institutional foodservice establishments; therefore, menu planning from a nutritional point of view is very important. Often, eating out may be a social rather than a physiological need. It can eliminate boredom, help pass the time, and provide a change of atmosphere. Food thus becomes an important reason for elderly persons to dress up and spend some time outside of their place of residence. They prefer easily chewable, tasty, and relatively inexpensive foods. Several factors need to be considered when providing foods and services to these patrons. One consideration is portion sizes. Medium-sized to small servings are normally preferred. Foods should be attractive and of desirable texture since these persons often have a diminished appetite. Heavy meals are generally avoided, particularly for dinner—the main meal usually being lunch. Fried foods and dairy products are frequently avoided. The elderly prefer foods that are cooked simply, with few spices, and semiliquid foods such as soups, stews, or casseroles. It is advisable to add soft-textured fresh fruits and vegetables to their meals whenever possible. Frequent criticisms of contemporary meal patterns may be expected since their food habits are set and it is difficult to introduce new foods to them. Monotony in menu items should be avoided as much as possible.

Tips for Planning Meals for the Elderly

- Fat intake should be moderate and foods that belong in the tip of the Food Guide Pyramid should be used sparingly.
- Foods with complex carbohydrates, such as bread, cereal, pasta, rice, vegetables, and beans, supply many nutrients as well as fiber.
- Fiber-rich foods especially should be included in the diet.

- Small portions of meat, poultry, and fish are good sources of protein that can be served in bite-sized pieces. Milk, cheese, and yogurt can be provided, either alone or mixed into other foods as ingredients.

- Calcium plays a very important role even at this stage of life. It helps keep the bones healthy, reducing the risk of osteoporosis. With age, the body does not absorb calcium from food as well as in earlier stages of life.

- Vitamin D is also needed at this stage; it can be provided by milk and other dairy products.

- Special attention should be paid to providing vitamin A, folic acid, vitamin B_{12}, and zinc.

- Water should be included in order to prevent dehydration, constipation, and kidney problems.

- In general, a well-balanced diet should consist of a variety of foods that are nutrient dense rather than those providing empty calories. Foods should be selected from different categories listed in the Food Guide Pyramid, minimizing the use of sodium and fat. Foods should be presented in an attractive form to make them more appealing.

NUTRITION FOR ATHLETES

With so many persons engaged in athletic activities, it is important to provide meals with appropriate nutritional contents. This knowledge is important for managers of school, college, and university foodservice operations; sports arenas; fitness centers; spa resorts; hotels; and other recreational facilities. Although the discussion in this section focuses on athletes, the factors discussed also apply to those who undertake other types of heavy physical activities.

Whether physical activity is due to daily work, recreational, or health reasons, it puts extra demands on the body. More energy and fluids are lost, and extra stress affects muscles, joints, and bones. One of the most important requirements to keep in mind is the replenishment of calories lost during athletic activities. The most important fuel for these activities should come from carbohydrates. These are stored as glycogen, which acts as fuel for immediate use during muscle activity. As discussed earlier, the use of carbohydrates or fats for energy spares the use or misuse of protein. During intense athletic activity, extra oxygen is needed by muscle cells. When the need for oxygen cannot be met, glucose is broken down anaerobically, and converted to pyruvic acid and finally to lactic acid. The accumulation of lactic acid causes muscle fatigue. When carbohydrate stores are depleted, exercise has to be decreased or discontinued. At this point, oxygen again becomes available and fat is used as the energy source. Thus, there is simultaneous use of aerobic and anaerobic activity, and the amount of oxygen available is very important. The capacity for oxygen consumption determines the amount of oxygen available to cells. As the intensity of activity increases, oxygen consumption by cells increases. A balance between the energy required and supplied should be achieved by alternating aerobic and anaerobic activities. Walking is an example of aerobic exercise, and weight lifting is an example of anaerobic exercise. For activities that require intense energy spurts, such as tennis, volleyball, baseball, weight lifting, and bowling, muscle glycogen is the main source of energy. For sports that require both intensity and endurance, such as basketball and football, muscle glycogen is used. For endurance activities, such as long-distance running or bicycling, the body first uses some glycogen and then relies on fat stores for fuel. Also, for endurance exercises, *carbohydrate loading* is done. Carbohydrate loading is stocking up of glycogen for use during endurance activity, since only a limited amount of glycogen is stored in the muscles and the liver. This is done by gradually increasing carbohydrate calories. When the body cannot get enough carbohydrates and fats, as in persons on low-calorie diets, needed protein can be lost. With exercise, the body develops enzymatic activity, which facilitates the burning of fats. Thus, well-exercised bodies not only store more glycogen but also burn fat more efficiently.

When planning meals for athletes, the nature and extent of the activity should be considered. A variety of foods should be selected from each food group listed in the Food Guide Pyramid. The consumption of calories with exercise also increases, depending on the intensity of activity. Foods should contain considerable amounts of carbohydrates with natural sugars. Natural sugars are found in fruits, fruit juices, and vegetables. Although refined simple sugars such as those found in candy, cakes, pastries and soft drinks are carbohydrates, they are not preferable. Most carbohydrate foods selected should contain complex carbohydrates, which are typically found in pasta, vegetables, whole-grain bread, cereal products, dried beans, peas, oats, corn, and rice. With an increase in physical activity, provision of fluids becomes very important. A lot of water is lost from the body with heavy physical activity and needs to be replenished. Dehydration can result in loss of endurance and strength. Water as a part of blood helps to carry the oxygen and glucose needed by muscles. Blood also helps to remove wasteful by-products from muscles. Fluid loss decreases the blood volume and puts an extra strain on the heart, which is striving to supply oxygen to the muscle cells. Fluids also cool the body by reducing the heat produced during exercises. Sweat evaporates on the body surface, producing a cooling effect. The fluid lost as sweat has to be replenished. Thus, drinking plenty of fluids is necessary before, during, and after any physical activity. Although cool water is sufficient, fluids can also be provided by fruit juices, sports drinks, and all other types of beverages. Sport drinks normally contain carbohydrates in the form of simple sugars, which supply energy. Some of them also supply electrolytes, which are lost during exercise. Vitamins are not lost through sweat, so there is no need to provide them through drinks.

Tips for Planning Meals for Athletes

- Menu items should be planned to meet the caloric needs of athletes. Most of the calories should come from carbohydrates found in foods made with or provided with breads, grains, cereals, and pastas. Specific foods include wild rice, whole-wheat breads, pita bread, oatmeal, and crackers. Also included are raw fresh fruits, fresh vegetables, baked potato, celery, and broccoli. Legumes such as chickpeas, kidney beans, split peas, pinto beans, black beans, and lentils also provide complex carbohydrates. About 60 to 65 percent of the total calories in meals should come from carbohydrates.

- Although fat is also needed for energy, there is no need to add extra fat to the diet. The general requirement of having no more than 30 percent of total calories from fat and no more than 10 percent from saturated fat also applies to meals for athletes.

- Adequate sources of protein should be present in all meals, although there is no need to increase the amount of protein in foods. Roughly 15 to 20 percent of the calories should come from protein. Low-fat protein foods should be selected since fat is not the most essential provider of energy. The recipes in general should be high in carbohydrates, moderate in protein, and low in fat.

- Eating a wide variety of foods will also provide necessary vitamins and minerals.

- Fluids and electrolytes should be included in meal plans. Enough fluids should be provided with meals, possibly with the electrolytes sodium, chloride, and potassium. Since enough sodium can be taken through daily meals, it is not necessary to add extra sodium. Potassium can be provided by fruits and vegetables.

- Iron in the diet is necessary since it is part of the red blood cells that carry oxygen to different body cells. Physical performance can be adversely affected in the absence of iron. Good sources include lean red meat, dark turkey meat, legumes, clams, oysters, and iron-fortified cereals.

- Since calcium is helpful in building and maintaining strong bones, it should be included in meals.

- The Food Guide Pyramid should be followed, selecting foods from different groups based on the needs of athletes discussed earlier. It should be considered that it is the number of calories that increase based on the endurance or nonendurance sports without a significant change in the other nutrient requirements.

- Some sports, like football, require weight gain, which can be achieved by providing extra calories from foods. An active athlete can easily consume over 4000 calories per day. These can be provided by eating frequent meals, increasing portion sizes, providing between-meal snacks, and getting most of the extra energy from nutrient-dense, high-carbohydrate foods. Good choices for snacks include bagels, crackers, fruit bars, and fresh fruits.

- Meals should be served at least three hours before athletic events. Plenty of cool liquids should be provided.

- After events, high-carbohydrate foods should be provided to restore the lost glycogen.

- Carbohydrates can be easily supplied for breakfast by including whole-grain breads, muffins, and hot and cold cereals, as well as fresh fruits and yogurt.

Fats, including butter and margarine, should be restricted. Tomato and other vegetable-based sauces should be used on pasta rather than cheese or cream-based toppings. Egg whites can replace whole eggs in some breakfast preparations.

- The general guidelines for nutritional meals should be followed. Baking or broiling should be used rather than frying.

NUTRITION FOR VEGETARIANS

Vegetarians have different motives. There is no single vegetarian eating pattern. For some, vetegarianism is a way of eating; for others, it is a complete lifestyle. There are also different restrictions based on the beliefs of vegetarians. In general, vegetarian meals exclude foods from animal sources such as meat, poultry, and fish. Instead, foods from plant sources such as vegetables, fruits, legumes, nuts, and grains are used. Some vegetarians eat dairy products and eggs, avoiding only meat and fish. Very few vegetarians avoid all food of animal origin. Based on food preferences, vegetarians can be classified as **lacto-ovo-vegetarians** (lacto = milk; ovo = egg), who select a diet with eggs and dairy products but no meat, poultry, or fish; **lacto-vegetarians,** who avoid meat, poultry, fish, and eggs but eat dairy products; **strict vegetarians,** or **vegans,** who eat no animal products, including meat, poultry, fish, eggs, milk, cheese, and other dairy products; **semivegetarians,** who avoid only selected kinds of meat, fish, and poultry; **macrobiotic vegetarians,** who progress through ten dietary stages, starting as widely inclusive and then becoming increasingly restricted; and **fruitarians,** who include fruit, nuts, honey, and/or olive oil. This exclusion also applies to ingredients made from animal products, such as lard, butter, and margarine. Some vegetarians follow a vegetarian diet much of the time and eat meat, poultry, and fish occasionally, whereas others totally eliminate red meats.

Although vegetarian diets are low in fat and high in fiber, they do not necessarily ensure a healthy eating style. Vegans are at special risk since they do not eat any foods of animal origin, which are primary sources of certain vitamins that cannot be obtained from plant foods, such as vitamin B_{12}, vitamin D, calcium, iron, and zinc. Careful meal planning is needed to overcome some of the drawbacks of excluding foods of animal origin. In fact, vetegarianism may lead to severe malnutrition if precautions are not taken. A vegetarian eating style can also be high in calories, high in fat and cholesterol, and low in fiber. It may not provide adequate amounts of nutrients. However, if carefully selected, vegetarian diets can provide enough energy and nutrients. These diets are usually high in fiber and complex carbohydrates, low in fat, and adequate in protein.

Since vegetarian diets provide enough proteins, adequate protein intake is not a problem in menu planning. The amount and quality of protein, however, are concerns, since animal products provide better-quality protein. Providing essential amino acids is also a problem. This involves combining major sources of vegetable protein from different plant sources. Also, for vegans, vitamin B_{12} is a concern. For vegan meals, alternative sources of this vitamin must be found. Products fortified with vitamin B_{12} should be considered, or it can be provided by vitamin supplementation. These fortified products include vegetarian or meatless burgers, cereals, meat analogues, and soy milk. Some seaweeds and yeast are also sources of vitamin B_{12}; however, the amount available may not be enough. Another vitamin of concern is vitamin D. This is not a problem if dairy products are included in the diet. Vitamin D–fortified products are available and can be added to vegetarian meals. Again, for vegans, alternative sources fortified with vitamin D should be considered. Calcium is another nutrient that may be lacking in vegan diets. It can be obtained from products derived from plant sources, including tofu processed with calcium, calcium-fortified soy beverages, broccoli, sunflower seeds, nuts, legumes, okra, rutabaga, dried figs, tortillas made from lime-processed corn, calcium-fortified orange juice, and calcium-fortified cereals.

Iron can also be a concern in vegetarian diets planned for children, women, and during pregnancy and lactation. Foods of plant origin contain nonheme iron. However, it is not absorbed as well as the heme iron obtained from meats and other foods of animal origin. Plant sources of food that contain iron include legumes; iron-fortified breads; iron-fortified cereals; tofu; some dark-green vegetables, such as spinach and beet greens; prune juice; and dried fruits. To help the absorption of iron, vitamin C–rich foods such as citrus fruits and juices, broccoli, tomatoes, and green peppers are necessary. For semivegetarian meals, adding meat dishes once in a while may provide heme iron from animal sources. Another nutrient that may be of concern in vegetarian meals is zinc. This is not a problem for lacto-ovo-vegetarians since milk, cheese, eggs, and yogurt supply adequate amounts. Foods of plant origin such as whole-wheat bread, whole grains, legumes, tofu, and nuts also provide zinc.

Calcium-rich foods should be added to vegetarian meals during pregnancy and lactation, along with vitamin B_{12} supplementation. Iron and folic acid should be provided by including leafy vegetables, legumes, fruits, wheat germ, yeast breads, and some fortified cereals. A variety of foods should be included to provide enough vitamins, minerals, and other nutrients.

Tips for Planning Vegetarian Meals

- The Food Guide Pyramid should be the guide in planning vegetarian meals and modifying menus.
- Whole-grain products, breakfast cereals, pasta, or brown rice should be included in every meal.
- Grain dishes can be important menu items and can be provided in large quantities. Rice, rice pilaf, noodles, barley, brown rice, and so on can be used to supplement main dishes.
- Different types of bread, such as tortillas, pita bread, chapatis, naan, and bagels, can be included to provide variety.

- Various spices can be added to vegetable dishes. In fact, more spices can be used in vegetarian dishes than in meat dishes.

- Stuffed vegetables (such as eggplant, bell peppers, and cabbage) with shredded vegetables, meat analogues, yogurt, and tofu are examples of the types of foods that can be provided.

- Fortified foods, particularly cereals, should be selected. Rice, flours, breads, and breakfast cereals are all available with fortified nutrients.

- Select vegetables that are good sources of calcium and iron. Complement vegetables that are high in vitamin C with plant sources of iron.

- Meals should be planned with different types and colors of vegetables. In addition to providing contrast and appeal, this ensures the inclusion of different types of nutrients.

- Fruits can be used in whole or in part and in different combinations as desserts and snacks. Fruits are also good sources of vitamin C.

- Legumes should be included as meat alternatives. They provide protein, complex carbohydrates, and iron.

- Include nuts, seeds, and seed spreads. Sesame seed spreads, for example, can be used with different types of breads.

- Herbs and spices can be added to enrich the flavor of vegetarian dishes. Soybean products in different forms also provide variety. Tofu, tempeh, cooked beans, nuts, and sesame seeds can be used in stir-fried dishes.

- Select a reliable source of vitamin B_{12}, such as fortified cereals, soy beverages, and a vitamin D supplement.

- Pasta sauces and pizza toppings can be made with vegetables and fruits, which can be used in different preparations.

- Tofu, soy milk, soy cheese, soy yogurt, and other soy products can be used in place of dairy products.

- Suggested daily servings are for breads, cereals, rice, and pasta—6 or more servings; for vegetables—4 or more servings; for legumes and other meat substitutes—2 to 3 servings; fruits—3 or more servings; dairy products—up to 3 servings; and eggs—optional.

NUTRITION AND SPECIAL DIETS

In earlier chapters, various nutrients, their role, and how to control them to maximize health benefits were discussed. In the following paragraphs, points to consider in planning special meals will be discussed. They focus on preparing meals for healthy persons and are not intended for therapeutic diets, which are beyond the scope of this chapter. Also, only important special diets are included, giving salient features and hints that should be considered when planning them.

Low-Fat Diets

- All visible fat should be trimmed from fat-containing foods such as meats and skimmed from liquid foods such as stews and sauces.
- Substitute or supplement meats with other foods such as vegetables, grains, and dairy products.
- Remove the skin from poultry before cooking.
- Purchase and use lean meats. Loin and round cuts of meat have less fat.
- Select meats that are low in fat, such as seafood, to alternate with other meats on the menu.
- Choose low-fat or nonfat dairy products that are fortified with nutrients. This will reduce the fat content without decreasing the calcium or vitamin content.
- Use less fat and oil in cooking. This reduction should involve all aspects of cooking, from greasing the pans to using them as ingredients or spreads.
- Nonfat or low-fat products should be purchased whenever possible.
- Use baking and broiling rather than frying.
- Herbs and spices can be used to flavor foods when fats have been reduced.
- Reduce the portion sizes of foods that contain fat and cholesterol.
- Evaluate recipes and meals to provide no more than 30 percent of the calories from fats.
- Refer to food fact labels when selecting foods that may contain fat.
- Use liquid vegetable oils whenever possible. Try using polyunsaturated or monounsaturated oil in recipes requiring butter or animal shortening.
- To control cholesterol, use fewer whole eggs and egg yolks. Egg whites or egg substitutes can take the place of whole eggs in baked goods.
- Assess the fat content when organ meats are used. As a general rule, reduce the use of organ meats with high cholesterol, such as liver.

Fiber-Rich Diets

Fiber-rich foods should be included in healthy meals, as well as for certain medical conditions. It is advisable to provide 20 to 35 grams of fiber daily in meals for healthy persons.

- Include a variety of foods, ensuring that they contain both soluble and insoluble fiber.
- Select high-fiber foods as both meals and snacks. Raw vegetables and fruits can be selected for different meals.
- Bran cereal and fiber-rich foods should be selected for breakfast or other meals. Bran can be added to baked goods and salads.

- Use whole-grain products such as breads, cereals, buns, bagels, pasta and other baked goods that have bran.
- Substitute whole-wheat flour for regular flour in baked goods. Replace low-fiber or refined ingredients with high-fiber ingredients in recipes whenever possible without sacrificing quality.
- Legumes are good sources of fiber and can be included in different forms in menus. They also provide flavor, nutrients, and variety.
- Providing fresh fruits and vegetables in meals adds fiber. If possible, the edible skin should be left on in such fruits as kiwi, peaches, and figs.
- Fruits and vegetables should be cooked with edible skin on, such as baked potatoes.
- Use the peel and pulp of fruits in drinks and baked products.

Low-Sodium Diets

- Select foods on the basis of sodium content and reduce the use of foods that contain indigenous or added sodium.
- Addition of fresh fruits and vegetables to meals controls the sodium content of meals since they generally are low in sodium.
- Use herbs, spices, vinegar, and fruit juices instead of table salt.
- Reduce the use of table salt in preparation and at the table.
- Use lightly salted or unsalted prepared foods in foodservice operations.
- Reduce the use of MSG and other additives containing sodium.
- Sodium is also added to some baking sodas, baking powder, and meat tenderizers; labels should be checked for their presence.
- Sodium is used in different forms as food additives in prepared foods and beverages. Food fact labels should be checked.

Foods and Nutrients for Sensitive Persons

Some people have food intolerances or food allergies for different metabolic reasons. These should be considered in providing meals.

Lactose-Reduced or Lactose-Free Diets

- Select lactose-reduced or lactose-free foods.
- Select calcium-rich foods that are low in lactose. Cheese products and other dairy foods containing lactose should be checked and those low in lactose selected.
- Reduce the portion sizes of foods that contain lactose.
- Prefer dairy foods with active cultures such as selected yogurts and buttermilk. They are easier to digest since the cultures help the digestion of lactose.

- Select calcium-rich foods other than dairy products, such as dark green leafy vegetables, broccoli, greens, sardines, and other calcium-fortified foods.

Other Food Sensitivities and Allergies

- Gluten intolerance is an intestinal disorder in which the body cannot digest gluten, a protein component in grains. Gluten normally breaks down into two substances, gliadin and glutenin, by metabolic processes. Gliadin damages the lining of the small intestine (where absorption of nutrients takes place) in persons with gluten intolerance. This results in malnutrition if grain products are excluded from the diet. Wheat, rye, oats, and barley are commonly used grains that contain gliadin. Although some grains, such as rice and corn, contain gluten, they do not have gliadin. For those with gluten intolerance, use of these grains should be reduced or eliminated. Among the grains listed above, wheat is most commonly used in foodservice operations; its elimination can be a problem when planning menus. Gliadin is also used as a food additive. Thus, gliadin-free grains and food ingredients should be used. Also, gliadin-free flours should be used in place of wheat flour in food preparation. Corn, rice, soy, tapioca, and potato flours can be used as substitutes.

- Some commonly used food additives belong to the sulfite group. Some persons are sensitive to sulfites; this should be verified. Sulfites are commonly used in fruits and vegetables to prevent certain foods from browning. They are also used in fermented foods. Sulfites are listed on food fact labels as sodium sulfite, potassium bisulfite, or potassium metabisulfite. They can result in severe, sometimes life-threatening, reactions in sensitive persons. Food labels should be checked and sulfite-containing foods or ingredients eliminated.

- MSG is another ingredient that can cause a sensitivity reaction. As mentioned earlier, MSG is a flavor enhancer used in different foods. Also, as the name implies, it contains sodium. Foods containing MSG should be restricted and other flavorings used instead.

Chapter 15

MANAGEMENT AND MARKETING FROM A NUTRITIONAL POINT OF VIEW

The success of providing a nutritional menu in any foodservice operation depends on effective management and marketing. All foodservice management involves the utilization of six resources: human power, money, material, time, machinery, and methods. Different definitions of management focus on the following factors: (1) management has goals to fulfill; (2) management has to utilize all available resources in the most efficient manner; (3) management has to be active at all times; and (4) management should coordinate the efforts of all persons directly involved. Keeping this in mind, this chapter will focus on the management of preparing and serving nutritious meals. The resources available in any type of foodservice operation have to be managed effectively to achieve the desired goals. The mission and the goal of foodservice operations should be based on the demands of market segments. In making management decisions, these demands should be taken into consideration. The goals of the organization should be based on solid nutritional principles. The various functions of management to be considered in serving nutritious meals will now be briefly discussed.

The mission of any organization should be clearly set and followed. The goal of providing healthy meals should be clearly indicated in the mission statement of the organization, which should be conveyed to every worker. Management functions are (1) decision making, (2) planning, (3) organization, (4) communication, (5) direction, and (6) controlling. This mission should also be considered in every *decision-making* process. *Planning* is another important management function in developing a course of action to meet the desired goal. The questions that need to be answered include the following: Will the patrons prefer a fixed menu or choices? How can specific menus be introduced? What type of clientele can be attracted? What changes will be necessary to offer healthy menu choices? One of the most important plans of a foodservice organization is the menu plan, which should establish nutrition as a major goal. Good plans are clear, concise, complete, and specific to the objectives to be achieved. If nutrition is the primary concern, then it should be easily understood by all concerned. This requires proper training of both employees and management in the nutritional aspects of menus. Plans that are well thought out and executed should produce the desired results. Once the plans are finalized, they should be conveyed to everyone in the organization. Normally, an organization chart shows the functions and levels of activities to be carried out by different individuals. This chart shows the flow of authority and consequently the distribution of responsibility and accountability. The organization should therefore include trained nutritionists and dietitians in key positions to provide technical assistance. Another function of management is *communication*. This keeps the entire organization functioning smoothly and unites all the workers. Every critical aspect of the focus on nutrition should be conveyed to all concerned. Communications should be well planned and delivered in the most appropriate way. Open communication between management and employees is desirable. Management should be willing to listen to all concerns of the employees, as well as convey effectively the motivation behind major decisions. Some points to consider while communicating, either orally or in writing, are these:

1. Plan the message. Gather all points to be mentioned and select the main idea of the message carefully.

2. Select the most appropriate time for communicating.

3. Begin the message with words that will draw the attention of the receiver.

4. Clarify and outline what needs to be discussed at the beginning.

5. Personalize the message as much as possible.

6. Use words that are commonly understood by the receiver. This is particularly important when technical information on nutrition is included in the communication.

7. Cite examples whenever possible to clarify statements and enable the receiver to relate to them.

8. Anticipate questions and objections, and be prepared to answer them satisfactorily and politely.

9. Provide ample time for communication and pay attention to receivers' comments.

10. Repeat and close with an emphasis on the key points of the message.

Management must also ensure that the organization's activities are properly *directed*. Finally, there should be enough *controls* to fulfill the organization's goals, as well as to maintain the quality of foods and service. The menu is one of the major instruments of control; it is commonly said that any foodservice operation "starts with a menu and ends with a menu." The menu determines the labor, food, service, facility, equipment, and other systems that need to be set in operation, as well as the controls needed for proper functioning.

HUMAN RESOURCE MANAGEMENT

Job descriptions and specifications should also reflect the nutritional significance of the organization's goals and objectives. Each job that is needed should be analyzed by obtaining all pertinent information about the components of the job. A *job description* is a list of duties and responsibilities indicating the skills required. Things to be included in the job description include the job title; location; summary of work; duties; machines, tools, or equipment involved; materials used; supervision required; work conditions; and desired controls. A *job specification* is a statement or list of the minimum standards that an applicant must meet to qualify for a particular job. It normally includes education, experience, training, physical efforts, judgment, abilities, skills, responsibilities, and communication skills. Job descriptions and specifications are helpful in recruitment, training, accountability, and distribution of responsibilities. After careful recruitment, orientation and training must be provided.

TRAINING

The most important challenge for the management is to train the employees; this is essential for successful implementation of the nutritional program. A well-trained employee is more likely to be motivated. Training also reduces employee turnover. The orientation should involve a tour of the facility and information related to the job. The organization's goals and objectives should also be explained at this point. Orientation should be followed by training, which can be done either by a manager, a supervisor, a senior employee, or a training specialist. Training the new employee is an investment and should be done in a way that yields maximum benefits over the long term. On-the-job demonstrations and hands-on experience are important. Training programs should be carefully planned and should include all components of the operation. There are two important components in a training program: (1) providing instructions pertaining to nutritional knowledge and (2) developing the required skills. Instruction should include all aspects of foodservice operations, from the back of the house to the front. All systems throughout the operation should be included. The **training program** should be carefully designed, with measurable objectives. It should be flexible and suitable for the ability of the trainees. Although the training program can vary in length and content, the following list describes the components of a comprehensive training program. Not all the parts may be applicable; the training program will depend on the responsibilities of the individuals. The training program can be customized, selecting the most applicable components. The following program is typical of all types of foodservice operations; however, the emphasis in each part should be on the nutritional aspects.

PART ONE: Introduction

Mission and goals of the organization

Description of the nutritional concepts

Historical development of the operation

Organization charts and administration

Roles and responsibilities

PART TWO: General Rules

Quality expectations

Customer relations

Policies and procedures

Controls and inspections

Warranties

Maintenance requirements

PART THREE: Menus and Menu Plans

Nutrition basics

Menu details

Nutritional components of menus

Recipes

Ingredients

Computerized menu controls

Menu design and display

Mechanics of menu planning

PART FOUR: Equipment Use and Care

Types of equipment

Equipment use and precautions

Equipment cleaning

Equipment maintenance

PART FIVE: Food Purchasing

Specifications

Commodities used

List of supplies

Purchase of nutritional ingredients

Supplier list

Buying methods

Regulatory agencies and controls

Ethics in buying

PART SIX: Receiving and Storage

Mechanism of receiving

Storage requirements

Issuing supplies

Inventory procedures

Inventory controls

Inventory levels

PART SEVEN: Sanitation Requirements

Food-borne illnesses and precautions

Safe handling of foods

Safe temperatures and critical points

Personal hygiene and procedures

PART EIGHT: Food Preparation

Procedures for preparing different items

Critical control points

Time and temperature controls

Precautions in preparation

Quality of the products

Production forecasting and planning

Production schedules

Control of leftovers

PART NINE: Delivery and Service of Foods

Portion control methods

Consumer aspects

Dress code and personal appearance

Service procedures

Delivery procedures

PART TEN: Financial Aspects

Cost sheets

Financial statements

Food costing

Labor costing

Profit-and-loss statement

Balance sheets

Other financial controls

PART ELEVEN: *Management*

Employee–supervisor relations

Recruitment and selection procedures

Performance appraisal

Employee rules, grievance procedures, and turnover

Motivation and job enrichment

Control of human resources

Stress management

PART TWELVE: *Foodservice Operation*

Opening and closing procedures

Register operation

Maintenance and housekeeping

Handling consumers' complaints and special requests

Lighting, signage, and atmosphere control

PART THIRTEEN: *Marketing*

Advertising policies and procedures

Promotional activities

Community programs

Long- and short-term marketing plans

PART FOURTEEN: *Maintenance*

Utilities control

Fire protection

Pest control

Garbage disposal

Parking and drive-in maintenance

Electrical, mechanical, construction, and plumbing maintenance

Heating, ventilation, and air conditioning

Alarms, locks, and security

Audio-video control

Repairs and maintenance

Computer problems and controls

Training programs should also be evaluated and, if necessary, revised from time to time. All operational aspects should be adequately covered and updated, particularly the use of software for the nutritional assessment of recipes and menus. It is also important to get feedback from trainees. All necessary handouts should be provided to employees. The latest training methods and audiovisual aids should be used to increase the effectiveness of the training program. Role playing and hands-on experience are particularly important.

For the nutritional program to be effective, back-of-the-house and front-of-the-house staff should be well trained since the preparation and marketing of the program will depend on their performance. In fact, all employees should understand the healthful characteristics of the menu, and should be well aware of the items that are different from those on conventional menus and the reasons for them. Those in charge of **purchasing, receiving, storage, and issuing** should be trained to understand the ingredient and product specifications. They should understand the alternative items that can be substituted. They should also be able to check the overall quality of the products, particularly from the nutritional point of view. The products should be stored in a way that preserves their nutrient quality, and any conditions that will have an adverse impact should be eliminated. An understanding of temperature, humidity, and food safety is essential.

The **kitchen staff** should have a strong basic knowledge of nutrition and should be well aware of the recipes. Critical factors in prepreparation and preparation of menu items from a nutritional point of view should be clearly explained. All methods of preparation and service should be included in the training program. The kitchen staff should be trained in ingredient substitutions and in selecting appropriate, nutrient-rich foods. They should also have enough practice in the preparation of recipes and should be able to modify recipes whenever necessary. They should also be trained in the use of different equipment and preparation methods when recipes need to be modified. Training for special products, methods, and procedures should be included. Also important is the art of food display and plate presentation. In short, after the training, the kitchen staff should be able to prepare healthy meals.

The training of the **waitstaff** is also very important. They play an important role in describing, suggesting, and selling nutritionally rich menus. Cleanliness, uniforms, and employee attitudes should reflect the philosophy of the organization and can be an important aspect of the success of the operation. The waitstaff should be trained to be good salespersons by knowing the menu items; their ingredients and cooking methods; and the number of calories and nutrients provided by every item. They should be able to communicate effectively with the guests. It may be preferable to provide the waitstaff with a fact sheet or a small brochure describing different terms and special items that they should know pertaining to the menus. Some of the questions frequently asked by guests are

Table 15.1   Questions Commonly Asked About Healthy Menus

- What are the special healthy items?
- Which are the low-calorie products?
- What type of shortening (vegetable or animal) is used?
- Are the vegetables fresh or frozen?
- How big are the servings?
- Will the dressing be available on the side?
- How is the food cooked?
- Are low-fat or nonfat dairy products used?
- Is butter or margarine used in preparation?
- What cut of meat is used?
- Are egg yolks or eggs used in any way?
- Do the products contain sodium or related items?
- Are artificial sweeteners, flavors, or other additives used?
- Do the products contain milk, wheat, eggs, nuts, and/or shellfish?
- What are the primary ingredients in the item?
- Is the skin removed from poultry before or after cooking?
- Are fruits available for dessert?
- Can smaller servings of desserts be served or extra plates provided?
- Are there special symbols for healthy menu items?

listed in Table 15.1. The waitstaff should have the following information so that it can be conveyed to the consumers:

1. Menu suggestions including special items for diets such as low-calorie, low-sodium, low-fat, low-cholesterol, and high-fiber diets.

2. Ingredients, cooking methods, preparation methods, and portion sizes of the items being served.

3. The nutritional contents of menu items and any special nutrients provided by different items.

4. Special items included on the menu and substitutions/accommodations that can be made if the patrons so desire.

5. Information about items that complement menu choices and the various serving sizes.

6. Suggestive selling of the items that are prepared for nutritional menus.

Waitpersons should also be trained to report feedback from the guests so that popular items can be offered and to make any necessary menu modifications. Feedback is helpful in assessing guests' attitudes, opinions, and desires, all of which are helpful in future planning and changes.

Theoretical training should be followed by on-the-job training. The training program should be an ongoing activity for permanent as well as new employees.

MARKETING A NUTRITIONALLY HEALTHY MENU

The success of any foodservice operation depends on the extent to which consumers' demands and needs are fulfilled. Consumers are primarily interested in the menu, but other factors such as convenience, atmosphere, entertainment, and service are also important. Because consumers represent all age groups, their needs and wants have individual variations, which may be physiological or sociological in origin. It is important to understand the market segment before marketing the plan. Some of the major market segments and their demands and needs will now be briefly described.

Children

Children are a special and important group of consumers since they are major influences when families eat out. They are also influenced by advertisements and promotions, particularly when gifts and discounts are offered. Special programs and facilities can be planned for them, such as birthday parties, animatronics, computer games, videos, and gift packages. These can also be used to provide nutritional information and to promote nutritional menus. Children prefer relatively fast service and like menu items that are not usually served at home. It is important to know that usually the children themselves, not their parents, decide what they order, a fact to be considered when planning promotions.

Adolescents

Adolescents are a special group of consumers in whom physiological changes are taking place and social awareness is developing. They often become calorie-conscious at this stage and should be particularly interested in healthy menus. They often prefer salads, vegetables, and low-calorie items. On the other hand, some prefer hamburgers and french fries only, requiring special attention. Special dietary foods like vegetarian dishes, baked potatoes, salad bars, yogurt, and vegetables are becoming more popular among this group. Special entertainment and sports bars are also gaining popularity. Since this group is often health conscious, special menus should be planned for them.

Young and Middle-Aged Adults

Adults are a very broad category of consumers with different needs. Single persons who are largely independent often eat away from home, as many of them do not care to cook or clean up after meals. They also prefer to eat at restaurants where they will not feel lonely. They often look for a variety of food choices on menus. Ethnic foods that are hard to prepare at home, like Chinese or Mexican foods, are preferred. Singles also buy many take-out and home-delivered meals. Married persons have other priorities. Because marital status greatly affects economic status, the frequency with which married couples eat out depends on the total income of the family, the time available for outings, and the family size. Most families prefer visiting mid-priced restaurants, primarily for economic reasons. They should also be provided with healthy choices on menus.

Senior Citizens

Senior citizens represent a distinct group of consumers and an ever-growing market for the foodservice industry. Factors that affect their food habits and preferences were discussed in Chapter 14. Eating out is often a satisfying social event as well as a physiological need. It can eliminate boredom, pass the time, and provide a change of atmosphere since elderly persons may live alone or spend many hours with few persons. They may also prefer convenience and often do not like to cook or clean up. They prefer tasty, easily chewable foods, possibly due to a diminishing sense of taste and dental problems. Economy is often a main concern because many of them have limited incomes. They often avail themselves of special offers, coupons, early-bird specials, and other bargains. They prefer staying for long periods of time while eating and often patronize coffee shops, cafeterias, and food counters within malls or shopping centers. These places provide an appealing atmosphere by providing them with an opportunity to socialize. Soft-textured foods are preferred. Medium-sized to small portions are normally preferred, and older persons may order special menu items. Their big meal is usually lunch. Fried foods and dairy product are generally avoided. They like foods cooked with few spices and prefer such semiliquid foods as soups, stews, and casseroles. Comfort may be the single most important factor in the selection of a restaurant. Comfort may be derived from such factors as accessibility, a pleasant atmosphere in a dining area with bright lighting, little congestion and traffic, no waiting lines, an easy-to-read menu, provision of ambulatory facilities, a location within a mall or shopping center, good heating and/or air conditioning, cordial service, light entertainment, television, and newspapers. Elderly persons are loyal customers. Since eating out is influenced by weather conditions, the season may play an important role in the frequency of their decision to eat out.

Students

College students often prefer convenience when selecting restaurants, mainly because they may lack the time, the motivation, or the facilities to prepare meals. A limited budget influences their selection of eating places. Lack of transportation causes this group to patronize eating establishments close to the campus. They often visit local restaurants, particularly on weekends. High school students also prefer eating lunch out at places close to their school. This group may be the one most likely to use healthy menus. They are value conscious and seriously consider the quality and quantity of foods provided for the price. Consideration should be given to the fact that students love to eat out after supper or take foods away late at night.

Shoppers

Shoppers are another group that is growing in number. Since shopping is their primary motive, food becomes secondary, although at times shopping and dining may be combined. Since these consumers are interested in shopping, a convenient location of the restaurant is highly desirable. Fast service is also important, particularly during peak shopping hours and holiday seasons. In addition to shoppers, persons who work in or near shopping centers avail themselves of these restaurants, particularly during lunch time.

Workers

Both blue- and white-collar workers represent a loyal and growing class of consumers for many types of foodservice. Restaurants serving workers should be relaxing and have quick, efficient service, as there is a need to unwind quickly from the tensions of work. Many workers prefer to eat hot meals rather than a cold "brown-bag" lunch. They can also be attracted for both breakfast and lunch. Carry-out items for breakfast are also preferred.

Travelers

Persons travel for business, leisure, or family visits. Travel is at a peak during vacations, conventions, national holidays, other important events, and the summer months. Certain travelers, like truck drivers, are constantly on the move and are therefore a continuous source of income for restaurants on or near highways. Many restaurants try to attract these year-round customers by providing efficient and pleasant service or discounts. Discounts may also be extended to bus drivers when they bring in busloads of passengers. As far as travelers are concerned, their main incentive is to take a break; a fine dining experience is not their motive. Cleanliness and uncrowded conditions are preferred. Facilities such as adequate washrooms and dining areas are considered when selecting food stops while traveling. Hot foods and cold beverages, generally carbonated, are preferred. Most of the items selected are medium-priced, particularly the foods purchased by those traveling in large groups or with families. Restaurants at bus stops, train stations, or airports cater to the needs of passengers, their guests, and transportation personnel. Passengers in transit find these restaurants convenient because they often have time between transportation connections; passing time is often the primary motive of these consumers. They may want to sit in a convenient and comfortable spot and refresh themselves while waiting for their next ride or flight. Some prefer a drink or two between flights. The crew and staff of the transportation services are among the regular customers of these foodservice operations. When flights are delayed or canceled, airlines depend on these restaurants to provide food and beverages to detained passengers. Although these customers are not particular about menus, they prefer healthy foods, if available, and are willing to try new types of foods.

The marketing strategy should be based on the segment of the population to be served. Nutrition information is increasingly being used by different types of restaurants to promote lighter and healthier menu items. This information varies from restaurant to restaurant. Some franchisors and chain restaurants provide nutritional information on all the items they serve. Nutritional information in the form of labels is also provided by some restaurants. This information is displayed on menu boards, in brochures, or in printed menus, is posted, or is provided on request. Most fast-food restaurants provide more detailed nutritional information. An increased emphasis on nutrients is being demonstrated by restaurants and hotels. The caloric value of special items may be given, or special symbols such as a heart or an apple may be used to indicate healthy items. Sometimes the presence or absence of special ingredients is indicated.

Providing healthy menus with an emphasis on nutrition can be successful, particularly if special items are used. These restaurants can become popular as well as financially profitable. Nutrition information should be provided in an easy-to-understand way, focusing on nutrients that are needed by consumers. This information should be based on the market segments to which it is targeted, emphasizing the nutrition concerns and needs of the consumers. The foods provided should compete with other types of foods available in the market from the point of view of quality, quantity, and price.

PROMOTING NUTRITION

Special promotions should be based on specific objectives, such as increasing patronage, publicizing the restaurant, adding a new item, or increasing the sales of item(s). Promotion includes advertising (both verbal and written), which can be carried out by different means. Successful promotions are designed with a particular segment of the market in mind. They should be developed to take advantage of the special foods and services offered, with the intent of enhancing, modifying, or changing them. Creativity is a key to success in promoting. Management, employees, and guests can all be helpful in determining the type of promotion to be undertaken. Enough resources should be available for the promotion campaign. Careful planning should precede promotion, with enough time allocated for planning, execution, and evaluation.

Merchandising a Healthy Menu

Merchandising should be included in the formal plan of any foodservice operation. A healthy menu is itself an important merchandising medium. It should therefore reflect the organization's philosophy and policies about healthy foods. Merchandising should be carefully planned so that the menu items are based on these goals. Even the most creative, appealing, and nutritious menu will be ineffective if patrons are unaware of it. Communication between an operation and a guest occurs primarily through the menu. In addition to information provided to the waitstaff during training, other information can be printed in the menu and displayed within the eating area or made available on request. If healthy choices are included in a menu with other items, they should be clearly marked or designated. If many of the menu items are healthy, a separate menu or an insert can be used. The description of these items should be accurate and appealing. Avoid using any information that exaggerates or inappropriately describes menu items. Correct terminology should be used. According to FDA, certain terms describe different products, and they must be used appropriately. The information provided should be specific, concise, and descriptive. Avoid making any health claims, although the presence or absence of an ingredient can be emphasized. Do not provide information that is based on estimation, such as calorie contents, or provide any advice from a dietary point of view.

Consumers who are health conscious are looking for detailed information and may have additional questions. A common question is whether the vegetables or fruits are fresh. It will save a lot of time if the word *fresh* is used for the menu item or included in the description. Another popular question concerns portion sizes. An accurate description or a picture of the actual serving can address this concern. Some of the information that can be included in the printed menu is listed in Table 15.2. Commonly asked questions should be addressed satisfactorily. Symbols are often used to designate special healthy menu items, ranging from asterisks to hearts, apples, stars, and carrots. A "heart" symbol against menu items that are designed for health/heart-conscious consumers is often used. Footnotes are also helpful in communicating information on healthy foods.

Promotion can be done by the waitstaff, paid advertising, providing free samples, point-of-sale messages, endorsements by professional organizations, and by word of mouth. Some of these methods are described below. The waitstaff is very important in selling the menu items, and should be encouraged and trained to sell. Advertisement using all available media is another form of promotion, which may involve newspapers, radio, TV, the Internet, coupons, and so on. Point-of-sale messages can be provided by graphics, flyers, table tents, clip-ons, posters, electronic flashes, product wraps, packaging, napkins, and other such means. Endorsements from organizations, dietitians, physicians, and fitness/sports specialists are also used. Finally, word of mouth is an influential form of promotion.

Creative merchandising often involves state-of-the-art computerized techniques. Graphics should be chosen to enhance the message, and a variety of audiovisual techniques should be used. Merchandising should be planned to highlight the nature of the food items. In short, promotion and marketing should be carefully planned, executed, and periodically evaluated for its success. Pricing

Table 15.2 Suggested Menu Description for Healthy Items

- A descriptive name of the item (e.g., "Fresh baked catfish," not "Catch of the day")
- Accompaniments (fresh vegetables, brown rice, whole-wheat rolls, etc.)
- Portion size (indicate options if available)
- The grade and quality of the product, if applicable
- Processing and prepreparation method (peeling, skinless, breaded, trimmed, etc.)
- Preparation/cooking method(s) (indicate if alternative cooking methods are available)
- Fats/shortening/alcohol used in preparation or during service
- Special spices or ingredients used
- Types of dairy or egg products used
- The way it is served (on a hot skillet, flambéd, etc.)
- Nutrient values and calorie contents (if available)

should also be competitive. Market analysis should be conducted from time to time, and strategies should be based on strengths, weaknesses, threats, and opportunities. Problems should be paid special attention, and customer feedback should be taken into account in future planning. Menu items should be constantly changed based on consumer demand. The quality of the products and services is always important for the success of any foodservice operation.

Appendix A

RETENTION OF NUTRIENTS

Appendix A.1 Retention[a] of Nutrients in Cooked Vegetables (Percent)

Food	Calcium	Iron	Magnesium	Phosphorus	Potassium	Sodium	Zinc	Copper	Manganese
Potatoes									
Prepared from raw									
Baked in skin	100	100	100	100	100	100	100	100	100
Boiled in skin	95	95	95	95	90	95	95	95	95
Boiled, without skin	95	95	95	95	90	95	95	95	95
Fried	100	100	100	100	100	100	100	100	100
Hashed-brown[b]	95	95	95	95	90	95	95	95	95
Mashed	95	95	95	95	90	95	95	95	95
Scalloped and au gratin	100	100	100	100	100	100	100	100	100
Prepared from frozen									
French fried, heated	100	100	100	100	100	100	100	100	100
Baked, stuffed, heated	100	100	100	100	100	100	100	100	100
Hashed-brown	100	100	100	100	100	100	100	100	100
Sweet potatoes									
Prepared from raw									
Baked in skin	100	100	100	100	100	100	100	100	100
Boiled in skin	95	95	95	95	90	95	95	95	95
Prepared from frozen									
Baked	100	100	100	100	100	100	100	100	100
Boiled	95	95	95	95	90	95	95	95	95
Tomatoes, prepared from raw, baked, boiled, or stewed	100	100	100	100	100	100	100	100	100
Vegetables, other than potatoes, sweet potatoes and tomatoes (cooked in small or moderate amount of water until tender)									
Prepared from raw, drained									
Greens, dark and leafy[c]	95	95	95	90	90	95	95	95	95
Roots, bulbs, other vegetables of high starch and/or sugar content[d]	95	95	95	90	90	95	95	95	95
Other[e]	95	95	95	90	90	95	95	95	95
Prepared from frozen, drained	95	95	95	90	90	95	95	95	95
Greens, dark and leafy[c]									
Roots, bulbs, other vegetables of high starch and/or sugar content[d]	95	95	95	90	90	95	95	95	95
Other[e]	95	95	95	90	90	95	95	95	95

Appendix A.1 *(Continued)*

Food	Ascorbic Acid	Thiamin	Ribo-flavin	Niacin	Pantothenic Acid[f]	Vitamin B_6	Folacin[g]	Vitamin A
Potatoes								
Prepared from raw								
Baked in skin	80	85	95	95	90	95	90	—
Boiled in skin	75	80	95	95	90	95	90	—
Boiled, without skin	75	80	95	95	90	95	75	—
Fried	80	80	95	95	90	95	75	—
Hashed-brown[b]	25	40	85	80	—	—	65	—
Mashed	75	80	95	95	90	95	75	—
Scalloped and au gratin	80	80	95	95	90	95	75	—
Prepared from frozen								
French fried, heated	50	75	95	95	90	95	75	—
Baked, stuffed, heated	80	85	95	95	90	95	80	—
Hashed-brown	80	80	95	95	90	95	80	—
Sweet potatoes								
Prepared from raw								
Baked in skin	80	85	95	95	90	95	90	90
Boiled in skin	75	80	95	95	90	95	90	85
Prepared from frozen								
Baked	80	80	95	95	90	95	80	90
Boiled	75	80	95	95	90	95	80	85
Tomatoes, prepared from raw, baked, boiled, or stewed	95	95	95	95	95	95	70	95
Vegetables, other than potatoes, sweet potatoes and tomatoes (cooked in small or moderate amount of water until tender)								
Prepared from raw, drained								
Greens, dark and leafy[c]	60	85	95	90	95	90	65	95
Roots, bulbs, other vegetables of high starch and/or sugar content[d]	70	85	95	95	90	95	70	90
Other[e]	80	85	95	90	90	90	70	90
Prepared from frozen, drained Greens, dark and leafy[c]	60	90	95	90	95	90	55	95
Roots, bulbs, other vegetables of high starch and/or sugar content[d]	70	90	95	95	90	95	70	90
Other[e]	80	90	95	90	90	90	70	90

[a] % true retention = $\dfrac{\text{Nutrient content per g of cooked food} \times \text{g of food after cooking}}{\text{Nutrient content per g of raw food} \times \text{g of food before cooking}} \times 100$

[b] Potatoes were pared, boiled, and held overnight before hashed-browning.

[c] Vegetables such as beet greens, Chinese cabbage, collards, mustard greens, spinach, Swiss chard, turnip greens, and other wild greens.

[d] Vegetables such as beets, carrots, green peas, lima beans, onions, parsnips, rutabagas, salsify, turnips, summer and winter squash, and other immature seeds of the legume group.

[e] Vegetables such as asparagus, bean sprouts, broccoli, brussels sprouts, cabbage, cauliflower, eggplant, kohlrabi, okra, and sweet peppers.

[f] Due to limited data, values are based on nutrient retention data from other cooked plant products.

[g] Values are based on limited data.

[h] Dashes denote lack of reliable data.

Source: USDA: *Composition of Foods: Vegetables and Vegetable Products.* Agriculture Handbook #8–11.

Appendix A.2 Retention of Nutrients in Cooked Fish[a,b]

Cooking Procedure	Thiamin	Riboflavin	Niacin	Pantothenic Acid	Vitamin B_6	Folacin	Vitamin B_{12}	Vitamin A
				Percent retained				
Dry heat								
Finfish:								
Less than 5% fat	90	95	95	90	90	90	90	90
More than 5% fat	95	100	100	90	90	90	75	85
Shellfish	85	95	95	80	90	85	85	95
Moist heat								
Finfish, more than 5% fat	90	100	95	90	90	90	95	95
Shellfish	95	100	95	95	95	90	100	95
Fried with coating								
Finfish, less than 5% fat	85	95	100	90	90	90	90	85
Shellfish	85	95	95	85	90	80	85	95

[a] Retention of minerals is 100 percent for all cooking procedures.

[b] Values developed for USDA food consumption surveys and based on data from National Food Processors Association studies.

Source: USDA: *Composition of Foods: Finfish and Shellfish Products.* Agriculture Handbook #8–15.

Appendix A.3   Retention of Nutrients in Cooked Separable Lean of Beef Products

Nutrients	Braised Mean (%)	Braised Standard Error (%)	Braised No. of Samples	Broiled Mean (%)	Broiled Standard Error (%)	Broiled No. of Samples	Roasted Mean (%)	Roasted Standard Error (%)	Roasted No. of Samples
Water	50	0.85	64	63	0.77	59	65	1.20	40
Protein	98	1.04	58	99	.99	56	99	1.65	38
Total Lipid 0-inch trim cuts	105	—	180	102	—	120	106	—	120
¼- and ½-inch trim cuts	117	—	227	109	—	165	118	—	149
Ash	65	1.87	45	87	1.10	48	84	1.81	35
Calcium	84	3.54	46	103	4.83	47	91	4.06	38
Iron	102	2.19	44	94	1.67	47	99	2.50	38
Magnesium	66	1.29	46	86	1.09	47	83	1.56	38
Phosphorus[a]	81	—	—	83	—	—	84	—	—
Potassium	57	1.21	46	83	1.10	47	80	1.54	39
Sodium	59	1.36	46	85	1.30	46	83	2.21	38
Manganese[b]	80	—	—	85	—	—	85	—	—
Thiamin	45	2.45	47	70	2.35	46	58	2.25	37
Riboflavin	86	3.22	32	92	1.77	35	98	2.89	26
Niacin	61	3.01	49	78	2.48	48	75	3.55	37
Pantothenic acid	69	5.21	8	79	3.03	4	97	5.70	4
Vitamin B_6	46	2.46	8	74	5.58	4	66	3.54	4
Folate	72	5.34	48	87	3.93	49	88	4.98	38
Vitamin B_{12}	67	3.69	49	75	2.89	50	72	2.55	41
Cholesterol	103	1.91	35	106	1.49	37	103	2.43	30

[a]Limited data available.
[b]Imputed.
Source: USDA: *Composition of Foods: Beef Products.* Agriculture Handbook #8–13.

Appendix B

DIETARY FIBER CONTENTS OF FOODS

Appendix B.1   Dietary Fiber Content of Selected Foods

Food	Measure	Total Weight (g)	Fiber Content (g)	% of Fiber Content
Fruits				
Apple, fresh, with skin	1 medium	138	3.7	2.68
Apple, cooked, peeled	1 medium	128	2.4	1.88
Banana	1 medium	114	2.7	2.37
Blackberries, fresh	¾ cup	108	3.7	3.42
Blueberries, frozen	½ cup	72	3.6	5.00
Cantaloupe	½ cup	80	0.6	0.75
Cranberries, fresh	½ cup	55	2.3	4.18
Figs, dried, cooked	½ cup	130	6.2	4.77
Figs, fresh	½ cup	100	9.2	9.20
Fruit cocktail, canned, water packed	½ cup	123	1.4	1.14
Guava, fresh	One	90	4.9	5.44
Grapes, green, seedless, fresh	½ cup	46	0.5	1.09
Mango, fresh, pulp	One	207	3.7	1.79
Orange, fresh	1 medium	131	3.1	2.37
Peach, fresh	1 medium	87	1.7	1.95
Peach, canned, water packed	½ cup	122	1.2	0.98
Peach, cooked	½ cup	130	3.2	2.46
Pear, fresh	1 medium	166	4.0	2.41
Pineapple, fresh	½ cup	76	0.9	1.18
Prunes, dried	½ cup	106	7.0	6.60
Raisins, seedless	½ cup	73	2.9	3.97
Raspberries, fresh	1 cup	123	8.4	6.83
Rhubarb, fresh	1 cup	122	2.2	1.80
Strawberries, fresh	1 cup	149	3.4	2.28
V-8 juice	½ cup	121	0.7	0.58
Vegetables				
Asparagus, cooked	½ cup	90	1.8	2.00
Beans, green, frozen, cooked	½ cup	68	2.2	3.24
Bean sprouts, fresh	½ cup	52	0.9	1.73
Broccoli, raw	½ cup	44	1.3	2.95
Brussels sprouts, cooked	½ cup	78	3.8	4.87
Cabbage, fresh	½ cup	35	0.5	1.43
Carrots, fresh	1 medium	72	2.2	3.06
Cauliflower, fresh	½ cup	62	1.7	2.74
Celery, fresh, diced	1 cup	120	2.0	1.67
Corn, whole kernel, canned	½ cup	82	1.6	1.95
Corn, whole kernel, frozen	½ cup	82	2.0	2.44
Cucumber, fresh	1 cup	104	0.8	0.77
Eggplant, fresh	1 cup	82	2.1	2.56
Green beans, canned	½ cup	120	2.0	1.67

Appendix B.1 *(Continued)*

Food	Measure	Total Weight (g)	Fiber Content (g)	% of Fiber Content
Vegetables (cont.)				
Lettuce, fresh	1 cup	55	0.7	1.27
Mushrooms, fresh	½ cup	35	0.8	2.29
Okra, fresh	1 cup	113	2.0	1.77
Onion, fresh, chopped	¼ cup	40	0.7	1.75
Peas, green, canned	½ cup	85	3.5	4.12
Peas, green, cooked	½ cup	80	4.4	5.50
Potato, sweet, flesh, cooked	⅓ cup	114	3.4	2.98
Potatoes, boiled, peeled	One	136	2.5	1.84
Pumpkin, fresh	1 cup	116	2.1	1.81
Radish, fresh	10	45	0.7	1.56
Spinach, frozen, cooked	½ cup	95	2.9	3.05
Squash, zucchini, fresh	½ cup	65	0.8	1.23
Tomato, fresh	1 medium	123	1.4	1.14
Tomato, cooked	½ cup	51	0.9	1.76
Turnip, cooked	½ cup	78	1.6	2.05
Yam, flesh only, cooked	⅓ cup	45	1.7	3.78
Zucchini, fresh	1 cup	130	1.6	1.23
Grains and Grain Products				
Bagel, plain	One	71	1.5	2.11
Barley, pearled, cooked	½ cup	79	3.0	3.80
Bran	1 cup	56	7.3	13.04
Bread, rye	1 slice	32	1.9	5.94
Bread, pita, white	½ pocket	30	0.5	1.67
Bread, pita, whole wheat	½ pocket	32	2.4	7.50
Bread, wheat	1 slice	25	1.1	4.40
Bread, white	1 slice	25	0.6	2.40
Bread, whole wheat	1 slice	25	2.2	8.80
Corn flakes	1 cup	30	1.0	3.33
Crackers, saltine	6	18	0.2	1.11
Crackers, wheat	5	9	0.6	6.67
Cream of wheat	1 cup	251	0.9	0.34
Flour, whole wheat	½ cup	60	7.3	12.17
Granola	¼ cup	48	1.1	2.29
Macaroni, white, cooked	½ cup	70	1.1	1.57
Macaroni, whole wheat, cooked	½ cup	70	3.1	4.43
Noodles, cooked	½ cup	80	0.9	1.13
Oatmeal, cooked	½ cup	117	2.0	1.71
Popcorn	1 cup	8	1.2	15.00
Rice Krispies	1 cup	24	0.8	3.33
Rice, puffed	1 cup	14	0.2	1.43

Appendix B.1 *(Continued)*

Food	Measure	Total Weight (g)	Fiber Content (g)	% of Fiber Content
Grains and Grain Products (cont.)				
Rice, brown, cooked	½ cup	98	1.8	1.84
Rice, white, cooked	½ cup	79	0.3	0.38
Shredded wheat	1 biscuit	21	2.3	10.95
Spaghetti, white, cooked	½ cup	70	2.2	3.14
Spaghetti, whole wheat, cooked	½ cup	70	3.2	4.57
Taco shell	2	26	2.1	8.08
Tortilla, corn	1	25	1.3	5.20
Tortilla, flour	1	35	1.1	3.14
Wheat bran	½ cup	28	3.6	12.86
Legumes				
Beans, black, cooked	½ cup	86	7.5	8.72
Beans, kidney, canned	½ cup	127	4.9	3.86
Beans, lima, cooked	½ cup	226	15.9	7.04
Chick peas, canned	½ cup	14	0.7	5.00
Garbanzo beans	½ cup	50	6.0	12.00
Kidney beans, cooked	½ cup	88	6.7	7.61
Lentils, cooked	½ cup	99	7.8	7.88
Lima beans, cooked	½ cup	85	4.5	5.29
Mung beans, cooked	½ cup	101	7.7	7.62
Navy beans, canned	½ cup	131	6.7	5.11
Peas, canned	½ cup	125	4.0	3.20
Pinto beans, cooked	½ cup	85	7.4	8.71
Snap beans, cooked	½ cup	63	2.0	3.17
Nuts and Seeds				
Almonds, slivered	½ cup	68	7.4	10.88
Brazilnuts	½ cup	70	4.0	5.71
Chestnuts, Chinese, raw	½ cup	62	1.9	3.06
Hazelnuts	½ cup	58	3.5	6.03
Peanuts, roasted	½ cup	73	5.9	8.08
Sesame seeds	¼ cup	36	4.2	11.67
Sunflower seeds	¼ cup	36	3.7	10.28
Walnuts	¼ cup	31	1.6	5.16

Note: Much of the information presented in this table is derived from USDA food composition tables. Calculations were made to show the comparison between different foods. However, this list is not exhaustive and keeps changing with advanced analytical techniques that become available.

Appendix B.2 Dietary Fiber Contents of Selected Cereal Grains and Pasta (g/100 g Edible Portion)

Food Item	Total Dietary Fiber (AOAC)
Cereal Grains	
Amaranth	15.2
Arrowroot flour	3.4
Barley	17.3
Barley, pearled, raw	15.6
Bulgur, dry	18.3
Corn bran, crude	84.6
Corn flour, whole-grain	13.4
Cornmeal	
Whole-grain	11.0
Degermed	5.2
Cornstarch	.9
Farina	
Dry	2.7
Cooked	1.4
Oat bran, raw	15.9
Oats, rolled or oatmeal, dry	10.3
Rice, brown	
Long-grain, raw	3.5
Long-grain, cooked	1.7
Rice, white	
Long-grain	
Regular, raw	1.0
Parboiled	
Dry	1.8
Cooked	.5
Precooked or instant	
Dry	1.6
Cooked	.8
Medium-grain, raw	1.4
Glutinous, raw	2.8
Rice bran, crude	21.7
Rice flour	
Brown	4.6
White	2.4
Rye flour, medium or light	14.6
Semolina	3.9
Tapioca, pearl, dry	1.1
Triticale	18.1
Triticale flour, whole-grain	14.6
Wheat bran, crude	42.4
Wheat germ	
Crude	15.0
Toasted	12.9
Wheat flour	
Whole-grain	12.6
White, all-purpose	2.7
Wild rice, raw	5.2

Appendix B.2 *(Continued)*

Food Item	Total Dietary Fiber (AOAC)
Pasta	
Macaroni (see Spaghetti)	
Macaroni, protein-fortified, dry	4.3
Macaroni, vegetable, dry	4.3
Noodles, egg	
Dry	2.7
Cooked	2.2
Spinach, dry	6.8
Noodles, Chinese, chow mein	3.9
Noodles, Japanese, Somen, dry	4.3
Spaghetti or macaroni	
Dry	2.4
Cooked	1.6
Spaghetti, spinach, dry	10.6
Spaghetti, whole-wheat, dry	11.8

Source: USDA: *Composition of Foods: Cereal Grains and Pasta.*
Agriculture Handbook #8–20.

Appendix B.3 **Total Dietary Fiber Content of Selected Nuts and Seeds (Amount in 100 g, edible portion)**

Food	Total Dietary Fiber (g)
Almonds, oil roasted, unblanched and blanched	11.2
Cashews, oil roasted	6.0
Coconut meat, raw	9.0
Filberts or Hazelnuts, oil roasted, unblanched	6.4
Mixed nuts, oil roasted, with peanuts	9.0
Peanuts	
Dry roasted	8.0
Oil roasted	8.8
Peanut butter	
Chunk style	6.6
Smooth style	6.0
Pecans, dried	6.5
Pistachio nuts, dried	10.8
Sunflower seed kernels, oil roasted	6.8
Sesame butter, Tahini	9.3
Walnuts	
Black, dried	5.0
English, dried	4.8

Source: USDA: *Composition of Food: Nuts and Seed Products.* Agriculture
Handbook #8–12.

Appendix B.4   Total Dietary Fiber Content of Selected Fruits and Fruit Juices (Amount in 100 g, edible portion)

Food	Total Dietary Fiber (g)
Apples, raw	
With skin	2.2
Without skin	1.9
Apple juice, unsweetened	0.1
Applesauce	
Sweetened	1.2
Unsweetened	1.5
Apricots, dried	7.8
Apricot nectar	0.6
Bananas, raw	1.6
Blueberries, raw	2.3
Figs, dried	9.3
Grapefruit, raw	0.6
Grapes, European type, raw	0.7
Kiwifruit, raw	3.4
Melons, cantaloup, raw	0.8
Nectarines, raw	1.6
Olives	
Green	2.6
Ripe	3.0
Oranges, raw	2.4
Orange juice, frozen concentrate	
Undiluted	0.8
Prepared	0.2
Peaches	
Raw	1.6
Dried	8.2
Pears, raw	2.6
Pineapple	
Raw	1.2
Prunes	
Dried	7.2
Stewed	6.6
Prune juice	1.0
Raisins	5.3
Strawberries	2.6
Watermelon	0.4

Source: USDA: *Composition of Foods: Fruits and Fruit Juices.* Agriculture Handbook #8–9.

Appendix B.5 Total Dietary Fiber Content of Selected Vegetables and Vegetable Products (Amount in 100 g, edible portion)

Food	Total Dietary Fiber (g)
Artichokes, raw	5.2
Beans, snap	
Raw	1.8
Canned	
Drained solids	1.3
Solids and liquid	0.8
Beets, canned	
Drained solids, sliced	1.7
Solids and liquid	1.7
Broccoli	
Raw	2.8
Cooked	2.6
Brussels sprouts, boiled	4.3
Cabbage, Chinese	
Raw	1.0
Cooked	1.6
Cabbage, red	
Raw	2.0
Cooked	2.4
Carrots	
Raw	3.2
Canned, drained solids	1.5
Cauliflower	
Raw	2.4
Cooked	2.2
Celery, raw	1.6
Chives	3.2
Corn, sweet	
Raw	3.2
Cooked	3.7
Canned	
Brine pack	
Drained solids	1.4
Solids and liquid	0.8
Cream-style	1.2
Cucumbers, raw	1.0
Lettuce	
Butterhead or iceberg	1.0
Romaine	1.7
Mushrooms	
Raw	1.3
Boiled	2.2
Onions, raw	1.6
Onions, spring, raw	2.4
Parsley, raw	4.4
Peas, edible-podded	
Raw	2.6
Cooked	2.8

Food	Total Dietary Fiber (g)
Peas, green, canned	
Drained solids	3.4
Solids and liquid	2.0
Peppers, sweet, raw	1.6
Pickles	
Dill	1.2
Sweet	1.1
Potatoes	
Raw	
Flesh	1.6
Baked	
Flesh	1.5
Skin	4.0
Boiled	1.5
French-fried, home-prepared from frozen	4.2
Hashed brown	2.0
Potato chips	4.8
Potato chips, formulated	3.6
Spinach	
Raw	2.6
Boiled	2.2
Squash	
Summer	
Raw	1.2
Cooked	1.4
Winter	
Raw	1.8
Cooked	2.8
Sweet potatoes	
Raw	3.0
Cooked	3.0
Canned, drained solids	1.8
Tomatoes, raw	1.3
Tomato products	
Catsup	1.6
Paste	4.3
Puree	2.3
Sauce	1.5
Turnip greens	
Raw	2.4
Boiled	3.1
Turnips	
Raw	1.8
Boiled	2.0
Vegetables, mixed, frozen, cooked	3.8
Watercress	2.3

Source: USDA: *Composition of Foods: Vegetables and Vegetable Products.* Agriculture Handbook #8–11.

NUTRIENT COMPOSITION OF FOODS

Source of this information is Home and Garden Bulletin #72, revised 1991, based on *USDA Nutritive Value of Foods* by Susan E. Gebhardt. Please refer to Appendix E for latest information that can be obtained electronically.

Item No.	Foods, approximate measures, units, and weight (weight of edible portion only)		Water	Food energy	Pro-tein	Fat	Fatty acids		
							Satu-rated	Mono-unsatu-rated	Poly-unsatu-rated
		Grams	Per-cent	Cal-ories	Grams	Grams	Grams	Grams	Grams

Beverages

Item No.	Foods, approximate measures, units, and weight	measure	Grams	Per-cent Water	Cal-ories Food energy	Grams Pro-tein	Grams Fat	Grams Satu-rated	Grams Mono-unsatu-rated	Grams Poly-unsatu-rated
	Alcoholic:									
	Beer:									
1	Regular----------------------	12 fl oz--------	360	92	150	1	0	0.0	0.0	0.0
2	Light------------------------	12 fl oz--------	355	95	95	1	0	0.0	0.0	0.0
	Gin, rum, vodka, whiskey:									
3	80-proof--------------------	1-1/2 fl oz-----	42	67	95	0	0	0.0	0.0	0.0
4	86-proof--------------------	1-1/2 fl oz-----	42	64	105	0	0	0.0	0.0	0.0
5	90-proof--------------------	1-1/2 fl oz-----	42	62	110	0	0	0.0	0.0	0.0
	Wines:									
6	Dessert---------------------	3-1/2 fl oz-----	103	77	140	Tr	0	0.0	0.0	0.0
	Table:									
7	Red------------------------	3-1/2 fl oz-----	102	88	75	Tr	0	0.0	0.0	0.0
8	White----------------------	3-1/2 fl oz-----	102	87	80	Tr	0	0.0	0.0	0.0
	Carbonated:[2]									
9	Club soda-------------------	12 fl oz--------	355	100	0	0	0	0.0	0.0	0.0
	Cola type:									
10	Regular--------------------	12 fl oz--------	369	89	160	0	0	0.0	0.0	0.0
11	Diet, artificially sweetened	12 fl oz--------	355	100	Tr	0	0	0.0	0.0	0.0
12	Ginger ale------------------	12 fl oz--------	366	91	125	0	0	0.0	0.0	0.0
13	Grape-----------------------	12 fl oz--------	372	88	180	0	0	0.0	0.0	0.0
14	Lemon-lime------------------	12 fl oz--------	372	89	155	0	0	0.0	0.0	0.0
15	Orange----------------------	12 fl oz--------	372	88	180	0	0	0.0	0.0	0.0
16	Pepper type-----------------	12 fl oz--------	369	89	160	0	0	0.0	0.0	0.0
17	Root beer--------------------	12 fl oz--------	370	89	165	0	0	0.0	0.0	0.0
	Cocoa and chocolate-flavored bev-erages. See Dairy Products (items 95-98).									
	Coffee:									
18	Brewed----------------------	6 fl oz---------	180	100	Tr	Tr	Tr	Tr	Tr	Tr
19	Instant, prepared (2 tsp powder plus 6 fl oz water)---------	6 fl oz---------	182	99	Tr	Tr	Tr	Tr	Tr	Tr
	Fruit drinks, noncarbonated:									
	Canned:									
20	Fruit punch drink------------	6 fl oz---------	190	88	85	Tr	0	0.0	0.0	0.0
21	Grape drink------------------	6 fl oz---------	187	86	100	Tr	0	0.0	0.0	0.0
22	Pineapple-grapefruit juice drink--------------------	6 fl oz---------	187	87	90	Tr	Tr	Tr	Tr	Tr
	Frozen:									
	Lemonade concentrate:									
23	Undiluted-----------------	6-fl-oz can-----	219	49	425	Tr	Tr	Tr	Tr	Tr
24	Diluted with 4-1/3 parts water by volume---------	6 fl oz---------	185	89	80	Tr	Tr	Tr	Tr	Tr
	Limeade concentrate:									
25	Undiluted-----------------	6-fl-oz can-----	218	50	410	Tr	Tr	Tr	Tr	Tr
26	Diluted with 4-1/3 parts water by volume---------	6 fl oz---------	185	89	75	Tr	Tr	Tr	Tr	Tr
	Fruit juices. See type under Fruits and Fruit Juices.									
	Milk beverages. See Dairy Prod-ucts (items 92-105).									
	Tea:									
27	Brewed----------------------	8 fl oz---------	240	100	Tr	Tr	Tr	Tr	Tr	Tr
	Instant, powder, prepared:									
28	Unsweetened (1 tsp powder plus 8 fl oz water)--------	8 fl oz---------	241	100	Tr	Tr	Tr	Tr	Tr	Tr
29	Sweetened (3 tsp powder plus 8 fl oz water)-------------	8 fl oz---------	262	91	85	Tr	Tr	Tr	Tr	Tr

[1] Value not determined.
[2] Mineral content varies depending on water source.

							Vitamin A value						Item No.
Cho-les-terol	Carbo-hydrate	Calcium	Phos-phorus	Iron	Potas-sium	Sodium	(IU)	(RE)	Thiamin	Ribo-flavin	Niacin	Ascorbic acid	
Milli-grams	Grams	Milli-grams	Milli-grams	Milli-grams	Milli-grams	Milli-grams	Inter-national units	Retinol equiva-lents	Milli-grams	Milli-grams	Milli-grams	Milli-grams	
0	13	14	50	0.1	115	18	0	0	0.02	0.09	1.8	0	1
0	5	14	43	0.1	64	11	0	0	0.03	0.11	1.4	0	2
0	Tr	Tr	Tr	Tr	1	Tr	0	0	Tr	Tr	Tr	0	3
0	Tr	Tr	Tr	Tr	1	Tr	0	0	Tr	Tr	Tr	0	4
0	Tr	Tr	Tr	Tr	1	Tr	0	0	Tr	Tr	Tr	0	5
0	8	8	9	0.2	95	9	(1)	(1)	0.01	0.02	0.2	0	6
0	3	8	18	0.4	113	5	(1)	(1)	0.00	0.03	0.1	0	7
0	3	9	14	0.3	83	5	(1)	(1)	0.00	0.01	0.1	0	8
0	0	18	0	Tr	0	78	0	0	0.00	0.00	0.0	0	9
0	41	11	52	0.2	7	18	0	0	0.00	0.00	0.0	0	10
0	Tr	14	39	0.2	7	[3]32	0	0	0.00	0.00	0.0	0	11
0	32	11	0	0.1	4	29	0	0	0.00	0.00	0.0	0	12
0	46	15	0	0.4	4	48	0	0	0.00	0.00	0.0	0	13
0	39	7	0	0.4	4	33	0	0	0.00	0.00	0.0	0	14
0	46	15	4	0.3	7	52	0	0	0.00	0.00	0.0	0	15
0	41	11	41	0.1	4	37	0	0	0.00	0.00	0.0	0	16
0	42	15	0	0.2	4	48	0	0	0.00	0.00	0.0	0	17
0	Tr	4	2	Tr	124	2	0	0	0.00	0.02	0.4	0	18
0	1	2	6	0.1	71	Tr	0	0	0.00	0.03	0.6	0	19
0	22	15	2	0.4	48	15	20	2	0.03	0.04	Tr	[4]61	20
0	26	2	2	0.3	9	11	Tr	Tr	0.01	0.01	Tr	[4]64	21
0	23	13	7	0.9	97	24	60	6	0.06	0.04	0.5	[4]110	22
0	112	9	13	0.4	153	4	40	4	0.04	0.07	0.7	66	23
0	21	2	2	0.1	30	1	10	1	0.01	0.02	0.2	13	24
0	108	11	13	0.2	129	Tr	Tr	Tr	0.02	0.02	0.2	26	25
0	20	2	2	Tr	24	Tr	Tr	Tr	Tr	Tr	Tr	4	26
0	Tr	0	2	Tr	36	1	0	0	0.00	0.03	Tr	0	27
0	1	1	4	Tr	61	1	0	0	0.00	0.02	0.1	0	28
0	22	1	3	Tr	49	Tr	0	0	0.00	0.04	0.1	0	29

[3]Blend of aspartame and saccharin; if only sodium saccharin is used, sodium is 75 mg; if only aspartame is used, sodium is 23 mg.
[4]With added ascorbic acid.

Item No.	Foods, approximate measures, units, and weight (weight of edible portion only)		Water	Food energy	Pro-tein	Fat	Fatty acids		
							Satu-rated	Mono-unsatu-rated	Poly-unsatu-rated
	Dairy Products	Grams	Per-cent	Cal-ories	Grams	Grams	Grams	Grams	Grams
	Butter. See Fats and Oils (items 128-130).								
	Cheese:								
	Natural:								
30	Blue------------------------ 1 oz------------	28	42	100	6	8	5.3	2.2	0.2
31	Camembert (3 wedges per 4-oz container)----------------- 1 wedge--------	38	52	115	8	9	5.8	2.7	0.3
	Cheddar:								
32	Cut pieces---------------- 1 oz------------	28	37	115	7	9	6.0	2.7	0.3
33	1 in³-----------	17	37	70	4	6	3.6	1.6	0.2
34	Shredded------------------- 1 cup-----------	113	37	455	28	37	23.8	10.6	1.1
	Cottage (curd not pressed down):								
	Creamed (cottage cheese, 4% fat):								
35	Large curd--------------- 1 cup-----------	225	79	235	28	10	6.4	2.9	0.3
36	Small curd--------------- 1 cup-----------	210	79	215	26	9	6.0	2.7	0.3
37	With fruit-------------- 1 cup-----------	226	72	280	22	8	4.9	2.2	0.2
38	Lowfat (2%)---------------- 1 cup-----------	226	79	205	31	4	2.8	1.2	0.1
39	Uncreamed (cottage cheese dry curd, less than 1/2% fat)-------------------- 1 cup-----------	145	80	125	25	1	0.4	0.2	Tr
40	Cream----------------------- 1 oz------------	28	54	100	2	10	6.2	2.8	0.4
41	Feta------------------------ 1 oz------------	28	55	75	4	6	4.2	1.3	0.2
	Mozzarella, made with:								
42	Whole milk---------------- 1 oz------------	28	54	80	6	6	3.7	1.9	0.2
43	Part skim milk (low moisture)---------------- 1 oz------------	28	49	80	8	5	3.1	1.4	0.1
44	Muenster-------------------- 1 oz------------	28	42	105	7	9	5.4	2.5	0.2
	Parmesan, grated:								
45	Cup, not pressed down------ 1 cup-----------	100	18	455	42	30	19.1	8.7	0.7
46	Tablespoon---------------- 1 tbsp----------	5	18	25	2	2	1.0	0.4	Tr
47	Ounce-------------------- 1 oz------------	28	18	130	12	9	5.4	2.5	0.2
48	Provolone------------------- 1 oz------------	28	41	100	7	8	4.8	2.1	0.2
	Ricotta, made with:								
49	Whole milk---------------- 1 cup-----------	246	72	430	28	32	20.4	8.9	0.9
50	Part skim milk------------ 1 cup-----------	246	74	340	28	19	12.1	5.7	0.6
51	Swiss----------------------- 1 oz------------	28	37	105	8	8	5.0	2.1	0.3
	Pasteurized process cheese:								
52	American-------------------- 1 oz------------	28	39	105	6	9	5.6	2.5	0.3
53	Swiss----------------------- 1 oz------------	28	42	95	7	7	4.5	2.0	0.2
54	Pasteurized process cheese food, American -------------- 1 oz------------	28	43	95	6	7	4.4	2.0	0.2
55	Pasteurized process cheese spread, American------------ 1 oz------------	28	48	80	5	6	3.8	1.8	0.2
	Cream, sweet:								
56	Half-and-half (cream and milk) 1 cup-----------	242	81	315	7	28	17.3	8.0	1.0
57	1 tbsp----------	15	81	20	Tr	2	1.1	0.5	0.1
58	Light, coffee, or table------- 1 cup-----------	240	74	470	6	46	28.8	13.4	1.7
59	1 tbsp----------	15	74	30	Tr	3	1.8	0.8	0.1
	Whipping, unwhipped (volume about double when whipped):								
60	Light----------------------- 1 cup-----------	239	64	700	5	74	46.2	21.7	2.1
61	1 tbsp----------	15	64	45	Tr	5	2.9	1.4	0.1
62	Heavy----------------------- 1 cup-----------	238	58	820	5	88	54.8	25.4	3.3
63	1 tbsp----------	15	58	50	Tr	6	3.5	1.6	0.2
64	Whipped topping, (pressurized) 1 cup-----------	60	61	155	2	13	8.3	3.9	0.5
65	1 tbsp----------	3	61	10	Tr	1	0.4	0.2	Tr
66	Cream, sour---------------------- 1 cup-----------	230	71	495	7	48	30.0	13.9	1.8
67	1 tbsp---------	12	71	25	Tr	3	1.6	0.7	0.1

							Nutrients in Indicated Quantity						
Cho-les-terol	Carbo-hydrate	Calcium	Phos-phorus	Iron	Potas-sium	Sodium	Vitamin A value (IU)	Vitamin A value (RE)	Thiamin	Ribo-flavin	Niacin	Ascorbic acid	Item No.
Milli-grams	Grams	Milli-grams	Milli-grams	Milli-grams	Milli-grams	Milli-grams	Inter-national units	Retinol equiva-lents	Milli-grams	Milli-grams	Milli-grams	Milli-grams	
21	1	150	110	0.1	73	396	200	65	0.01	0.11	0.3	0	30
27	Tr	147	132	0.1	71	320	350	96	0.01	0.19	0.2	0	31
30	Tr	204	145	0.2	28	176	300	86	0.01	0.11	Tr	0	32
18	Tr	123	87	0.1	17	105	180	52	Tr	0.06	Tr	0	33
119	1	815	579	0.8	111	701	1,200	342	0.03	0.42	0.1	0	34
34	6	135	297	0.3	190	911	370	108	0.05	0.37	0.3	Tr	35
31	6	126	277	0.3	177	850	340	101	0.04	0.34	0.3	Tr	36
25	30	108	236	0.2	151	915	280	81	0.04	0.29	0.2	Tr	37
19	8	155	340	0.4	217	918	160	45	0.05	0.42	0.3	Tr	38
10	3	46	151	0.3	47	19	40	12	0.04	0.21	0.2	0	39
31	1	23	30	0.3	34	84	400	124	Tr	0.06	Tr	0	40
25	1	140	96	0.2	18	316	130	36	0.04	0.24	0.3	0	41
22	1	147	105	0.1	19	106	220	68	Tr	0.07	Tr	0	42
15	1	207	149	0.1	27	150	180	54	0.01	0.10	Tr	0	43
27	Tr	203	133	0.1	38	178	320	90	Tr	0.09	Tr	0	44
79	4	1,376	807	1.0	107	1,861	700	173	0.05	0.39	0.3	0	45
4	Tr	69	40	Tr	5	93	40	9	Tr	0.02	Tr	0	46
22	1	390	229	0.3	30	528	200	49	0.01	0.11	0.1	0	47
20	1	214	141	0.1	39	248	230	75	0.01	0.09	Tr	0	48
124	7	509	389	0.9	257	207	1,210	330	0.03	0.48	0.3	0	49
76	13	669	449	1.1	307	307	1,060	278	0.05	0.46	0.2	0	50
26	1	272	171	Tr	31	74	240	72	0.01	0.10	Tr	0	51
27	Tr	174	211	0.1	46	406	340	82	0.01	0.10	Tr	0	52
24	1	219	216	0.2	61	388	230	65	Tr	0.08	Tr	0	53
18	2	163	130	0.2	79	337	260	62	0.01	0.13	Tr	0	54
16	2	159	202	0.1	69	381	220	54	0.01	0.12	Tr	0	55
89	10	254	230	0.2	314	98	1,050	259	0.08	0.36	0.2	2	56
6	1	16	14	Tr	19	6	70	16	0.01	0.02	Tr	Tr	57
159	9	231	192	0.1	292	95	1,730	437	0.08	0.36	0.1	2	58
10	1	14	12	Tr	18	6	110	27	Tr	0.02	Tr	Tr	59
265	7	166	146	0.1	231	82	2,690	705	0.06	0.30	0.1	1	60
17	Tr	10	9	Tr	15	5	170	44	Tr	0.02	Tr	Tr	61
326	7	154	149	0.1	179	89	3,500	1,002	0.05	0.26	0.1	1	62
21	Tr	10	9	Tr	11	6	220	63	Tr	0.02	Tr	Tr	63
46	7	61	54	Tr	88	78	550	124	0.02	0.04	Tr	0	64
2	Tr	3	3	Tr	4	4	30	6	Tr	Tr	Tr	0	65
102	10	268	195	0.1	331	123	1,820	448	0.08	0.34	0.2	2	66
5	1	14	10	Tr	17	6	90	23	Tr	0.02	Tr	Tr	67

Item No.	Foods, approximate measures, units, and weight (weight of edible portion only)			Water	Food energy	Pro-tein	Fat	Fatty acids		
								Satu-rated	Mono-unsatu-rated	Poly-unsatu-rated
			Grams	Per-cent	Cal-ories	Grams	Grams	Grams	Grams	Grams

Dairy Products—Con.

	Cream products, imitation (made with vegetable fat):									
	Sweet:									
	Creamers:									
68	Liquid (frozen)------------	1 tbsp----------	15	77	20	Tr	1	1.4	Tr	Tr
69	Powdered------------------	1 tsp-----------	2	2	10	Tr	1	0.7	Tr	Tr
	Whipped topping:									
70	Frozen--------------------	1 cup-----------	75	50	240	1	19	16.3	1.2	0.4
71		1 tbsp----------	4	50	15	Tr	1	0.9	0.1	Tr
	Powdered, made with whole									
72	milk--------------------	1 cup-----------	80	67	150	3	10	8.5	0.7	0.2
73		1 tbsp----------	4	67	10	Tr	Tr	0.4	Tr	Tr
74	Pressurized---------------	1 cup-----------	70	60	185	1	16	13.2	1.3	0.2
75		1 tbsp----------	4	60	10	Tr	1	0.8	0.1	Tr
76	Sour dressing (filled cream type product, nonbutterfat)--	1 cup-----------	235	75	415	8	39	31.2	4.6	1.1
77		1 tbsp----------	12	75	20	Tr	2	1.6	0.2	0.1
	Ice cream. See Milk desserts, frozen (items 106-111).									
	Ice milk. See Milk desserts, frozen (items 112-114).									
	Milk:									
	Fluid:									
78	Whole (3.3% fat)-------------	1 cup-----------	244	88	150	8	8	5.1	2.4	0.3
	Lowfat (2%):									
79	No milk solids added-------	1 cup-----------	244	89	120	8	5	2.9	1.4	0.2
80	Milk solids added, label claim less than 10 g of protein per cup----------	1 cup-----------	245	89	125	9	5	2.9	1.4	0.2
	Lowfat (1%):									
81	No milk solids added-------	1 cup-----------	244	90	100	8	3	1.6	0.7	0.1
82	Milk solids added, label claim less than 10 g of protein per cup----------	1 cup-----------	245	90	105	9	2	1.5	0.7	0.1
	Nonfat (skim):									
83	No milk solids added-------	1 cup-----------	245	91	85	8	Tr	0.3	0.1	Tr
84	Milk solids added, label claim less than 10 g of protein per cup----------	1 cup-----------	245	90	90	9	1	0.4	0.2	Tr
85	Buttermilk------------------	1 cup-----------	245	90	100	8	2	1.3	0.6	0.1
	Canned:									
86	Condensed, sweetened---------	1 cup-----------	306	27	980	24	27	16.8	7.4	1.0
	Evaporated:									
87	Whole milk-----------------	1 cup-----------	252	74	340	17	19	11.6	5.9	0.6
88	Skim milk------------------	1 cup-----------	255	79	200	19	1	0.3	0.2	Tr
	Dried:									
89	Buttermilk------------------	1 cup-----------	120	3	465	41	7	4.3	2.0	0.3
	Nonfat, instantized:									
90	Envelope, 3.2 oz, net wt.[6]	1 envelope------	91	4	325	32	1	0.4	0.2	Tr
91	Cup-----------------------	1 cup-----------	68	4	245	24	Tr	0.3	0.1	Tr
	Milk beverages:									
	Chocolate milk (commercial):									
92	Regular---------------------	1 cup-----------	250	82	210	8	8	5.3	2.5	0.3
93	Lowfat (2%)-----------------	1 cup-----------	250	84	180	8	5	3.1	1.5	0.2
94	Lowfat (1%)-----------------	1 cup-----------	250	85	160	8	3	1.5	0.8	0.1

[5] Vitamin A value is largely from beta-carotene used for coloring.
[6] Yields 1 qt of fluid milk when reconstituted according to package directions.

Nutrients in Indicated Quantity

Cho-les-terol	Carbo-hydrate	Calcium	Phos-phorus	Iron	Potas-sium	Sodium	Vitamin A value		Thiamin	Ribo-flavin	Niacin	Ascorbic acid	Item No.
							(IU)	(RE)					
Milli-grams	Grams	Milli-grams	Milli-grams	Milli-grams	Milli-grams	Milli-grams	Inter-national units	Retinol equiva-lents	Milli-grams	Milli-grams	Milli-grams	Milli-grams	
0	2	1	10	Tr	29	12	[5]10	[5]1	0.00	0.00	0.0	0	68
0	1	Tr	8	Tr	16	4	Tr	Tr	0.00	Tr	0.0	0	69
0	17	5	6	0.1	14	19	[5]650	[5]65	0.00	0.00	0.0	0	70
0	1	Tr	Tr	Tr	1	1	[5]30	[5]3	0.00	0.00	0.0	0	71
8	13	72	69	Tr	121	53	[5]290	[5]39	0.02	0.09	Tr	1	72
Tr	1	4	3	Tr	6	3	[5]10	[5]2	Tr	Tr	Tr	Tr	73
0	11	4	13	Tr	13	43	[5]330	[5]33	0.00	0.00	0.0	0	74
0	1	Tr	1	Tr	1	2	[5]20	[5]2	0.00	0.00	0.0	0	75
13	11	266	205	0.1	380	113	20	5	0.09	0.38	0.2	2	76
1	1	14	10	Tr	19	6	Tr	Tr	Tr	0.02	Tr	Tr	77
33	11	291	228	0.1	370	120	310	76	0.09	0.40	0.2	2	78
18	12	297	232	0.1	377	122	500	139	0.10	0.40	0.2	2	79
18	12	313	245	0.1	397	128	500	140	0.10	0.42	0.2	2	80
10	12	300	235	0.1	381	123	500	144	0.10	0.41	0.2	2	81
10	12	313	245	0.1	397	128	500	145	0.10	0.42	0.2	2	82
4	12	302	247	0.1	406	126	500	149	0.09	0.34	0.2	2	83
5	12	316	255	0.1	418	130	500	149	0.10	0.43	0.2	2	84
9	12	285	219	0.1	371	257	80	20	0.08	0.38	0.1	2	85
104	166	868	775	0.6	1,136	389	1,000	248	0.28	1.27	0.6	8	86
74	25	657	510	0.5	764	267	610	136	0.12	0.80	0.5	5	87
9	29	738	497	0.7	845	293	1,000	298	0.11	0.79	0.4	3	88
83	59	1,421	1,119	0.4	1,910	621	260	65	0.47	1.89	1.1	7	89
17	47	1,120	896	0.3	1,552	499	[7]2,160	[7]646	0.38	1.59	0.8	5	90
12	35	837	670	0.2	1,160	373	[7]1,610	[7]483	0.28	1.19	0.6	4	91
31	26	280	251	0.6	417	149	300	73	0.09	0.41	0.3	2	92
17	26	284	254	0.6	422	151	500	143	0.09	0.41	0.3	2	93
7	26	287	256	0.6	425	152	500	148	0.10	0.42	0.3	2	94

[7]With added vitamin A.

Item No.	Foods, approximate measures, units, and weight (weight of edible portion only)			Water	Food energy	Pro-tein	Fat	Fatty acids		
								Satu-rated	Mono-unsatu-rated	Poly-unsatu-rated
			Grams	Per-cent	Cal-ories	Grams	Grams	Grams	Grams	Grams
	Dairy Products—Con.									
	Milk beverages:									
	Cocoa and chocolate-flavored beverages:									
95	Powder containing nonfat dry milk-----------------	1 oz------------	28	1	100	3	1	0.6	0.3	Tr
96	Prepared (6 oz water plus 1 oz powder)-------------	1 serving-------	206	86	100	3	1	0.6	0.3	Tr
97	Powder without nonfat dry milk-----------------	3/4 oz----------	21	1	75	1	1	0.3	0.2	Tr
98	Prepared (8 oz whole milk plus 3/4 oz powder)------	1 serving-------	265	81	225	9	9	5.4	2.5	0.3
99	Eggnog (commercial)------------	1 cup-----------	254	74	340	10	19	11.3	5.7	0.9
	Malted milk:									
	Chocolate:									
100	Powder---------------------	3/4 oz ---------	21	2	85	1	1	0.5	0.3	0.1
101	Prepared (8 oz whole milk plus 3/4 oz powder)----	1 serving-------	265	81	235	9	9	5.5	2.7	0.4
	Natural:									
102	Powder---------------------	3/4 oz----------	21	3	85	3	2	0.9	0.5	0.3
103	Prepared (8 oz whole milk plus 3/4 oz powder)----	1 serving-------	265	81	235	11	10	6.0	2.9	0.6
	Shakes, thick:									
104	Chocolate--------------------	10-oz container	283	72	335	9	8	4.8	2.2	0.3
105	Vanilla----------------------	10-oz container	283	74	315	11	9	5.3	2.5	0.3
	Milk desserts, frozen:									
	Ice cream, vanilla:									
	Regular (about 11% fat):									
106	Hardened-------------------	1/2 gal---------	1,064	61	2,155	38	115	71.3	33.1	4.3
107		1 cup-----------	133	61	270	5	14	8.9	4.1	0.5
108		3 fl oz---------	50	61	100	2	5	3.4	1.6	0.2
109	Soft serve (frozen custard)	1 cup-----------	173	60	375	7	23	13.5	6.7	1.0
110	Rich (about 16% fat), hardened-------------------	1/2 gal---------	1,188	59	2,805	33	190	118.3	54.9	7.1
111		1 cup-----------	148	59	350	4	24	14.7	6.8	0.9
	Ice milk, vanilla:									
112	Hardened (about 4% fat)------	1/2 gal---------	1,048	69	1,470	41	45	28.1	13.0	1.7
113		1 cup-----------	131	69	185	5	6	3.5	1.6	0.2
114	Soft serve (about 3% fat)----	1 cup-----------	175	70	225	8	5	2.9	1.3	0.2
115	Sherbet (about 2% fat)---------	1/2 gal---------	1,542	66	2,160	17	31	19.0	8.8	1.1
116		1 cup-----------	193	66	270	2	4	2.4	1.1	0.1
	Yogurt:									
	With added milk solids:									
	Made with lowfat milk:									
117	Fruit-flavored[8]------------	8-oz container--	227	74	230	10	2	1.6	0.7	0.1
118	Plain----------------------	8-oz container--	227	85	145	12	4	2.3	1.0	0.1
119	Made with nonfat milk--------	8-oz container--	227	85	125	13	Tr	0.3	0.1	Tr
	Without added milk solids:									
120	Made with whole milk---------	8-oz container--	227	88	140	8	7	4.8	2.0	0.2
	Eggs									
	Eggs, large (24 oz per dozen):									
	Raw:									
121	Whole, without shell---------	1 egg-----------	50	75	75	6	5	1.6	1.9	0.7
122	White-----------------------	1 white---------	33	88	15	4	0	0.0	0.0	0.0
123	Yolk------------------------	1 yolk----------	17	49	60	3	5	1.6	1.9	0.7
	Cooked:									
124	Fried in margarine-----------	1 egg-----------	46	69	90	6	7	1.9	2.7	1.3
125	Hard-cooked, shell removed---	1 egg-----------	50	75	75	6	5	1.6	2.0	0.7
126	Poached---------------------	1 egg-----------	50	75	75	6	5	1.5	1.9	0.7
127	Scrambled (milk added) in margarine-------------------	1 egg-----------	61	73	100	7	7	2.2	2.9	1.3

[8]Carbohydrate content varies widely because of amount of sugar added and amount and solids content of added flavoring. Consult the label if more precise values for carbohydrate and calories are needed.

							Nutrients in Indicated Quantity						

Cho-les-terol	Carbo-hydrate	Calcium	Phos-phorus	Iron	Potas-sium	Sodium	Vitamin A value		Thiamin	Ribo-flavin	Niacin	Ascorbic acid	Item No.
							(IU)	(RE)					
Milli-grams	Grams	Milli-grams	Milli-grams	Milli-grams	Milli-grams	Milli-grams	Inter-national units	Retinol equiva-lents	Milli-grams	Milli-grams	Milli-grams	Milli-grams	
1	22	90	88	0.3	223	139	Tr	Tr	0.03	0.17	0.2	Tr	95
1	22	90	88	0.3	223	139	Tr	Tr	0.03	0.17	0.2	Tr	96
0	19	7	26	0.7	136	56	Tr	Tr	Tr	0.03	0.1	Tr	97
33	30	298	254	0.9	508	176	310	76	0.10	0.43	0.3	3	98
149	34	330	278	0.5	420	138	890	203	0.09	0.48	0.3	4	99
1	18	13	37	0.4	130	49	20	5	0.04	0.04	0.4	0	100
34	29	304	265	0.5	500	168	330	80	0.14	0.43	0.7	2	101
4	15	56	79	0.2	159	96	70	17	0.11	0.14	1.1	0	102
37	27	347	307	0.3	529	215	380	93	0.20	0.54	1.3	2	103
30	60	374	357	0.9	634	314	240	59	0.13	0.63	0.4	0	104
33	50	413	326	0.3	517	270	320	79	0.08	0.55	0.4	0	105
476	254	1,406	1,075	1.0	2,052	929	4,340	1,064	0.42	2.63	1.1	6	106
59	32	176	134	0.1	257	116	540	133	0.05	0.33	0.1	1	107
22	12	66	51	Tr	96	44	200	50	0.02	0.12	0.1	Tr	108
153	38	236	199	0.4	338	153	790	199	0.08	0.45	0.2	1	109
703	256	1,213	927	0.8	1,771	868	7,200	1,758	0.36	2.27	0.9	5	110
88	32	151	115	0.1	221	108	900	219	0.04	0.28	0.1	1	111
146	232	1,409	1,035	1.5	2,117	836	1,710	419	0.61	2.78	0.9	6	112
18	29	176	129	0.2	265	105	210	52	0.08	0.35	0.1	1	113
13	38	274	202	0.3	412	163	175	44	0.12	0.54	0.2	1	114
113	469	827	594	2.5	1,585	706	1,480	308	0.26	0.71	1.0	31	115
14	59	103	74	0.3	198	88	190	39	0.03	0.09	0.1	4	116
10	43	345	271	0.2	442	133	100	25	0.08	0.40	0.2	1	117
14	16	415	326	0.2	531	159	150	36	0.10	0.49	0.3	2	118
4	17	452	355	0.2	579	174	20	5	0.11	0.53	0.3	2	119
29	11	274	215	0.1	351	105	280	68	0.07	0.32	0.2	1	120
213	1	25	89	0.7	60	63	320	95	0.03	0.25	Tr	0	121
0	Tr	2	4	Tr	48	55	0	0	Tr	0.15	Tr	0	122
213	Tr	23	81	0.6	16	7	320	97	0.03	0.11	Tr	0	123
211	1	25	89	0.7	61	162	390	114	0.03	0.24	Tr	0	124
213	1	25	86	0.6	63	62	280	84	0.03	0.26	Tr	0	125
212	1	25	89	0.7	60	140	320	95	0.02	0.22	Tr	0	126
215	1	44	104	0.7	84	171	420	119	0.03	0.27	Tr	Tr	127

Item No.	Foods, approximate measures, units, and weight (weight of edible portion only)		Water	Food energy	Pro-tein	Fat	Fatty acids		
							Satu-rated	Mono-unsatu-rated	Poly-unsatu-rated
	Fats and Oils	Grams	Per-cent	Cal-ories	Grams	Grams	Grams	Grams	Grams
	Butter (4 sticks per lb):								
128	Stick-------------------------- 1/2 cup----------	113	16	810	1	92	57.1	26.4	3.4
129	Tablespoon (1/8 stick)-------- 1 tbsp-----------	14	16	100	Tr	11	7.1	3.3	0.4
130	Pat (1 in square, 1/3 in								
	high; 90 per lb)------------ 1 pat-----------	5	16	35	Tr	4	2.5	1.2	0.2
131	Fats, cooking (vegetable								
	shortenings)------------------ 1 cup-----------	205	0	1,810	0	205	51.3	91.2	53.5
132	1 tbsp----------	13	0	115	0	13	3.3	5.8	3.4
133	Lard-------------------------- 1 cup-----------	205	0	1,850	0	205	80.4	92.5	23.0
134	1 tbsp----------	13	0	115	0	13	5.1	5.9	1.5
135	Margarine:								
	Imitation (about 40% fat), soft 8-oz container--	227	58	785	1	88	17.5	35.6	31.3
136	1 tbsp----------	14	58	50	Tr	5	1.1	2.2	1.9
	Regular (about 80% fat):								
	Hard (4 sticks per lb):								
137	Stick--------------------- 1/2 cup----------	113	16	810	1	91	17.9	40.5	28.7
138	Tablespoon (1/8 stick)----- 1 tbsp----------	14	16	100	Tr	11	2.2	5.0	3.6
139	Pat (1 in square, 1/3 in								
	high; 90 per lb)-------- 1 pat-----------	5	16	35	Tr	4	0.8	1.8	1.3
140	Soft----------------------- 8-oz container--	227	16	1,625	2	183	31.3	64.7	78.5
141	1 tbsp----------	14	16	100	Tr	11	1.9	4.0	4.8
	Spread (about 60% fat):								
	Hard (4 sticks per lb):								
142	Stick--------------------- 1/2 cup----------	113	37	610	1	69	15.9	29.4	20.5
143	Tablespoon (1/8 stick)----- 1 tbsp----------	14	37	75	Tr	9	2.0	3.6	2.5
144	Pat (1 in square, 1/3 in								
	high; 90 per lb)-------- 1 pat-----------	5	37	25	Tr	3	0.7	1.3	0.9
145	Soft----------------------- 8-oz container--	227	37	1,225	1	138	29.1	71.5	31.3
146	1 tbsp----------	14	37	75	Tr	9	1.8	4.4	1.9
	Oils, salad or cooking:								
147	Corn--------------------------- 1 cup-----------	218	0	1,925	0	218	27.7	52.8	128.0
148	1 tbsp----------	14	0	125	0	14	1.8	3.4	8.2
149	Olive-------------------------- 1 cup-----------	216	0	1,910	0	216	29.2	159.2	18.1
150	1 tbsp----------	14	0	125	0	14	1.9	10.3	1.2
151	Peanut------------------------- 1 cup-----------	216	0	1,910	0	216	36.5	99.8	69.1
152	1 tbsp----------	14	0	125	0	14	2.4	6.5	4.5
153	Safflower---------------------- 1 cup-----------	218	0	1,925	0	218	19.8	26.4	162.4
154	1 tbsp----------	14	0	125	0	14	1.3	1.7	10.4
155	Soybean oil, hydrogenated								
	(partially hardened)-------- 1 cup-----------	218	0	1,925	0	218	32.5	93.7	82.0
156	1 tbsp----------	14	0	125	0	14	2.1	6.0	5.3
157	Soybean-cottonseed oil blend,								
	hydrogenated---------------- 1 cup-----------	218	0	1,925	0	218	39.2	64.3	104.9
158	1 tbsp----------	14	0	125	0	14	2.5	4.1	6.7
159	Sunflower---------------------- 1 cup-----------	218	0	1,925	0	218	22.5	42.5	143.2
160	1 tbsp----------	14	0	125	0	14	1.4	2.7	9.2
	Salad dressings:								
	Commercial:								
161	Blue cheese------------------ 1 tbsp----------	15	32	75	1	8	1.5	1.8	4.2
	French:								
162	Regular-------------------- 1 tbsp----------	16	35	85	Tr	9	1.4	4.0	3.5
163	Low calorie---------------- 1 tbsp----------	16	75	25	Tr	2	0.2	0.3	1.0
	Italian:								
164	Regular-------------------- 1 tbsp----------	15	34	80	Tr	9	1.3	3.7	3.2
165	Low calorie---------------- 1 tbsp----------	15	86	5	Tr	Tr	Tr	Tr	Tr
	Mayonnaise:								
166	Regular-------------------- 1 tbsp----------	14	15	100	Tr	11	1.7	3.2	5.8
167	Imitation------------------ 1 tbsp----------	15	63	35	Tr	3	0.5	0.7	1.6
168	Mayonnaise type-------------- 1 tbsp----------	15	40	60	Tr	5	0.7	1.4	2.7
169	Tartar sauce---------------- 1 tbsp----------	14	34	75	Tr	8	1.2	2.6	3.9
	Thousand island:								
170	Regular-------------------- 1 tbsp----------	16	46	60	Tr	6	1.0	1.3	3.2
171	Low calorie---------------- 1 tbsp----------	15	69	25	Tr	2	0.2	0.4	0.9

[9] For salted butter; unsalted butter contains 12 mg sodium per stick, 2 mg per tbsp, or 1 mg per pat.
[10] Values for vitamin A are year-round average.

Nutrients in Indicated Quantity

Cholesterol	Carbohydrate	Calcium	Phosphorus	Iron	Potassium	Sodium	Vitamin A value (IU)	Vitamin A value (RE)	Thiamin	Riboflavin	Niacin	Ascorbic acid	Item No.
Milligrams	Grams	Milligrams	Milligrams	Milligrams	Milligrams	Milligrams	International units	Retinol equivalents	Milligrams	Milligrams	Milligrams	Milligrams	
247	Tr	27	26	0.2	29	[9]933	[10]3,460	[10]852	0.01	0.04	Tr	0	128
31	Tr	3	3	Tr	4	[9]116	[10]430	[10]106	Tr	Tr	Tr	0	129
11	Tr	1	1	Tr	1	[9]41	[10]150	[10]38	Tr	Tr	Tr	0	130
0	0	0	0	0.0	0	0	0	0	0.00	0.00	0.0	0	131
0	0	0	0	0.0	0	0	0	0	0.00	0.00	0.0	0	132
195	0	0	0	0.0	0	0	0	0	0.00	0.00	0.0	0	133
12	0	0	0	0.0	0	0	0	0	0.00	0.00	0.0	0	134
0	1	40	31	0.0	57	[11]2,178	[12]7,510	[12]2,254	0.01	0.05	Tr	Tr	135
0	Tr	2	2	0.0	4	[11]134	[12]460	[12]139	Tr	Tr	Tr	Tr	136
0	1	34	26	0.1	48	[11]1,066	[12]3,740	[12]1,122	0.01	0.04	Tr	Tr	137
0	Tr	4	3	Tr	6	[11]132	[12]460	[12]139	Tr	0.01	Tr	Tr	138
0	Tr	1	1	Tr	2	[11]47	[12]170	[12]50	Tr	Tr	Tr	Tr	139
0	1	60	46	0.0	86	[11]2,449	[12]7,510	[12]2,254	0.02	0.07	Tr	Tr	140
0	Tr	4	3	0.0	5	[11]151	[12]460	[12]139	Tr	Tr	Tr	Tr	141
0	0	24	18	0.0	34	[11]1,123	[12]3,740	[12]1,122	0.01	0.03	Tr	Tr	142
0	0	3	2	0.0	4	[11]139	[12]460	[12]139	Tr	Tr	Tr	Tr	143
0	0	1	1	0.0	1	[11]50	[12]170	[12]50	Tr	Tr	Tr	Tr	144
0	0	47	37	0.0	68	[11]2,256	[12]7,510	[12]2,254	0.02	0.06	Tr	Tr	145
0	0	3	2	0.0	4	[11]139	[12]460	[12]139	Tr	Tr	Tr	Tr	146
0	0	0	0	0.0	0	0	0	0	0.00	0.00	0.0	0	147
0	0	0	0	0.0	0	0	0	0	0.00	0.00	0.0	0	148
0	0	0	0	0.0	0	0	0	0	0.00	0.00	0.0	0	149
0	0	0	0	0.0	0	0	0	0	0.00	0.00	0.0	0	150
0	0	0	0	0.0	0	0	0	0	0.00	0.00	0.0	0	151
0	0	0	0	0.0	0	0	0	0	0.00	0.00	0.0	0	152
0	0	0	0	0.0	0	0	0	0	0.00	0.00	0.0	0	153
0	0	0	0	0.0	0	0	0	0	0.00	0.00	0.0	0	154
0	0	0	0	0.0	0	0	0	0	0.00	0.00	0.0	0	155
0	0	0	0	0.0	0	0	0	0	0.00	0.00	0.0	0	156
0	0	0	0	0.0	0	0	0	0	0.00	0.00	0.0	0	157
0	0	0	0	0.0	0	0	0	0	0.00	0.00	0.0	0	158
0	0	0	0	0.0	0	0	0	0	0.00	0.00	0.0	0	159
0	0	0	0	0.0	0	0	0	0	0.00	0.00	0.0	0	160
3	1	12	11	Tr	6	164	30	10	Tr	0.02	Tr	Tr	161
0	1	2	1	Tr	2	188	Tr	Tr	Tr	Tr	Tr	Tr	162
0	2	6	5	Tr	3	306	Tr	Tr	Tr	Tr	Tr	Tr	163
0	1	1	1	Tr	5	162	30	3	Tr	Tr	Tr	Tr	164
0	2	1	1	Tr	4	136	Tr	Tr	Tr	Tr	Tr	Tr	165
8	Tr	3	4	0.1	5	80	40	12	0.00	0.00	Tr	0	166
4	2	Tr	Tr	0.0	2	75	0	0	0.00	0.00	0.0	0	167
4	4	2	4	Tr	1	107	30	13	Tr	Tr	Tr	0	168
4	1	3	4	0.1	11	182	30	9	Tr	Tr	0.0	Tr	169
4	2	2	3	0.1	18	112	50	15	Tr	Tr	Tr	0	170
2	2	2	3	0.1	17	150	50	14	Tr	Tr	Tr	0	171

[11]For salted margarine.
[12]Based on average vitamin A content of fortified margarine. Federal specifications for fortified margarine require a minimum of 15,000 IU per pound.

Item No.	Foods, approximate measures, units, and weight (weight of edible portion only)			Water	Food energy	Pro-tein	Fat	Fatty acids		
								Satu-rated	Mono-unsatu-rated	Poly-unsatu-rated
	Fats and Oils—Con.		Grams	Per-cent	Cal-ories	Grams	Grams	Grams	Grams	Grams
	Salad dressings:									
	Prepared from home recipe:									
172	Cooked type[13]	1 tbsp	16	69	25	1	2	0.5	0.6	0.3
173	Vinegar and oil	1 tbsp	16	47	70	0	8	1.5	2.4	3.9
	Fish and Shellfish									
	Clams:									
174	Raw, meat only	3 oz	85	82	65	11	1	0.3	0.3	0.3
175	Canned, drained solids	3 oz	85	77	85	13	2	0.5	0.5	0.4
176	Crabmeat, canned	1 cup	135	77	135	23	3	0.5	0.8	1.4
177	Fish sticks, frozen, reheated, (stick, 4 by 1 by 1/2 in)	1 fish stick	28	52	70	6	3	0.8	1.4	0.8
	Flounder or Sole, baked, with lemon juice:									
178	With butter	3 oz	85	73	120	16	6	3.2	1.5	0.5
179	With margarine	3 oz	85	73	120	16	6	1.2	2.3	1.9
180	Without added fat	3 oz	85	78	80	17	1	0.3	0.2	0.4
181	Haddock, breaded, fried[14]	3 oz	85	61	175	17	9	2.4	3.9	2.4
182	Halibut, broiled, with butter and lemon juice	3 oz	85	67	140	20	6	3.3	1.6	0.7
183	Herring, pickled	3 oz	85	59	190	17	13	4.3	4.6	3.1
184	Ocean perch, breaded, fried[14]	1 fillet	85	59	185	16	11	2.6	4.6	2.8
	Oysters:									
185	Raw, meat only (13-19 medium Selects)	1 cup	240	85	160	20	4	1.4	0.5	1.4
186	Breaded, fried[14]	1 oyster	45	65	90	5	5	1.4	2.1	1.4
	Salmon:									
187	Canned (pink), solids and liquid	3 oz	85	71	120	17	5	0.9	1.5	2.1
188	Baked (red)	3 oz	85	67	140	21	5	1.2	2.4	1.4
189	Smoked	3 oz	85	59	150	18	8	2.6	3.9	0.7
190	Sardines, Atlantic, canned in oil, drained solids	3 oz	85	62	175	20	9	2.1	3.7	2.9
191	Scallops, breaded, frozen, reheated	6 scallops	90	59	195	15	10	2.5	4.1	2.5
	Shrimp:									
192	Canned, drained solids	3 oz	85	70	100	21	1	0.2	0.2	0.4
193	French fried (7 medium)[16]	3 oz	85	55	200	16	10	2.5	4.1	2.6
194	Trout, broiled, with butter and lemon juice	3 oz	85	63	175	21	9	4.1	2.9	1.6
	Tuna, canned, drained solids:									
195	Oil pack, chunk light	3 oz	85	61	165	24	7	1.4	1.9	3.1
196	Water pack, solid white	3 oz	85	63	135	30	1	0.3	0.2	0.3
197	Tuna salad[17]	1 cup	205	63	375	33	19	3.3	4.9	9.2
	Fruits and Fruit Juices									
	Apples:									
	Raw:									
	Unpeeled, without cores:									
198	2-3/4-in diam. (about 3 per lb with cores)	1 apple	138	84	80	Tr	Tr	0.1	Tr	0.1
199	3-1/4-in diam. (about 2 per lb with cores)	1 apple	212	84	125	Tr	1	0.1	Tr	0.2
200	Peeled, sliced	1 cup	110	84	65	Tr	Tr	0.1	Tr	0.1
201	Dried, sulfured	10 rings	64	32	155	1	Tr	Tr	Tr	0.1
202	Apple juice, bottled or canned[19]	1 cup	248	88	115	Tr	Tr	Tr	Tr	0.1
	Applesauce, canned:									
203	Sweetened	1 cup	255	80	195	Tr	Tr	0.1	Tr	0.1
204	Unsweetened	1 cup	244	88	105	Tr	Tr	Tr	Tr	Tr

[13] Fatty acid values apply to product made with regular margarine.
[14] Dipped in egg, milk, and breadcrumbs; fried in vegetable shortening.
[15] If bones are discarded, value for calcium will be greatly reduced.
[16] Dipped in egg, breadcrumbs, and flour; fried in vegetable shortening.

Nutrients in Indicated Quantity

Cho-les-terol	Carbo-hydrate	Calcium	Phos-phorus	Iron	Potas-sium	Sodium	Vitamin A value		Thiamin	Ribo-flavin	Niacin	Ascorbic acid	Item No.
							(IU)	(RE)					
Milli-grams	Grams	Milli-grams	Milli-grams	Milli-grams	Milli-grams	Milli-grams	Inter-national units	Retinol equiva-lents	Milli-grams	Milli-grams	Milli-grams	Milli-grams	
9	2	13	14	0.1	19	117	70	20	0.01	0.02	Tr	Tr	172
0	Tr	0	0	0.0	1	Tr	0	0	0.00	0.00	0.0	0	173
43	2	59	138	2.6	154	102	90	26	0.09	0.15	1.1	9	174
54	2	47	116	3.5	119	102	90	26	0.01	0.09	0.9	3	175
135	1	61	246	1.1	149	1,350	50	14	0.11	0.11	2.6	0	176
26	4	11	58	0.3	94	53	20	5	0.03	0.05	0.6	0	177
68	Tr	13	187	0.3	272	145	210	54	0.05	0.08	1.6	1	178
55	Tr	14	187	0.3	273	151	230	69	0.05	0.08	1.6	1	179
59	Tr	13	197	0.3	286	101	30	10	0.05	0.08	1.7	1	180
75	7	34	183	1.0	270	123	70	20	0.06	0.10	2.9	0	181
62	Tr	14	206	0.7	441	103	610	174	0.06	0.07	7.7	1	182
85	0	29	128	0.9	85	850	110	33	0.04	0.18	2.8	0	183
66	7	31	191	1.2	241	138	70	20	0.10	0.11	2.0	0	184
120	8	226	343	15.6	290	175	740	223	0.34	0.43	6.0	24	185
35	5	49	73	3.0	64	70	150	44	0.07	0.10	1.3	4	186
34	0	[15]167	243	0.7	307	443	60	18	0.03	0.15	6.8	0	187
60	0	26	269	0.5	305	55	290	87	0.18	0.14	5.5	0	188
51	0	12	208	0.8	327	1,700	260	77	0.17	0.17	6.8	0	189
85	0	[15]371	424	2.6	349	425	190	56	0.03	0.17	4.6	0	190
70	10	39	203	2.0	369	298	70	21	0.11	0.11	1.6	0	191
128	1	98	224	1.4	104	1,955	50	15	0.01	0.03	1.5	0	192
168	11	61	154	2.0	189	384	90	26	0.06	0.09	2.8	0	193
71	Tr	26	259	1.0	297	122	230	60	0.07	0.07	2.3	1	194
55	0	7	199	1.6	298	303	70	20	0.04	0.09	10.1	0	195
48	0	17	202	0.6	255	468	110	32	0.03	0.10	13.4	0	196
80	19	31	281	2.5	531	877	230	53	0.06	0.14	13.3	6	197
0	21	10	10	0.2	159	Tr	70	7	0.02	0.02	0.1	8	198
0	32	15	15	0.4	244	Tr	110	11	0.04	0.03	0.2	12	199
0	16	4	8	0.1	124	Tr	50	5	0.02	0.01	0.1	4	200
0	42	9	24	0.9	288	[18]56	0	0	0.00	0.10	0.6	2	201
0	29	17	17	0.9	295	7	Tr	Tr	0.05	0.04	0.2	[20]2	202
0	51	10	18	0.9	156	8	30	3	0.03	0.07	0.5	[20]4	203
0	28	7	17	0.3	183	5	70	7	0.03	0.06	0.5	[20]3	204

[17] Made with drained chunk light tuna, celery, onion, pickle relish, and mayonnaise-type salad dressing.
[18] Sodium bisulfite used to preserve color; unsulfited product would contain less sodium.
[19] Also applies to pasteurized apple cider.
[20] Without added ascorbic acid. For value with added ascorbic acid, refer to label.

Item No.	Foods, approximate measures, units, and weight (weight of edible portion only)		Grams	Water	Food energy	Pro-tein	Fat	Fatty acids		
								Satu-rated	Mono-unsatu-rated	Poly-unsatu-rated
	Fruits and Fruit Juices—Con.		Grams	Per-cent	Cal-ories	Grams	Grams	Grams	Grams	Grams
	Apricots:									
205	Raw, without pits (about 12 per lb with pits)--------------	3 apricots------	106	86	50	1	Tr	Tr	0.2	0.1
	Canned (fruit and liquid):									
206	Heavy syrup pack------------	1 cup-----------	258	78	215	1	Tr	Tr	0.1	Tr
207		3 halves--------	85	78	70	Tr	Tr	Tr	Tr	Tr
208	Juice pack------------------	1 cup-----------	248	87	120	2	Tr	Tr	Tr	Tr
209		3 halves--------	84	87	40	1	Tr	Tr	Tr	Tr
	Dried:									
210	Uncooked (28 large or 37 medium halves per cup)-----	1 cup-----------	130	31	310	5	1	Tr	0.3	0.1
211	Cooked, unsweetened, fruit and liquid----------------	1 cup-----------	250	76	210	3	Tr	Tr	0.2	0.1
212	Apricot nectar, canned-----------	1 cup-----------	251	85	140	1	Tr	Tr	0.1	Tr
	Avocados, raw, whole, without skin and seed:									
213	California (about 2 per lb with skin and seed)--------------	1 avocado-------	173	73	305	4	30	4.5	19.4	3.5
214	Florida (about 1 per lb with skin and seed)--------------	1 avocado-------	304	80	340	5	27	5.3	14.8	4.5
	Bananas, raw, without peel:									
215	Whole (about 2-1/2 per lb with peel)----------------------	1 banana--------	114	74	105	1	1	0.2	Tr	0.1
216	Sliced------------------------	1 cup-----------	150	74	140	2	1	0.3	0.1	0.1
217	Blackberries, raw---------------	1 cup-----------	144	86	75	1	1	0.2	0.1	0.1
	Blueberries:									
218	Raw--------------------------	1 cup-----------	145	85	80	1	1	Tr	0.1	0.3
219	Frozen, sweetened-------------	10-oz container	284	77	230	1	Tr	Tr	0.1	0.2
220		1 cup-----------	230	77	185	1	Tr	Tr	Tr	0.1
	Cantaloup. See Melons (item 251).									
	Cherries:									
221	Sour, red, pitted, canned, water pack------------------	1 cup-----------	244	90	90	2	Tr	0.1	0.1	0.1
222	Sweet, raw, without pits and stems------------------------	10 cherries-----	68	81	50	1	1	0.1	0.2	0.2
223	Cranberry juice cocktail, bottled, sweetened------------	1 cup-----------	253	85	145	Tr	Tr	Tr	Tr	0.1
224	Cranberry sauce, sweetened, canned, strained--------------	1 cup-----------	277	61	420	1	Tr	Tr	0.1	0.2
	Dates:									
225	Whole, without pits-----------	10 dates--------	83	23	230	2	Tr	0.1	0.1	Tr
226	Chopped----------------------	1 cup-----------	178	23	490	4	1	0.3	0.2	Tr
227	Figs, dried---------------------	10 figs---------	187	28	475	6	2	0.4	0.5	1.0
	Fruit cocktail, canned, fruit and liquid:									
228	Heavy syrup pack---------------	1 cup-----------	255	80	185	1	Tr	Tr	Tr	0.1
229	Juice pack--------------------	1 cup-----------	248	87	115	1	Tr	Tr	Tr	Tr
	Grapefruit:									
230	Raw, without peel, membrane and seeds (3-3/4-in diam., 1 lb 1 oz, whole, with refuse)----	1/2 grapefruit--	120	91	40	1	Tr	Tr	Tr	Tr
231	Canned, sections with syrup----	1 cup-----------	254	84	150	1	Tr	Tr	Tr	0.1
	Grapefruit juice:									
232	Raw---------------------------	1 cup-----------	247	90	95	1	Tr	Tr	Tr	0.1
	Canned:									
233	Unsweetened------------------	1 cup-----------	247	90	95	1	Tr	Tr	Tr	0.1
234	Sweetened--------------------	1 cup-----------	250	87	115	1	Tr	Tr	Tr	0.1
	Frozen concentrate, unsweetened									
235	Undiluted--------------------	6-fl-oz can-----	207	62	300	4	1	0.1	0.1	0.2
236	Diluted with 3 parts water by volume--------------------	1 cup-----------	247	89	100	1	Tr	Tr	Tr	0.1

[20] Without added ascorbic acid. For value with added ascorbic acid, refer to label.
[21] With added ascorbic acid.

Nutrients in Indicated Quantity

Cho-les-terol	Carbo-hydrate	Calcium	Phos-phorus	Iron	Potas-sium	Sodium	Vitamin A value		Thiamin	Ribo-flavin	Niacin	Ascorbic acid	Item No.
							(IU)	(RE)					
Milli-grams	Grams	Milli-grams	Milli-grams	Milli-grams	Milli-grams	Milli-grams	Inter-national units	Retinol equiva-lents	Milli-grams	Milli-grams	Milli-grams	Milli-grams	
0	12	15	20	0.6	314	1	2,770	277	0.03	0.04	0.6	11	205
0	55	23	31	0.8	361	10	3,170	317	0.05	0.06	1.0	8	206
0	18	8	10	0.3	119	3	1,050	105	0.02	0.02	0.3	3	207
0	31	30	50	0.7	409	10	4,190	419	0.04	0.05	0.9	12	208
0	10	10	17	0.3	139	3	1,420	142	0.02	0.02	0.3	4	209
0	80	59	152	6.1	1,791	13	9,410	941	0.01	0.20	3.9	3	210
0	55	40	103	4.2	1,222	8	5,910	591	0.02	0.08	2.4	4	211
0	36	18	23	1.0	286	8	3,300	330	0.02	0.04	0.7	[20]2	212
0	12	19	73	2.0	1,097	21	1,060	106	0.19	0.21	3.3	14	213
0	27	33	119	1.6	1,484	15	1,860	186	0.33	0.37	5.8	24	214
0	27	7	23	0.4	451	1	90	9	0.05	0.11	0.6	10	215
0	35	9	30	0.5	594	2	120	12	0.07	0.15	0.8	14	216
0	18	46	30	0.8	282	Tr	240	24	0.04	0.06	0.4	30	217
0	20	9	15	0.2	129	9	150	15	0.07	0.07	0.5	19	218
0	62	17	20	1.1	170	3	120	12	0.06	0.15	0.7	3	219
0	50	14	16	0.9	138	2	100	10	0.05	0.12	0.6	2	220
0	22	27	24	3.3	239	17	1,840	184	0.04	0.10	0.4	5	221
0	11	10	13	0.3	152	Tr	150	15	0.03	0.04	0.3	5	222
0	38	8	3	0.4	61	10	10	1	0.01	0.04	0.1	[21]108	223
0	108	11	17	0.6	72	80	60	6	0.04	0.06	0.3	6	224
0	61	27	33	1.0	541	2	40	4	0.07	0.08	1.8	0	225
0	131	57	71	2.0	1,161	5	90	9	0.16	0.18	3.9	0	226
0	122	269	127	4.2	1,331	21	250	25	0.13	0.16	1.3	1	227
0	48	15	28	0.7	224	15	520	52	0.05	0.05	1.0	5	228
0	29	20	35	0.5	236	10	760	76	0.03	0.04	1.0	7	229
0	10	14	10	0.1	167	Tr	[22]10	[22]1	0.04	0.02	0.3	41	230
0	39	36	25	1.0	328	5	Tr	Tr	0.10	0.05	0.6	54	231
0	23	22	37	0.5	400	2	20	2	0.10	0.05	0.5	94	232
0	22	17	27	0.5	378	2	20	2	0.10	0.05	0.6	72	233
0	28	20	28	0.9	405	5	20	2	0.10	0.06	0.8	67	234
0	72	56	101	1.0	1,002	6	60	6	0.30	0.16	1.6	248	235
0	24	20	35	0.3	336	2	20	2	0.10	0.05	0.5	83	236

[22]For white grapefruit; pink grapefruit have about 310 IU or 31 RE.

Item No.	Foods, approximate measures, units, and weight (weight of edible portion only)			Water	Food energy	Pro-tein	Fat	Fatty acids		
								Satu-rated	Mono-unsatu-rated	Poly-unsatu-rated
			Grams	Per-cent	Cal-ories	Grams	Grams	Grams	Grams	Grams

Fruits and Fruit Juices—Con.

	Grapes, European type (adherent skin), raw:									
237	Thompson Seedless	10 grapes	50	81	35	Tr	Tr	0.1	Tr	0.1
238	Tokay and Emperor, seeded types	10 grapes	57	81	40	Tr	Tr	0.1	Tr	0.1
	Grape juice:									
239	Canned or bottled	1 cup	253	84	155	1	Tr	0.1	Tr	0.1
	Frozen concentrate, sweetened:									
240	Undiluted	6-fl-oz can	216	54	385	1	1	0.2	Tr	0.2
241	Diluted with 3 parts water by volume	1 cup	250	87	125	Tr	Tr	0.1	Tr	0.1
242	Kiwifruit, raw, without skin (about 5 per lb with skin)	1 kiwifruit	76	83	45	1	Tr	Tr	0.1	0.1
243	Lemons, raw, without peel and seeds (about 4 per lb with peel and seeds)	1 lemon	58	89	15	1	Tr	Tr	Tr	0.1
	Lemon juice:									
244	Raw	1 cup	244	91	60	1	Tr	Tr	Tr	Tr
245	Canned or bottled, unsweetened	1 cup	244	92	50	1	1	0.1	Tr	0.2
246		1 tbsp	15	92	5	Tr	Tr	Tr	Tr	Tr
247	Frozen, single-strength, unsweetened	6-fl-oz can	244	92	55	1	1	0.1	Tr	0.2
	Lime juice:									
248	Raw	1 cup	246	90	65	1	Tr	Tr	Tr	0.1
249	Canned, unsweetened	1 cup	246	93	50	1	1	0.1	0.1	0.2
250	Mangos, raw, without skin and seed (about 1-1/2 per lb with skin and seed)	1 mango	207	82	135	1	1	0.1	0.2	0.1
	Melons, raw, without rind and cavity contents:									
251	Cantaloup, orange-fleshed (5-in diam., 2-1/3 lb, whole, with rind and cavity contents)	1/2 melon	267	90	95	2	1	0.1	0.1	0.3
252	Honeydew (6-1/2-in diam., 5-1/4 lb, whole, with rind and cavity contents)	1/10 melon	129	90	45	1	Tr	Tr	Tr	0.1
253	Nectarines, raw, without pits (about 3 per lb with pits)	1 nectarine	136	86	65	1	1	0.1	0.2	0.3
	Oranges, raw:									
254	Whole, without peel and seeds (2-5/8-in diam., about 2-1/2 per lb, with peel and seeds)	1 orange	131	87	60	1	Tr	Tr	Tr	Tr
255	Sections without membranes	1 cup	180	87	85	2	Tr	Tr	Tr	Tr
	Orange juice:									
256	Raw, all varieties	1 cup	248	88	110	2	Tr	0.1	0.1	0.1
257	Canned, unsweetened	1 cup	249	89	105	1	Tr	Tr	0.1	0.1
258	Chilled	1 cup	249	88	110	2	1	0.1	0.1	0.2
	Frozen concentrate:									
259	Undiluted	6-fl-oz can	213	58	340	5	Tr	0.1	0.1	0.1
260	Diluted with 3 parts water by volume	1 cup	249	88	110	2	Tr	Tr	Tr	Tr
261	Orange and grapefruit juice, canned	1 cup	247	89	105	1	Tr	Tr	Tr	Tr
262	Papayas, raw, 1/2-in cubes	1 cup	140	86	65	1	Tr	0.1	0.1	Tr
	Peaches:									
	Raw:									
263	Whole, 2-1/2-in diam., peeled, pitted (about 4 per lb with peels and pits)	1 peach	87	88	35	1	Tr	Tr	Tr	Tr
264	Sliced	1 cup	170	88	75	1	Tr	Tr	0.1	0.1
	Canned, fruit and liquid:									
265	Heavy syrup pack	1 cup	256	79	190	1	Tr	Tr	0.1	0.1
266		1 half	81	79	60	Tr	Tr	Tr	Tr	Tr
267	Juice pack	1 cup	248	87	110	2	Tr	Tr	Tr	Tr
268		1 half	77	87	35	Tr	Tr	Tr	Tr	Tr

[20]Without added ascorbic acid. For value with added ascorbic acid, refer to label.
[21]With added ascorbic acid.

Nutrients in Indicated Quantity

Cholesterol	Carbohydrate	Calcium	Phosphorus	Iron	Potassium	Sodium	Vitamin A value (IU)	Vitamin A value (RE)	Thiamin	Riboflavin	Niacin	Ascorbic acid	Item No.
Milligrams	Grams	Milligrams	Milligrams	Milligrams	Milligrams	Milligrams	International units	Retinol equivalents	Milligrams	Milligrams	Milligrams	Milligrams	
0	9	6	7	0.1	93	1	40	4	0.05	0.03	0.2	5	237
0	10	6	7	0.1	105	1	40	4	0.05	0.03	0.2	6	238
0	38	23	28	0.6	334	8	20	2	0.07	0.09	0.7	[20]Tr	239
0	96	28	32	0.8	160	15	60	6	0.11	0.20	0.9	[21]179	240
0	32	10	10	0.3	53	5	20	2	0.04	0.07	0.3	[21]60	241
0	11	20	30	0.3	252	4	130	13	0.02	0.04	0.4	74	242
0	5	15	9	0.3	80	1	20	2	0.02	0.01	0.1	31	243
0	21	17	15	0.1	303	2	50	5	0.07	0.02	0.2	112	244
0	16	27	22	0.3	249	[23]51	40	4	0.10	0.02	0.5	61	245
0	1	2	1	Tr	15	[23]3	Tr	Tr	0.01	Tr	Tr	4	246
0	16	20	20	0.3	217	2	30	3	0.14	0.03	0.3	77	247
0	22	22	17	0.1	268	2	20	2	0.05	0.02	0.2	72	248
0	16	30	25	0.6	185	[23]39	40	4	0.08	0.01	0.4	16	249
0	35	21	23	0.3	323	4	8,060	806	0.12	0.12	1.2	57	250
0	22	29	45	0.6	825	24	8,610	861	0.10	0.06	1.5	113	251
0	12	8	13	0.1	350	13	50	5	0.10	0.02	0.8	32	252
0	16	7	22	0.2	288	Tr	1,000	100	0.02	0.06	1.3	7	253
0	15	52	18	0.1	237	Tr	270	27	0.11	0.05	0.4	70	254
0	21	72	25	0.2	326	Tr	370	37	0.16	0.07	0.5	96	255
0	26	27	42	0.5	496	2	500	50	0.22	0.07	1.0	124	256
0	25	20	35	1.1	436	5	440	44	0.15	0.07	0.8	86	257
0	25	25	27	0.4	473	2	190	19	0.28	0.05	0.7	82	258
0	81	68	121	0.7	1,436	6	590	59	0.60	0.14	1.5	294	259
0	27	22	40	0.2	473	2	190	19	0.20	0.04	0.5	97	260
0	25	20	35	1.1	390	7	290	29	0.14	0.07	0.8	72	261
0	17	35	12	0.3	247	9	400	40	0.04	0.04	0.5	92	262
0	10	4	10	0.1	171	Tr	470	47	0.01	0.04	0.9	6	263
0	19	9	20	0.2	335	Tr	910	91	0.03	0.07	1.7	11	264
0	51	8	28	0.7	236	15	850	85	0.03	0.06	1.6	7	265
0	16	2	9	0.2	75	5	270	27	0.01	0.02	0.5	2	266
0	29	15	42	0.7	317	10	940	94	0.02	0.04	1.4	9	267
0	9	5	13	0.2	99	3	290	29	0.01	0.01	0.4	3	268

[23]Sodium benzoate and sodium bisulfite added as preservatives.

Item No.	Foods, approximate measures, units, and weight (weight of edible portion only)		Water	Food energy	Pro-tein	Fat	Fatty acids		
							Satu-rated	Mono-unsatu-rated	Poly-unsatu-rated
		Grams	Per-cent	Cal-ories	Grams	Grams	Grams	Grams	Grams

Fruits and Fruit Juices—Con.

	Peaches:								
	Dried:								
269	Uncooked--------------------- 1 cup-----------	160	32	380	6	1	0.1	0.4	0.6
270	Cooked, unsweetened, fruit and liquid----------------- 1 cup-----------	258	78	200	3	1	0.1	0.2	0.3
271	Frozen, sliced, sweetened------ 10-oz container	284	75	265	2	Tr	Tr	0.1	0.2
272	1 cup-----------	250	75	235	2	Tr	Tr	0.1	0.2
	Pears:								
	Raw, with skin, cored:								
273	Bartlett, 2-1/2-in diam. (about 2-1/2 per lb with cores and stems)----------- 1 pear----------	166	84	100	1	1	Tr	0.1	0.2
274	Bosc, 2-1/2-in diam. (about 3 per lb with cores and stems)--------------------- 1 pear----------	141	84	85	1	1	Tr	0.1	0.1
275	D'Anjou, 3-in diam. (about 2 per lb with cores and stems)--------------------- 1 pear----------	200	84	120	1	1	Tr	0.2	0.2
	Canned, fruit and liquid:								
276	Heavy syrup pack------------- 1 cup-----------	255	80	190	1	Tr	Tr	0.1	0.1
277	1 half----------	79	80	60	Tr	Tr	Tr	Tr	Tr
278	Juice pack------------------- 1 cup-----------	248	86	125	1	Tr	Tr	Tr	Tr
279	1 half----------	77	86	40	Tr	Tr	Tr	Tr	Tr
	Pineapple:								
280	Raw, diced--------------------- 1 cup-----------	155	87	75	1	1	Tr	0.1	0.2
	Canned, fruit and liquid:								
	Heavy syrup pack:								
281	Crushed, chunks, tidbits--- 1 cup-----------	255	79	200	1	Tr	Tr	Tr	0.1
282	Slices--------------------- 1 slice---------	58	79	45	Tr	Tr	Tr	Tr	Tr
	Juice pack:								
283	Chunks or tidbits---------- 1 cup-----------	250	84	150	1	Tr	Tr	Tr	0.1
284	Slices--------------------- 1 slice---------	58	84	35	Tr	Tr	Tr	Tr	Tr
285	Pineapple juice, unsweetened, canned------------------------ 1 cup-----------	250	86	140	1	Tr	Tr	Tr	0.1
	Plantains, without peel:								
286	Raw------------------------- 1 plantain------	179	65	220	2	1	0.3	0.1	0.1
287	Cooked, boiled, sliced-------- 1 cup-----------	154	67	180	1	Tr	0.1	Tr	0.1
	Plums, without pits:								
	Raw:								
288	2-1/8-in diam. (about 6-1/2 per lb with pits)---------- 1 plum----------	66	85	35	1	Tr	Tr	0.3	0.1
289	1-1/2-in diam. (about 15 per lb with pits)-------------- 1 plum----------	28	85	15	Tr	Tr	Tr	0.1	Tr
	Canned, purple, fruit and liquid:								
290	Heavy syrup pack------------- 1 cup-----------	258	76	230	1	Tr	Tr	0.2	0.1
291	3 plums---------	133	76	120	Tr	Tr	Tr	0.1	Tr
292	Juice pack------------------- 1 cup-----------	252	84	145	1	Tr	Tr	Tr	Tr
293	3 plums---------	95	84	55	Tr	Tr	Tr	Tr	Tr
	Prunes, dried:								
294	Uncooked---------------------- 4 extra large or 5 large prunes	49	32	115	1	Tr	Tr	0.2	0.1
295	Cooked, unsweetened, fruit and liquid---------------------- 1 cup-----------	212	70	225	2	Tr	Tr	0.3	0.1
296	Prune juice, canned or bottled--- 1 cup-----------	256	81	180	2	Tr	Tr	0.1	Tr
	Raisins, seedless:								
297	Cup, not pressed down---------- 1 cup-----------	145	15	435	5	1	0.2	Tr	0.2
298	Packet, 1/2 oz (1-1/2 tbsp)---- 1 packet--------	14	15	40	Tr	Tr	Tr	Tr	Tr
	Raspberries:								
299	Raw------------------------- 1 cup-----------	123	87	60	1	1	Tr	0.1	0.4
300	Frozen, sweetened-------------- 10-oz container	284	73	295	2	Tr	Tr	Tr	0.3
301	1 cup-----------	250	73	255	2	Tr	Tr	Tr	0.2

[21] With added ascorbic acid.

Nutrients in Indicated Quantity

Cho-les-terol	Carbo-hydrate	Calcium	Phos-phorus	Iron	Potas-sium	Sodium	Vitamin A value		Thiamin	Ribo-flavin	Niacin	Ascorbic acid	Item No.
							(IU)	(RE)					
Milli-grams	Grams	Milli-grams	Milli-grams	Milli-grams	Milli-grams	Milli-grams	Inter-national units	Retinol equiva-lents	Milli-grams	Milli-grams	Milli-grams	Milli-grams	
0	98	45	190	6.5	1,594	11	3,460	346	Tr	0.34	7.0	8	269
0	51	23	98	3.4	826	5	510	51	0.01	0.05	3.9	10	270
0	68	9	31	1.1	369	17	810	81	0.04	0.10	1.9	[21]268	271
0	60	8	28	0.9	325	15	710	71	0.03	0.09	1.6	[21]236	272
0	25	18	18	0.4	208	Tr	30	3	0.03	0.07	0.2	7	273
0	21	16	16	0.4	176	Tr	30	3	0.03	0.06	0.1	6	274
0	30	22	22	0.5	250	Tr	40	4	0.04	0.08	0.2	8	275
0	49	13	18	0.6	166	13	10	1	0.03	0.06	0.6	3	276
0	15	4	6	0.2	51	4	Tr	Tr	0.01	0.02	0.2	1	277
0	32	22	30	0.7	238	10	10	1	0.03	0.03	0.5	4	278
0	10	7	9	0.2	74	3	Tr	Tr	0.01	0.01	0.2	1	279
0	19	11	11	0.6	175	2	40	4	0.14	0.06	0.7	24	280
0	52	36	18	1.0	265	3	40	4	0.23	0.06	0.7	19	281
0	12	8	4	0.2	60	1	10	1	0.05	0.01	0.2	4	282
0	39	35	15	0.7	305	3	100	10	0.24	0.05	0.7	24	283
0	9	8	3	0.2	71	1	20	2	0.06	0.01	0.2	6	284
0	34	43	20	0.7	335	3	10	1	0.14	0.06	0.6	27	285
0	57	5	61	1.1	893	7	2,020	202	0.09	0.10	1.2	33	286
0	48	3	43	0.9	716	8	1,400	140	0.07	0.08	1.2	17	287
0	9	3	7	0.1	114	Tr	210	21	0.03	0.06	0.3	6	288
0	4	1	3	Tr	48	Tr	90	9	0.01	0.03	0.1	3	289
0	60	23	34	2.2	235	49	670	67	0.04	0.10	0.8	1	290
0	31	12	17	1.1	121	25	340	34	0.02	0.05	0.4	1	291
0	38	25	38	0.9	388	3	2,540	254	0.06	0.15	1.2	7	292
0	14	10	14	0.3	146	1	960	96	0.02	0.06	0.4	3	293
0	31	25	39	1.2	365	2	970	97	0.04	0.08	1.0	2	294
0	60	49	74	2.4	708	4	650	65	0.05	0.21	1.5	6	295
0	45	31	64	3.0	707	10	10	1	0.04	0.18	2.0	10	296
0	115	71	141	3.0	1,089	17	10	1	0.23	0.13	1.2	5	297
0	11	7	14	0.3	105	2	Tr	Tr	0.02	0.01	0.1	Tr	298
0	14	27	15	0.7	187	Tr	160	16	0.04	0.11	1.1	31	299
0	74	43	48	1.8	324	3	170	17	0.05	0.13	0.7	47	300
0	65	38	43	1.6	285	3	150	15	0.05	0.11	0.6	41	301

Item No.	Foods, approximate measures, units, and weight (weight of edible portion only)			Water	Food energy	Pro- tein	Fat	Fatty acids		
								Satu- rated	Mono- unsatu- rated	Poly- unsatu- rated
	Fruits and Fruit Juices—Con.		Grams	Per- cent	Cal- ories	Grams	Grams	Grams	Grams	Grams
302	Rhubarb, cooked, added sugar-----	1 cup----------	240	68	280	1	Tr	Tr	Tr	0.1
	Strawberries:									
303	Raw, capped, whole-------------	1 cup----------	149	92	45	1	1	Tr	0.1	0.3
304	Frozen, sweetened, sliced------	10-oz container	284	73	275	2	Tr	Tr	0.1	0.2
305		1 cup----------	255	73	245	1	Tr	Tr	Tr	0.2
	Tangerines:									
306	Raw, without peel and seeds (2-3/8-in diam., about 4 per 1b, with peel and seeds)-----	1 tangerine-----	84	88	35	1	Tr	Tr	Tr	Tr
307	Canned, light syrup, fruit and liquid----------------------	1 cup----------	252	83	155	1	Tr	Tr	Tr	0.1
308	Tangerine juice, canned, sweet- ened----------------------	1 cup----------	249	87	125	1	Tr	Tr	Tr	0.1
	Watermelon, raw, without rind and seeds:									
309	Piece (4 by 8 in wedge with rind and seeds; 1/16 of 32-2/3-1b melon, 10 by 16 in)	1 piece---------	482	92	155	3	2	0.3	0.2	1.0
310	Diced-------------------------	1 cup----------	160	92	50	1	1	0.1	0.1	0.3
	Grain Products									
311	Bagels, plain or water, enriched, 3-1/2-in diam.[24]	1 bagel---------	68	29	200	7	2	0.3	0.5	0.7
312	Barley, pearled, light, uncooked	1 cup----------	200	11	700	16	2	0.3	0.2	0.9
	Biscuits, baking powder, 2-in diam. (enriched flour, vege- table shortening):									
313	From home recipe---------------	1 biscuit-------	28	28	100	2	5	1.2	2.0	1.3
314	From mix----------------------	1 biscuit-------	28	29	95	2	3	0.8	1.4	0.9
315	From refrigerated dough--------	1 biscuit-------	20	30	65	1	2	0.6	0.9	0.6
	Breadcrumbs, enriched:									
316	Dry, grated-------------------	1 cup----------	100	7	390	13	5	1.5	1.6	1.0
	Soft. See White bread (item 351).									
	Breads:									
317	Boston brown bread, canned, slice, 3-1/4 in by 1/2 in[25]--	1 slice---------	45	45	95	2	1	0.3	0.1	0.1
	Cracked-wheat bread (3/4 en- riched wheat flour, 1/4 cracked wheat flour):[25]									
318	Loaf, 1 lb-------------------	1 loaf----------	454	35	1,190	42	16	3.1	4.3	5.7
319	Slice (18 per loaf)----------	1 slice---------	25	35	65	2	1	0.2	0.2	0.3
320	Toasted---------------------	1 slice---------	21	26	65	2	1	0.2	0.2	0.3
	French or vienna bread, en- riched:[25]									
321	Loaf, 1 lb-------------------	1 loaf----------	454	34	1,270	43	18	3.8	5.7	5.9
	Slice:									
322	French, 5 by 2-1/2 by 1 in	1 slice---------	35	34	100	3	1	0.3	0.4	0.5
323	Vienna, 4-3/4 by 4 by 1/2 in----------------------	1 slice---------	25	34	70	2	1	0.2	0.3	0.3
	Italian bread, enriched:									
324	Loaf, 1 lb-------------------	1 loaf----------	454	32	1,255	41	4	0.6	0.3	1.6
325	Slice, 4-1/2 by 3-1/4 by 3/4 in-------------------------	1 slice---------	30	32	85	3	Tr	Tr	Tr	0.1
	Mixed grain bread, enriched:[25]									
326	Loaf, 1 lb-------------------	1 loaf----------	454	37	1,165	45	17	3.2	4.1	6.5
327	Slice (18 per loaf)----------	1 slice---------	25	37	65	2	1	0.2	0.2	0.4
328	Toasted---------------------	1 slice---------	23	27	65	2	1	0.2	0.2	0.4

[24] Egg bagels have 44 mg cholesterol and 22 IU or 7 RE vitamin A per bagel.
[25] Made with vegetable shortening.

							Nutrients in Indicated Quantity						
Cho-les-terol	Carbo-hydrate	Calcium	Phos-phorus	Iron	Potas-sium	Sodium	Vitamin A value		Thiamin	Ribo-flavin	Niacin	Ascorbic acid	Item No.
							(IU)	(RE)					
Milli-grams	Grams	Milli-grams	Milli-grams	Milli-grams	Milli-grams	Milli-grams	Inter-national units	Retinol equiva-lents	Milli-grams	Milli-grams	Milli-grams	Milli-grams	
0	75	348	19	0.5	230	2	170	17	0.04	0.06	0.5	8	302
0	10	21	28	0.6	247	1	40	4	0.03	0.10	0.3	84	303
0	74	31	37	1.7	278	9	70	7	0.05	0.14	1.1	118	304
0	66	28	33	1.5	250	8	60	6	0.04	0.13	1.0	106	305
0	9	12	8	0.1	132	1	770	77	0.09	0.02	0.1	26	306
0	41	18	25	0.9	197	15	2,120	212	0.13	0.11	1.1	50	307
0	30	45	35	0.5	443	2	1,050	105	0.15	0.05	0.2	55	308
0	35	39	43	0.8	559	10	1,760	176	0.39	0.10	1.0	46	309
0	11	13	14	0.3	186	3	590	59	0.13	0.03	0.3	15	310
0	38	29	46	1.8	50	245	0	0	0.26	0.20	2.4	0	311
0	158	32	378	4.2	320	6	0	0	0.24	0.10	6.2	0	312
Tr	13	47	36	0.7	32	195	10	3	0.08	0.08	0.8	Tr	313
Tr	14	58	128	0.7	56	262	20	4	0.12	0.11	0.8	Tr	314
1	10	4	79	0.5	18	249	0	0	0.08	0.05	0.7	0	315
5	73	122	141	4.1	152	736	0	0	0.35	0.35	4.8	0	316
3	21	41	72	0.9	131	113	[26]0	[26]0	0.06	0.04	0.7	0	317
0	227	295	581	12.1	608	1,966	Tr	Tr	1.73	1.73	15.3	Tr	318
0	12	16	32	0.7	34	106	Tr	Tr	0.10	0.09	0.8	Tr	319
0	12	16	32	0.7	34	106	Tr	Tr	0.07	0.09	0.8	Tr	320
0	230	499	386	14.0	409	2,633	Tr	Tr	2.09	1.59	18.2	Tr	321
0	18	39	30	1.1	32	203	Tr	Tr	0.16	0.12	1.4	Tr	322
0	13	28	21	0.8	23	145	Tr	Tr	0.12	0.09	1.0	Tr	323
0	256	77	350	12.7	336	2,656	0	0	1.80	1.10	15.0	0	324
0	17	5	23	0.8	22	176	0	0	0.12	0.07	1.0	0	325
0	212	472	962	14.8	990	1,870	Tr	Tr	1.77	1.73	18.9	Tr	326
0	12	27	55	0.8	56	106	Tr	Tr	0.10	0.10	1.1	Tr	327
0	12	27	55	0.8	56	106	Tr	Tr	0.08	0.10	1.1	Tr	328

[26] Made with white cornmeal. If made with yellow cornmeal, value is 32 IU or 3 RE.

Item No.	Foods, approximate measures, units, and weight (weight of edible portion only)			Water	Food energy	Pro-tein	Fat	Fatty acids		
								Satu-rated	Mono-unsatu-rated	Poly-unsatu-rated
			Grams	Per-cent	Cal-ories	Grams	Grams	Grams	Grams	Grams

Grain Products—Con.

	Breads:									
	Oatmeal bread, enriched:[25]									
329	Loaf, 1 lb	1 loaf	454	37	1,145	38	20	3.7	7.1	8.2
330	Slice (18 per loaf)	1 slice	25	37	65	2	1	0.2	0.4	0.5
331	Toasted	1 slice	23	30	65	2	1	0.2	0.4	0.5
332	Pita bread, enriched, white, 6-1/2-in diam.	1 pita	60	31	165	6	1	0.1	0.1	0.4
	Pumpernickel (2/3 rye flour, 1/3 enriched wheat flour):[25]									
333	Loaf, 1 lb	1 loaf	454	37	1,160	42	16	2.6	3.6	6.4
334	Slice, 5 by 4 by 3/8 in	1 slice	32	37	80	3	1	0.2	0.3	0.5
335	Toasted	1 slice	29	28	80	3	1	0.2	0.3	0.5
	Raisin bread, enriched:[25]									
336	Loaf, 1 lb	1 loaf	454	33	1,260	37	18	4.1	6.5	6.7
337	Slice (18 per loaf)	1 slice	25	33	65	2	1	0.2	0.3	0.4
338	Toasted	1 slice	21	24	65	2	1	0.2	0.3	0.4
	Rye bread, light (2/3 enriched wheat flour, 1/3 rye flour):[25]									
339	Loaf, 1 lb	1 loaf	454	37	1,190	38	17	3.3	5.2	5.5
340	Slice, 4-3/4 by 3-3/4 by 7/16 in	1 slice	25	37	65	2	1	0.2	0.3	0.3
341	Toasted	1 slice	22	28	65	2	1	0.2	0.3	0.3
	Wheat bread, enriched:[25]									
342	Loaf, 1 lb	1 loaf	454	37	1,160	43	19	3.9	7.3	4.5
343	Slice (18 per loaf)	1 slice	25	37	65	2	1	0.2	0.4	0.3
344	Toasted	1 slice	23	28	65	3	1	0.2	0.4	0.3
	White bread, enriched:[25]									
345	Loaf, 1 lb	1 loaf	454	37	1,210	38	18	5.6	6.5	4.2
346	Slice (18 per loaf)	1 slice	25	37	65	2	1	0.3	0.4	0.2
347	Toasted	1 slice	22	28	65	2	1	0.3	0.4	0.2
348	Slice (22 per loaf)	1 slice	20	37	55	2	1	0.2	0.3	0.2
349	Toasted	1 slice	17	28	55	2	1	0.2	0.3	0.2
350	Cubes	1 cup	30	37	80	2	1	0.4	0.4	0.3
351	Crumbs, soft	1 cup	45	37	120	4	2	0.6	0.6	0.4
	Whole-wheat bread:[25]									
352	Loaf, 1 lb	1 loaf	454	38	1,110	44	20	5.8	6.8	5.2
353	Slice (16 per loaf)	1 slice	28	38	70	3	1	0.4	0.4	0.3
354	Toasted	1 slice	25	29	70	3	1	0.4	0.4	0.3
	Bread stuffing (from enriched bread), prepared from mix:									
355	Dry type	1 cup	140	33	500	9	31	6.1	13.3	9.6
356	Moist type	1 cup	203	61	420	9	26	5.3	11.3	8.0
	Breakfast cereals:									
	Hot type, cooked:									
	Corn (hominy) grits:									
357	Regular and quick, enriched	1 cup	242	85	145	3	Tr	Tr	0.1	0.2
358	Instant, plain	1 pkt	137	85	80	2	Tr	Tr	Tr	0.1
	Cream of Wheat®:									
359	Regular, quick, instant	1 cup	244	86	140	4	Tr	0.1	Tr	0.2
360	Mix'n Eat, plain	1 pkt	142	82	100	3	Tr	Tr	Tr	0.1
361	Malt-O-Meal®	1 cup	240	88	120	4	Tr	Tr	Tr	0.1
	Oatmeal or rolled oats:									
362	Regular, quick, instant, nonfortified	1 cup	234	85	145	6	2	0.4	0.8	1.0
	Instant, fortified:									
363	Plain	1 pkt	177	86	105	4	2	0.3	0.6	0.7
364	Flavored	1 pkt	164	76	160	5	2	0.3	0.7	0.8

[25] Made with vegetable shortening.
[27] Nutrient added.
[28] Cooked without salt. If salt is added according to label recommendations, sodium content is 540 mg.
[29] For white corn grits. Cooked yellow grits contain 145 IU or 14 RE.
[30] Value based on label declaration for added nutrients.

Nutrients in Indicated Quantity

Cho-les-terol	Carbo-hydrate	Calcium	Phos-phorus	Iron	Potas-sium	Sodium	Vitamin A value (IU)	Vitamin A value (RE)	Thiamin	Ribo-flavin	Niacin	Ascorbic acid	Item No.
Milli-grams	Grams	Milli-grams	Milli-grams	Milli-grams	Milli-grams	Milli-grams	Inter-national units	Retinol equiva-lents	Milli-grams	Milli-grams	Milli-grams	Milli-grams	
0	212	267	563	12.0	707	2,231	0	0	2.09	1.20	15.4	0	329
0	12	15	31	0.7	39	124	0	0	0.12	0.07	0.9	0	330
0	12	15	31	0.7	39	124	0	0	0.09	0.07	0.9	0	331
0	33	49	60	1.4	71	339	0	0	0.27	0.12	2.2	0	332
0	218	322	990	12.4	1,966	2,461	0	0	1.54	2.36	15.0	0	333
0	16	23	71	0.9	141	177	0	0	0.11	0.17	1.1	0	334
0	16	23	71	0.9	141	177	0	0	0.09	0.17	1.1	0	335
0	239	463	395	14.1	1,058	1,657	Tr	Tr	1.50	2.81	18.6	Tr	336
0	13	25	22	0.8	59	92	Tr	Tr	0.08	0.15	1.0	Tr	337
0	13	25	22	0.8	59	92	Tr	Tr	0.06	0.15	1.0	Tr	338
0	218	363	658	12.3	926	3,164	0	0	1.86	1.45	15.0	0	339
0	12	20	36	0.7	51	175	0	0	0.10	0.08	0.8	0	340
0	12	20	36	0.7	51	175	0	0	0.08	0.08	0.8	0	341
0	213	572	835	15.8	627	2,447	Tr	Tr	2.09	1.45	20.5	Tr	342
0	12	32	47	0.9	35	138	Tr	Tr	0.12	0.08	1.2	Tr	343
0	12	32	47	0.9	35	138	Tr	Tr	0.10	0.08	1.2	Tr	344
0	222	572	490	12.9	508	2,334	Tr	Tr	2.13	1.41	17.0	Tr	345
0	12	32	27	0.7	28	129	Tr	Tr	0.12	0.08	0.9	Tr	346
0	12	32	27	0.7	28	129	Tr	Tr	0.09	0.08	0.9	Tr	347
0	10	25	21	0.6	22	101	Tr	Tr	0.09	0.06	0.7	Tr	348
0	10	25	21	0.6	22	101	Tr	Tr	0.07	0.06	0.7	Tr	349
0	15	38	32	0.9	34	154	Tr	Tr	0.14	0.09	1.1	Tr	350
0	22	57	49	1.3	50	231	Tr	Tr	0.21	0.14	1.7	Tr	351
0	206	327	1,180	15.5	799	2,887	Tr	Tr	1.59	0.95	17.4	Tr	352
0	13	20	74	1.0	50	180	Tr	Tr	0.10	0.06	1.1	Tr	353
0	13	20	74	1.0	50	180	Tr	Tr	0.08	0.06	1.1	Tr	354
0	50	92	136	2.2	126	1,254	910	273	0.17	0.20	2.5	0	355
67	40	81	134	2.0	118	1,023	850	256	0.10	0.18	1.6	0	356
0	31	0	29	[27]1.5	53	[28]0	[29]0	[29]0	[27]0.24	[27]0.15	[27]2.0	0	357
0	18	7	16	[27]1.0	29	343	0	0	[27]0.18	[27]0.08	[27]1.3	0	358
0	29	[30]54	[31]43	[30]10.9	46	[31,32]5	0	0	[30]0.24	[30]0.07	[30]1.5	0	359
0	21	[30]20	[30]20	[30]8.1	38	241	[30]1,250	[30]376	[30]0.43	[30]0.28	[30]5.0	0	360
0	26	5	[30]24	[30]9.6	31	[33]2	0	0	[30]0.48	[30]0.24	[30]5.8	0	361
0	25	19	178	1.6	131	[34]2	40	4	0.26	0.05	0.3	0	362
0	18	[27]163	133	[27]6.3	99	[27]285	[27]1,510	[27]453	[27]0.53	[27]0.28	[27]5.5	0	363
0	31	[27]168	148	[27]6.7	137	[27]254	[27]1,530	[27]460	[27]0.53	[27]0.38	[27]5.9	Tr	364

[31] For regular and instant cereal. For quick cereal, phosphorus is 102 mg and sodium is 142 mg.
[32] Cooked without salt. If salt is added according to label recommendations, sodium content is 390 mg.
[33] Cooked without salt. If salt is added according to label recommendations, sodium content is 324 mg.
[34] Cooked without salt. If salt is added according to label recommendations, sodium content is 374 mg.

Item No.	Foods, approximate measures, units, and weight (weight of edible portion only)		Grams	Water Percent	Food energy Calories	Protein Grams	Fat Grams	Fatty acids Saturated Grams	Mono-unsaturated Grams	Poly-unsaturated Grams

Grain Products—Con.

Breakfast cereals:
Ready to eat:

Item No.	Food	Measure	Grams	Water %	Cal	Protein	Fat	Sat	Mono	Poly
365	All-Bran® (about 1/3 cup)	1 oz	28	3	70	4	1	0.1	0.1	0.3
366	Cap'n Crunch® (about 3/4 cup)	1 oz	28	3	120	1	3	1.7	0.3	0.4
367	Cheerios® (about 1-1/4 cup)	1 oz	28	5	110	4	2	0.3	0.6	0.7
	Corn Flakes (about 1-1/4 cup):									
368	Kellogg's®	1 oz	28	3	110	2	Tr	Tr	Tr	Tr
369	Toasties®	1 oz	28	3	110	2	Tr	Tr	Tr	Tr
	40% Bran Flakes:									
370	Kellogg's® (about 3/4 cup)	1 oz	28	3	90	4	1	0.1	0.1	0.3
371	Post® (about 2/3 cup)	1 oz	28	3	90	3	Tr	0.1	0.1	0.2
372	Froot Loops® (about 1 cup)	1 oz	28	3	110	2	1	0.2	0.1	0.1
373	Golden Grahams® (about 3/4 cup)	1 oz	28	2	110	2	1	0.7	0.1	0.2
374	Grape-Nuts® (about 1/4 cup)	1 oz	28	3	100	3	Tr	Tr	Tr	0.1
375	Honey Nut Cheerios® (about 3/4 cup)	1 oz	28	3	105	3	1	0.1	0.3	0.3
376	Lucky Charms® (about 1 cup)	1 oz	28	3	110	3	1	0.2	0.4	0.4
377	Nature Valley® Granola (about 1/3 cup)	1 oz	28	4	125	3	5	3.3	0.7	0.7
378	100% Natural Cereal (about 1/4 cup)	1 oz	28	2	135	3	6	4.1	1.2	0.5
379	Product 19® (about 3/4 cup)	1 oz	28	3	110	3	Tr	Tr	Tr	0.1
	Raisin Bran:									
380	Kellogg's® (about 3/4 cup)	1 oz	28	8	90	3	1	0.1	0.1	0.3
381	Post® (about 1/2 cup)	1 oz	28	9	85	3	1	0.1	0.1	0.3
382	Rice Krispies® (about 1 cup)	1 oz	28	2	110	2	Tr	Tr	Tr	0.1
383	Shredded Wheat (about 2/3 cup)	1 oz	28	5	100	3	1	0.1	0.1	0.3
384	Special K® (about 1-1/3 cup)	1 oz	28	2	110	6	Tr	Tr	Tr	Tr
385	Super Sugar Crisp® (about 7/8 cup)	1 oz	28	2	105	2	Tr	Tr	Tr	0.1
386	Sugar Frosted Flakes, Kellogg's® (about 3/4 cup)	1 oz	28	3	110	1	Tr	Tr	Tr	Tr
387	Sugar Smacks® (about 3/4 cup)	1 oz	28	3	105	2	1	0.1	0.1	0.2
388	Total® (about 1 cup)	1 oz	28	4	100	3	1	0.1	0.1	0.3
389	Trix® (about 1 cup)	1 oz	28	3	110	2	Tr	0.2	0.1	0.1
390	Wheaties® (about 1 cup)	1 oz	28	5	100	3	Tr	0.1	Tr	0.2
391	Buckwheat flour, light, sifted	1 cup	98	12	340	6	1	0.2	0.4	0.4
392	Bulgur, uncooked	1 cup	170	10	600	19	3	1.2	0.3	1.2
	Cakes prepared from cake mixes with enriched flour:[35]									
	Angelfood:									
393	Whole cake, 9-3/4-in diam. tube cake	1 cake	635	38	1,510	38	2	0.4	0.2	1.0
394	Piece, 1/12 of cake	1 piece	53	38	125	3	Tr	Tr	Tr	0.1
	Coffeecake, crumb:									
395	Whole cake, 7-3/4 by 5-5/8 by 1-1/4 in	1 cake	430	30	1,385	27	41	11.8	16.7	9.6
396	Piece, 1/6 of cake	1 piece	72	30	230	5	7	2.0	2.8	1.6
	Devil's food with chocolate frosting:									
397	Whole, 2-layer cake, 8- or 9-in diam.	1 cake	1,107	24	3,755	49	136	55.6	51.4	19.7
398	Piece, 1/16 of cake	1 piece	69	24	235	3	8	3.5	3.2	1.2
399	Cupcake, 2-1/2-in diam.	1 cupcake	35	24	120	2	4	1.8	1.6	0.6
	Gingerbread:									
400	Whole cake, 8 in square	1 cake	570	37	1,575	18	39	9.6	16.4	10.5
401	Piece, 1/9 of cake	1 piece	63	37	175	2	4	1.1	1.8	1.2

[27] Nutrient added.
[30] Value based on label declaration for added nutrients.

Nutrients in Indicated Quantity

Cho-les-terol	Carbo-hydrate	Calcium	Phos-phorus	Iron	Potas-sium	Sodium	Vitamin A value (IU)	(RE)	Thiamin	Ribo-flavin	Niacin	Ascorbic acid	Item No.
Milli-grams	Grams	Milli-grams	Milli-grams	Milli-grams	Milli-grams	Milli-grams	Inter-national units	Retinol equiva-lents	Milli-grams	Milli-grams	Milli-grams	Milli-grams	
0	21	23	264	[30]4.5	350	320	[30]1,250	[30]375	[30]0.37	[30]0.43	[30]5.0	[30]15	365
0	23	5	36	[27]7.5	37	213	[30]40	[30]4	[27]0.50	[27]0.55	[276]6.6	[30]0	366
0	20	48	134	[30]4.5	101	307	[30]1,250	[30]375	[30]0.37	[30]0.43	[30]5.0	[30]15	367
0	24	1	18	[30]1.8	26	351	[30]1,250	[30]375	[30]0.37	[30]0.43	[30]5.0	[30]15	368
0	24	1	12	[27]0.7	33	297	[30]1,250	[30]375	[30]0.37	[30]0.43	[30]5.0	0	369
0	22	14	139	[30]8.1	180	264	[30]1,250	[30]375	[30]0.37	[30]0.43	[30]5.0	0	370
0	22	12	179	[30]4.5	151	260	[30]1,250	[30]375	[30]0.37	[30]0.43	[30]5.0	0	371
0	25	3	24	[30]4.5	26	145	[30]1,250	[30]375	[30]0.37	[30]0.43	[30]5.0	[30]15	372
Tr	24	17	41	[30]4.5	63	346	[30]1,250	[30]375	[30]0.37	[30]0.43	[30]5.0	[30]15	373
0	23	11	71	1.2	95	197	[30]1,250	[30]375	[30]0.37	[30]0.43	[30]5.0	0	374
0	23	20	105	[30]4.5	99	257	[30]1,250	[30]375	[30]0.37	[30]0.43	[30]5.0	[30]15	375
0	23	32	79	[30]4.5	59	201	[30]1,250	[30]375	[30]0.37	[30]0.43	[30]5.0	[30]15	376
0	19	18	89	0.9	98	58	20	2	0.10	0.05	0.2	0	377
Tr	18	49	104	0.8	140	12	20	2	0.09	0.15	0.6	0	378
0	24	3	40	[30]18.0	44	325	[30]5,000	[30]1,501	[30]1.50	[30]1.70	[30]20.0	[30]60	379
0	21	10	105	[30]3.5	147	207	[30]960	[30]288	[30]0.28	[30]0.34	[30]3.9	0	380
0	21	13	119	[30]4.5	175	185	[30]1,250	[30]375	[30]0.37	[30]0.43	[30]5.0	0	381
0	25	4	34	[30]1.8	29	340	[30]1,250	[30]375	[30]0.37	[30]0.43	[30]5.0	[30]15	382
0	23	11	100	1.2	102	3	0	0	0.07	0.08	1.5	0	383
Tr	21	8	55	[30]4.5	49	265	[30]1,250	[30]375	[30]0.37	[30]0.43	[30]5.0	[30]15	384
0	26	6	52	[30]1.8	105	25	[30]1,250	[30]375	[30]0.37	[30]0.43	[30]5.0	0	385
0	26	1	21	[30]1.8	18	230	[30]1,250	[30]375	[30]0.37	[30]0.43	[30]5.0	[30]15	386
0	25	3	31	[30]1.8	42	75	[30]1,250	[30]375	[30]0.37	[30]0.43	[30]5.0	[30]15	387
0	22	48	118	[30]18.0	106	352	[30]5,000	[30]1,501	[30]1.50	[30]1.70	[30]20.0	[30]60	388
0	25	6	19	[30]4.5	27	181	[30]1,250	[30]375	[30]0.37	[30]0.43	[30]5.0	[30]15	389
0	23	43	98	[30]4.5	106	354	[30]1,250	[30]375	[30]0.37	[30]0.43	[30]5.0	[30]15	390
0	78	11	86	1.0	314	2	0	0	0.08	0.04	0.4	0	391
0	129	49	575	9.5	389	7	0	0	0.48	0.24	7.7	0	392
0	342	527	1,086	2.7	845	3,226	0	0	0.32	1.27	1.6	0	393
0	29	44	91	0.2	71	269	0	0	0.03	0.11	0.1	0	394
279	225	262	748	7.3	469	1,853	690	194	0.82	0.90	7.7	1	395
47	38	44	125	1.2	78	310	120	32	0.14	0.15	1.3	Tr	396
598	645	653	1,162	22.1	1,439	2,900	1,660	498	1.11	1.66	10.0	1	397
37	40	41	72	1.4	90	181	100	31	0.07	0.10	0.6	Tr	398
19	20	21	37	0.7	46	92	50	16	0.04	0.05	0.3	Tr	399
6	291	513	570	10.8	1,562	1,733	0	0	0.86	1.03	7.4	1	400
1	32	57	63	1.2	173	192	0	0	0.09	0.11	0.8	Tr	401

[35] Excepting angelfood cake, cakes were made from mixes containing vegetable shortening and frostings were made with margarine.

Item No.	Foods, approximate measures, units, and weight (weight of edible portion only)			Water	Food energy	Pro-tein	Fat	Fatty acids		
								Satu-rated	Mono-unsatu-rated	Poly-unsatu-rated
	Grain Products—Con.		Grams	Per-cent	Cal-ories	Grams	Grams	Grams	Grams	Grams
	Cakes prepared from cake mixes with enriched flour:[35]									
	Yellow with chocolate frosting:									
402	Whole, 2-layer cake, 8- or 9-in diam.	1 cake	1,108	26	3,735	45	125	47.8	48.8	21.8
403	Piece, 1/16 of cake	1 piece	69	26	235	3	8	3.0	3.0	1.4
	Cakes prepared from home recipes using enriched flour:									
	Carrot, with cream cheese frosting:[36]									
404	Whole cake, 10-in diam. tube cake	1 cake	1,536	23	6,175	63	328	66.0	135.2	107.5
405	Piece, 1/16 of cake	1 piece	96	23	385	4	21	4.1	8.4	6.7
	Fruitcake, dark:[36]									
406	Whole cake, 7-1/2-in diam., 2-1/4-in high tube cake	1 cake	1,361	18	5,185	74	228	47.6	113.0	51.7
407	Piece, 1/32 of cake, 2/3-in arc	1 piece	43	18	165	2	7	1.5	3.6	1.6
	Plain sheet cake:[37]									
	Without frosting:									
408	Whole cake, 9-in square	1 cake	777	25	2,830	35	108	29.5	45.1	25.6
409	Piece, 1/9 of cake	1 piece	86	25	315	4	12	3.3	5.0	2.8
	With uncooked white frosting:									
410	Whole cake, 9-in square	1 cake	1,096	21	4,020	37	129	41.6	50.4	26.3
411	Piece, 1/9 of cake	1 piece	121	21	445	4	14	4.6	5.6	2.9
	Pound:[38]									
412	Loaf, 8-1/2 by 3-1/2 by 3-1/4 in	1 loaf	514	22	2,025	33	94	21.1	40.9	26.7
413	Slice, 1/17 of loaf	1 slice	30	22	120	2	5	1.2	2.4	1.6
	Cakes, commercial, made with en-riched flour:									
	Pound:									
414	Loaf, 8-1/2 by 3-1/2 by 3 in	1 loaf	500	24	1,935	26	94	52.0	30.0	4.0
415	Slice, 1/17 of loaf	1 slice	29	24	110	2	5	3.0	1.7	0.2
	Snack cakes:									
416	Devil's food with creme filling (2 small cakes per pkg)	1 small cake	28	20	105	1	4	1.7	1.5	0.6
417	Sponge with creme filling (2 small cakes per pkg)	1 small cake	42	19	155	1	5	2.3	2.1	0.5
	White with white frosting:									
418	Whole, 2-layer cake, 8- or 9-in diam.	1 cake	1,140	24	4,170	43	148	33.1	61.6	42.2
419	Piece, 1/16 of cake	1 piece	71	24	260	3	9	2.1	3.8	2.6
	Yellow with chocolate frosting:									
420	Whole, 2-layer cake, 8- or 9-in diam.	1 cake	1,108	23	3,895	40	175	92.0	58.7	10.0
421	Piece, 1/16 of cake	1 piece	69	23	245	2	11	5.7	3.7	0.6
	Cheesecake:									
422	Whole cake, 9-in diam.	1 cake	1,110	46	3,350	60	213	119.9	65.5	14.4
423	Piece, 1/12 of cake	1 piece	92	46	280	5	18	9.9	5.4	1.2
	Cookies made with enriched flour:									
	Brownies with nuts:									
424	Commercial, with frosting, 1-1/2 by 1-3/4 by 7/8 in	1 brownie	25	13	100	1	4	1.6	2.0	0.6
425	From home recipe, 1-3/4 by 1-3/4 by 7/8 in[36]	1 brownie	20	10	95	1	6	1.4	2.8	1.2
	Chocolate chip:									
426	Commercial, 2-1/4-in diam., 3/8 in thick	4 cookies	42	4	180	2	9	2.9	3.1	2.6

[35] Excepting angelfood cake, cakes were made from mixes containing vegetable shortening and frostings were made with margarine.
[36] Made with vegetable oil.

							Vitamin A value						
Cho-les-terol	Carbo-hydrate	Calcium	Phos-phorus	Iron	Potas-sium	Sodium	(IU)	(RE)	Thiamin	Ribo-flavin	Niacin	Ascorbic acid	Item No.
Milli-grams	Grams	Milli-grams	Milli-grams	Milli-grams	Milli-grams	Milli-grams	Inter-national units	Retinol equiva-lents	Milli-grams	Milli-grams	Milli-grams	Milli-grams	
576	638	1,008	2,017	15.5	1,208	2,515	1,550	465	1.22	1.66	11.1	1	402
36	40	63	126	1.0	75	157	100	29	0.08	0.10	0.7	Tr	403
1183	775	707	998	21.0	1,720	4,470	2,240	246	1.83	1.97	14.7	23	404
74	48	44	62	1.3	108	279	140	15	0.11	0.12	0.9	1	405
640	783	1,293	1,592	37.6	6,138	2,123	1,720	422	2.41	2.55	17.0	504	406
20	25	41	50	1.2	194	67	50	13	0.08	0.08	0.5	16	407
552	434	497	793	11.7	614	2,331	1,320	373	1.24	1.40	10.1	2	408
61	48	55	88	1.3	68	258	150	41	0.14	0.15	1.1	Tr	409
636	694	548	822	11.0	669	2,488	2,190	647	1.21	1.42	9.9	2	410
70	77	61	91	1.2	74	275	240	71	0.13	0.16	1.1	Tr	411
555	265	339	473	9.3	483	1,645	3,470	1,033	0.93	1.08	7.8	1	412
32	15	20	28	0.5	28	96	200	60	0.05	0.06	0.5	Tr	413
1100	257	146	517	8.0	443	1,857	2,820	715	0.96	1.12	8.1	0	414
64	15	8	30	0.5	26	108	160	41	0.06	0.06	0.5	0	415
15	17	21	26	1.0	34	105	20	4	0.06	0.09	0.7	0	416
7	27	14	44	0.6	37	155	30	9	0.07	0.06	0.6	0	417
46	670	536	1,585	15.5	832	2,827	640	194	3.19	2.05	27.6	0	418
3	42	33	99	1.0	52	176	40	12	0.20	0.13	1.7	0	419
609	620	366	1,884	19.9	1,972	3,080	1,850	488	0.78	2.22	10.0	0	420
38	39	23	117	1.2	123	192	120	30	0.05	0.14	0.6	0	421
2053	317	622	977	5.3	1,088	2,464	2,820	833	0.33	1.44	5.1	56	422
170	26	52	81	0.4	90	204	230	69	0.03	0.12	0.4	5	423
14	16	13	26	0.6	50	59	70	18	0.08	0.07	0.3	Tr	424
18	11	9	26	0.4	35	51	20	6	0.05	0.05	0.3	Tr	425
5	28	13	41	0.8	68	140	50	15	0.10	0.23	1.0	Tr	426

[37]Cake made with vegetable shortening; frosting with margarine.
[38]Made with margarine.

Item No.	Foods, approximate measures, units, and weight (weight of edible portion only)			Water	Food energy	Pro-tein	Fat	Fatty acids		
								Satu-rated	Mono-unsatu-rated	Poly-unsatu-rated
			Grams	Per-cent	Cal-ories	Grams	Grams	Grams	Grams	Grams

Grain Products—Con.

	Cookies made with enriched flour:									
	Chocolate chip:									
427	From home recipe, 2-1/3-in diam.[25]	4 cookies	40	3	185	2	11	3.9	4.3	2.0
428	From refrigerated dough, 2-1/4-in diam., 3/8 in thick	4 cookies	48	5	225	2	11	4.0	4.4	2.0
429	Fig bars, square, 1-5/8 by 1-5/8 by 3/8 in or rectangular, 1-1/2 by 1-3/4 by 1/2 in	4 cookies	56	12	210	2	4	1.0	1.5	1.0
430	Oatmeal with raisins, 2-5/8-in diam., 1/4 in thick	4 cookies	52	4	245	3	10	2.5	4.5	2.8
431	Peanut butter cookie, from home recipe, 2-5/8-in diam.[25]	4 cookies	48	3	245	4	14	4.0	5.8	2.8
432	Sandwich type (chocolate or vanilla), 1-3/4-in diam., 3/8 in thick	4 cookies	40	2	195	2	8	2.0	3.6	2.2
	Shortbread:									
433	Commercial	4 small cookies	32	6	155	2	8	2.9	3.0	1.1
434	From home recipe [38]	2 large cookies	28	3	145	2	8	1.3	2.7	3.4
435	Sugar cookie, from refrigerated dough, 2-1/2-in diam., 1/4 in thick	4 cookies	48	4	235	2	12	2.3	5.0	3.6
436	Vanilla wafers, 1-3/4-in diam., 1/4 in thick	10 cookies	40	4	185	2	7	1.8	3.0	1.8
437	Corn chips	1-oz package	28	1	155	2	9	1.4	2.4	3.7
	Cornmeal:									
438	Whole-ground, unbolted, dry form	1 cup	122	12	435	11	5	0.5	1.1	2.5
439	Bolted (nearly whole-grain), dry form	1 cup	122	12	440	11	4	0.5	0.9	2.2
	Degermed, enriched:									
440	Dry form	1 cup	138	12	500	11	2	0.2	0.4	0.9
441	Cooked	1 cup	240	88	120	3	Tr	Tr	0.1	0.2
	Crackers:[39]									
	Cheese:									
442	Plain, 1 in square	10 crackers	10	4	50	1	3	0.9	1.2	0.3
443	Sandwich type (peanut butter)	1 sandwich	8	3	40	1	2	0.4	0.8	0.3
444	Graham, plain, 2-1/2 in square	2 crackers	14	5	60	1	1	0.4	0.6	0.4
445	Melba toast, plain	1 piece	5	4	20	1	Tr	0.1	0.1	0.1
446	Rye wafers, whole-grain, 1-7/8 by 3-1/2 in	2 wafers	14	5	55	1	1	0.3	0.4	0.3
447	Saltines [40]	4 crackers	12	4	50	1	1	0.5	0.4	0.2
448	Snack-type, standard	1 round cracker	3	3	15	Tr	1	0.2	0.4	0.1
449	Wheat, thin	4 crackers	8	3	35	1	1	0.5	0.5	0.4
450	Whole-wheat wafers	2 crackers	8	4	35	1	2	0.5	0.6	0.4
451	Croissants, made with enriched flour, 4-1/2 by 4 by 1-3/4 in	1 croissant	57	22	235	5	12	3.5	6.7	1.4
	Danish pastry, made with enriched flour:									
	Plain without fruit or nuts:									
452	Packaged ring, 12 oz	1 ring	340	27	1,305	21	71	21.8	28.6	15.6
453	Round piece, about 4-1/4-in diam., 1 in high	1 pastry	57	27	220	4	12	3.6	4.8	2.6
454	Ounce	1 oz	28	27	110	2	6	1.8	2.4	1.3
455	Fruit, round piece	1 pastry	65	30	235	4	13	3.9	5.2	2.9
	Doughnuts, made with enriched flour:									
456	Cake type, plain, 3-1/4-in diam., 1 in high	1 doughnut	50	21	210	3	12	2.8	5.0	3.0
457	Yeast-leavened, glazed, 3-3/4-in diam., 1-1/4 in high	1 doughnut	60	27	235	4	13	5.2	5.5	0.9
458	English muffins, plain, enriched	1 muffin	57	42	140	5	1	0.3	0.2	0.3
459	Toasted	1 muffin	50	29	140	5	1	0.3	0.2	0.3

[25]Made with vegetable shortening.
[38]Made with margarine.

							Vitamin A value						
Cho-les-terol	Carbo-hydrate	Calcium	Phos-phorus	Iron	Potas-sium	Sodium	(IU)	(RE)	Thiamin	Ribo-flavin	Niacin	Ascorbic acid	Item No.
Milli-grams	Grams	Milli-grams	Milli-grams	Milli-grams	Milli-grams	Milli-grams	Inter-national units	Retinol equiva-lents	Milli-grams	Milli-grams	Milli-grams	Milli-grams	
18	26	13	34	1.0	82	82	20	5	0.06	0.06	0.6	0	427
22	32	13	34	1.0	62	173	30	8	0.06	0.10	0.9	0	428
27	42	40	34	1.4	162	180	60	6	0.08	0.07	0.7	Tr	429
2	36	18	58	1.1	90	148	40	12	0.09	0.08	1.0	0	430
22	28	21	60	1.1	110	142	20	5	0.07	0.07	1.9	0	431
0	29	12	40	1.4	66	189	0	0	0.09	0.07	0.8	0	432
27	20	13	39	0.8	38	123	30	8	0.10	0.09	0.9	0	433
0	17	6	31	0.6	18	125	300	89	0.08	0.06	0.7	Tr	434
29	31	50	91	0.9	33	261	40	11	0.09	0.06	1.1	0	435
25	29	16	36	0.8	50	150	50	14	0.07	0.10	1.0	0	436
0	16	35	52	0.5	52	233	110	11	0.04	0.05	0.4	1	437
0	90	24	312	2.2	346	1	620	62	0.46	0.13	2.4	0	438
0	91	21	272	2.2	303	1	590	59	0.37	0.10	2.3	0	439
0	108	8	137	5.9	166	1	610	61	0.61	0.36	4.8	0	440
0	26	2	34	1.4	38	0	140	14	0.14	0.10	1.2	0	441
6	6	11	17	0.3	17	112	20	5	0.05	0.04	0.4	0	442
1	5	7	25	0.3	17	90	Tr	Tr	0.04	0.03	0.6	0	443
0	11	6	20	0.4	36	86	0	0	0.02	0.03	0.6	0	444
0	4	6	10	0.1	11	44	0	0	0.01	0.01	0.1	0	445
0	10	7	44	0.5	65	115	0	0	0.06	0.03	0.5	0	446
4	9	3	12	0.5	17	165	0	0	0.06	0.05	0.6	0	447
0	2	3	6	0.1	4	30	Tr	Tr	0.01	0.01	0.1	0	448
0	5	3	15	0.3	17	69	Tr	Tr	0.04	0.03	0.4	0	449
0	5	3	22	0.2	31	59	0	0	0.02	0.03	0.4	0	450
13	27	20	64	2.1	68	452	50	13	0.17	0.13	1.3	0	451
292	152	360	347	6.5	316	1,302	360	99	0.95	1.02	8.5	Tr	452
49	26	60	58	1.1	53	218	60	17	0.16	0.17	1.4	Tr	453
24	13	30	29	0.5	26	109	30	8	0.08	0.09	0.7	Tr	454
56	28	17	80	1.3	57	233	40	11	0.16	0.14	1.4	Tr	455
20	24	22	111	1.0	58	192	20	5	0.12	0.12	1.1	Tr	456
21	26	17	55	1.4	64	222	Tr	Tr	0.28	0.12	1.8	0	457
0	27	96	67	1.7	331	378	0	0	0.26	0.19	2.2	0	458
0	27	96	67	1.7	331	378	0	0	0.23	0.19	2.2	0	459

[39]Crackers made with enriched flour except for rye wafers and whole-wheat wafers.
[40]Made with lard.

Item No.	Foods, approximate measures, units, and weight (weight of edible portion only)		Grams	Water Per-cent	Food energy Cal-ories	Pro-tein Grams	Fat Grams	Fatty acids		
								Satu-rated Grams	Mono-unsatu-rated Grams	Poly-unsatu-rated Grams
	Grain Products—Con.									
460	French toast, from home recipe---	1 slice---------	65	53	155	6	7	1.6	2.0	1.6
	Macaroni, enriched, cooked (cut lengths, elbows, shells):									
461	Firm stage (hot)---------------	1 cup-----------	130	64	190	7	1	0.1	0.1	0.3
	Tender stage:									
462	Cold------------------------	1 cup-----------	105	72	115	4	Tr	0.1	0.1	0.2
463	Hot-------------------------	1 cup-----------	140	72	155	5	1	0.1	0.1	0.2
	Muffins made with enriched flour, 2-1/2-in diam., 1-1/2 in high:									
	From home recipe:									
464	Blueberry [25]-----------------	1 muffin--------	45	37	135	3	5	1.5	2.1	1.2
465	Bran [36] ---------------------	1 muffin--------	45	35	125	3	6	1.4	1.6	2.3
466	Corn (enriched, degermed cornmeal and flour) [25] ------	1 muffin--------	45	33	145	3	5	1.5	2.2	1.4
	From commercial mix (egg and water added):									
467	Blueberry--------------------	1 muffin--------	45	33	140	3	5	1.4	2.0	1.2
468	Bran------------------------	1 muffin--------	45	28	140	3	4	1.3	1.6	1.0
469	Corn------------------------	1 muffin--------	45	30	145	3	6	1.7	2.3	1.4
470	Noodles (egg noodles), enriched, cooked------------------------	1 cup-----------	160	70	200	7	2	0.5	0.6	0.6
471	Noodles, chow mein, canned-------	1 cup-----------	45	11	220	6	11	2.1	7.3	0.4
	Pancakes, 4-in diam.:									
472	Buckwheat, from mix (with buck-wheat and enriched flours), egg and milk added-----------	1 pancake-------	27	58	55	2	2	0.9	0.9	0.5
	Plain:									
473	From home recipe using enriched flour-------------	1 pancake-------	27	50	60	2	2	0.5	0.8	0.5
474	From mix (with enriched flour), egg, milk, and oil added--------------------	1 pancake-------	27	54	60	2	2	0.5	0.9	0.5
	Piecrust, made with enriched flour and vegetable shorten-ing, baked:									
475	From home recipe, 9-in diam.---	1 pie shell-----	180	15	900	11	60	14.8	25.9	15.7
476	From mix, 9-in diam.-----------	Piecrust for 2-crust pie-----	320	19	1,485	20	93	22.7	41.0	25.0
	Pies, piecrust made with enriched flour, vegetable shortening, 9-in diam.:									
	Apple:									
477	Whole----------------------	1 pie----------	945	48	2,420	21	105	27.4	44.4	26.5
478	Piece, 1/6 of pie-----------	1 piece--------	158	48	405	3	18	4.6	7.4	4.4
	Blueberry:									
479	Whole----------------------	1 pie----------	945	51	2,285	23	102	25.5	44.4	27.4
480	Piece, 1/6 of pie-----------	1 piece--------	158	51	380	4	17	4.3	7.4	4.6
	Cherry:									
481	Whole----------------------	1 pie----------	945	47	2,465	25	107	28.4	46.3	27.4
482	Piece, 1/6 of pie-----------	1 piece--------	158	47	410	4	18	4.7	7.7	4.6
	Creme:									
483	Whole----------------------	1 pie----------	910	43	2,710	20	139	90.1	23.7	6.4
484	Piece, 1/6 of pie-----------	1 piece--------	152	43	455	3	23	15.0	4.0	1.1
	Custard:									
485	Whole----------------------	1 pie----------	910	58	1,985	56	101	33.7	40.0	19.1
486	Piece, 1/6 of pie-----------	1 piece--------	152	58	330	9	17	5.6	6.7	3.2
	Lemon meringue:									
487	Whole----------------------	1 pie----------	840	47	2,140	31	86	26.0	34.4	17.6
488	Piece, 1/6 of pie-----------	1 piece--------	140	47	355	5	14	4.3	5.7	2.9
	Peach:									
489	Whole----------------------	1 pie----------	945	48	2,410	24	101	24.6	43.5	26.5
490	Piece, 1/6 of pie-----------	1 piece--------	158	48	405	4	17	4.1	7.3	4.4

[25] Made with vegetable shortening.

									Nutrients in Indicated Quantity					

Cho-les-terol	Carbo-hydrate	Calcium	Phos-phorus	Iron	Potas-sium	Sodium	Vitamin A value		Thiamin	Ribo-flavin	Niacin	Ascorbic acid	Item No.
							(IU)	(RE)					
Milli-grams	Grams	Milli-grams	Milli-grams	Milli-grams	Milli-grams	Milli-grams	Inter-national units	Retinol equiva-lents	Milli-grams	Milli-grams	Milli-grams	Milli-grams	
112	17	72	85	1.3	86	257	110	32	0.12	0.16	1.0	Tr	460
0	39	14	85	2.1	103	1	0	0	0.23	0.13	1.8	0	461
0	24	8	53	1.3	64	1	0	0	0.15	0.08	1.2	0	462
0	32	11	70	1.7	85	1	0	0	0.20	0.11	1.5	0	463
19	20	54	46	0.9	47	198	40	9	0.10	0.11	0.9	1	464
24	19	60	125	1.4	99	189	230	30	0.11	0.13	1.3	3	465
23	21	66	59	0.9	57	169	80	15	0.11	0.11	0.9	Tr	466
45	22	15	90	0.9	54	225	50	11	0.10	0.17	1.1	Tr	467
28	24	27	182	1.7	50	385	100	14	0.08	0.12	1.9	0	468
42	22	30	128	1.3	31	291	90	16	0.09	0.09	0.8	Tr	469
50	37	16	94	2.6	70	3	110	34	0.22	0.13	1.9	0	470
5	26	14	41	0.4	33	450	0	0	0.05	0.03	0.6	0	471
20	6	59	91	0.4	66	125	60	17	0.04	0.05	0.2	Tr	472
16	9	27	38	0.5	33	115	30	10	0.06	0.07	0.5	Tr	473
16	8	36	71	0.7	43	160	30	7	0.09	0.12	0.8	Tr	474
0	79	25	90	4.5	90	1,100	0	0	0.54	0.40	5.0	0	475
0	141	131	272	9.3	179	2,602	0	0	1.06	0.80	9.9	0	476
0	360	76	208	9.5	756	2,844	280	28	1.04	0.76	9.5	9	477
0	60	13	35	1.6	126	476	50	5	0.17	0.13	1.6	2	478
0	330	104	217	12.3	945	2,533	850	85	1.04	0.85	10.4	38	479
0	55	17	36	2.1	158	423	140	14	0.17	0.14	1.7	6	480
0	363	132	236	9.5	992	2,873	4,160	416	1.13	0.85	9.5	0	481
0	61	22	40	1.6	166	480	700	70	0.19	0.14	1.6	0	482
46	351	273	919	6.8	796	2,207	1,250	391	0.36	0.89	6.4	0	483
8	59	46	154	1.1	133	369	210	65	0.06	0.15	1.1	0	484
1010	213	874	1,028	9.1	1,247	2,612	2,090	573	0.82	1.91	5.5	0	485
169	36	146	172	1.5	208	436	350	96	0.14	0.32	0.9	0	486
857	317	118	412	8.4	420	2,369	1,430	395	0.59	0.84	5.0	25	487
143	53	20	69	1.4	70	395	240	66	0.10	0.14	0.8	4	488
0	361	95	274	11.3	1,408	2,533	6,900	690	1.04	0.95	14.2	28	489
0	60	16	46	1.9	235	423	1,150	115	0.17	0.16	2.4	5	490

[36] Made with vegetable oil.

Item No.	Foods, approximate measures, units, and weight (weight of edible portion only)		Water	Food energy	Pro-tein	Fat	Fatty acids		
							Satu-rated	Mono-unsatu-rated	Poly-unsatu-rated
		Grams	Per-cent	Cal-ories	Grams	Grams	Grams	Grams	Grams

Grain Products—Con.

	Pies, piecrust made with enriched flour, vegetable shortening, 9-inch diam.:								
	Pecan:								
491	Whole----------------------- 1 pie----------	825	20	3,450	42	189	28.1	101.5	47.0
492	Piece, 1/6 of pie----------- 1 piece--------	138	20	575	7	32	4.7	17.0	7.9
	Pumpkin:								
493	Whole----------------------- 1 pie----------	910	59	1,920	36	102	38.2	40.0	18.2
494	Piece, 1/6 of pie----------- 1 piece--------	152	59	320	6	17	6.4	6.7	3.0
	Pies, fried:								
495	Apple----------------------- 1 pie----------	85	43	255	2	14	5.8	6.6	0.6
496	Cherry---------------------- 1 pie----------	85	42	250	2	14	5.8	6.7	0.6
	Popcorn, popped:								
497	Air-popped, unsalted---------- 1 cup----------	8	4	30	1	Tr	Tr	0.1	0.2
498	Popped in vegetable oil, salted 1 cup----------	11	3	55	1	3	0.5	1.4	1.2
499	Sugar syrup coated------------ 1 cup----------	35	4	135	2	1	0.1	0.3	0.6
	Pretzels, made with enriched flour:								
500	Stick, 2-1/4 in long---------- 10 pretzels-----	3	3	10	Tr	Tr	Tr	Tr	Tr
501	Twisted, dutch, 2-3/4 by 2-5/8 in------------------------ 1 pretzel-------	16	3	65	2	1	0.1	0.2	0.2
502	Twisted, thin, 3-1/4 by 2-1/4 by 1/4 in---------------- 10 pretzels-----	60	3	240	6	2	0.4	0.8	0.6
	Rice:								
503	Brown, cooked, served hot------ 1 cup----------	195	70	230	5	1	0.3	0.3	0.4
	White, enriched:								
	Commercial varieties, all types:								
504	Raw------------------------ 1 cup----------	185	12	670	12	1	0.2	0.2	0.3
505	Cooked, served hot--------- 1 cup----------	205	73	225	4	Tr	0.1	0.1	0.1
506	Instant, ready-to-serve, hot 1 cup----------	165	73	180	4	0	0.1	0.1	0.1
	Parboiled:								
507	Raw------------------------ 1 cup----------	185	10	685	14	1	0.1	0.1	0.2
508	Cooked, served hot--------- 1 cup----------	175	73	185	4	Tr	Tr	Tr	0.1
	Rolls, enriched:								
	Commercial:								
509	Dinner, 2-1/2-in diam., 2 in high-------------------- 1 roll----------	28	32	85	2	2	0.5	0.8	0.6
510	Frankfurter and hamburger (8 per 11-1/2-oz pkg.)-------- 1 roll----------	40	34	115	3	2	0.5	0.8	0.6
511	Hard, 3-3/4-in diam., 2 in high-------------------- 1 roll----------	50	25	155	5	2	0.4	0.5	0.6
512	Hoagie or submarine, 11-1/2 by 3 by 2-1/2 in---------- 1 roll----------	135	31	400	11	8	1.8	3.0	2.2
	From home recipe:								
513	Dinner, 2-1/2-in diam., 2 in high-------------------- 1 roll----------	35	26	120	3	3	0.8	1.2	0.9
	Spaghetti, enriched, cooked:								
514	Firm stage, "al dente," served hot------------------------- 1 cup----------	130	64	190	7	1	0.1	0.1	0.3
515	Tender stage, served hot------- 1 cup----------	140	73	155	5	1	0.1	0.1	0.2
516	Toaster pastries----------------- 1 pastry--------	54	13	210	2	6	1.7	3.6	0.4
517	Tortillas, corn----------------- 1 tortilla------	30	45	65	2	1	0.1	0.3	0.6
	Waffles, made with enriched flour, 7-in diam.:								
518	From home recipe---------------- 1 waffle--------	75	37	245	7	13	4.0	4.9	2.6
519	From mix, egg and milk added--- 1 waffle--------	75	42	205	7	8	2.7	2.9	1.5
	Wheat flours:								
	All-purpose or family flour, enriched:								
520	Sifted, spooned-------------- 1 cup----------	115	12	420	12	1	0.2	0.1	0.5
521	Unsifted, spooned------------ 1 cup----------	125	12	455	13	1	0.2	0.1	0.5
522	Cake or pastry flour, enriched, sifted, spooned-------------- 1 cup----------	96	12	350	7	1	0.1	0.1	0.3
523	Self-rising, enriched, unsifted, spooned----------- 1 cup----------	125	12	440	12	1	0.2	0.1	0.5
524	Whole-wheat, from hard wheats, stirred--------------------- 1 cup----------	120	12	400	16	2	0.3	0.3	1.1

							Vitamin A value						
Cho-les-terol	Carbo-hydrate	Calcium	Phos-phorus	Iron	Potas-sium	Sodium	(IU)	(RE)	Thiamin	Ribo-flavin	Niacin	Ascorbic acid	Item No.
Milli-grams	Grams	Milli-grams	Milli-grams	Milli-grams	Milli-grams	Milli-grams	Inter-national units	Retinol equiva-lents	Milli-grams	Milli-grams	Milli-grams	Milli-grams	
569	423	388	850	27.2	1,015	1,823	1,320	322	1.82	0.99	6.6	0	491
95	71	65	142	4.6	170	305	220	54	0.30	0.17	1.1	0	492
655	223	464	628	8.2	1,456	1,947	22,480	2,493	0.82	1.27	7.3	0	493
109	37	78	105	1.4	243	325	3,750	416	0.14	0.21	1.2	0	494
14	31	12	34	0.9	42	326	30	3	0.09	0.06	1.0	1	495
13	32	11	41	0.7	61	371	190	19	0.06	0.06	0.6	1	496
0	6	1	22	0.2	20	Tr	10	1	0.03	0.01	0.2	0	497
0	6	3	31	0.3	19	86	20	2	0.01	0.02	0.1	0	498
0	30	2	47	0.5	90	Tr	30	3	0.13	0.02	0.4	0	499
0	2	1	3	0.1	3	48	0	0	0.01	0.01	0.1	0	500
0	13	4	15	0.3	16	258	0	0	0.05	0.04	0.7	0	501
0	48	16	55	1.2	61	966	0	0	0.19	0.15	2.6	0	502
0	50	23	142	1.0	137	0	0	0	0.18	0.04	2.7	0	503
0	149	44	174	5.4	170	9	0	0	0.81	0.06	6.5	0	504
0	50	21	57	1.8	57	0	0	0	0.23	0.02	2.1	0	505
0	40	5	31	1.3	0	0	0	0	0.21	0.02	1.7	0	506
0	150	111	370	5.4	278	17	0	0	0.81	0.07	6.5	0	507
0	41	33	100	1.4	75	0	0	0	0.19	0.02	2.1	0	508
Tr	14	33	44	0.8	36	155	Tr	Tr	0.14	0.09	1.1	Tr	509
Tr	20	54	44	1.2	56	241	Tr	Tr	0.20	0.13	1.6	Tr	510
Tr	30	24	46	1.4	49	313	0	0	0.20	0.12	1.7	0	511
Tr	72	100	115	3.8	128	683	0	0	0.54	0.33	4.5	0	512
12	20	16	36	1.1	41	98	30	8	0.12	0.12	1.2	0	513
0	39	14	85	2.0	103	1	0	0	0.23	0.13	1.8	0	514
0	32	11	70	1.7	85	1	0	0	0.20	0.11	1.5	0	515
0	38	104	104	2.2	91	248	520	52	0.17	0.18	2.3	4	516
0	13	42	55	0.6	43	1	80	8	0.05	0.03	0.4	0	517
102	26	154	135	1.5	129	445	140	39	0.18	0.24	1.5	Tr	518
59	27	179	257	1.2	146	515	170	49	0.14	0.23	0.9	Tr	519
0	88	18	100	5.1	109	2	0	0	0.73	0.46	6.1	0	520
0	95	20	109	5.5	119	3	0	0	0.80	0.50	6.6	0	521
0	76	16	70	4.2	91	2	0	0	0.58	0.38	5.1	0	522
0	93	331	583	5.5	113	1,349	0	0	0.80	0.50	6.6	0	523
0	85	49	446	5.2	444	4	0	0	0.66	0.14	5.2	0	524

Item No.	Foods, approximate measures, units, and weight (weight of edible portion only)			Water	Food energy	Pro-tein	Fat	Fatty acids		
								Satu-rated	Mono-unsatu-rated	Poly-unsatu-rated
	Legumes, Nuts, and Seeds		Grams	Per-cent	Cal-ories	Grams	Grams	Grams	Grams	Grams
	Almonds, shelled:									
525	Slivered, packed---------------	1 cup-----------	135	4	795	27	70	6.7	45.8	14.8
526	Whole--------------------------	1 oz-----------	28	4	165	6	15	1.4	9.6	3.1
	Beans, dry:									
	Cooked, drained:									
527	Black--------------------	1 cup-----------	171	66	225	15	1	0.1	0.1	0.5
528	Great Northern-----------	1 cup-----------	180	69	210	14	1	0.1	0.1	0.6
529	Lima---------------------	1 cup-----------	190	64	260	16	1	0.2	0.1	0.5
530	Pea (navy)---------------	1 cup-----------	190	69	225	15	1	0.1	0.1	0.7
531	Pinto--------------------	1 cup-----------	180	65	265	15	1	0.1	0.1	0.5
	Canned, solids and liquid:									
	White with:									
532	Frankfurters (sliced)------	1 cup-----------	255	71	365	19	18	7.4	8.8	0.7
533	Pork and tomato sauce------	1 cup-----------	255	71	310	16	7	2.4	2.7	0.7
534	Pork and sweet sauce-------	1 cup-----------	255	66	385	16	12	4.3	4.9	1.2
535	Red kidney-----------------	1 cup-----------	255	76	230	15	1	0.1	0.1	0.6
536	Black-eyed peas, dry, cooked (with residual cooking liquid)	1 cup-----------	250	80	190	13	1	0.2	Tr	0.3
537	Brazil nuts, shelled-------------	1 oz-----------	28	3	185	4	19	4.6	6.5	6.8
538	Carob flour----------------------	1 cup-----------	140	3	255	6	Tr	Tr	0.1	0.1
	Cashew nuts, salted:									
539	Dry roasted---------------------	1 cup-----------	137	2	785	21	63	12.5	37.4	10.7
540		1 oz-----------	28	2	165	4	13	2.6	7.7	2.2
541	Roasted in oil-----------------	1 cup-----------	130	4	750	21	63	12.4	36.9	10.6
542		1 oz-----------	28	4	165	5	14	2.7	8.1	2.3
543	Chestnuts, European (Italian), roasted, shelled---------------	1 cup-----------	143	40	350	5	3	0.6	1.1	1.2
544	Chickpeas, cooked, drained-------	1 cup-----------	163	60	270	15	4	0.4	0.9	1.9
	Coconut:									
	Raw:									
545	Piece, about 2 by 2 by 1/2 in	1 piece---------	45	47	160	1	15	13.4	0.6	0.2
546	Shredded or grated-----------	1 cup-----------	80	47	285	3	27	23.8	1.1	0.3
547	Dried, sweetened, shredded-----	1 cup-----------	93	13	470	3	33	29.3	1.4	0.4
548	Filberts (hazelnuts), chopped----	1 cup-----------	115	5	725	15	72	5.3	56.5	6.9
549		1 oz-----------	28	5	180	4	18	1.3	13.9	1.7
550	Lentils, dry, cooked-------------	1 cup-----------	200	72	215	16	1	0.1	0.2	0.5
551	Macadamia nuts, roasted in oil, salted------------------	1 cup-----------	134	2	960	10	103	15.4	80.9	1.8
552		1 oz-----------	28	2	205	2	22	3.2	17.1	0.4
	Mixed nuts, with peanuts, salted:									
553	Dry roasted---------------------	1 oz-----------	28	2	170	5	15	2.0	8.9	3.1
554	Roasted in oil-----------------	1 oz-----------	28	2	175	5	16	2.5	9.0	3.8
555	Peanuts, roasted in oil, salted--	1 cup-----------	145	2	840	39	71	9.9	35.5	22.6
556		1 oz-----------	28	2	165	8	14	1.9	6.9	4.4
557	Peanut butter--------------------	1 tbsp----------	16	1	95	5	8	1.4	4.0	2.5
558	Peas, split, dry, cooked---------	1 cup-----------	200	70	230	16	1	0.1	0.1	0.3
559	Pecans, halves-------------------	1 cup-----------	108	5	720	8	73	5.9	45.5	18.1
560		1 oz-----------	28	5	190	2	19	1.5	12.0	4.7
561	Pine nuts (pinyons), shelled-----	1 oz-----------	28	6	160	3	17	2.7	6.5	7.3
562	Pistachio nuts, dried, shelled----	1 oz-----------	28	4	165	6	14	1.7	9.3	2.1
563	Pumpkin and squash kernels, dry, hulled-------------------------	1 oz-----------	28	7	155	7	13	2.5	4.0	5.9
564	Refried beans, canned------------	1 cup-----------	290	72	295	18	3	0.4	0.6	1.4
565	Sesame seeds, dry, hulled--------	1 tbsp----------	8	5	45	2	4	0.6	1.7	1.9
566	Soybeans, dry, cooked, drained---	1 cup-----------	180	71	235	20	10	1.3	1.9	5.3
	Soy products:									
567	Miso-----------------------------	1 cup-----------	276	53	470	29	13	1.8	2.6	7.3
568	Tofu, piece 2-1/2 by 2-3/4 by 1 in----------------------	1 piece--------	120	85	85	9	5	0.7	1.0	2.9
569	Sunflower seeds, dry, hulled-----	1 oz-----------	28	5	160	6	14	1.5	2.7	9.3
570	Tahini---------------------------	1 tbsp----------	15	3	90	3	8	1.1	3.0	3.5

[41] Cashews without salt contain 21 mg sodium per cup or 4 mg per oz.
[42] Cashews without salt contain 22 mg sodium per cup or 5 mg per oz.
[43] Macadamia nuts without salt contain 9 mg sodium per cup or 2 mg per oz.

							Nutrients in Indicated Quantity						
Cho-les-terol	Carbo-hydrate	Calcium	Phos-phorus	Iron	Potas-sium	Sodium	Vitamin A value		Thiamin	Ribo-flavin	Niacin	Ascorbic acid	Item No.
							(IU)	(RE)					
Milli-grams	Grams	Milli-grams	Milli-grams	Milli-grams	Milli-grams	Milli-grams	Inter-national units	Retinol equiva-lents	Milli-grams	Milli-grams	Milli-grams	Milli-grams	
0	28	359	702	4.9	988	15	0	0	0.28	1.05	4.5	1	525
0	6	75	147	1.0	208	3	0	0	0.06	0.22	1.0	Tr	526
0	41	47	239	2.9	608	1	Tr	Tr	0.43	0.05	0.9	0	527
0	38	90	266	4.9	749	13	0	0	0.25	0.13	1.3	0	528
0	49	55	293	5.9	1,163	4	0	0	0.25	0.11	1.3	0	529
0	40	95	281	5.1	790	13	0	0	0.27	0.13	1.3	0	530
0	49	86	296	5.4	882	3	Tr	Tr	0.33	0.16	0.7	0	531
30	32	94	303	4.8	668	1,374	330	33	0.18	0.15	3.3	Tr	532
10	48	138	235	4.6	536	1,181	330	33	0.20	0.08	1.5	5	533
10	54	161	291	5.9	536	969	330	33	0.15	0.10	1.3	5	534
0	42	74	278	4.6	673	968	10	1	0.13	0.10	1.5	0	535
0	35	43	238	3.3	573	20	30	3	0.40	0.10	1.0	0	536
0	4	50	170	1.0	170	1	Tr	Tr	0.28	0.03	0.5	Tr	537
0	126	390	102	5.7	1,275	24	Tr	Tr	0.07	0.07	2.2	Tr	538
0	45	62	671	8.2	774	[41]877	0	0	0.27	0.27	1.9	0	539
0	9	13	139	1.7	160	[41]181	0	0	0.06	0.06	0.4	0	540
0	37	53	554	5.3	689	[42]814	0	0	0.55	0.23	2.3	0	541
0	8	12	121	1.2	150	[42]177	0	0	0.12	0.05	0.5	0	542
0	76	41	153	1.3	847	3	30	3	0.35	0.25	1.9	37	543
0	45	80	273	4.9	475	11	Tr	Tr	0.18	0.09	0.9	0	544
0	7	6	51	1.1	160	9	0	0	0.03	0.01	0.2	1	545
0	12	11	90	1.9	285	16	0	0	0.05	0.02	0.4	3	546
0	44	14	99	1.8	313	244	0	0	0.03	0.02	0.4	1	547
0	18	216	359	3.8	512	3	80	8	0.58	0.13	1.3	1	548
0	4	53	88	0.9	126	1	20	2	0.14	0.03	0.3	Tr	549
0	38	50	238	4.2	498	26	40	4	0.14	0.12	1.2	0	550
0	17	60	268	2.4	441	[43]348	10	1	0.29	0.15	2.7	0	551
0	4	13	57	0.5	93	[43]74	Tr	Tr	0.06	0.03	0.6	0	552
0	7	20	123	1.0	169	[44]190	Tr	Tr	0.06	0.06	1.3	0	553
0	6	31	131	0.9	165	[44]185	10	1	0.14	0.06	1.4	Tr	554
0	27	125	734	2.8	1,019	[45]626	0	0	0.42	0.15	21.5	0	555
0	5	24	143	0.5	199	[45]122	0	0	0.08	0.03	4.2	0	556
0	3	5	60	0.3	110	75	0	0	0.02	0.02	2.2	0	557
0	42	22	178	3.4	592	26	80	8	0.30	0.18	1.8	0	558
0	20	39	314	2.3	423	1	140	14	0.92	0.14	1.0	2	559
0	5	10	83	0.6	111	Tr	40	4	0.24	0.04	0.3	1	560
0	5	2	10	0.9	178	20	10	1	0.35	0.06	1.2	1	561
0	7	38	143	1.9	310	2	70	7	0.23	0.05	0.3	Tr	562
0	5	12	333	4.2	229	5	110	11	0.06	0.09	0.5	Tr	563
0	51	141	245	5.1	1,141	1,228	0	0	0.14	0.16	1.4	17	564
0	1	11	62	0.6	33	3	10	1	0.06	0.01	0.4	0	565
0	19	131	322	4.9	972	4	50	5	0.38	0.16	1.1	0	566
0	65	188	853	4.7	922	8,142	110	11	0.17	0.28	0.8	0	567
0	3	108	151	2.3	50	8	0	0	0.07	0.04	0.1	0	568
0	5	33	200	1.9	195	1	10	1	0.65	0.07	1.3	Tr	569
0	3	21	119	0.7	69	5	10	1	0.24	0.02	0.8	1	570

[44]Mixed nuts without salt contain 3 mg sodium per oz.
[45]Peanuts without salt contain 22 mg sodium per cup or 4 mg per oz.

Item No.	Foods, approximate measures, units, and weight (weight of edible portion only)			Water	Food energy	Pro-tein	Fat	Fatty acids		
								Satu-rated	Mono-unsatu-rated	Poly-unsatu-rated
			Grams	Per-cent	Cal-ories	Grams	Grams	Grams	Grams	Grams
	Legumes, Nuts, and Seeds—Con.									
	Walnuts:									
571	Black, chopped-----------------	1 cup-----------	125	4	760	30	71	4.5	15.9	46.9
572		1 oz-----------	28	4	170	7	16	1.0	3.6	10.6
573	English or Persian, pieces or chips-----------------------	1 cup-----------	120	4	770	17	74	6.7	17.0	47.0
574		1 oz-----------	28	4	180	4	18	1.6	4.0	11.1
	Meat and Meat Products									
	Beef, cooked:[46]									
	Cuts braised, simmered, or pot roasted:									
	Relatively fat such as chuck blade:									
575	Lean and fat, piece, 2-1/2 by 2-1/2 by 3/4 in-------	3 oz-----------	85	43	325	22	26	10.8	11.7	0.9
576	Lean only from item 575----	2.2 oz----------	62	53	170	19	9	3.9	4.2	0.3
	Relatively lean, such as bottom round:									
577	Lean and fat, piece, 4-1/8 by 2-1/4 by 1/2 in-------	3 oz-----------	85	54	220	25	13	4.8	5.7	0.5
578	Lean only from item 577----	2.8 oz----------	78	57	175	25	8	2.7	3.4	0.3
	Ground beef, broiled, patty, 3 by 5/8 in:									
579	Lean-----------------------	3 oz-----------	85	56	230	21	16	6.2	6.9	0.6
580	Regular---------------------	3 oz-----------	85	54	245	20	18	6.9	7.7	0.7
581	Heart, lean, braised------------	3 oz-----------	85	65	150	24	5	1.2	0.8	1.6
582	Liver, fried, slice, 6-1/2 by 2-3/8 by 3/8 in[47]------------	3 oz-----------	85	56	185	23	7	2.5	3.6	1.3
	Roast, oven cooked, no liquid added:									
	Relatively fat, such as rib:									
583	Lean and fat, 2 pieces, 4-1/8 by 2-1/4 by 1/4 in	3 oz-----------	85	46	315	19	26	10.8	11.4	0.9
584	Lean only from item 583----	2.2 oz----------	61	57	150	17	9	3.6	3.7	0.3
	Relatively lean, such as eye of round:									
585	Lean and fat, 2 pieces, 2-1/2 by 2-1/2 by 3/8 in	3 oz-----------	85	57	205	23	12	4.9	5.4	0.5
586	Lean only from item 585----	2.6 oz----------	75	63	135	22	5	1.9	2.1	0.2
	Steak:									
	Sirloin, broiled:									
587	Lean and fat, piece, 2-1/2 by 2-1/2 by 3/4 in-------	3 oz-----------	85	53	240	23	15	6.4	6.9	0.6
588	Lean only from item 587----	2.5 oz----------	72	59	150	22	6	2.6	2.8	0.3
589	Beef, canned, corned-----------	3 oz-----------	85	59	185	22	10	4.2	4.9	0.4
590	Beef, dried, chipped------------	2.5 oz----------	72	48	145	24	4	1.8	2.0	0.2
	Lamb, cooked:									
	Chops, (3 per lb with bone):									
	Arm, braised:									
591	Lean and fat--------------	2.2 oz----------	63	44	220	20	15	6.9	6.0	0.9
592	Lean only from item 591----	1.7 oz----------	48	49	135	17	7	2.9	2.6	0.4
	Loin, broiled:									
593	Lean and fat--------------	2.8 oz----------	80	54	235	22	16	7.3	6.4	1.0
594	Lean only from item 593----	2.3 oz----------	64	61	140	19	6	2.6	2.4	0.4
	Leg, roasted:									
595	Lean and fat, 2 pieces, 4-1/8 by 2-1/4 by 1/4 in-------	3 oz-----------	85	59	205	22	13	5.6	4.9	0.8
596	Lean only from item 595------	2.6 oz----------	73	64	140	20	6	2.4	2.2	0.4
	Rib, roasted:									
597	Lean and fat, 3 pieces, 2-1/2 by 2-1/2 by 1/4 in--------	3 oz-----------	85	47	315	18	26	12.1	10.6	1.5
598	Lean only from item 597------	2 oz-----------	57	60	130	15	7	3.2	3.0	0.5

[46] Outer layer of fat was removed to within approximately 1/2 inch of the lean. Deposits of fat within the cut were not removed.
[47] Fried in vegetable shortening.

						Nutrients in Indicated Quantity							
Cho-les-terol	Carbo-hydrate	Calcium	Phos-phorus	Iron	Potas-sium	Sodium	Vitamin A value		Thiamin	Ribo-flavin	Niacin	Ascorbic acid	Item No.
							(IU)	(RE)					
Milli-grams	Grams	Milli-grams	Milli-grams	Milli-grams	Milli-grams	Milli-grams	Inter-national units	Retinol equiva-lents	Milli-grams	Milli-grams	Milli-grams	Milli-grams	
0	15	73	580	3.8	655	1	370	37	0.27	0.14	0.9	Tr	571
0	3	16	132	0.9	149	Tr	80	8	0.06	0.03	0.2	Tr	572
0	22	113	380	2.9	602	12	150	15	0.46	0.18	1.3	4	573
0	5	27	90	0.7	142	3	40	4	0.11	0.04	0.3	1	574
87	0	11	163	2.5	163	53	Tr	Tr	0.06	0.19	2.0	0	575
66	0	8	146	2.3	163	44	Tr	Tr	0.05	0.17	1.7	0	576
81	0	5	217	2.8	248	43	Tr	Tr	0.06	0.21	3.3	0	577
75	0	4	212	2.7	240	40	Tr	Tr	0.06	0.20	3.0	0	578
74	0	9	134	1.8	256	65	Tr	Tr	0.04	0.18	4.4	0	579
76	0	9	144	2.1	248	70	Tr	Tr	0.03	0.16	4.9	0	580
164	0	5	213	6.4	198	54	Tr	Tr	0.12	1.31	3.4	5	581
410	7	9	392	5.3	309	90	[48]30,690	[48]9,120	0.18	3.52	12.3	23	582
72	0	8	145	2.0	246	54	Tr	Tr	0.06	0.16	3.1	0	583
49	0	5	127	1.7	218	45	Tr	Tr	0.05	0.13	2.7	0	584
62	0	5	177	1.6	308	50	Tr	Tr	0.07	0.14	3.0	0	585
52	0	3	170	1.5	297	46	Tr	Tr	0.07	0.13	2.8	0	586
77	0	9	186	2.6	306	53	Tr	Tr	0.10	0.23	3.3	0	587
64	0	8	176	2.4	290	48	Tr	Tr	0.09	0.22	3.1	0	588
80	0	17	90	3.7	51	802	Tr	Tr	0.02	0.20	2.9	0	589
46	0	14	287	2.3	142	3,053	Tr	Tr	0.05	0.23	2.7	0	590
77	0	16	132	1.5	195	46	Tr	Tr	0.04	0.16	4.4	0	591
59	0	12	111	1.3	162	36	Tr	Tr	0.03	0.13	3.0	0	592
78	0	16	162	1.4	272	62	Tr	Tr	0.09	0.21	5.5	0	593
60	0	12	145	1.3	241	54	Tr	Tr	0.08	0.18	4.4	0	594
78	0	8	162	1.7	273	57	Tr	Tr	0.09	0.24	5.5	0	595
65	0	6	150	1.5	247	50	Tr	Tr	0.08	0.20	4.6	0	596
77	0	19	139	1.4	224	60	Tr	Tr	0.08	0.18	5.5	0	597
50	0	12	111	1.0	179	46	Tr	Tr	0.05	0.13	3.5	0	598

[48] Value varies widely.

Item No.	Foods, approximate measures, units, and weight (weight of edible portion only)		Grams	Water Per-cent	Food energy Cal-ories	Pro-tein Grams	Fat Grams	Fatty acids Satu-rated Grams	Mono-unsatu-rated Grams	Poly-unsatu-rated Grams
	Meat and Meat Products—Con.									
	Pork, cured, cooked:									
	Bacon:									
599	Regular-----------------------	3 medium slices	19	13	110	6	9	3.3	4.5	1.1
600	Canadian-style---------------	2 slices--------	46	62	85	11	4	1.3	1.9	0.4
	Ham, light cure, roasted:									
601	Lean and fat, 2 pieces, 4-1/8 by 2-1/4 by 1/4 in-------	3 oz------------	85	58	205	18	14	5.1	6.7	1.5
602	Lean only from item 601------	2.4 oz----------	68	66	105	17	4	1.3	1.7	0.4
603	Ham, canned, roasted, 2 pieces, 4-1/8 by 2-1/4 by 1/4 in-----	3 oz------------	85	67	140	18	7	2.4	3.5	0.8
	Luncheon meat:									
604	Canned, spiced or unspiced, slice, 3 by 2 by 1/2 in----	2 slices--------	42	52	140	5	13	4.5	6.0	1.5
605	Chopped ham (8 slices per 6 oz pkg)--------------------	2 slices--------	42	64	95	7	7	2.4	3.4	0.9
	Cooked ham (8 slices per 8-oz pkg):									
606	Regular------------------	2 slices--------	57	65	105	10	6	1.9	2.8	0.7
607	Extra lean--------------	2 slices--------	57	71	75	11	3	0.9	1.3	0.3
	Pork, fresh, cooked:									
	Chop, loin (cut 3 per lb with bone):									
	Broiled:									
608	Lean and fat--------------	3.1 oz----------	87	50	275	24	19	7.0	8.8	2.2
609	Lean only from item 608----	2.5 oz----------	72	57	165	23	8	2.6	3.4	0.9
	Pan fried:									
610	Lean and fat--------------	3.1 oz----------	89	45	335	21	27	9.8	12.5	3.1
611	Lean only from item 610----	2.4 oz----------	67	54	180	19	11	3.7	4.8	1.3
	Ham (leg), roasted:									
612	Lean and fat, piece, 2-1/2 by 2-1/2 by 3/4 in-------	3 oz------------	85	53	250	21	18	6.4	8.1	2.0
613	Lean only from item 612------	2.5 oz----------	72	60	160	20	8	2.7	3.6	1.0
	Rib, roasted:									
614	Lean and fat, piece, 2-1/2 by 3/4 in---------------------	3 oz------------	85	51	270	21	20	7.2	9.2	2.3
615	Lean only from item 614------	2.5 oz----------	71	57	175	20	10	3.4	4.4	1.2
	Shoulder cut, braised:									
616	Lean and fat, 3 pieces, 2-1/2 by 2-1/2 by 1/4 in---------	3 oz------------	85	47	295	23	22	7.9	10.0	2.4
617	Lean only from item 616------	2.4 oz----------	67	54	165	22	8	2.8	3.7	1.0
	Sausages (See also Luncheon meats, items 604-607):									
618	Bologna, slice (8 per 8-oz pkg)	2 slices--------	57	54	180	7	16	6.1	7.6	1.4
619	Braunschweiger, slice (6 per 6-oz pkg)--------------------	2 slices--------	57	48	205	8	18	6.2	8.5	2.1
620	Brown and serve (10-11 per 8-oz pkg), browned--------	1 link----------	13	45	50	2	5	1.7	2.2	0.5
621	Frankfurter (10 per 1-lb pkg), cooked (reheated)------------	1 frankfurter---	45	54	145	5	13	4.8	6.2	1.2
622	Pork link (16 per 1-lb pkg), cooked[50] ---------------------	1 link----------	13	45	50	3	4	1.4	1.8	0.5
	Salami:									
623	Cooked type, slice (8 per 8-oz pkg)-------------------	2 slices--------	57	60	145	8	11	4.6	5.2	1.2
624	Dry type, slice (12 per 4-oz pkg)------------------------	2 slices--------	20	35	85	5	7	2.4	3.4	0.6
625	Sandwich spread (pork, beef)---	1 tbsp----------	15	60	35	1	3	0.9	1.1	0.4
626	Vienna sausage (7 per 4-oz can)	1 sausage-------	16	60	45	2	4	1.5	2.0	0.3
	Veal, medium fat, cooked, bone removed:									
627	Cutlet, 4-1/8 by 2-1/4 by 1/2 in, braised or broiled-------	3 oz------------	85	60	185	23	9	4.1	4.1	0.6
628	Rib, 2 pieces, 4-1/8 by 2-1/4 by 1/4 in, roasted----------	3 oz------------	85	55	230	23	14	6.0	6.0	1.0

[49] Contains added sodium ascorbate. If sodium ascorbate is not added, ascorbic acid content is negligible.

							Vitamin A value						
Nutrients in Indicated Quantity													
Cho-les-terol	Carbo-hydrate	Calcium	Phos-phorus	Iron	Potas-sium	Sodium	(IU)	(RE)	Thiamin	Ribo-flavin	Niacin	Ascorbic acid	Item No.
Milli-grams	Grams	Milli-grams	Milli-grams	Milli-grams	Milli-grams	Milli-grams	Inter-national units	Retinol equiva-lents	Milli-grams	Milli-grams	Milli-grams	Milli-grams	
16	Tr	2	64	0.3	92	303	0	0	0.13	0.05	1.4	6	599
27	1	5	136	0.4	179	711	0	0	0.38	0.09	3.2	10	600
53	0	6	182	0.7	243	1,009	0	0	0.51	0.19	3.8	0	601
37	0	5	154	0.6	215	902	0	0	0.46	0.17	3.4	0	602
35	Tr	6	188	0.9	298	908	0	0	0.82	0.21	4.3	[49]19	603
26	1	3	34	0.3	90	541	0	0	0.15	0.08	1.3	Tr	604
21	0	3	65	0.3	134	576	0	0	0.27	0.09	1.6	[49]8	605
32	2	4	141	0.6	189	751	0	0	0.49	0.14	3.0	[49]16	606
27	1	4	124	0.4	200	815	0	0	0.53	0.13	2.8	[49]15	607
84	0	3	184	0.7	312	61	10	3	0.87	0.24	4.3	Tr	608
71	0	4	176	0.7	302	56	10	1	0.83	0.22	4.0	Tr	609
92	0	4	190	0.7	323	64	10	3	0.91	0.24	4.6	Tr	610
72	0	3	178	0.7	305	57	10	1	0.84	0.22	4.0	Tr	611
79	0	5	210	0.9	280	50	10	2	0.54	0.27	3.9	Tr	612
68	0	5	202	0.8	269	46	10	1	0.50	0.25	3.6	Tr	613
69	0	9	190	0.8	313	37	10	3	0.50	0.24	4.2	Tr	614
56	0	8	182	0.7	300	33	10	2	0.45	0.22	3.8	Tr	615
93	0	6	162	1.4	286	75	10	3	0.46	0.26	4.4	Tr	616
76	0	5	151	1.3	271	68	10	1	0.40	0.24	4.0	Tr	617
31	2	7	52	0.9	103	581	0	0	0.10	0.08	1.5	[49]12	618
89	2	5	96	5.3	113	652	8,010	2,405	0.14	0.87	4.8	[49]6	619
9	Tr	1	14	0.1	25	105	0	0	0.05	0.02	0.4	0	620
23	1	5	39	0.5	75	504	0	0	0.09	0.05	1.2	[49]12	621
11	Tr	4	24	0.2	47	168	0	0	0.10	0.03	0.6	Tr	622
37	1	7	66	1.5	113	607	0	0	0.14	0.21	2.0	[49]7	623
16	1	2	28	0.3	76	372	0	0	0.12	0.06	1.0	[49]5	624
6	2	2	9	0.1	17	152	10	1	0.03	0.02	0.3	0	625
8	Tr	2	8	0.1	16	152	0	0	0.01	0.02	0.3	0	626
109	0	9	196	0.8	258	56	Tr	Tr	0.06	0.21	4.6	0	627
109	0	10	211	0.7	259	57	Tr	Tr	0.11	0.26	6.6	0	628

[50] One patty (8 per pound) of bulk sausage is equivalent to 2 links.

Item No.	Foods, approximate measures, units, and weight (weight of edible portion only)		Water	Food energy	Pro-tein	Fat	Fatty acids		
							Satu-rated	Mono-unsatu-rated	Poly-unsatu-rated
	Mixed Dishes and Fast Foods	Grams	Per-cent	Cal-ories	Grams	Grams	Grams	Grams	Grams
	Mixed dishes:								
629	Beef and vegetable stew, from home recipe-----------------	1 cup-----------	245	82	220	16	11	4.4	4.5	0.5
630	Beef potpie, from home recipe, baked, piece, 1/3 of 9-in diam. pie[51] ------------------	1 piece---------	210	55	515	21	30	7.9	12.9	7.4
631	Chicken a la king, cooked, from home recipe-------------	1 cup-----------	245	68	470	27	34	12.9	13.4	6.2
632	Chicken and noodles, cooked, from home recipe-------------	1 cup-----------	240	71	365	22	18	5.1	7.1	3.9
	Chicken chow mein:								
633	Canned----------------------	1 cup-----------	250	89	95	7	Tr	0.1	0.1	0.8
634	From home recipe-------------	1 cup-----------	250	78	255	31	10	4.1	4.9	3.5
635	Chicken potpie, from home recipe, baked, piece, 1/3 of 9-in diam. pie[51] -------------	1 piece---------	232	57	545	23	31	10.3	15.5	6.6
636	Chili con carne with beans, canned----------------------	1 cup-----------	255	72	340	19	16	5.8	7.2	1.0
637	Chop suey with beef and pork, from home recipe-------------	1 cup-----------	250	75	300	26	17	4.3	7.4	4.2
	Macaroni (enriched) and cheese:								
638	Canned[52] -------------------	1 cup-----------	240	80	230	9	10	4.7	2.9	1.3
639	From home recipe[38] -----------	1 cup-----------	200	58	430	17	22	9.8	7.4	3.6
640	Quiche Lorraine, 1/8 of 8-in diam. quiche[51] ---------------	1 slice---------	176	47	600	13	48	23.2	17.8	4.1
	Spaghetti (enriched) in tomato sauce with cheese:								
641	Canned----------------------	1 cup-----------	250	80	190	6	2	0.4	0.4	0.5
642	From home recipe-------------	1 cup-----------	250	77	260	9	9	3.0	3.6	1.2
	Spaghetti (enriched) with meat-balls and tomato sauce:								
643	Canned----------------------	1 cup-----------	250	78	260	12	10	2.4	3.9	3.1
644	From home recipe-------------	1 cup-----------	248	70	330	19	12	3.9	4.4	2.2
	Fast food entrees:								
	Cheeseburger:								
645	Regular----------------------	1 sandwich------	112	46	300	15	15	7.3	5.6	1.0
646	4 oz patty-------------------	1 sandwich------	194	46	525	30	31	15.1	12.2	1.4
	Chicken, fried. See Poultry and Poultry Products (items 656-659).								
647	Enchilada---------------------	1 enchilada-----	230	72	235	20	16	7.7	6.7	0.6
648	English muffin, egg, cheese, and bacon--------------------	1 sandwich------	138	49	360	18	18	8.0	8.0	0.7
	Fish sandwich:								
649	Regular, with cheese---------	1 sandwich------	140	43	420	16	23	6.3	6.9	7.7
650	Large, without cheese--------	1 sandwich------	170	48	470	18	27	6.3	8.7	9.5
	Hamburger:								
651	Regular----------------------	1 sandwich------	98	46	245	12	11	4.4	5.3	0.5
652	4 oz patty-------------------	1 sandwich------	174	50	445	25	21	7.1	11.7	0.6
653	Pizza, cheese, 1/8 of 15-in diam. pizza[51] ----------------	1 slice---------	120	46	290	15	9	4.1	2.6	1.3
654	Roast beef sandwich-----------	1 sandwich------	150	52	345	22	13	3.5	6.9	1.8
655	Taco-------------------------	1 taco----------	81	55	195	9	11	4.1	5.5	0.8

[38] Made with margarine.
[51] Crust made with vegetable shortening and enriched flour.

							Nutrients in Indicated Quantity						
Cho-les-terol	Carbo-hydrate	Calcium	Phos-phorus	Iron	Potas-sium	Sodium	Vitamin A value		Thiamin	Ribo-flavin	Niacin	Ascorbic acid	Item No.
							(IU)	(RE)					
Milli-grams	Grams	Milli-grams	Milli-grams	Milli-grams	Milli-grams	Milli-grams	Inter-national units	Retinol equiva-lents	Milli-grams	Milli-grams	Milli-grams	Milli-grams	
71	15	29	184	2.9	613	292	5,690	568	0.15	0.17	4.7	17	629
42	39	29	149	3.8	334	596	4,220	517	0.29	0.29	4.8	6	630
221	12	127	358	2.5	404	760	1,130	272	0.10	0.42	5.4	12	631
103	26	26	247	2.2	149	600	430	130	0.05	0.17	4.3	Tr	632
8	18	45	85	1.3	418	725	150	28	0.05	0.10	1.0	13	633
75	10	58	293	2.5	473	718	280	50	0.08	0.23	4.3	10	634
56	42	70	232	3.0	343	594	7,220	735	0.32	0.32	4.9	5	635
28	31	82	321	4.3	594	1,354	150	15	0.08	0.18	3.3	8	636
68	13	60	248	4.8	425	1,053	600	60	0.28	0.38	5.0	33	637
24	26	199	182	1.0	139	730	260	72	0.12	0.24	1.0	Tr	638
44	40	362	322	1.8	240	1,086	860	232	0.20	0.40	1.8	1	639
285	29	211	276	1.0	283	653	1,640	454	0.11	0.32	Tr	Tr	640
3	39	40	88	2.8	303	955	930	120	0.35	0.28	4.5	10	641
8	37	80	135	2.3	408	955	1,080	140	0.25	0.18	2.3	13	642
23	29	53	113	3.3	245	1,220	1,000	100	0.15	0.18	2.3	5	643
89	39	124	236	3.7	665	1,009	1,590	159	0.25	0.30	4.0	22	644
44	28	135	174	2.3	219	672	340	65	0.26	0.24	3.7	1	645
104	40	236	320	4.5	407	1,224	670	128	0.33	0.48	7.4	3	646
19	24	97	198	3.3	653	1,332	2,720	352	0.18	0.26	Tr	Tr	647
213	31	197	290	3.1	201	832	650	160	0.46	0.50	3.7	1	648
56	39	132	223	1.8	274	667	160	25	0.32	0.26	3.3	2	649
91	41	61	246	2.2	375	621	110	15	0.35	0.23	3.5	1	650
32	28	56	107	2.2	202	463	80	14	0.23	0.24	3.8	1	651
71	38	75	225	4.8	404	763	160	28	0.38	0.38	7.8	1	652
56	39	220	216	1.6	230	699	750	106	0.34	0.29	4.2	2	653
55	34	60	222	4.0	338	757	240	32	0.40	0.33	6.0	2	654
21	15	109	134	1.2	263	456	420	57	0.09	0.07	1.4	1	655

[52]Made with corn oil.

Item No.	Foods, approximate measures, units, and weight (weight of edible portion only)		Water	Food energy	Pro-tein	Fat	Fatty acids		
							Satu-rated	Mono-unsatu-rated	Poly-unsatu-rated
	Poultry and Poultry Products	Grams	Per-cent	Cal-ories	Grams	Grams	Grams	Grams	Grams
	Chicken:								
	Fried, flesh, with skin:[53]								
	Batter dipped:								
656	Breast, 1/2 breast (5.6 oz with bones)	4.9 oz	140	52	365	35	18	4.9	7.6	4.3
657	Drumstick (3.4 oz with bones)	2.5 oz	72	53	195	16	11	3.0	4.6	2.7
	Flour coated:								
658	Breast, 1/2 breast (4.2 oz with bones)	3.5 oz	98	57	220	31	9	2.4	3.4	1.9
659	Drumstick (2.6 oz with bones)	1.7 oz	49	57	120	13	7	1.8	2.7	1.6
	Roasted, flesh only:								
660	Breast, 1/2 breast (4.2 oz with bones and skin)	3.0 oz	86	65	140	27	3	0.9	1.1	0.7
661	Drumstick, (2.9 oz with bones and skin)	1.6 oz	44	67	75	12	2	0.7	0.8	0.6
662	Stewed, flesh only, light and dark meat, chopped or diced	1 cup	140	67	250	38	9	2.6	3.3	2.2
663	Chicken liver, cooked	1 liver	20	68	30	5	1	0.4	0.3	0.2
664	Duck, roasted, flesh only	1/2 duck	221	64	445	52	25	9.2	8.2	3.2
	Turkey, roasted, flesh only:								
665	Dark meat, piece, 2-1/2 by 1-5/8 by 1/4 in	4 pieces	85	63	160	24	6	2.1	1.4	1.8
666	Light meat, piece, 4 by 2 by 1/4 in	2 pieces	85	66	135	25	3	0.9	0.5	0.7
	Light and dark meat:								
667	Chopped or diced	1 cup	140	65	240	41	7	2.3	1.4	2.0
668	Pieces (1 slice white meat, 4 by 2 by 1/4 in and 2 slices dark meat, 2-1/2 by 1-5/8 by 1/4 in)	3 pieces	85	65	145	25	4	1.4	0.9	1.2
	Poultry food products:								
	Chicken:								
669	Canned, boneless	5 oz	142	69	235	31	11	3.1	4.5	2.5
670	Frankfurter (10 per 1-lb pkg)	1 frankfurter	45	58	115	6	9	2.5	3.8	1.8
671	Roll, light (6 slices per 6 oz pkg)	2 slices	57	69	90	11	4	1.1	1.7	0.9
	Turkey:								
672	Gravy and turkey, frozen	5-oz package	142	85	95	8	4	1.2	1.4	0.7
673	Ham, cured turkey thigh meat (8 slices per 8-oz pkg)	2 slices	57	71	75	11	3	1.0	0.7	0.9
674	Loaf, breast meat (8 slices per 6-oz pkg)	2 slices	42	72	45	10	1	0.2	0.2	0.1
675	Patties, breaded, battered, fried (2.25 oz)	1 patty	64	50	180	9	12	3.0	4.8	3.0
676	Roast, boneless, frozen, sea-soned, light and dark meat, cooked	3 oz	85	68	130	18	5	1.6	1.0	1.4
	Soups, Sauces, and Gravies								
	Soups:								
	Canned, condensed:								
	Prepared with equal volume of milk:								
677	Clam chowder, New England	1 cup	248	85	165	9	7	3.0	2.3	1.1
678	Cream of chicken	1 cup	248	85	190	7	11	4.6	4.5	1.6
679	Cream of mushroom	1 cup	248	85	205	6	14	5.1	3.0	4.6
680	Tomato	1 cup	248	85	160	6	6	2.9	1.6	1.1

[53] Fried in vegetable shortening.

Nutrients in Indicated Quantity

Cho-les-terol	Carbo-hydrate	Calcium	Phos-phorus	Iron	Potas-sium	Sodium	Vitamin A value		Thiamin	Ribo-flavin	Niacin	Ascorbic acid	Item No.
							(IU)	(RE)					
Milli-grams	Grams	Milli-grams	Milli-grams	Milli-grams	Milli-grams	Milli-grams	Inter-national units	Retinol equiva-lents	Milli-grams	Milli-grams	Milli-grams	Milli-grams	
119	13	28	259	1.8	281	385	90	28	0.16	0.20	14.7	0	656
62	6	12	106	1.0	134	194	60	19	0.08	0.15	3.7	0	657
87	2	16	228	1.2	254	74	50	15	0.08	0.13	13.5	0	658
44	1	6	86	0.7	112	44	40	12	0.04	0.11	3.0	0	659
73	0	13	196	0.9	220	64	20	5	0.06	0.10	11.8	0	660
41	0	5	81	0.6	108	42	30	8	0.03	0.10	2.7	0	661
116	0	20	210	1.6	252	98	70	21	0.07	0.23	8.6	0	662
126	Tr	3	62	1.7	28	10	3,270	983	0.03	0.35	0.9	3	663
197	0	27	449	6.0	557	144	170	51	0.57	1.04	11.3	0	664
72	0	27	173	2.0	246	67	0	0	0.05	0.21	3.1	0	665
59	0	16	186	1.1	259	54	0	0	0.05	0.11	5.8	0	666
106	0	35	298	2.5	417	98	0	0	0.09	0.25	7.6	0	667
65	0	21	181	1.5	253	60	0	0	0.05	0.15	4.6	0	668
88	0	20	158	2.2	196	714	170	48	0.02	0.18	9.0	3	669
45	3	43	48	0.9	38	616	60	17	0.03	0.05	1.4	0	670
28	1	24	89	0.6	129	331	50	14	0.04	0.07	3.0	0	671
26	7	20	115	1.3	87	787	60	18	0.03	0.18	2.6	0	672
32	Tr	6	108	1.6	184	565	0	0	0.03	0.14	2.0	0	673
17	0	3	97	0.2	118	608	0	0	0.02	0.05	3.5	[54]0	674
40	10	9	173	1.4	176	512	20	7	0.06	0.12	1.5	0	675
45	3	4	207	1.4	253	578	0	0	0.04	0.14	5.3	0	676
22	17	186	156	1.5	300	992	160	40	0.07	0.24	1.0	3	677
27	15	181	151	0.7	273	1,047	710	94	0.07	0.26	0.9	1	678
20	15	179	156	0.6	270	1,076	150	37	0.08	0.28	0.9	2	679
17	22	159	149	1.8	449	932	850	109	0.13	0.25	1.5	68	680

[54]If sodium ascorbate is added, product contains 11 mg ascorbic acid.

Item No.	Foods, approximate measures, units, and weight (weight of edible portion only)			Water	Food energy	Pro-tein	Fat	Fatty acids		
								Satu-rated	Mono-unsatu-rated	Poly-unsatu-rated
			Grams	Per-cent	Cal-ories	Grams	Grams	Grams	Grams	Grams
	Soups, Sauces, and Gravies—Con.									
	Soups:									
	Canned, condensed:									
	Prepared with equal volume of water:									
681	Bean with bacon------------	1 cup-----------	253	84	170	8	6	1.5	2.2	1.8
682	Beef broth, bouillon, consomme----------------	1 cup-----------	240	98	15	3	1	0.3	0.2	Tr
683	Beef noodle----------------	1 cup-----------	244	92	85	5	3	1.1	1.2	0.5
684	Chicken noodle-------------	1 cup-----------	241	92	75	4	2	0.7	1.1	0.6
685	Chicken rice--------------	1 cup-----------	241	94	60	4	2	0.5	0.9	0.4
686	Clam chowder, Manhattan----	1 cup-----------	244	90	80	4	2	0.4	0.4	1.3
687	Cream of chicken----------	1 cup-----------	244	91	115	3	7	2.1	3.3	1.5
688	Cream of mushroom----------	1 cup-----------	244	90	130	2	9	2.4	1.7	4.2
689	Minestrone----------------	1 cup-----------	241	91	80	4	3	0.6	0.7	1.1
690	Pea, green----------------	1 cup-----------	250	83	165	9	3	1.4	1.0	0.4
691	Tomato-------------------	1 cup-----------	244	90	85	2	2	0.4	0.4	1.0
692	Vegetable beef------------	1 cup-----------	244	92	80	6	2	0.9	0.8	0.1
693	Vegetarian----------------	1 cup-----------	241	92	70	2	2	0.3	0.8	0.7
	Dehydrated:									
	Unprepared:									
694	Bouillon------------------	1 pkt----------	6	3	15	1	1	0.3	0.2	Tr
695	Onion--------------------	1 pkt----------	7	4	20	1	Tr	0.1	0.2	Tr
	Prepared with water:									
696	Chicken noodle-------------	1 pkt (6-fl-oz)	188	94	40	2	1	0.2	0.4	0.3
697	Onion--------------------	1 pkt (6-fl-oz)	184	96	20	1	Tr	0.1	0.2	0.1
698	Tomato vegetable----------	1 pkt (6-fl-oz)	189	94	40	1	1	0.3	0.2	0.1
	Sauces:									
	From dry mix:									
699	Cheese, prepared with milk---	1 cup-----------	279	77	305	16	17	9.3	5.3	1.6
700	Hollandaise, prepared with water------------------	1 cup-----------	259	84	240	5	20	11.6	5.9	0.9
701	White sauce, prepared with milk------------------	1 cup-----------	264	81	240	10	13	6.4	4.7	1.7
	From home recipe:									
702	White sauce, medium[55]--------	1 cup-----------	250	73	395	10	30	9.1	11.9	7.2
	Ready to serve:									
703	Barbecue-------------------	1 tbsp----------	16	81	10	Tr	Tr	Tr	0.1	0.1
704	Soy-----------------------	1 tbsp----------	18	68	10	2	0	0.0	0.0	0.0
	Gravies:									
	Canned:									
705	Beef----------------------	1 cup-----------	233	87	125	9	5	2.7	2.3	0.2
706	Chicken-------------------	1 cup-----------	238	85	190	5	14	3.4	6.1	3.6
707	Mushroom------------------	1 cup-----------	238	89	120	3	6	1.0	2.8	2.4
	From dry mix:									
708	Brown---------------------	1 cup-----------	261	91	80	3	2	0.9	0.8	0.1
709	Chicken-------------------	1 cup-----------	260	91	85	3	2	0.5	0.9	0.4
	Sugars and Sweets									
	Candy:									
710	Caramels, plain or chocolate---	1 oz------------	28	8	115	1	3	2.2	0.3	0.1
	Chocolate:									
711	Milk, plain----------------	1 oz-----------	28	1	145	2	9	5.4	3.0	0.3
712	Milk, with almonds-----------	1 oz-----------	28	2	150	3	10	4.8	4.1	0.7
713	Milk, with peanuts-----------	1 oz-----------	28	1	155	4	11	4.2	3.5	1.5
714	Milk, with rice cereal-------	1 oz-----------	28	2	140	2	7	4.4	2.5	0.2
715	Semisweet, small pieces (60 per oz)-----------------	1 cup or 6 oz---	170	1	860	7	61	36.2	19.9	1.9
716	Sweet (dark)---------------	1 oz-----------	28	1	150	1	10	5.9	3.3	0.3
717	Fondant, uncoated (mints, candy corn, other)-----------------	1 oz-----------	28	3	105	Tr	0	0.0	0.0	0.0
718	Fudge, chocolate, plain--------	1 oz-----------	28	8	115	1	3	2.1	1.0	0.1
719	Gum drops---------------------	1 oz-----------	28	12	100	Tr	Tr	Tr	Tr	0.1

[55] Made with enriched flour, margarine, and whole milk.

Nutrients in Indicated Quantity

Cholesterol	Carbohydrate	Calcium	Phosphorus	Iron	Potassium	Sodium	Vitamin A value		Thiamin	Riboflavin	Niacin	Ascorbic acid	Item No.
							(IU)	(RE)					
Milligrams	Grams	Milligrams	Milligrams	Milligrams	Milligrams	Milligrams	International units	Retinol equivalents	Milligrams	Milligrams	Milligrams	Milligrams	
3	23	81	132	2.0	402	951	890	89	0.09	0.03	0.6	2	681
Tr	Tr	14	31	0.4	130	782	0	0	Tr	0.05	1.9	0	682
5	9	15	46	1.1	100	952	630	63	0.07	0.06	1.1	Tr	683
7	9	17	36	0.8	55	1,106	710	71	0.05	0.06	1.4	Tr	684
7	7	17	22	0.7	101	815	660	66	0.02	0.02	1.1	Tr	685
2	12	34	59	1.9	261	1,808	920	92	0.06	0.05	1.3	3	686
10	9	34	37	0.6	88	986	560	56	0.03	0.06	0.8	Tr	687
2	9	46	49	0.5	100	1,032	0	0	0.05	0.09	0.7	1	688
2	11	34	55	0.9	313	911	2,340	234	0.05	0.04	0.9	1	689
0	27	28	125	2.0	190	988	200	20	0.11	0.07	1.2	2	690
0	17	12	34	1.8	264	871	690	69	0.09	0.05	1.4	66	691
5	10	17	41	1.1	173	956	1,890	189	0.04	0.05	1.0	2	692
0	12	22	34	1.1	210	822	3,010	301	0.05	0.05	0.9	1	693
1	1	4	19	0.1	27	1,019	Tr	Tr	Tr	0.01	0.3	0	694
Tr	4	10	23	0.1	47	627	Tr	Tr	0.02	0.04	0.4	Tr	695
2	6	24	24	0.4	23	957	50	5	0.05	0.04	0.7	Tr	696
0	4	9	22	0.1	48	635	Tr	Tr	0.02	0.04	0.4	Tr	697
0	8	6	23	0.5	78	856	140	14	0.04	0.03	0.6	5	698
53	23	569	438	0.3	552	1,565	390	117	0.15	0.56	0.3	2	699
52	14	124	127	0.9	124	1,564	730	220	0.05	0.18	0.1	Tr	700
34	21	425	256	0.3	444	797	310	92	0.08	0.45	0.5	3	701
32	24	292	238	0.9	381	888	1,190	340	0.15	0.43	0.8	2	702
0	2	3	3	0.1	28	130	140	14	Tr	Tr	0.1	1	703
0	2	3	38	0.5	64	1,029	0	0	0.01	0.02	0.6	0	704
7	11	14	70	1.6	189	1,305	0	0	0.07	0.08	1.5	0	705
5	13	48	69	1.1	259	1,373	880	264	0.04	0.10	1.1	0	706
0	13	17	36	1.6	252	1,357	0	0	0.08	0.15	1.6	0	707
2	14	66	47	0.2	61	1,147	0	0	0.04	0.09	0.9	0	708
3	14	39	47	0.3	62	1,134	0	0	0.05	0.15	0.8	3	709
1	22	42	35	0.4	54	64	Tr	Tr	0.01	0.05	0.1	Tr	710
6	16	50	61	0.4	96	23	30	10	0.02	0.10	0.1	Tr	711
5	15	65	77	0.5	125	23	30	8	0.02	0.12	0.2	Tr	712
5	13	49	83	0.4	138	19	30	8	0.07	0.07	1.4	Tr	713
6	18	48	57	0.2	100	46	30	8	0.01	0.08	0.1	Tr	714
0	97	51	178	5.8	593	24	30	3	0.10	0.14	0.9	Tr	715
0	16	7	41	0.6	86	5	10	1	0.01	0.04	0.1	Tr	716
0	27	2	Tr	0.1	1	57	0	0	Tr	Tr	Tr	0	717
1	21	22	24	0.3	42	54	Tr	Tr	0.01	0.03	0.1	Tr	718
0	25	2	Tr	0.1	1	10	0	0	0.00	Tr	Tr	0	719

Item No.	Foods, approximate measures, units, and weight (weight of edible portion only)		Grams	Water	Food energy	Protein	Fat	Fatty acids		
								Saturated	Mono- unsaturated	Poly- unsaturated
			Grams	Percent	Calories	Grams	Grams	Grams	Grams	Grams

Sugars and Sweets—Con.

	Candy:									
720	Hard	1 oz	28	1	110	0	0	0.0	0.0	0.0
721	Jelly beans	1 oz	28	6	105	Tr	Tr	Tr	Tr	0.1
722	Marshmallows	1 oz	28	17	90	1	0	0.0	0.0	0.0
723	Custard, baked	1 cup	265	77	305	14	15	6.8	5.4	0.7
724	Gelatin dessert prepared with gelatin dessert powder and water	1/2 cup	120	84	70	2	0	0.0	0.0	0.0
725	Honey, strained or extracted	1 cup	339	17	1,030	1	0	0.0	0.0	0.0
726		1 tbsp	21	17	65	Tr	0	0.0	0.0	0.0
727	Jams and preserves	1 tbsp	20	29	55	Tr	Tr	0.0	Tr	Tr
728		1 packet	14	29	40	Tr	Tr	0.0	Tr	Tr
729	Jellies	1 tbsp	18	28	50	Tr	Tr	Tr	Tr	Tr
730		1 packet	14	28	40	Tr	Tr	Tr	Tr	Tr
731	Popsicle, 3-fl-oz size	1 popsicle	95	80	70	0	0	0.0	0.0	0.0
	Puddings:									
	Canned:									
732	Chocolate	5-oz can	142	68	205	3	11	9.5	0.5	0.1
733	Tapioca	5-oz can	142	74	160	3	5	4.8	Tr	Tr
734	Vanilla	5-oz can	142	69	220	2	10	9.5	0.2	0.1
	Dry mix, prepared with whole milk:									
	Chocolate:									
735	Instant	1/2 cup	130	71	155	4	4	2.3	1.1	0.2
736	Regular (cooked)	1/2 cup	130	73	150	4	4	2.4	1.1	0.1
737	Rice	1/2 cup	132	73	155	4	4	2.3	1.1	0.1
738	Tapioca	1/2 cup	130	75	145	4	4	2.3	1.1	0.1
	Vanilla:									
739	Instant	1/2 cup	130	73	150	4	4	2.2	1.1	0.2
740	Regular (cooked)	1/2 cup	130	74	145	4	4	2.3	1.0	0.1
	Sugars:									
741	Brown, pressed down	1 cup	220	2	820	0	0	0.0	0.0	0.0
	White:									
742	Granulated	1 cup	200	1	770	0	0	0.0	0.0	0.0
743		1 tbsp	12	1	45	0	0	0.0	0.0	0.0
744		1 packet	6	1	25	0	0	0.0	0.0	0.0
745	Powdered, sifted, spooned into cup	1 cup	100	1	385	0	0	0.0	0.0	0.0
	Syrups:									
	Chocolate-flavored syrup or topping:									
746	Thin type	2 tbsp	38	37	85	1	Tr	0.2	0.1	0.1
747	Fudge type	2 tbsp	38	25	125	2	5	3.1	1.7	0.2
748	Molasses, cane, blackstrap	2 tbsp	40	24	85	0	0	0.0	0.0	0.0
749	Table syrup (corn and maple)	2 tbsp	42	25	122	0	0	0.0	0.0	0.0

Vegetables and Vegetable Products

750	Alfalfa seeds, sprouted, raw	1 cup	33	91	10	1	Tr	Tr	Tr	0.1
751	Artichokes, globe or French, cooked, drained	1 artichoke	120	87	55	3	Tr	Tr	Tr	0.1
	Asparagus, green:									
	Cooked, drained:									
	From raw:									
752	Cuts and tips	1 cup	180	92	45	5	1	0.1	Tr	0.2
753	Spears, 1/2-in diam. at base	4 spears	60	92	15	2	Tr	Tr	Tr	0.1
	From frozen:									
754	Cuts and tips	1 cup	180	91	50	5	1	0.2	Tr	0.3
755	Spears, 1/2-in diam. at base	4 spears	60	91	15	2	Tr	0.1	Tr	0.1
756	Canned, spears, 1/2-in diam. at base	4 spears	80	95	10	1	Tr	Tr	Tr	0.1
757	Bamboo shoots, canned, drained	1 cup	131	94	25	2	1	0.1	Tr	0.2

[56] For regular pack; special dietary pack contains 3 mg sodium.

Nutrients in Indicated Quantity

Cho-les-terol	Carbo-hydrate	Calcium	Phos-phorus	Iron	Potas-sium	Sodium	Vitamin A value		Thiamin	Ribo-flavin	Niacin	Ascorbic acid	Item No.
							(IU)	(RE)					
Milli-grams	Grams	Milli-grams	Milli-grams	Milli-grams	Milli-grams	Milli-grams	Inter-national units	Retinol equiva-lents	Milli-grams	Milli-grams	Milli-grams	Milli-grams	
0	28	Tr	2	0.1	1	7	0	0	0.10	0.00	0.0	0	720
0	26	1	1	0.3	11	7	0	0	0.00	Tr	Tr	0	721
0	23	1	2	0.5	2	25	0	0	0.00	Tr	Tr	0	722
278	29	297	310	1.1	387	209	530	146	0.11	0.50	0.3	1	723˙
0	17	2	23	Tr	Tr	55	0	0	0.00	0.00	0.0	0	724
0	279	17	20	1.7	173	17	0	0	0.02	0.14	1.0	3	725
0	17	1	1	0.1	11	1	0	0	Tr	0.01	0.1	Tr	726
0	14	4	2	0.2	18	2	Tr	Tr	Tr	0.01	Tr	Tr	727
0	10	3	1	0.1	12	2	Tr	Tr	Tr	Tr	Tr	Tr	728
0	13	2	Tr	0.1	16	5	Tr	Tr	Tr	0.01	Tr	1	729
0	10	1	Tr	Tr	13	4	Tr	Tr	Tr	Tr	Tr	1	730
0	18	0	0	Tr	4	11	0	0	0.00	0.00	0.0	0	731
1	30	74	117	1.2	254	285	100	31	0.04	0.17	0.6	Tr	732
Tr	28	119	113	0.3	212	252	Tr	Tr	0.03	0.14	0.4	Tr	733
1	33	79	94	0.2	155	305	Tr	Tr	0.03	0.12	0.6	Tr	734
14	27	130	329	0.3	176	440	130	33	0.04	0.18	0.1	1	735
15	25	146	120	0.2	190	167	140	34	0.05	0.20	0.1	1	736
15	27	133	110	0.5	165	140	140	33	0.10	0.18	0.6	1	737
15	25	131	103	0.1	167	152	140	34	0.04	0.18	0.1	1	738
15	27	129	273	0.1	164	375	140	33	0.04	0.17	0.1	1	739
15	25	132	102	0.1	166	178	140	34	0.04	0.18	0.1	1	740
0	212	187	56	4.8	757	97	0	0	0.02	0.07	0.2	0	741
0	199	3	Tr	0.1	7	5	0	0	0.00	0.00	0.0	0	742
0	12	Tr	Tr	Tr	Tr	Tr	0	0	0.00	0.00	0.0	0	743
0	6	Tr	Tr	Tr	Tr	Tr	0	0	0.00	0.00	0.0	0	744
0	100	1	Tr	Tr	4	2	0	0	0.00	0.00	0.0	0	745
0	22	6	49	0.8	85	36	Tr	Tr	Tr	0.02	0.1	0	746
0	21	38	60	0.5	82	42	40	13	0.02	0.08	0.1	0	747
0	22	274	34	10.1	1,171	38	0	0	0.04	0.08	0.8	0	748
0	32	1	4	Tr	7	19	0	0	0.00	0.00	0.0	0	749
0	1	11	23	0.3	26	2	50	5	0.03	0.04	0.2	3	750
0	12	47	72	1.6	316	79	170	17	0.07	0.06	0.7	9	751
0	8	43	110	1.2	558	7	1,490	149	0.18	0.22	1.9	49	752
0	3	14	37	0.4	186	2	500	50	0.06	0.07	0.6	16	753
0	9	41	99	1.2	392	7	1,470	147	0.12	0.19	1.9	44	754
0	3	14	33	0.4	131	2	490	49	0.04	0.06	0.6	15	755
0	2	11	30	0.5	122	[56]278	380	38	0.04	0.07	0.7	13	756
0	4	10	33	0.4	105	9	10	1	0.03	0.03	0.2	1	757

Item No.	Foods, approximate measures, units, and weight (weight of edible portion only)		Grams	Water	Food energy	Pro-tein	Fat	Fatty acids		
								Satu-rated	Mono-unsatu-rated	Poly-unsatu-rated
	Vegetables and Vegetable Products—Con.		Grams	Per-cent	Cal-ories	Grams	Grams	Grams	Grams	Grams
	Beans:									
	Lima, immature seeds, frozen, cooked, drained:									
758	Thick-seeded types (Ford-hooks)---------------------	1 cup-----------	170	74	170	10	1	0.1	Tr	0.3
759	Thin-seeded types (baby limas)--------------------	1 cup-----------	180	72	190	12	1	0.1	Tr	0.3
	Snap:									
	Cooked, drained:									
760	From raw (cut and French style)-----------------	1 cup-----------	125	89	45	2	Tr	0.1	Tr	0.2
761	From frozen (cut)----------	1 cup-----------	135	92	35	2	Tr	Tr	Tr	0.1
762	Canned, drained solids (cut)	1 cup-----------	135	93	25	2	Tr	Tr	Tr	0.1
	Beans, mature. See Beans, dry (items 527-535) and Black-eyed peas, dry (item 536).									
	Bean sprouts (mung):									
763	Raw-----------------------	1 cup-----------	104	90	30	3	Tr	Tr	Tr	0.1
764	Cooked, drained----------------	1 cup-----------	124	93	25	3	Tr	Tr	Tr	Tr
	Beets:									
	Cooked, drained:									
765	Diced or sliced-------------	1 cup-----------	170	91	55	2	Tr	Tr	Tr	Tr
766	Whole beets, 2-in diam.------	2 beets---------	100	91	30	1	Tr	Tr	Tr	Tr
767	Canned, drained solids, diced or sliced--------------------	1 cup-----------	170	91	55	2	Tr	Tr	Tr	0.1
768	Beet greens, leaves and stems, cooked, drained-------------	1 cup-----------	144	89	40	4	Tr	Tr	0.1	0.1
	Black-eyed peas, immature seeds, cooked and drained:									
769	From raw-------------------	1 cup-----------	165	72	180	13	1	0.3	0.1	0.6
770	From frozen-------------------	1 cup-----------	170	66	225	14	1	0.3	0.1	0.5
	Broccoli:									
771	Raw-------------------------	1 spear---------	151	91	40	4	1	0.1	Tr	0.3
	Cooked, drained:									
	From raw:									
772	Spear, medium--------------	1 spear---------	180	90	50	5	1	0.1	Tr	0.2
773	Spears, cut into 1/2-in pieces-------------------	1 cup-----------	155	90	45	5	Tr	0.1	Tr	0.2
	From frozen:									
774	Piece, 4-1/2 to 5 in long--	1 piece---------	30	91	10	1	Tr	Tr	Tr	Tr
775	Chopped--------------------	1 cup-----------	185	91	50	6	Tr	Tr	Tr	0.1
	Brussels sprouts, cooked, drained:									
776	From raw, 7-8 sprouts, 1-1/4 to 1-1/2-in diam.------------	1 cup-----------	155	87	60	4	1	0.2	0.1	0.4
777	From frozen-------------------	1 cup-----------	155	87	65	6	1	0.1	Tr	0.3
	Cabbage, common varieties:									
778	Raw, coarsely shredded or sliced--------------------	1 cup-----------	70	93	15	1	Tr	Tr	Tr	0.1
779	Cooked, drained----------------	1 cup-----------	150	94	30	1	Tr	Tr	Tr	0.2
	Cabbage, Chinese:									
780	Pak-choi, cooked, drained------	1 cup-----------	170	96	20	3	Tr	Tr	Tr	0.1
781	Pe-tsai, raw, 1-in pieces------	1 cup-----------	76	94	10	1	Tr	Tr	Tr	0.1
782	Cabbage, red, raw, coarsely shredded or sliced------------	1 cup-----------	70	92	20	1	Tr	Tr	Tr	0.1
783	Cabbage, savoy, raw, coarsely shredded or sliced------------	1 cup-----------	70	91	20	1	Tr	Tr	Tr	Tr

[57] For green varieties; yellow varieties contain 101 IU or 10 RE.
[58] For green varieties; yellow varieties contain 151 IU or 15 RE.
[59] For regular pack; special dietary pack contains 3 mg sodium.

							Nutrients in Indicated Quantity						
Cho-les-terol	Carbo-hydrate	Calcium	Phos-phorus	Iron	Potas-sium	Sodium	Vitamin A value		Thiamin	Ribo-flavin	Niacin	Ascorbic acid	Item No.
							(IU)	(RE)					
Milli-grams	Grams	Milli-grams	Milli-grams	Milli-grams	Milli-grams	Milli-grams	Inter-national units	Retinol equiva-lents	Milli-grams	Milli-grams	Milli-grams	Milli-grams	
0	32	37	107	2.3	694	90	320	32	0.13	0.10	1.8	22	758
0	35	50	202	3.5	740	52	300	30	0.13	0.10	1.4	10	759
0	10	58	49	1.6	374	4	[57]830	[57]83	0.09	0.12	0.8	12	760
0	8	61	32	1.1	151	18	[58]710	[58]71	0.06	0.10	0.6	11	761
0	6	35	26	1.2	147	[59]339	[60]470	[60]47	0.02	0.08	0.3	6	762
0	6	14	56	0.9	155	6	20	2	0.09	0.13	0.8	14	763
0	5	15	35	0.8	125	12	20	2	0.06	0.13	1.0	14	764
0	11	19	53	1.1	530	83	20	2	0.05	0.02	0.5	9	765
0	7	11	31	0.6	312	49	10	1	0.03	0.01	0.3	6	766
0	12	26	29	3.1	252	[61]466	20	2	0.02	0.07	0.3	7	767
0	8	164	59	2.7	1,309	347	7,340	734	0.17	0.42	0.7	36	768
0	30	46	196	2.4	693	7	1,050	105	0.11	0.18	1.8	3	769
0	40	39	207	3.6	638	9	130	13	0.44	0.11	1.2	4	770
0	8	72	100	1.3	491	41	2,330	233	0.10	0.18	1.0	141	771
0	10	82	86	2.1	293	20	2,540	254	0.15	0.37	1.4	113	772
0	9	71	74	1.8	253	17	2,180	218	0.13	0.32	1.2	97	773
0	2	15	17	0.2	54	7	570	57	0.02	0.02	0.1	12	774
0	10	94	102	1.1	333	44	3,500	350	0.10	0.15	0.8	74	775
0	13	56	87	1.9	491	33	1,110	111	0.17	0.12	0.9	96	776
0	13	37	84	1.1	504	36	910	91	0.16	0.18	0.8	71	777
0	4	33	16	0.4	172	13	90	9	0.04	0.02	0.2	33	778
0	7	50	38	0.6	308	29	130	13	0.09	0.08	0.3	36	779
0	3	158	49	1.8	631	58	4,370	437	0.05	0.11	0.7	44	780
0	2	59	22	0.2	181	7	910	91	0.03	0.04	0.3	21	781
0	4	36	29	0.3	144	8	30	3	0.04	0.02	0.2	40	782
0	4	25	29	0.3	161	20	700	70	0.05	0.02	0.2	22	783

[60] For green varieties; yellow varieties contain 142 IU or 14 RE.
[61] For regular pack; special dietary pack contains 78 mg sodium.

Item No.	Foods, approximate measures, units, and weight (weight of edible portion only)			Water	Food energy	Pro-tein	Fat	Fatty acids		
								Satu-rated	Mono-unsatu-rated	Poly-unsatu-rated
			Grams	Per-cent	Cal-ories	Grams	Grams	Grams	Grams	Grams
	Vegetables and Vegetable Products—Con.									
	Carrots:									
	Raw, without crowns and tips, scraped:									
784	Whole, 7-1/2 by 1-1/8 in, or strips, 2-1/2 to 3 in long	1 carrot or 18 strips--------	72	88	30	1	Tr	Tr	Tr	0.1
785	Grated----------------------	1 cup----------	110	88	45	1	Tr	Tr	Tr	0.1
	Cooked, sliced, drained:									
786	From raw-------------------	1 cup----------	156	87	70	2	Tr	0.1	Tr	0.1
787	From frozen----------------	1 cup----------	146	90	55	2	Tr	Tr	Tr	0.1
788	Canned, sliced, drained solids	1 cup----------	146	93	35	1	Tr	0.1	Tr	0.1
	Cauliflower:									
789	Raw, (flowerets)--------------	1 cup----------	100	92	25	2	Tr	Tr	Tr	0.1
	Cooked, drained:									
790	From raw (flowerets)---------	1 cup----------	125	93	30	2	Tr	Tr	Tr	0.1
791	From frozen (flowerets)------	1 cup----------	180	94	35	3	Tr	0.1	Tr	0.2
	Celery, pascal type, raw:									
792	Stalk, large outer, 8 by 1-1/2 in (at root end)------------	1 stalk--------	40	95	5	Tr	Tr	Tr	Tr	Tr
793	Pieces, diced------------------	1 cup----------	120	95	20	1	Tr	Tr	Tr	0.1
	Collards, cooked, drained:									
794	From raw (leaves without stems)	1 cup----------	190	96	25	2	Tr	0.1	Tr	0.2
795	From frozen (chopped)----------	1 cup----------	170	88	60	5	1	0.1	0.1	0.4
	Corn, sweet:									
	Cooked, drained:									
796	From raw, ear 5 by 1-3/4 in--	1 ear----------	77	70	85	3	1	0.2	0.3	0.5
	From frozen:									
797	Ear, trimmed to about 3-1/2 in long------------------	1 ear----------	63	73	60	2	Tr	0.1	0.1	0.2
798	Kernels--------------------	1 cup----------	165	76	135	5	Tr	Tr	Tr	0.1
	Canned:									
799	Cream style----------------	1 cup----------	256	79	185	4	1	0.2	0.3	0.5
800	Whole kernel, vacuum pack----	1 cup----------	210	77	165	5	1	0.2	0.3	0.5
	Cowpeas. See Black-eyed peas, immature (items 769,770), mature (item 536).									
801	Cucumber, with peel, slices, 1/8 in thick (large, 2-1/8-in diam.; small, 1-3/4-in diam.)--	6 large or 8 small slices	28	96	5	Tr	Tr	Tr	Tr	Tr
802	Dandelion greens, cooked, drained	1 cup----------	105	90	35	2	1	0.1	Tr	0.3
803	Eggplant, cooked, steamed-------	1 cup----------	96	92	25	1	Tr	Tr	Tr	0.1
804	Endive, curly (including esca-role), raw, small pieces-------	1 cup----------	50	94	10	1	Tr	Tr	Tr	Tr
805	Jerusalem-artichoke, raw, sliced	1 cup----------	150	78	115	3	Tr	0.0	Tr	Tr
	Kale, cooked, drained:									
806	From raw, chopped--------------	1 cup----------	130	91	40	2	1	0.1	Tr	0.3
807	From frozen, chopped-----------	1 cup----------	130	91	40	4	1	0.1	Tr	0.3
808	Kohlrabi, thickened bulb-like stems, cooked, drained, diced--	1 cup----------	165	90	50	3	Tr	Tr	Tr	0.1
	Lettuce, raw:									
	Butterhead, as Boston types:									
809	Head, 5-in diam--------------	1 head----------	163	96	20	2	Tr	Tr	Tr	0.2
810	Leaves----------------------	1 outer or 2 inner leaves--	15	96	Tr	Tr	Tr	Tr	Tr	Tr
	Crisphead, as iceberg:									
811	Head, 6-in diam-------------	1 head----------	539	96	70	5	1	0.1	Tr	0.5
812	Wedge, 1/4 of head----------	1 wedge---------	135	96	20	1	Tr	Tr	Tr	0.1
813	Pieces, chopped or shredded--	1 cup----------	55	96	5	1	Tr	Tr	Tr	0.1
814	Looseleaf (bunching varieties including romaine or cos), chopped or shredded pieces---	1 cup----------	56	94	10	1	Tr	Tr	Tr	0.1

[62] For regular pack; special dietary pack contains 61 mg sodium.
[63] For yellow varieties; white varieties contain only a trace of vitamin A.

Nutrients in Indicated Quantity

Cho-les-terol	Carbo-hydrate	Calcium	Phos-phorus	Iron	Potas-sium	Sodium	Vitamin A value		Thiamin	Ribo-flavin	Niacin	Ascorbic acid	Item No.
							(IU)	(RE)					
Milli-grams	Grams	Milli-grams	Milli-grams	Milli-grams	Milli-grams	Milli-grams	Inter-national units	Retinol equiva-lents	Milli-grams	Milli-grams	Milli-grams	Milli-grams	
0	7	19	32	0.4	233	25	20,250	2,025	0.07	0.04	0.7	7	784
0	11	30	48	0.6	355	39	30,940	3,094	0.11	0.06	1.0	10	785
0	16	48	47	1.0	354	103	38,300	3,830	0.05	0.09	0.8	4	786
0	12	41	38	0.7	231	86	25,850	2,585	0.04	0.05	0.6	4	787
0	8	37	35	0.9	261	[62]352	20,110	2,011	0.03	0.04	0.8	4	788
0	5	29	46	0.6	355	15	20	2	0.08	0.06	0.6	72	789
0	6	34	44	0.5	404	8	20	2	0.08	0.07	0.7	69	790
0	7	31	43	0.7	250	32	40	4	0.07	0.10	0.6	56	791
0	1	14	10	0.2	114	35	50	5	0.01	0.01	0.1	3	792
0	4	43	31	0.6	341	106	150	15	0.04	0.04	0.4	8	793
0	5	148	19	0.8	177	36	4,220	422	0.03	0.08	0.4	19	794
0	12	357	46	1.9	427	85	10,170	1,017	0.08	0.20	1.1	45	795
0	19	2	79	0.5	192	13	[63]170	[63]17	0.17	0.06	1.2	5	796
0	14	2	47	0.4	158	3	[63]130	[63]13	0.11	0.04	1.0	3	797
0	34	3	78	0.5	229	8	[63]410	[63]41	0.11	0.12	2.1	4	798
0	46	8	131	1.0	343	[64]730	[63]250	[63]25	0.06	0.14	2.5	12	799
0	41	11	134	0.9	391	[65]571	[63]510	[63]51	0.09	0.15	2.5	17	800
0	1	4	5	0.1	42	1	10	1	0.01	0.01	0.1	1	801
0	7	147	44	1.9	244	46	12,290	1,229	0.14	0.18	0.5	19	802
0	6	6	21	0.3	238	3	60	6	0.07	0.02	0.6	1	803
0	2	26	14	0.4	157	11	1,030	103	0.04	0.04	0.2	3	804
0	26	21	117	5.1	644	6	30	3	0.30	0.09	2.0	6	805
0	7	94	36	1.2	296	30	9,620	962	0.07	0.09	0.7	53	806
0	7	179	36	1.2	417	20	8,260	826	0.06	0.15	0.9	33	807
0	11	41	74	0.7	561	35	60	6	0.07	0.03	0.6	89	808
0	4	52	38	0.5	419	8	1,580	158	0.10	0.10	0.5	13	809
0	Tr	5	3	Tr	39	1	150	15	0.01	0.01	Tr	1	810
0	11	102	108	2.7	852	49	1,780	178	0.25	0.16	1.0	21	811
0	3	26	27	0.7	213	12	450	45	0.06	0.04	0.3	5	812
0	1	10	11	0.3	87	5	180	18	0.03	0.02	0.1	2	813
0	2	38	14	0.8	148	5	1,060	106	0.03	0.04	0.2	10	814

[64]For regular pack; special dietary pack contains 8 mg sodium.
[65]For regular pack; special dietary pack contains 6 mg sodium.

Item No.	Foods, approximate measures, units, and weight (weight of edible portion only)		Grams	Water Per-cent	Food energy Cal-ories	Pro-tein Grams	Fat Grams	Fatty acids Satu-rated Grams	Mono-unsatu-rated Grams	Poly-unsatu-rated Grams
	Vegetables and Vegetable Products—Con.									
	Mushrooms:									
815	Raw, sliced or chopped---------	1 cup----------	70	92	20	1	Tr	Tr	Tr	0.1
816	Cooked, drained----------------	1 cup----------	156	91	40	3	1	0.1	Tr	0.3
817	Canned, drained solids---------	1 cup----------	156	91	35	3	Tr	0.1	Tr	0.2
818	Mustard greens, without stems and midribs, cooked, drained------	1 cup----------	140	94	20	3	Tr	Tr	0.2	0.1
819	Okra pods, 3 by 5/8 in, cooked---	8 pods----------	85	90	25	2	Tr	Tr	Tr	Tr
	Onions:									
	Raw:									
820	Chopped----------------------	1 cup----------	160	91	55	2	Tr	0.1	0.1	0.2
821	Sliced-----------------------	1 cup----------	115	91	40	1	Tr	0.1	Tr	0.1
822	Cooked (whole or sliced), drained----------------------	1 cup----------	210	92	60	2	Tr	0.1	Tr	0.1
823	Onions, spring, raw, bulb (3/8-in diam.) and white portion of top	6 onions--------	30	92	10	1	Tr	Tr	Tr	Tr
824	Onion rings, breaded, par-fried, frozen, prepared--------------	2 rings---------	20	29	80	1	5	1.7	2.2	1.0
	Parsley:									
825	Raw--------------------------	10 sprigs-------	10	88	5	Tr	Tr	Tr	Tr	Tr
826	Freeze-dried------------------	1 tbsp----------	0.4	2	Tr	Tr	Tr	Tr	Tr	Tr
827	Parsnips, cooked (diced or 2 in lengths), drained------------	1 cup----------	156	78	125	2	Tr	0.1	0.2	0.1
828	Peas, edible pod, cooked, drained	1 cup----------	160	89	65	5	Tr	0.1	Tr	0.2
	Peas, green:									
829	Canned, drained solids---------	1 cup----------	170	82	115	8	1	0.1	0.1	0.3
830	Frozen, cooked, drained--------	1 cup----------	160	80	125	8	Tr	0.1	Tr	0.2
	Peppers:									
831	Hot chili, raw----------------	1 pepper--------	45	88	20	1	Tr	Tr	Tr	Tr
	Sweet (about 5 per lb, whole), stem and seeds removed:									
832	Raw--------------------------	1 pepper--------	74	93	20	1	Tr	Tr	Tr	0.2
833	Cooked, drained--------------	1 pepper--------	73	95	15	Tr	Tr	Tr	Tr	0.1
	Potatoes, cooked:									
	Baked (about 2 per lb, raw):									
834	With skin--------------------	1 potato--------	202	71	220	5	Tr	0.1	Tr	0.1
835	Flesh only-------------------	1 potato--------	156	75	145	3	Tr	Tr	Tr	0.1
	Boiled (about 3 per lb, raw):									
836	Peeled after boiling---------	1 potato--------	136	77	120	3	Tr	Tr	Tr	0.1
837	Peeled before boiling--------	1 potato--------	135	77	115	2	Tr	Tr	Tr	0.1
	French fried, strip, 2 to 3-1/2 in long, frozen:									
838	Oven heated------------------	10 strips-------	50	53	110	2	4	2.1	1.8	0.3
839	Fried in vegetable oil-------	10 strips-------	50	38	160	2	8	2.5	1.6	3.8
	Potato products, prepared:									
	Au gratin:									
840	From dry mix-----------------	1 cup----------	245	79	230	6	10	6.3	2.9	0.3
841	From home recipe-------------	1 cup----------	245	74	325	12	19	11.6	5.3	0.7
842	Hashed brown, from frozen------	1 cup----------	156	56	340	5	18	7.0	8.0	2.1
	Mashed:									
	From home recipe:									
843	Milk added-----------------	1 cup----------	210	78	160	4	1	0.7	0.3	0.1
844	Milk and margarine added---	1 cup----------	210	76	225	4	9	2.2	3.7	2.5
845	From dehydrated flakes (without milk), water, milk, butter, and salt added---------------------	1 cup----------	210	76	235	4	12	7.2	3.3	0.5
846	Potato salad, made with mayonnaise-------------------	1 cup----------	250	76	360	7	21	3.6	6.2	9.3
	Scalloped:									
847	From dry mix-----------------	1 cup----------	245	79	230	5	11	6.5	3.0	0.5
848	From home recipe-------------	1 cup----------	245	81	210	7	9	5.5	2.5	0.4

[66] For regular pack; special dietary pack contains 3 mg sodium.
[67] For red peppers; green peppers contain 350 IU or 35 RE.
[68] For green peppers; red peppers contain 4,220 IU or 422 RE.

	Nutrients in Indicated Quantity												
Cho-les-terol	Carbo-hydrate	Calcium	Phos-phorus	Iron	Potas-sium	Sodium	Vitamin A value (IU)	(RE)	Thiamin	Ribo-flavin	Niacin	Ascorbic acid	Item No.
Milli-grams	Grams	Milli-grams	Milli-grams	Milli-grams	Milli-grams	Milli-grams	Inter-national units	Retinol equiva-lents	Milli-grams	Milli-grams	Milli-grams	Milli-grams	
0	3	4	73	0.9	259	3	0	0	0.07	0.31	2.9	2	815
0	8	9	136	2.7	555	3	0	0	0.11	0.47	7.0	6	816
0	8	17	103	1.2	201	663	0	0	0.13	0.03	2.5	0	817
0	3	104	57	1.0	283	22	4,240	424	0.06	0.09	0.6	35	818
0	6	54	48	0.4	274	4	490	49	0.11	0.05	0.7	14	819
0	12	40	46	0.6	248	3	0	0	0.10	0.02	0.2	13	820
0	8	29	33	0.4	178	2	0	0	0.07	0.01	0.1	10	821
0	13	57	48	0.4	319	17	0	0	0.09	0.02	0.2	12	822
0	2	18	10	0.6	77	1	1,500	150	0.02	0.04	0.1	14	823
0	8	6	16	0.3	26	75	50	5	0.06	0.03	0.7	Tr	824
0	1	13	4	0.6	54	4	520	52	0.01	0.01	0.1	9	825
0	Tr	1	2	0.2	25	2	250	25	Tr	0.01	Tr	1	826
0	30	58	108	0.9	573	16	0	0	0.13	0.08	1.1	20	827
0	11	67	88	3.2	384	6	210	21	0.20	0.12	0.9	77	828
0	21	34	114	1.6	294	[66]372	1,310	131	0.21	0.13	1.2	16	829
0	23	38	144	2.5	269	139	1,070	107	0.45	0.16	2.4	16	830
0	4	8	21	0.5	153	3	[67]4,840	[67]484	0.04	0.04	0.4	109	831
0	4	4	16	0.9	144	2	[68]390	[68]39	0.06	0.04	0.4	[69]95	832
0	3	3	11	0.6	94	1	[70]280	[70]28	0.04	0.03	0.3	[71]81	833
0	51	20	115	2.7	844	16	0	0	0.22	0.07	3.3	26	834
0	34	8	78	0.5	610	8	0	0	0.16	0.03	2.2	20	835
0	27	7	60	0.4	515	5	0	0	0.14	0.03	2.0	18	836
0	27	11	54	0.4	443	7	0	0	0.13	0.03	1.8	10	837
0	17	5	43	0.7	229	16	0	0	0.06	0.02	1.2	5	838
0	20	10	47	0.4	366	108	0	0	0.09	0.01	1.6	5	839
12	31	203	233	0.8	537	1,076	520	76	0.05	0.20	2.3	8	840
56	28	292	277	1.6	970	1,061	650	93	0.16	0.28	2.4	24	841
0	44	23	112	2.4	680	53	0	0	0.17	0.03	3.8	10	842
4	37	55	101	0.6	628	636	40	12	0.18	0.08	2.3	14	843
4	35	55	97	0.5	607	620	360	42	0.18	0.08	2.3	13	844
29	32	103	118	0.5	489	697	380	44	0.23	0.11	1.4	20	845
170	28	48	130	1.6	635	1,323	520	83	0.19	0.15	2.2	25	846
27	31	88	137	0.9	497	835	360	51	0.05	0.14	2.5	8	847
29	26	140	154	1.4	926	821	330	47	0.17	0.23	2.6	26	848

[69]For green peppers; red peppers contain 141 mg ascorbic acid.
[70]For green peppers; red peppers contain 2,740 IU or 274 RE.
[71]For green peppers; red peppers contain 121 mg ascorbic acid.

Item No.	Foods, approximate measures, units, and weight (weight of edible portion only)		Water	Food energy	Pro-tein	Fat	Fatty acids		
							Satu-rated	Mono-unsatu-rated	Poly-unsatu-rated
		Grams	Per-cent	Cal-ories	Grams	Grams	Grams	Grams	Grams
	Vegetables and Vegetable Products—Con.								
849	Potato chips-------------------- 10 chips--------	20	3	105	1	7	1.8	1.2	3.6
	Pumpkin:								
850	Cooked from raw, mashed-------- 1 cup-----------	245	94	50	2	Tr	0.1	Tr	Tr
851	Canned------------------------- 1 cup-----------	245	90	85	3	1	0.4	0.1	Tr
852	Radishes, raw, stem ends, rootlets cut off--------------- 4 radishes------	18	95	5	Tr	Tr	Tr	Tr	Tr
853	Sauerkraut, canned, solids and liquid------------------------- 1 cup-----------	236	93	45	2	Tr	0.1	Tr	0.1
	Seaweed:								
854	Kelp, raw---------------------- 1 oz------------	28	82	10	Tr	Tr	0.1	Tr	Tr
855	Spirulina, dried--------------- 1 oz------------	28	5	80	16	2	0.8	0.2	0.6
	Southern peas. See Black-eyed peas, immature (items 769,770), mature (item 536).								
	Spinach:								
856	Raw, chopped------------------- 1 cup-----------	55	92	10	2	Tr	Tr	Tr	0.1
	Cooked, drained:								
857	From raw--------------------- 1 cup-----------	180	91	40	5	Tr	0.1	Tr	0.2
858	From frozen (leaf)----------- 1 cup-----------	190	90	55	6	Tr	0.1	Tr	0.2
859	Canned, drained solids-------- 1 cup-----------	214	92	50	6	1	0.2	Tr	0.4
860	Spinach souffle---------------- 1 cup-----------	136	74	220	11	18	7.1	6.8	3.1
	Squash, cooked:								
861	Summer (all varieties), sliced, drained--------------------- 1 cup-----------	180	94	35	2	1	0.1	Tr	0.2
862	Winter (all varieties), baked, cubes------------------------- 1 cup-----------	205	89	80	2	1	0.3	0.1	0.5
	Sunchoke. See Jerusalem-arti-choke (item 805).								
	Sweetpotatoes:								
	Cooked (raw, 5 by 2 in; about 2-1/2 per lb):								
863	Baked in skin, peeled-------- 1 potato--------	114	73	115	2	Tr	Tr	Tr	0.1
864	Boiled, without skin--------- 1 potato--------	151	73	160	2	Tr	0.1	Tr	0.2
865	Candied, 2-1/2 by 2-in piece--- 1 piece---------	105	67	145	1	3	1.4	0.7	0.2
	Canned:								
866	Solid pack (mashed)---------- 1 cup-----------	255	74	260	5	1	0.1	Tr	0.2
867	Vacuum pack, piece 2-3/4 by 1 in---------------------- 1 piece---------	40	76	35	1	Tr	Tr	Tr	Tr
	Tomatoes:								
868	Raw, 2-3/5-in diam. (3 per 12 oz pkg.)-------------------- 1 tomato--------	123	94	25	1	Tr	Tr	Tr	0.1
869	Canned, solids and liquid------ 1 cup-----------	240	94	50	2	1	0.1	0.1	0.2
870	Tomato juice, canned------------ 1 cup-----------	244	94	40	2	Tr	Tr	Tr	0.1
	Tomato products, canned:								
871	Paste-------------------------- 1 cup-----------	262	74	220	10	2	0.3	0.4	0.9
872	Puree-------------------------- 1 cup-----------	250	87	105	4	Tr	Tr	Tr	0.1
873	Sauce-------------------------- 1 cup-----------	245	89	75	3	Tr	0.1	0.1	0.2
874	Turnips, cooked, diced---------- 1 cup-----------	156	94	30	1	Tr	Tr	Tr	0.1
	Turnip greens, cooked, drained:								
875	From raw (leaves and stems)---- 1 cup-----------	144	93	30	2	Tr	0.1	Tr	0.1
876	From frozen (chopped)---------- 1 cup-----------	164	90	50	5	1	0.2	Tr	0.3
877	Vegetable juice cocktail, canned 1 cup-----------	242	94	45	2	Tr	Tr	Tr	0.1
	Vegetables, mixed:								
878	Canned, drained solids--------- 1 cup-----------	163	87	75	4	Tr	0.1	Tr	0.2
879	Frozen, cooked, drained-------- 1 cup-----------	182	83	105	5	Tr	0.1	Tr	0.1
880	Waterchestnuts, canned---------- 1 cup-----------	140	86	70	1	Tr	Tr	Tr	Tr

[1] Value not determined.
[72] With added salt; if none is added, sodium content is 58 mg.
[73] For regular pack; special dietary pack contains 31 mg sodium.
[74] With added salt; if none is added, sodium content is 24 mg.

Nutrients in Indicated Quantity

Cho-les-terol	Carbo-hydrate	Calcium	Phos-phorus	Iron	Potas-sium	Sodium	Vitamin A value		Thiamin	Ribo-flavin	Niacin	Ascorbic acid	Item No.
							(IU)	(RE)					
Milli-grams	Grams	Milli-grams	Milli-grams	Milli-grams	Milli-grams	Milli-grams	Inter-national units	Retinol equiva-lents	Milli-grams	Milli-grams	Milli-grams	Milli-grams	
0	10	5	31	0.2	260	94	0	0	0.03	Tr	0.8	8	849
0	12	37	74	1.4	564	2	2,650	265	0.08	0.19	1.0	12	850
0	20	64	86	3.4	505	12	54,040	5,404	0.06	0.13	0.9	10	851
0	1	4	3	0.1	42	4	Tr	Tr	Tr	0.01	0.1	4	852
0	10	71	47	3.5	401	1,560	40	4	0.05	0.05	0.3	35	853
0	3	48	12	0.8	25	66	30	3	0.01	0.04	0.1	(1)	854
0	7	34	33	8.1	386	297	160	16	0.67	1.04	3.6	3	855
0	2	54	27	1.5	307	43	3,690	369	0.04	0.10	0.4	15	856
0	7	245	101	6.4	839	126	14,740	1,474	0.17	0.42	0.9	18	857
0	10	277	91	2.9	566	[72]163	14,790	1,479	0.11	0.32	0.8	23	858
0	7	272	94	4.9	740	[72]683	18,780	1,878	0.03	0.30	0.8	31	859
184	3	230	231	1.3	201	763	3,460	675	0.09	0.30	0.5	3	860
0	8	49	70	0.6	346	2	520	52	0.08	0.07	0.9	10	861
0	18	29	41	0.7	896	2	7,290	729	0.17	0.05	1.4	20	862
0	28	32	63	0.5	397	11	24,880	2,488	0.08	0.14	0.7	28	863
0	37	32	41	0.8	278	20	25,750	2,575	0.08	0.21	1.0	26	864
8	29	27	27	1.2	198	74	4,400	440	0.02	0.04	0.4	7	865
0	59	77	133	3.4	536	191	38,570	3,857	0.07	0.23	2.4	13	866
0	8	9	20	0.4	125	21	3,190	319	0.01	0.02	0.3	11	867
0	5	9	28	0.6	255	10	1,390	139	0.07	0.06	0.7	22	868
0	10	62	46	1.5	530	[73]391	1,450	145	0.11	0.07	1.8	36	869
0	10	22	46	1.4	537	[74]881	1,360	136	0.11	0.08	1.6	45	870
0	49	92	207	7.8	2,442	[75]170	6,470	647	0.41	0.50	8.4	111	871
0	25	38	100	2.3	1,050	[76]50	3,400	340	0.18	0.14	4.3	88	872
0	18	34	78	1.9	909	[77]1,482	2,400	240	0.16	0.14	2.8	32	873
0	8	34	30	0.3	211	78	0	0	0.04	0.04	0.5	18	874
0	6	197	42	1.2	292	42	7,920	792	0.06	0.10	0.6	39	875
0	8	249	56	3.2	367	25	13,080	1,308	0.09	0.12	0.8	36	876
0	11	27	41	1.0	467	883	2,830	283	0.10	0.07	1.8	67	877
0	15	44	68	1.7	474	243	18,990	1,899	0.08	0.08	0.9	8	878
0	24	46	93	1.5	308	64	7,780	778	0.13	0.22	1.5	6	879
0	17	6	27	1.2	165	11	10	1	0.02	0.03	0.5	2	880

[75] With no added salt; if salt is added, sodium content is 2,070 mg.
[76] With no added salt; if salt is added, sodium content is 998 mg.
[77] With salt added.

Item No.	Foods, approximate measures, units, and weight (weight of edible portion only)		Water	Food energy	Protein	Fat	Fatty acids		
							Saturated	Mono-unsaturated	Poly-unsaturated
			Grams	Percent	Calories	Grams	Grams	Grams	Grams	Grams

Miscellaneous Items

Item No.	Foods, approximate measures, units, and weight	measure	Water (Grams)	Percent	Calories	Protein (Grams)	Fat (Grams)	Saturated	Mono-unsaturated	Poly-unsaturated
	Baking powders for home use:									
	Sodium aluminum sulfate:									
881	With monocalcium phosphate monohydrate---------------	1 tsp-----------	3	2	5	Tr	0	0.0	0.0	0.0
882	With monocalcium phosphate monohydrate, calcium sulfate--------------------	1 tsp-----------	2.9	1	5	Tr	0	0.0	0.0	0.0
883	Straight phosphate------------	1 tsp-----------	3.8	2	5	Tr	0	0.0	0.0	0.0
884	Low sodium--------------------	1 tsp-----------	4.3	1	5	Tr	0	0.0	0.0	0.0
885	Catsup------------------------	1 cup-----------	273	69	290	5	1	0.2	0.2	0.4
886		1 tbsp----------	15	69	15	Tr	Tr	Tr	Tr	Tr
887	Celery seed-------------------	1 tsp-----------	2	6	10	Tr	1	Tr	0.3	0.1
888	Chili powder------------------	1 tsp-----------	2.6	8	10	Tr	Tr	0.1	0.1	0.2
	Chocolate:									
889	Bitter or baking-------------	1 oz------------	28	2	145	3	15	9.0	4.9	0.5
	Semisweet, see Candy, (item 715).									
890	Cinnamon----------------------	1 tsp-----------	2.3	10	5	Tr	Tr	Tr	Tr	Tr
891	Curry powder------------------	1 tsp-----------	2	10	5	Tr	Tr	([1])	([1])	([1])
892	Garlic powder-----------------	1 tsp-----------	2.8	6	10	Tr	Tr	Tr	Tr	Tr
893	Gelatin, dry------------------	1 envelope------	7	13	25	6	Tr	Tr	Tr	Tr
894	Mustard, prepared, yellow--------	1 tsp or individual packet---	5	80	5	Tr	Tr	Tr	0.2	Tr
	Olives, canned:									
895	Green-------------------------	4 medium or 3 extra large	13	78	15	Tr	2	0.2	1.2	0.1
896	Ripe, Mission, pitted----------	3 small or 2 large-------	9	73	15	Tr	2	0.3	1.3	0.2
897	Onion powder------------------	1 tsp-----------	2.1	5	5	Tr	Tr	Tr	Tr	Tr
898	Oregano-----------------------	1 tsp-----------	1.5	7	5	Tr	Tr	Tr	Tr	0.1
899	Paprika-----------------------	1 tsp-----------	2.1	10	5	Tr	Tr	Tr	Tr	0.2
900	Pepper, black-----------------	1 tsp-----------	2.1	11	5	Tr	Tr	Tr	Tr	Tr
	Pickles, cucumber:									
901	Dill, medium, whole, 3-3/4 in long, 1-1/4-in diam.---------	1 pickle--------	65	93	5	Tr	Tr	Tr	Tr	0.1
902	Fresh-pack, slices 1-1/2-in diam., 1/4 in thick----------	2 slices--------	15	79	10	Tr	Tr	Tr	Tr	Tr
903	Sweet, gherkin, small, whole, about 2-1/2 in long, 3/4-in diam.-----------------------	1 pickle--------	15	61	20	Tr	Tr	Tr	Tr	Tr
	Popcorn. See Grain Products, (items 497-499).									
904	Relish, finely chopped, sweet----	1 tbsp----------	15	63	20	Tr	Tr	Tr	Tr	Tr
905	Salt--------------------------	1 tsp-----------	5.5	0	0	0	0	0.0	0.0	0.0
906	Vinegar, cider----------------	1 tbsp----------	15	94	Tr	Tr	0	0.0	0.0	0.0
	Yeast:									
907	Baker's, dry, active-----------	1 pkg-----------	7	5	20	3	Tr	Tr	0.1	Tr
908	Brewer's, dry-----------------	1 tbsp----------	8	5	25	3	Tr	Tr	Tr	0.0

[1]Value not determined.

							Nutrients in Indicated Quantity						
Cho-les-terol	Carbo-hydrate	Calcium	Phos-phorus	Iron	Potas-sium	Sodium	Vitamin A value		Thiamin	Ribo-flavin	Niacin	Ascorbic acid	Item No.
							(IU)	(RE)					
Milli-grams	Grams	Milli-grams	Milli-grams	Milli-grams	Milli-grams	Milli-grams	Inter-national units	Retinol equiva-lents	Milli-grams	Milli-grams	Milli-grams	Milli-grams	
0	1	58	87	0.0	5	329	0	0	0.00	0.00	0.0	0	881
0	1	183	45	0.0	4	290	0	0	0.00	0.00	0.0	0	882
0	1	239	359	0.0	6	312	0	0	0.00	0.00	0.0	0	883
0	1	207	314	0.0	891	Tr	0	0	0.00	0.00	0.0	0	884
0	69	60	137	2.2	991	2,845	3,820	382	0.25	0.19	4.4	41	885
0	4	3	8	0.1	54	156	210	21	0.01	0.01	0.2	2	886
0	1	35	11	0.9	28	3	Tr	Tr	0.01	0.01	0.1	Tr	887
0	1	7	8	0.4	50	26	910	91	0.01	0.02	0.2	2	888
0	8	22	109	1.9	235	1	10	1	0.01	0.07	0.4	0	889
0	2	28	1	0.9	12	1	10	1	Tr	Tr	Tr	1	890
0	1	10	7	0.6	31	1	20	2	0.01	0.01	0.1	Tr	891
0	2	2	12	0.1	31	1	0	0	0.01	Tr	Tr	Tr	892
0	0	1	0	0.0	2	6	0	0	0.00	0.00	0.0	0	893
0	Tr	4	4	0.1	7	63	0	0	Tr	0.01	Tr	Tr	894
0	Tr	8	2	0.2	7	312	40	4	Tr	Tr	Tr	0	895
0	Tr	10	2	0.2	2	68	10	1	Tr	Tr	Tr	0	896
0	2	8	7	0.1	20	1	Tr	Tr	0.01	Tr	Tr	Tr	897
0	1	24	3	0.7	25	Tr	100	10	0.01	Tr	0.1	1	898
0	1	4	7	0.5	49	1	1,270	127	0.01	0.04	0.3	1	899
0	1	9	4	0.6	26	1	Tr	Tr	Tr	0.01	Tr	0	900
0	1	17	14	0.7	130	928	70	7	Tr	0.01	Tr	4	901
0	3	5	4	0.3	30	101	20	2	Tr	Tr	Tr	1	902
0	5	2	2	0.2	30	107	10	1	Tr	Tr	Tr	1	903
0	5	3	2	0.1	30	107	20	2	Tr	Tr	0.0	1	904
0	0	14	3	Tr	Tr	2,132	0	0	0.00	0.00	0.0	0	905
0	1	1	1	0.1	15	Tr	0	0	0.00	0.00	0.0	0	906
0	3	3	90	1.1	140	4	Tr	Tr	0.16	0.38	2.6	Tr	907
0	3	[78]17	140	1.4	152	10	Tr	Tr	1.25	0.34	3.0	Tr	908

[78]Value may vary from 6 to 60 mg.

NUTRIENT COMPOSITION OF FOODS AVAILABLE ELECTRONICALLY*

*This appendix explains how information related to nutrient composition of foods can be obtained through the Internet. All information is provided on the Internet by U.S.D.A. and affiliated agencies. The information included is directly downloaded from the Internet.

Appendix D.1 Food Composition Resource List for Professionals (January 1997)

The resources selected for this list contain reliable information and are available nation-wide. Your local library or bookstore can help you locate these books, journals, and audiovisuals. Other items can be obtained from the source listed. The call numbers provided are for the National Agricultural Library. Lending information is provided at the end of this document.

Books and Miscellaneous Publications (in alphabetical order)

Bowes and Church's Food Values of Portions Commonly Used, 16th edition
Jean A.T. Pennington
Philadelphia, PA: Lippincott, 1994. 483 pp.
Call no.: TX551.B64-1994

"Chinese Food Composition Tables."
A.G. Ershow
Journal of Food Composition and Analysis
Sept./Dec. 1990, vol. 3/4. pp. 191–434.
Call no.: TX501.J68

The Complete Book of Food Counts, 3rd edition
Connie T. Netzer
New York, NY: Dell Publishing, 1994. 672 pp.
Call no.: TX551.N38-1994

The Complete Food Count Guide
Editors of Consumer Guide with the Nutrient Analysis Center, Chicago Center for
    Clinical Research
Lincolnwood, IL: Publications, International, 1996. 704 pp.

Composition of Foods, Australia
Karen Cashel, Ruth English, and Janine Lewis (editors)
Canberra: Australian Government Pub. Service, 1989. 5 volumes.

Composition of New Zealand Foods
F.R. Visser and J.K. Burrows
DSIR Bulletin 0077-961X, 235
Wellington: New Zealand Dept. of Scientific and Industrial Research, 1983. 5 volumes.

The Concise New Zealand Food Composition Tables, 2nd edition
B.A. Burlingame, et al.
Palmerston North, NZ: New Zealand Institute for Crop & Food Research; Wellington,
    NZ: Public Health Commission, 1994. 162 pp.

The Connie T. Netzer Encyclopedia of Food Values
Connie T. Netzer
New York, NY: Dell Publishing, 1992. 903 pp.
Call no.: TX551.N42-1992

Convenience Food Facts: Help for Planning Quick, Healthy, and Convenient Meals, 3rd
    edition
A. Monk and M.J. Franz
Minneapolis, MN: International Diabetes Center, 1991. 457 pp.
Call no.: TX551.M56-1991

Fast Food Facts (Revised edition)
Office of Minnesota Attorney General Hubert H. Humphrey III
St. Paul, MN: Minnesota Attorney General's Office, 1994. 15 pp.
Call no.: TX551.F37–1993

Fast Food Facts: Complete Nutritional Information on More than 1500 Menu Items in 37 of
    the Largest Fast Food Chains, 4th edition
Marion J. Franz
Chronimed Publishing, 1994. 112 pp.
Call no.: TX551.F74–1994

The Fast-Food Guide. 2nd edition, completely revised and updated
Michael Jacobson and Sarah Fritschner
New York, NY: Workman Pub., 1991. 333 pp.
Call no.: TX945.J3–1991

Fast Foods: Eating In and Eating Out
Monte Florman and Marjorie Florman
Mount Vernon, NY: Consumers Union, 1990. 326 pp.
Call no.: TX370.F56–1990

Food Composition and Nutrition Tables, 1989/90 Revised
S.W. Souci, W. Fachmann, and H. Kraut
Stuttgart: Wissenschafliche Verlagsgesellschaft, 1989. 1029 pp.
Call no.: TX551.S735–1994

Food Composition Data: Production, Management and Use
H. Greenfield and D.A.T. Southgate
Elsevier Applied Science, New York, 1992. 243 pp.

Food Composition Tables for the Near East
Food & Agriculture Organization, United States Department of Agriculture, Human
    Nutrition Information Division
Rome: FAO Food and Nutrition Paper No. 26, 1982. 265 pp.

Food Finder: Food Sources of Vitamins and Minerals, 2nd edition
Elizabeth S. Hands
Salem, OR: ESHA Research, 1995.

Fruit and Nuts: First Supplement to the Fifth Edition of Mccance and Widdowson's The Composition of Foods
B. Holland, I.D. Unwin, and D.H. Buss
Cambridge: Royal Society of Chemistry; [London]: Ministry of Agriculture, Fisheries and Food, 1992. 136 pp.
Call no.: TX551.H64-1992

INFOODS Food Composition Data Series (available from: United Nations University Press. The United Nations University, 2-15-1 Sbibuya, Shibuya-yu, Tokyo 150, Japan.)

INFOODS Food Composition Data Interchange Handbook. John C. Klensin. 1992. 165 pp.

Food Composition Data: a User's Perspective. William M. Rand, Carol T. Windham, Bonita W. Wyse, and Vernon R. Young (editors). 1992 (2nd printing). 236 pp.

Identification of Food Components for INFOODS Data Interchange. John C. Klensin, et al. 1992. 112 pp.

Compiling Data for Food Composition Data Bases. William M. Rand, Jean A.T. Pennington, Suzanne P. Murphy, and John C. Klensin. 1991. 68 pp.

International Directory of Food Composition Databases
Available From: INFOODS Secretariat, Charles Street Station, Box 500, Boston, MA 02114–0500. Fax: (617) 227–9405, Tel: (617) 227-8747. (Latest version available on INFOODS home page listed below under Web sites)

McCance and Widdowson's the Composition of Foods, 5th edition
B. Holland, et al.
Cambridge: UK. Royal Society of Chemistry, 1991. 462 pp.
Call no.: TX551.M32-1991

The Nutribase Nutrition Facts Desk Reference
Art Ulene
Garden City Park NY: Avery Pub. Group, 1995. 789 pp.
Call no.: TX551.U43-1995

Nutrient Data Bank Directory, 9th edition
Jack L. Smith
Newark, DE: University of Delaware, 1993. 119 pp.
Available from the University of Delaware, Dept. of Nutrition and Dietetics, Alison Hall, Newark, DE
19715-3360
Call no.: QP141.N83 1993

Nutrient Value of Alaska Native Foods
Elizabeth Nobmann
Anchorage, Alaska: Alaska Area Native Health Service.
Available from the Health Sciences Information Service, University of Alaska Anchorage, 1993. 31 pp.

Nutritional Cereal Counter; Over 250 Ready-to-Eat Cereals
St. Paul, MN: Product Information and Analysis. Revised quarterly.

Nutritive Value of Foods, Revised
Susan E. Gebhardt and Ruth H. Matthews
Home and Garden Bulletin Number 72, 1991. 72 pp.
Available from United States Department of Agriculture, Superintendent of Documents,
    U.S. Government Printing Office, Washington D.C. 20402. (202) 512-1800.
Call no.: A1.77.72/991

Pearson's Composition and Analysis of Foods, 9th edition
Ronald S. Kirk and Ronald Sawyer
Essex, England: Longman Scientific & Technical; New York, NY: Wiley, 1991. 708 pp.
Call no.: TX545.K53-1991

The Pacific Islands Food Composition Tables
C.A. Dignan, et al.
Noumea Cedex, New Caledonia: South Pacific Commission; Palmerston North, NZ:
    New Zealand Institute for Crop & Food Research Ltd.; [Cambridge, MA?]: Interna-
    tional Network of Food Data Systems, 1994. 147 pp.
Call no.: TX360.177P33-1994

Tables of Composition of Australian Aboriginal Foods
Janette Brand Miller, Keith W. James, and Patricia M.A. Maggiore
Canberra, ACT: Aboriginal Studies Press, 1993. 256 pp.
Call no.: TX541.B73-1993

Quality and Accessibility of Food-Related Data
Proceedings of the First International Food Data Base Conference
AOAC International, Gaithersburg, MD, 1995. 311 pp.
Call no.: TX345.I634-1993

*Vegetables, Herbs and Spices: Fifth Supplement to McCance and Widdowson's the Composi-
    tion of Foods*
B. Holland, I.D. Unwin, and D.H. Buss
Letchworth, [England]: Royal Society of Chemistry and Ministry of Agriculture, Fisher-
    ies and Food, 1991. 163 pp.
Call no.: TX545.M2 1978 supplement 5

U.S. Government Publications (in alphabetical order)

Most of the Agriculture Handbook No. 8 series listed below are out-of-print, but may be
available at libraries affiliated with universities having food science and/or nutrition departments. Data from the USDA Nutrient Database for Standard Reference, which super-
sedes the printed handbooks are available from NDL's home page. See the section on
Home Pages below.

Composition of Foods . . . Raw, Processed, Prepared. U.S. Dept. of Agriculture, Human Nutrition Information Service. Washington, DC: U.S. Government Printing Office.
1976–1992.

AH-8–1 Dairy and Egg Products 158 pp. Rev. 1976
AH-8–2 Spices and Herbs 51 pp. Rev. 1977
AH-8–3 Baby Foods 255 pp. Rev. 1978
AH-8–4 Fats and Oils 142 pp. Rev. 1979
AH-8–5 Poultry Products 330 pp. Rev. 1979
AH-8–6 Soups, Sauces, and Gravies 228 pp. Rev. 1980
AH-8–7 Sausages and Luncheon Meats 92 pp. Rev. 1980
AH-8–8 Breakfast Cereals 160 pp. Rev. 1982
AH-8–9 Fruits and Fruit Juices 283 pp. Rev. 1982
AH-8–10 Pork Products 206 pp. Rev. 1992
AH-8–11 Vegetable and Vegetable Products 502 pp. Rev. 1984
AH-8–12 Nut and Seed Products 137 pp. Rev. 1984
AH-8–13 Beef Products 412 pp. Rev. 1990
AH-8–14 Beverages 173 pp. Rev. 1986
AH-8–15 Finfish and Shellfish Products 192 pp. Rev. 1987
AH-8–16 Legumes and Legume Products 156 pp. Rev. 1986
AH-8–17 Lamb, Veal, and Game Products 251 pp. Rev. 1989
AH-8–18 Baked Products 467 pp. Rev. 1992
AH-8–19 Snacks and Sweets 341 pp. Rev. 1991
AH-8–20 Cereal Grains and Pasta 137 pp. Rev. 1989
AH-8–21 Fast Foods 194 pp. Rev. 1988
AH-8 1989 Supplement 101 pp. Rev. 1990
AH-8 1990 Supplement 230 pp. Rev. 1991
AH-8 1991 Supplement 185 pp. Rev. 1992
AH-8 1992 Supplement 100 pp. Rev. 1993

Sugar Content of Selected Foods: Individual and Total Sugars. Ruth H. Matthews, Pamela R. Pehrsson, and Mojgan Farhat-Sabet. U.S. Department of Agriculture. Home Economics Research Report No. 48, 1987. 39 pp.

All provisional tables listed below are available from Nutrient Data Research Laboratory, 4700 River Road, Unit 89, Riverdale, MD 20737. (301) 734–8491.

HNIS/PT-108 *Provisional Table on the Vitamin D Content of Foods.*
John L. Weihrauch and Junko Tamaki. October 1991.

HNIS/PT-104 *Provisional Table on the Vitamin K Content of Foods.*
John L. Weihrauch and Shanthy A. Bowman. Revised June 1990.

HNIS/PT-109 *Provisional Table on the Selenium Content of Foods.*
Susan E. Gebhardt and Joanne M. Holden. Dec. 1992.

Food and Nutrition Software Database

The Food and Nutrition Information Center (FNIC) maintains the *Database of Food and Nutrition Software and Multimedia Programs* updated quarterly. This database lists food and nutrition-related software programs that are available commercially. This database is searchable on the FNIC Web site at http://www.nal.usda.gov/fnic. Print copies of four subject-specific reports are available: consumer-level diet analysis and recipe, nutrition education, nutrient analysis and clinical nutrition, and food service management and food industry. For more information, contact a FNIC nutritionist.

Journals

Archivos Latinoamericanos de Nutricion. Latin American Nutrition Society, Institue of Nutrition of Central America and Panama, Carretera Roosevelt, Apdo. Postal 11-88, Guatemala, Guatemala. Telex: 5696 INCAP-GU

Cereal Foods World. American Association of Cereal Chemists, Inc., 3340 Pilot Knob Rd., St. Paul, MN 55121-2097. (800) 328-7560.

European Journal of Clinical Nutrition. Stockton Press, Houndmills, Basingstroke, Hampshire, England. Telephone: 01256-817245 or FAX: 01256-28339.

FAO Food and Nutrition Series. Food and Agriculture Organization of the United Nations, c/o UNIPUB, 4611-F Assembly Dr., Lanham, MD 20706-4391.

Journal of The American Dietetic Association. The American Dietetic Association, 216 W. Jackson Blvd., Ste. 800, Chicago, IL 60606–6995. (312) 899-0040.

Journal of Food Composition and Analysis. Academic Press, Inc., Journal Division, 1250 Sixth Ave., San Diego, CA 92101. (619) 230-1840.

Journal of Food Science. Institute of Food Technologists, 221 N. LaSalle St., Chicago, IL 60601. (312) 782-8424.

Nutrition Today. Williams and Wilkins, 428 E. Preston St., Baltimore, MD 21202. (301) 528-4000.

Trends in Food Science Technology. Elsevier Science Publishing Co., Inc., Box 882, Madison Sq. Station, New York, NY 10159. (212) 989-5800.

Contacts for Assistance

National Contacts

Food and Nutrition Information Center, National Agricultural Library, ARS, USDA, 10301 Baltimore Ave., Room 304, Beltsville, MD 20705. (301) 504-5719. Fax: (301) 504–6409. E-mail: fnic@nal.usda.gov

Food companies, grocery chains, and restaurant franchises—contact the companies consumer affairs department concerning nutrient and energy (caloric) content of their products. Check food labels for addresses.

Nutrient Data Laboratory, Beltsville Human Nutrition Research Center, Agricultural Research Service, U.S. Department of Agriculture, 4700 River Road, Unit 89, Riverdale, MD 20737. Telephone: (301) 734-8491. E-mail: ndlinfo@rbhnrc.usda.gov

Penn State Nutrition Center, The Pennsylvania State University, Ruth Building, 417 E. Calder Way, University Park, PA 16801-5663. (814) 865-6323.

Internet Home Pages

USDA Food Composition Data
http://www.nal.usda.gov/fnic/foodcomp

USDA-NAL, Food and Nutrition Information Center
http://www.nal.usda.gov/fnic

INFOODS (International Network of Food Data Systems)
http://www.crop.cri.nz/foodinfo/infoods/infoods.htm

LANGUAL
http://food.ethz.ch:2000/Langual/langhome.html

Food and Agriculture Organization of the United Nations
http://www.fao.org

Nutrient Data Bank Bulletin Board

A service maintained by United States Dept. of Agriculture, Agricultural Research Service to provide information on its publications and data files. A number of data files are also available for downloading. You need a Personal Computer (PC), modem, and a communications package. The phone number is (301) 734-5078.

Resources were reviewed and selected by
David B. Haytowitz, M.Sc., Nutritionist,
Nutrient Data Laboratory, Beltsville Human Nutrition Research Center, ARS, USDA
with assistance from Shirley King Evans, Ed.M., R.D.,
Nutrition Information Specialist, Food and Nutrition Information Center

Food and Nutrition Information Center
Agricultural Research Service, USDA
National Agricultural Library, Room 304
10301 Baltimore Avenue
Beltsville, MD 20705-2351
Phone: 301-504-5719
Fax: 301-504-6409
TTY: 301-504-6856
e-mail:fnic@nal.usda.gov
Web site: http://www.nal.usda.gov/fnic/

The *National Agricultural Library* provides lending and photocopying services to USDA employees and some USDA program staff. Other users can obtain materials through interlibrary lending services at a local library. *For further information,* contact Document Delivery Services Branch, National Agricultural Library, 10301 Baltimore Ave., 6th floor, Beltsville, MD 20705-2351. Document Delivery can also be contacted by telephone: (301) 504-5755, or via Internet: circinfo@nal.usda.gov.

The *United States Department of Agriculture (USDA)* prohibits discrimination in its programs on the basis of race, color, national origin, sex, religion, age, disability, political beliefs, and marital or familial status. (Not all prohibited bases apply to all programs). Persons with disabilities who require alternative means for communication of program information (braille, large print, audiotape, etc.) should contact the USDA Office of Communications at (202) 720-2791 (voice) or (202) 720-7808 (TDD).

To file a complaint, write the Secretary of Agriculture, U.S. Department of Agriculture, Washington, D.C. 20250, or call 1-800-245-6340 (voice) or (202) 270-1127 (TDD). USDA is an equal employment opportunity employer.

Return to the Food and Nutrition Information Center

Appendix D.2   Answers to Frequently Asked Questions

Table of Contents

1. How do I get a copy of Agriculture Handbook No. 8?

The electronic version of Agriculture Handbook No. 8, the USDA Nutrient Database for Standard Reference can be downloaded from this Home Page. A program allowing you to search the database is also available. In the future, the database will be available on CD-ROM. Printed copies of Agriculture Handbook No. 8, Composition of Foods, are no longer available, though copies may be available at libraries in universities with departments of nutrition or food science. Since there is no copyright, you are free to make additional copies.

2. Is there a copyright on USDA food composition data?

USDA food composition data is in the public domain and there is no copyright. We would appreciate it if you would list us as the source of the data and when possible we would like to see the product which uses the data or be notified of its use.

3. How do I reference the USDA Nutrient Database for Standard Reference?

The suggested citation is:

> U.S. Department of Agriculture, Agricultural Research Service. 1997. USDA Nutrient Database for Standard Reference, Release 11–1. Nutrient Data Laboratory Home Page, http://www.nal.usda.gov/fnic/foodcomp

Note: Release numbers change as new versions are released.

4. I multiplied protein, fat and carbohydrate values by 4-9-4, but my energy value is different from USDA's. Why?

Calorie values are based on the Atwater system for determining energy values. The factors used in the calculation of energy in the database are given in the food description file of the USDA Nutrient Database for Standard Reference, Release 11–1. The basis and derivation of these factors are described in

> Merrill, A.L. and Watt, B.K. 1973. Energy Value of Foods . . . Basis and Derivation. Agriculture Handbook No. 74. U.S. Government Printing Office. Washington, DC. 105 p.

At the present time, this reference is out of print, but may be available at many university libraries. The Atwater system uses specific energy factors which have been determined for basic food commodities. These specific factors take into account the physiological availability of the energy from these foods. The more general factors of 4-9-4 were developed from the specific calorie factors determined by Professor Atwater and associates. For multi–ingredient foods which are listed by brand name, calorie values generally reflect industry practices of calculating calories from 4-9-4 kcal/g for protein, fat, and carbohydrate, respectively, or from 4-9-4 minus insoluble fiber. The latter method is frequently used for high-fiber foods because insoluble fiber is considered to provide no physiological energy. If the calorie factors are blank or zero for an item in the Database, energy was calculated by recipe from ingredients or was supplied by the manufacturer.

5. What is the difference between calories and kilocalories?

In the U.S., energy in foods is expressed in kilocalories (kcal). The scientific definition of a kilocalorie is the amount of energy needed to raise the temperature of 1 kilogram of water one degree Celsius from 15° to 16° at one atmosphere. The true calorie, sometimes referred to as a "small calorie," is the amount of energy needed to raise the temperature of one gram of water one degree Celsius from 15° to 16° at one atmosphere. A kilocalorie is equal to 1000 calories. While the term "calorie" technically applies to the "small calorie," in common usage, such as in reference to food energy, the term "calorie" is actually a kilocalorie. Internationally, most countries express food energy in kilojoules (kJ). One kcal equals 4.184 kJ. The USDA Nutrient Database for Standard Reference contains values for both kilocalories and kilojoules.

6. Why don't the individual fatty acids or the fatty acid classes add up to the total lipid (fat)?

The fatty acids are reported as grams of fatty acid per 100 grams of food. They may not add up to the total lipid value provided in a database because the fat value may include contains some non-fatty acid material, such as, glycerol, phosphate, sugar or sterol. In the case of vegetable oils that are 100% triglyceride, 95.6% is fatty acid and the remaining 4.4% is glycerol. For other fats, the percent of fatty acid will be even lower. Lipid conversion factors for specific fats define the amount of fatty acid (in grams) per gram of fat. The factor is 0.956 for triglycerides and lower for other fats. The factors used in each section of Agriculture Handbook No. 8 were published in an appendix table.

The same is true for the fatty acid classes (saturated, monounsaturated, and polyunsaturated) since they are the sum of the individual fatty acids of each type.

7. My son/daughter has a science fair project. How does he/she analyze a food for a particular nutrient?

Methods for determination of nutrients in foods are published in the "Official Methods of Analysis of AOAC International," The 16th edition comes in 2 volumes. If only earlier editions of the publication can be found, some methods such as the titrimetric method for vitamin C, have not changed in many years. There are also other publications which your child's science teacher can recommend. Caution: Many methods of analysis for foods require the use of strong chemicals, use of specialized equipment and adult supervision. Age and experience of the student should be considered when experiments are planned. Younger students may be encouraged to conduct simple experiments which are planned with the teacher's or parent's guidance.

8. Do you have a copy of the RDAs on your web site?

The Recommended Dietary Allowances (RDAs) are developed by the Food and Nutrition Board, Commission on Life Sciences, National Research Council and published by the *National Academy Press*. In 1973 the FDA developed the U.S. RDA system to replace the minimum daily requirements which had previously been used for nutrition labeling purposes. The U.S. RDAs were based on the Food and Nutrition Board's RDAs, but were not identical to them. The Daily Values (DV) used on current nutrition labels are based on the U.S. RDAs and can be found in the Code of Federal Regulations, Title 21, Part 101.9. Copies of the *RDA*s and *Daily Value* (DRVs and RDIs) tables are available through the National Agricultural Library's Food and Nutrition Information Center's Home Page.

9. Where do I get information on nutrition labeling?

USDA's *Food Safety and Inspection Service* (FSIS) regulates the labeling of meat and poultry. The Food and Drug Administration (FDA) is responsible for all other foods. Information on labeling is available from *FDA's Home Page,* or in a more consumer oriented *Q&A* section, or by *e-mail.*

10. Where can I find the Dietary Analysis Program?

The Dietary Analysis Program (DAP) was written by the Human Nutrition Information Service in cooperation with the Extension Service. It uses data from the Release 7 of the Survey Nutrient Database (used for the 1991 CSFII). In December 1994, when USDA's Center for Nutrition Policy and Promotion (CNPP) was formed, responsibility for this program was transferred to them. Questions on DAP should be referred to CNPP at:

> Center for Nutrition Policy and Promotion
> 1120 20th Street, NW
> Suite 200, North Lobby
> Washington, DC 20036
> Tel. 202-418-3139

DAP can be downloaded from *CNPP's Home Page*

Nutrient Data Laboratory
Agricultural Research Service
Beltsville Human Nutrition Research Center
4700 River Road, Unit 89
Riverdale, MD 20737

Send e-mail to: ndlinfo@rbhnrc.usda.gov
Phone: 301-734-8491, FAX: 301-734-5643

Last modified: August 29, 1997

Appendix D.3 Glossary of Terms Used By Nutrient Data Laboratory

This is a list of terms or acronyms with definitions used on this home page and in products developed by the Nutrient Data Laboratory.

Analytical	—	Data from laboratory analysis of one or more food samples
AOAC	—	Association of Official Analytical Chemists, independent scientific organization which published a reference of methods used in analyzing the composition of foods.
AMS	—	Agricultural Marketing Service, USDA
ARS	—	Agricultural Research Service, USDA
BHNRC	—	Beltsville Human Nutrition Research Center
Bulletin Board (BB)	—	USDA Nutrient Data Laboratory Bulletin Board
Calculated	—	Nutrient values computed or estimated by mathematical adjustment. Normalizing nutrients to an average moisture or fat value, use of retention factors, and substitution of similar ingredients in a formulation or recipe are examples of calculated values.
CFR	—	Code of Federal Regulations
CN Label	—	Approved Child Nutrition Label for food products under the USDA/FCS, Child Nutrition Labeling Program (precurser to NNDCNP)
Derivation code	—	A 4-character, alphabetic code used to document Standard Reference nutrient data source and quality.
Discontinued item	—	Food product no longer sold or available commercially; item removed from Standard Reference Database.
FCS	—	Food and Consumer Service, USDA
FDA	—	Food and Drug Administration, U.S. Department of Health and Human Services
Food Group	—	NDL categorizes foods into similar groups and assigns a Food Group Code, such as cereal grains and pasta (20), beverages (14), vegetables (11), etc.
Food Group Code	—	Two-digit numeric code identifying individual Food Groups. Food Groups are further classified by subcodes, to produce a four-digit numeric code. For example, fresh pork is 1010, while cured pork is 1020. Food group codes are independent of NDB numbers.
Food Survey	—	USDA Nationwide Food Surveys
Formulation	—	The estimated proportion by weight of ingredients in a multi-ingredient commercial food item when other characteristics of the food item are known or can be set. Characteristics which may be known or can be set include: order of predominance of ingredients, retention codes, target moisture level of individual ingredients and final product, and lower and upper bounds on the proportion of any individual ingredient. As a minimum, to derive a formulation, some nutrient values must be known and flagged for matching.
FSIS	—	Food Safety and Inspection Service, USDA
Handbook 8 (AH-8)	—	USDA Agriculture Handbook No. 8
Household measure	—	Standard weight (sometimes with dimensions) or portion of individual food. Sometimes called serving size.
IFDA	—	International Food Service Distributor's Association (IFDA), independent food industry organization

Imputed	—	Nutrient values developed when analytical values are unavailable. Nutrient values from another form of the same food, or another species of the same genus are examples of imputed values.
INFOODS	—	International Network of Food Data Systems
Item	—	Individual food or food product
Key Foods	—	Identification of foods most highly consumed and also best sources of nutrients deemed important to national dietary health. Key Foods are identified as those foods contributing up to 75% of any one nutrient. Key Foods are used by NDL to set priorities for our nutrient analysis contracts.
Label	—	Data printed on a food label, as supplied by its manufacturer. The values are primarily company analytical or imputed; however, the values have been rounded and/or adjusted to provide uniform serving size weights.
NDB	—	USDA Nutrient Database
NDB No.	—	Identification number for food item in USDA Nutrient Database
NFPA	—	National Food Processor's Association, independent food industry organization
NIST	—	National Institute of Standards and Technology, U.S. Department of Commerce
NLEA	—	National Labeling and Education Act of 1990. Refers to food labeling regulations promulgated by the FDA.
NNDCNP	—	National Nutrient Data Base for Child Nutrition Programs
NTIS	—	National Technical Information Service, U.S. Department of Commerce
PDS	—	Primary Data Set for USDA Nationwide Food Surveys
Recipe	—	The known weight or measure of ingredients in a multi-ingredient food item. Amounts of ingredients may be expressed in household volume measure units such as cups and tablespoons or may be expressed as gram weights. The term recipe is generally applied to a food item prepared from component ingredients in a household or institutional setting. The term may also apply to a commercial multi-ingredient food item for which the amounts of ingredients are set, rather than estimated (e.g., by Standards of Identity).
Refuse	—	Portion of food removed before consumption (meat bones, fruit pits, etc.).
RM	—	Reference Material used for evaluating the reliability of analytical methods
Source code	—	One-character numeric code to document source of nutrient data.
SRM	—	Standard Reference Material from NIST used for evaluating the reliability of analytical methods
Standard Reference (SR)	—	USDA Nutrient Database for Standard Reference
Tagname	—	INFOODS Tag Names identify individual nutrients for international interchange of nutrient data.
UPC	—	Universal Product Code is a unique product identification number found on most product labels, represented by bar and number codes.
USDA	—	U.S. Department of Agriculture
USDA Commodity	—	Foods donated, or available for donation, by the Department under authorizing legislation, for use in any State in child nutrition programs, nonprofit summer camps for children, charitable institutions, nutrition programs for the elderly, the Commodity Supplemental Nutrition Program for Women, Infants, and Children (WIC), the Food Distribution Programs on Indian Reservations and the assistance of needy people.
USDHHS	—	U.S. Department of Health and Human Services

Appendix D.4   Search the USDA Nutrient Database for Standard Reference
EXAMPLE 1

This interface allows simple searches. Enter one keyword which best describes your food item or the NDB No and press the enter or return key. If you don't get a match, check your spelling or try a related term. If you get too many items, try a more specific keyword. If you enter two or more keywords, the program will search for items which contain all of the keywords. They do not have to be adjacent or in the same order you entered them.

Nutrient Data Laboratory
Agricultural Research Service
Beltsville Human Nutrition Research Center
4700 River Road, Unit 89
Riverdale, MD 20737

Send e-mail to: **ndlinfo@rbhnrc.usda.gov**

Phone: 301-734-8491, FAX: 301-734-5643

STEP 1—ENTER THE KEYWORD EX. FAST FOODS

STEP 2—SELECT FAST FOODS

Search result from the USDA Nutrient Database for Standard Reference

Found 121 items about: ***Fast Foods***

- Fast foods, biscuit, with egg
- Fast foods, biscuit, with egg and bacon
- Fast foods, biscuit, with egg and ham
- Fast foods, biscuit, with egg, cheese, and bacon
- Fast foods, biscuit, with ham
- Fast foods, biscuit, with sausage
- Fast foods, biscuit, with steak
- Fast foods, croissant, with egg and cheese
- Fast foods, croissant, with egg, cheese, and bacon
- Fast foods, croissant, with egg, cheese, and ham
- Fast foods, croissant, with egg, cheese, and sausage
- Fast foods, danish pastry, cheese
- Fast foods, danish pastry, cinnamon
- Fast foods, danish pastry, fruit
- Fast foods, egg, scrambled
- Fast foods, english muffin, with butter
- Fast foods, english muffin, with cheese and sausage
- Fast foods, english muffin, with egg, cheese, and canadian bacon
- Fast foods, english muffin, with egg, cheese, and sausage
- Fast foods, french toast sticks
- Fast foods, pancakes with butter and syrup
- Fast foods, potatoes, hashed brown
- Fast foods, brownie
- Fast foods, ice milk, vanilla, soft-serve, with cone
- Fast foods, cookies, animal crackers

- Fast foods, cookies, chocolate chip
- Fast foods, fried pie, fruit (apple, cherry, or lemon)
- Fast foods, sundae, caramel
- Fast foods, sundae, hot fudge
- Fast foods, sundae, strawberry
- Fast foods, chicken, breaded and fried, dark meat (drumstick or thigh)
- Fast foods, chicken, breaded and fried, light meat (breast or wing)
- Fast foods, chicken, breaded and fried, boneless pieces, plain
- Fast foods, chicken, breaded and fried, boneless pieces, with barb. sauce
- Fast foods, chicken, breaded and fried, boneless pieces, with honey
- Fast foods, chicken, breaded and fried, boneless pieces, with mustard sauce
- Fast foods, chicken, breaded and fried, boneless pieces, with sweet and sour
- Fast foods, chili con carne
- Fast foods, clams, breaded and fried
- Fast foods, crab, soft-shell, fried
- Fast foods, oysters, battered or breaded, and fried
- Fast foods, salad, vegetable, tossed, without dressing
- Fast foods, salad, vegetable, tossed, without dressing, with cheese and egg
- Fast foods, salad, vegetable, tossed, without dressing, with chicken
- Fast foods, salad, vegetable, tossed, without dressing, with pasta and seafood
- Fast foods, salad, vegetable, tossed, without dressing, with shrimp
- Fast foods, salad, vegetables tossed, without dressing, with turkey, ham and cheese
- Fast foods, scallops, breaded and fried
- Fast foods, shrimp, breaded and fried

STEP 3—SELECT PORTION SIZE

Fast foods, chicken, breaded and fried, dark meat (drumstick or thigh)

Select weights to be reported. If you select 100 grams, number of samples (N) and standard error (SE) will also be reported. You may select up to 5 weights or 100 grams and up to 3 weights.

☒ 100 grams
☐ 2 pieces = 148.000 g

report   clear

STEP 4—REVIEW/PRINT REPORT
NDB No: 21035

Nutrient	Units	Value per 100 g, edible portion	N	SE
Proximates				
Water	g	48.990	50	445
Energy	kcal	291.000	0	0.000
Energy	kj	1218.000	0	0.000
Protein	g	20.320	54	.217
Total lipid (fat)	g	18.040	54	.264
Carbohydrate, by difference	g	10.610	0	0.000
Ash	g	2.050	49	.050

Nutrient	Units	Value per 100 g, edible portion	N	SE
Minerals				
Calcium, Ca	mg	24.000	6	4.081
Iron, Fe	mg	1.080	6	.029
Magnesium, Mg	mg	25.000	2	1.268
Phosphorus, P	mg	162.000	1	0.000
Potassium, K	mg	301.000	2	2.770
Sodium, Na	mg	510.000	9	29.877
Zinc, Zn	mg	2.190	2	.755
Copper, Cu	mg	.080	2	0.000
Manganese, Mn	mg	.086	2	.015
Vitamins				
Vitamin C, ascorbic acid	mg	0.000	1	0.000
Thiamin	mg	.090	50	.004
Riboflavin	mg	.290	51	.006
Niacin	mg	4.870	51	.128
Pantothenic acid	mg	1.660	47	.031
Vitamin B-6	mg	.220	47	.007
Folate	mcg	6.000	47	.332
Vitamin B-12	mcg	.560	47	.035
Vitamin A, IU	IU	150.000	1	0.000
Vitamin A, RE	mcg–RE	45.000	0	0.000
Lipids				
Fatty acids, saturated	g	4.763	0	0.000
12:0 lauric	g	.019	1	0.000
14:0 myristic	g	.108	1	0.000
16:0 palmitic	g	3.231	1	0.000
18:0 stearic	g	1.405	1	0.000
Fatty acids, monounsaturated	g	7.385	0	0.000
16:1 palmitoleic	g	.579	1	0.000
18:1 oleic	g	6.718	1	0.000
22:1 erucic	g	.088	1	0.000
Fatty acids, polyunsaturated	g	4.272	0	0.000
18:2 linoleic	g	3.890	1	0.000
18:3 linolenic	g	.206	1	0.000
20:4 arachidonic	g	.108	1	0.000
20:5 timnodonic	g	.010	1	0.000
22:5 clupanodonic	g	.019	1	0.000
22:6 docosahexaenoic	g	.040	1	0.000
Cholesterol	mg	112.000	5	10.942
Amino acids				
Tryptophan	g	.228	0	0.000
Threonine	g	.819	0	0.000
Isoleucine	g	.988	0	0.000
Leucine	g	1.466	0	0.000

Nutrient	Units	Value per 100 g, edible portion	N	SE
Amino acids (cont.)				
Lysine	g	1.570	0	0.000
Methionine	g	.527	0	0.000
Cystine	g	.283	0	0.000
Phenylalanine	g	.800	0	0.000
Tyrosine	g	.650	0	0.000
Valine	g	.975	0	0.000
Arginine	g	1.245	0	0.000
Histidine	g	.582	0	0.000
Alanine	g	1.154	0	0.000
Aspartic acid	g	1.749	0	0.000
Glutamic acid	g	3.160	0	0.000
Glycine	g	1.287	0	0.000
Proline	g	1.063	0	0.000
Serine	g	.738	0	0.000

USDA Nutrient Database for Standard Reference, Release 11–1 (August 1997)

Vegetables, mixed, frozen, cooked, boiled, drained, with salt

Select weights to be reported. If you select 100 grams, number of samples (N) and standard error (SE) will also be reported. You may select up to 5 weights or 100 grams and up to 3 weights.

- ☒ 100 grams
- ☐ 1 package (10 oz) yields = 275.000 g
- ☐ ½ cup = 91.000 g

report   clear

NDB No: 11894

Nutrient	Units	Value per 100 g, edible portion	N	SE
Proximates				
Water	g	83.230	0	0.000
Energy	kcal	59.000	0	0.000
Energy	kj	247.000	0	0.000
Protein	g	2.860	0	0.000
Total lipid (fat)	g	.150	0	0.000
Carbohydrate, by difference	g	13.090	0	0.000
Fiber, total dietary	g	4.400	0	0.000
Ash	g	.670	0	0.000
Minerals				
Calcium, Ca	mg	25.000	0	0.000
Iron, Fe	mg	.820	0	0.000
Magnesium, Mg	mg	22.000	0	0.000
Phosphorus, P	mg	51.000	0	0.000

Nutrient	Units	Value per 100 g, edible portion	N	SE
Minerals (cont.)				
Potassium, K	mg	169.000	0	0.000
Sodium, Na	mg	271.000	0	0.000
Zinc, Zn	mg	.490	0	0.000
Copper, Cu	mg	.083	0	0.000
Manganese, Mn	mg	.379	0	0.000
Vitamins				
Vitamin C, ascorbic acid	mg	3.200	0	0.000
Thiamin	mg	.071	2	.023
Riboflavin	mg	.120	2	.032
Niacin	mg	.851	0	0.000
Pantothenic acid	mg	.151	0	0.000
Vitamin B-6	mg	.074	2	.013
Folate	mcg	19.000	0	0.000
Vitamin B-12	mcg	0.000	0	0.000
Vitamin A, IU	IU	4277.000	0	0.000
Vitamin A, RE	mcg–RE	428.000	0	0.000
Lipids				
Fatty acids, saturated	g	.031	0	0.000
12:0 lauric	g	0.000	0	0.000
14:0 myristic	g	0.000	0	0.000
16:0 palmitic	g	.027	0	0.000
18:0 stearic	g	.003	0	0.000
Fatty acids, monounsaturated	g	.010	0	0.000
16:1 palmitoleic	g	0.000	0	0.000
18:1 oleic	g	.009	0	0.000
Fatty acids, polyunsaturated	g	.072	0	0.000
18:2 linoleic	g	.053	0	0.000
18:3 linolenic	g	.019	0	0.000
Cholesterol	mg	0.000	0	0.000
Amino acids				
Tryptophan	g	.029	0	0.000
Threonine	g	.115	0	0.000
Isoleucine	g	.139	0	0.000
Leucine	g	.190	0	0.000
Lysine	g	.170	0	0.000
Methionine	g	.034	0	0.000
Cystine	g	.026	0	0.000
Phenylalanine	g	.120	0	0.000
Tyrosine	g	.074	0	0.000
Valine	g	.149	0	0.000
Arginine	g	.193	0	0.000
Histidine	g	.073	0	0.000
Alanine	g	.123	0	0.000

Nutrient	Units	Value per 100 g, edible portion	N	SE
Amino acids (cont.)				
Aspartic acid	g	.303	0	0.000
Glutamic acid	g	.390	0	0.000
Glycine	g	.104	0	0.000
Proline	g	.070	0	0.000
Serine	g	.136	0	0.000

USDA Nutrient Database for Standard Reference, Release 11-1 (August 1997)

Lamb, domestic, composite of trimmed retail cuts, separable lean only, trimmed to ¼" fat, choice, cooked

Select weights to be reported. If you select 100 grams, number of samples (N) and standard error (SE) will also be reported. You may select up to 5 weights or 100 grams and up to 3 weights.

☒ 100 grams
☐ 1 lb raw with refuse, yields, excluding refuse = 187.000 g
☐ 3 oz = 85.000 g

report   clear

NDB No: 17004

Nutrient	Units	Value per 100 g, edible portion	N	SE
Proximates				
Water	g	61.960	16	.431
Energy	kcal	206.000	0	0.000
Energy	kj	862.000	0	0.000
Protein	g	28.220	16	.336
Total lipid (fat)	g	9.520	16	.357
Carbohydrate, by difference	g	0.000	0	0.000
Fiber, total dietary	g	0.000	0	0.000
Ash	g	1.140	16	.013
Minerals				
Calcium, Ca	mg	15.000	16	.599
Iron, Fe	mg	2.050	16	.063
Magnesium, Mg	mg	26.000	16	.340
Phosphorus, P	mg	210.000	16	3.519
Potassium, K	mg	344.000	16	3.940
Sodium, Na	mg	76.000	16	.861
Zinc, Zn	mg	5.270	16	.117
Copper, Cu	mg	.128	16	.006
Manganese, Mn	mg	.028	0	0.000
Vitamins				
Vitamin C, ascorbic acid	mg	0.000	0	0.000
Thiamin	mg	.100	16	.005
Riboflavin	mg	.280	16	.014

Nutrient	Units	Value per 100 g, edible portion	N	SE
Vitamins (cont.)				
Niacin	mg	6.320	16	.199
Pantothenic acid	mg	.690	16	.021
Vitamin B-6	mg	.160	0	0.000
Folate	mcg	23.000	16	.860
Vitamin B-12	mcg	2.610	16	.104
Vitamin A, IU	IU	0.000	0	0.000
Vitamin A, RE	mcg–RE	0.000	0	0.000
Vitamin E	mg–ATE	.190	0	0.000
Lipids				
Fatty acids, saturated	g	3.400	0	0.000
10:0 capric	g	.020	107	0.000
12:0 lauric	g	.030	107	0.000
14:0 myristic	g	.300	107	0.000
16:0 palmitic	g	1.830	107	0.000
18:0 stearic	g	1.170	107	0.000
Fatty acids, monounsaturated	g	4.170	0	0.000
16:1 palmitoleic	g	.280	107	0.000
18:1 oleic	g	3.860	107	0.000
Fatty acids, polyunsaturated	g	.620	0	0.000
18:2 linoleic	g	.510	107	0.000
18:3 linolenic	g	.060	107	0.000
20:4 arachidonic	g	.060	107	0.000
Cholesterol	mg	92.000	16	2.022
Amino acids				
Tryptophan	g	.330	0	0.000
Threonine	g	1.208	0	0.000
Isoleucine	g	1.361	0	0.000
Leucine	g	2.195	0	0.000
Lysine	g	2.492	0	0.000
Methionine	g	.724	0	0.000
Cystine	g	.337	0	0.000
Phenylalanine	g	1.149	0	0.000
Tyrosine	g	.948	0	0.000
Valine	g	1.523	0	0.000
Arginine	g	1.676	0	0.000
Histidine	g	.894	0	0.000
Alanine	g	1.697	0	0.000
Aspartic acid	g	2.484	0	0.000
Glutamic acid	g	4.095	0	0.000
Glycine	g	1.378	0	0.000
Proline	g	1.184	0	0.000
Serine	g	1.049	0	0.000

USDA Nutrient Database for Standard Reference, Release 11-1 (August 1997)

Cheesecake prepared from recipe

Select weights to be reported. If you select 100 grams, number of samples (N) and standard error (SE) will also be reported. You may select up to 5 weights or 100 grams and up to 3 weights.

☒ 100 grams
☐ 1 oz = 28.350 g
☐ 1 piece (1/12 of 9" dia) = 128.000 g

| report | | clear |

NDB No: 18149

Nutrient	Units	Value per 100 g, edible portion	N	SE
Proximates				
Water	g	40.900	0	0.000
Energy	kcal	357.000	0	0.000
Energy	kj	1494.000	0	0.000
Protein	g	6.800	0	0.000
Total lipid (fat)	g	26.000	0	0.000
Carbohydrate, by difference	g	25.200	0	0.000
Ash	g	1.100	0	0.000
Minerals				
Calcium, Ca	mg	58.000	0	0.000
Iron, Fe	mg	1.250	0	0.000
Magnesium, Mg	mg	8.000	0	0.000
Phosphorus, P	mg	96.000	0	0.000
Potassium, K	mg	102.000	0	0.000
Sodium, Na	mg	283.000	0	0.000
Zinc, Zn	mg	.550	0	0.000
Copper, Cu	mg	.037	0	0.000
Manganese, Mn	mg	.085	0	0.000
Vitamins				
Vitamin C, ascorbic acid	mg	.400	0	0.000
Thiamin	mg	.031	0	0.000
Riboflavin	mg	.211	0	0.000
Niacin	mg	.405	0	0.000
Pantothenic acid	mg	.184	0	0.000
Vitamin B-6	mg	.045	0	0.000
Folate	mcg	12.000	0	0.000
Vitamin B-12	mcg	.250	0	0.000
Vitamin A, IU	IU	1058.000	0	0.000
Vitamin A, RE	mcg–RE	321.000	0	0.000
Lipids				
Fatty acids, saturated	g	14.366	0	0.000
4:0 butyric	g	.623	0	0.000

Nutrient	Units	Value per 100 g, edible portion	N	SE
Lipids (cont.)				
6:0 caproic	g	.184	0	0.000
8:0 caprylic	g	.210	0	0.000
10:0 capric	g	.417	0	0.000
12:0 lauric	g	.292	0	0.000
14:0 myristic	g	2.270	0	0.000
16:0 palmitic	g	7.411	0	0.000
18:0 stearic	g	2.954	0	0.000
Fatty acids, monounsaturated	g	8.085	0	0.000
16:1 palmitoleic	g	.668	0	0.000
18:1 oleic	g	7.411	0	0.000
20:1 gadoleic	g	.004	0	0.000
22:1 erucic	g	0.000	0	0.000
Fatty acids, polyunsaturated	g	2.053	0	0.000
18:2 linoleic	g	1.668	0	0.000
18:3 linolenic	g	.361	0	0.000
18:4 parinaric	g	0.000	0	0.000
20:4 arachidonic	g	.019	0	0.000
20:5 timnodonic	g	0.000	0	0.000
22:5 clupanodonic	g	0.000	0	0.000
22:6 docosahexaenoic	g	.005	0	0.000
Cholesterol	mg	121.000	0	0.000
Amino acids				
Tryptophan	g	.067	0	0.000
Threonine	g	.279	0	0.000
Isoleucine	g	.340	0	0.000
Leucine	g	.601	0	0.000
Lysine	g	.519	0	0.000
Methionine	g	.166	0	0.000
Cystine	g	.089	0	0.000
Phenylalanine	g	.358	0	0.000
Tyrosine	g	.292	0	0.000
Valine	g	.379	0	0.000
Arginine	g	.288	0	0.000
Histidine	g	.207	0	0.000
Alanine	g	.243	0	0.000
Aspartic acid	g	.498	0	0.000
Glutamic acid	g	1.401	0	0.000
Glycine	g	.164	0	0.000
Proline	g	.530	0	0.000
Serine	g	.380	0	0.000

USDA Nutrient Database for Standard Reference, Release 11-1 (August 1997)

GLOSSARY

Absorption: The process of taking digested substances into the body.

Acid solution: A solution containing an excess amount of positively charged hydrogen ions.

Aerobic: Referring to the presence of oxygen.

Aging (meats): Holding meats in coolers under controlled conditions to allow natural tenderizing to take place.

Á la carte: Referring to a menu on which each item is listed with a separate price; or referring to cooking to order as opposed to cooking ahead in large batches.

Alkaline solution: A solution containing an excess amount of negatively charged hydroxyl ions.

Amino acids: The building blocks of proteins.

Anaerobic: Referring to the absence of oxygen.

Anemia: General term for a condition indicating that the concentration of blood hemoglobin or of red blood cells is lower than normal.

Anthocyanins: Red or purple pigments in vegetables and fruits.

Antibodies: Proteins that protect the body against antigens by binding to and inactivating them.

Antioxidant: Substance that prevents oxygen from combining with other substances that it may damage.

AP weight: As purchased; the weight of an item before trimming.

Arrowroot: A starch from the root of a tropical plant; used as a thickening agent.

Arteries: Vessels that carry blood away from the heart.

Aspartame: A sweet dipeptide composed of phenylalanine and aspartic acid used as a low-calorie sweetener.

Au gratin: Having a browned or crusted top, often made by topping food with bread crumbs, cheese, and/or a rich sauce and passing it under the broiler.

Au jus: Served with natural juices.

Back of the house: The part of the foodservice operation that is hidden from the customer; the part where food preparation takes place.

Baking powder: A chemical leavener composed of baking soda and acid; it releases carbon dioxide gas in the presence of moisture and acid.

Baking soda: Sodium bicarbonate; an alkaline chemical leavener; it releases carbon dioxide in the presence of moisture and heat.

Basal metabolic rate (BMR): The number of kcalories required to maintain life-sustaining activities for a specified amount of time, measured under very specific conditions.

Basal metabolism: Metabolic processes that must take place continuously to sustain life.

Basic solution: A solution containing an excess amount of negatively charged hydroxyl ions.

Batter: A semiliquid mixture containing flour or another starch used for the production of such products as cakes and breads and for coating products before frying; to batter is to coat with batter prior to frying.

Béchamel: A sauce made by thickening milk with a roux.

Beriberi: A disease resulting from thiamin deficiency.

Bile: A substance produced by the liver that emulsifies glycerides in the small intestine.

Binder: An ingredient that holds other ingredients together.

Bioavailability: The degree to which the body is able to use a substance in the form or amount present.

Bisque: A cream soup.

Blanching: Heating a food just long enough to destroy many of the enzymes that affect its palatability and nutritive value; cooking an item partially and very briefly in boiling water or in hot fat; usually a prepreparation technique to loosen peels from vegetables, fruits, nuts, and so on.

Bouillon: A seasoned stock; also available in the form of cubes and powders.

Bran: Tough outer layers of grain kernels in their whole form.

Breading: A coating for a product to be fried, usually consisting of a coat of a mixture of crumbs, eggs, and flour.

Brine: A salt solution used for pickling and canning vegetables.

Broth: The liquid in which a food is cooked.

Bulgar: A type of cracked wheat that has been partially cooked.

Burritos: Flour tortillas rolled around filling(s).

Calorie: Same as kilocalorie; the amount of heat needed to raise the temperature of 1 kilogram water 1°C; used as a measure of food energy.

Canapés: Bite-sized finger foods; tiny open-faced sandwiches, served as hors d'oeuvres.

Caramelization: The browning of sugars caused by heat; heating sugar until it liquefies.

Carcinogens: Factors believed to influence the development of cancer.

Carotenoids: Yellow or orange pigments in vegetables and fruits.

Casserole: A food or mixture of foods bound by a source and then baked or heated in the oven.

Caviar: Salted fish roe (eggs).

Cell: The smallest, simplest unit of living matter.

Cellulose: A form of carbohydrate found in fruits, grains, and vegetables that provides texture; makes up the cell wall in plants.

Chlorophyll: Green pigment in vegetables and fruits.

Cholesterol: A sterol that is both produced by the body and ingested by eating certain foods of animal origin.

Chowder: A hearty soup made from fish, shellfish, and/or vegetables, usually containing milk and potatoes.

Clarified butter: Purified butterfat, with water and milk solids removed.

Coagulation: The process by which proteins become firm, usually when heated.

Coenzymes: Vitamin-containing substances that unite with enzyme precursors to create active enzymes.

Collagen: A type of connective tissue in meats that dissolves when cooked with moisture.

Complementary proteins: Proteins supplied by foods that, if eaten together, supply all the amino acids necessary in the human diet.

Complete protein: A protein that supplies all the amino acids necessary in the human diet.

Conditioner: A chemical additive that makes a cake moister.

Consistency: The degree of thickness and smoothness of a product.

Consommé: A rich, flavorful, seasoned stock or broth that has been clarified to make it perfectly clear and transparent.

Convenience foods: Foods that are partially prepared.

Cream soup: A soup that is thickened with roux or another thickening agent and contains milk and/or cream.

Crepes: Very thin pancakes rolled around a filling.

Crustaceans: Sea animals with segmented shells and jointed legs, such as lobsters and shrimp.

Cuisine: Style of cooking of a particular region or country.

Curd: Coagulated milk proteins.

Custard: A liquid (egg and milk mixture) that is thickened or set firm by the coagulation of egg protein.

Cycle menu: A menu that changes every day for a certain period and then repeats the same daily items in the same order.

Deep-fry: To cook food by submerging it in hot fat.

Dehydration: Referring to the absence of water; removal of moisture from food.

Denaturation: Unfolding of the three-dimensional structure of a protein.

Dietary fiber (edible fiber): Food material that cannot be broken apart for absorption by human digestive processes.

Digestion: The process of breaking food down into substances small enough to be absorbed.

Disaccharides: Simple sugars consisting of two monosaccharide units linked together, such as in sucrose and lactose.

Dough: A flour-liquid mixture used in making breads, rolls, pies, biscuits, and pastries.

Drippings: Juices and fat from a cooked product.

Durum wheat: A type of wheat high in gluten.

Edible portion (EP): The portion, weight, or quantity of food remaining after peeling, trimming, or processing.

Elastin: A type of connective tissue in meats that does not dissolve when cooked.

Electrolytes: Substances that carry an electrical charge when dissolved in water.

Emulsifiers: Substances that mix with both fat-soluble and water-soluble materials to help create emulsions or suspensions.

Emulsify: To form an emulsion.

Emulsion: A uniform mixture of two unmixable liquids.

Enchiladas: Soft tortillas rolled around fillings and baked with a sauce.

Endosperm: The lighter, larger inner starchy portion of the grain kernel.

Energy: The capacity to do work, measured in kcalories; the power to affect physical changes.

Enrichment: The addition of nutrients already present in a food to levels that meet a specific requirement.

Entree: Main dish; main course on the menu.

Enzymes: Proteins that help to conduct as well as speed up biochemical reactions; organic substances within foods that soften or break down tissues.

EP weight: Edible portion: the weight of an item after all trimming and preparation is done.

Esophagus: A passageway that conducts food from the pharynx to the stomach.

Essential amino acids: Amino acids that the body needs for protein synthesis but cannot produce for itself, and so must be obtained from foods.

Fatty acids: Units attached to glycerol in glycerides.

Fermentation: The process in which microorganisms metabolize components of a food, changing its composition and taste; the process by which yeast acts on carbohydrates to change them into carbon dioxide gas and alcohol.

Fettuccine: Flat egg noodles.

Fiber: A component of plant foods that cannot be digested by humans.

Fillet: Meat that is boneless; a full segment of fish removed from bones; one side of fish; compressed meats.

Flavones: White pigments in vegetables and fruits.

Flavor enhancer: An ingredient added to a food to enhance or develop its flavor.

Florentine: Garnished/served with or containing spinach.

Fortification: Any addition of nutrients to foods in the course of processing.

French dressing: A salad dressing made of oil, vinegar, and seasonings.

Fricassee: A white stew in which the meat is cooked in fat without browning before liquid is added.

Frosting: A thick spread used on cakes and other desserts.

Garnish: An edible decorative item used to ornament or enhance the eye appeal of another food item; to add such a decorative item to food.

Gastrointestinal (GI) tract: The main part of the digestive system; a hollow tube beginning at the mouth and ending at the anus.

Gazpacho: A cold Spanish soup made of pureed raw vegetables.

Gelatin: A jellylike substance formed by the absorption of water.

Gelatinization: The process by which starch granules absorb water and swell in size.

Germ: The part of the grain kernel from which sprouting occurs.

Glucose: A simple sugar; a common product available as an energy source.

Gluten: A substance made up of proteins present in wheat flour that gives structure and strength to baked goods.

Glycerides: The most common lipids, consisting of one, two, or three fatty acids attached to a molecule of glycerol.

Glycerol: The three-carbon compound that is the backbone of glycerides.

Glycogen: A complex carbohydrate consisting of glucose units linked together; it serves as a storage form of glucose.

Glycogen loading: Controlling both exercise and food consumption in such a way as to maximize body stores of glycogen.

Glycolysis: The process in which body cells metabolize glucose without oxygen.

Goiter: Enlargement of the thyroid gland resulting primarily from iodine deficiency.

Gram: A metric unit of measure used for measuring macronutrients; equal to about 1/30 of an ounce.

Heme iron: A form of iron that is part of hemoglobin or myoglobin in meat, fish, and poultry.

Hemoglobin: Oxygen-carrying proteins found in blood.

Herbs: The leaves of certain plants, used in flavoring.

High density lipoprotein (HDL): A lipoprotein containing a high proportion of protein.

Hollandaise: A sauce made of butter, egg yolks, and flavorings (especially lemon juice).

Homogenized milk: Milk that has been processed so that the cream does not separate out.

Hormones: Chemical messengers produced in one region of the body that affect a process in another region.

Hors d'oeuvres: A variety of appetizers served in small portions.

Hydrogenation: Forcing hydrogen into unsaturated oils to make them firmer in order to prolong shelf life.

Hydrolysis: A chemical breakdown process in which water is one of the reacting substances.

Icing: A thin mixture of sugar and water used on cakes and other desserts.

Insulin: A hormone produced by the pancreas that helps to regulate the blood sugar level by promoting glucose utilization, protein synthesis, and the formation/storage of lipids.

Intrinsic factor: A substance produced by the stomach lining that promotes the absorption of vitamins.

Inventory: An itemized list of goods/stocks on hand.

Job description: A written description of responsibilities and requirements pertinent to a position or job.

Julienne: Cut in small, narrow strips; garnished with foods cut in this manner.

Kilo: Prefix in the metric system meaning "one thousand."

Kilocalorie (kcal): The amount of heat needed to raise the temperature of 1 kilogram of water 1°C; unit in which energy is measured.

Knead: To manipulate dough in order to develop gluten.

Kneading: A process by which dough is folded, pressed, and squeezed to strengthen the gluten strands.

Kwashiorkor: A serious form of protein-energy malnutrition in which liver damage results in fluid shifts that create a swollen appearance.

Lactose intolerance: Reduced ability to digest lactose.

Lard: The rendered fat of hogs; to insert strips of fat into meats low in marbling.

Lasagna: Broad, flat egg noodles or a baked, layered casserole made with these noodles.

Leaching: Dissolving of nutrients into a surrounding fluid.

Leavening: The production or incorporation of gases in baked products to increase their volume and to produce shape and texture.

Lecithin: A type of phospholipid that mixes well with both watery and oily substances.

Lipids: Fatty substances that usually do not dissolve in water.

Lipoproteins: Water-soluble aggregates of triglycerides, phospholipids, cholesterol, and protein that can be transported in the bloodstream.

Liter: The basic unit of volume in the metric system; equal to slightly more than a quart.

Low density lipoprotein (LDL):   A lipoprotein containing a high proportion of cholesterol.

Macaroni: Noodle product made of flour and water and dried.

Macrominerals: Minerals present in the body in amounts greater than 0.01 percent of body weight.

Malnutrition: Poor nutrition usually resulting from intakes either above or below the desirable range.

Marasmus: A serious form of protein-energy malnutrition characterized by progressive fat and muscle loss.

Marbling: Deposition of fat within muscle tissue.

Marinate: To soak a food in a seasoned liquid.

Mayonnaise: A semisolid cold sauce or dressing consisting of oil and vinegar emulsified with egg yolks.

Menu: A list of the dishes to be offered; physical write-up or display of items served; a list of choices offered.

Meringue: A foam made of beaten egg whites and sugar, used in making desserts.

Metabolism: The biochemical reactions that take place in a living organism.

Microgram (μg):   Metric unit of measure that is one-millionth of a gram. Commonly used for expressing micronutrients.

Milli-:   A prefix in the metric system meaning "one-thousandth."

Milligram (mg):   A metric unit of measure that is one-thousandth of a gram. Commonly used for expressing micronutrients.

Milling: The grinding of grain into flour.

Minerals: Chemical elements other than carbon, hydrogen, oxygen, and nitrogen that make up the body.

Minestrone: Italian vegetable soup.

Monosaccharides: The simplest sugars having five- or six-carbon skeletons, such as glucose or fructose.

Mousse: A soft, creamy food, either sweet or savory, that is made light by the addition of whipped cream, beaten egg whites, or both.

Mozzarella: A mild, unripened cheese used in pizzas and many other Italian-style dishes.

Myoglobin: Oxygen-carrying proteins found in muscle.

Nachos: Crisp tortillas dipped in or covered with a mixture of melted cheese.

Neutral solution: One containing equal numbers of hydrogen and hydroxyl ions.

Night blindness: Difficulty in shifting from bright light to darkness due to vitamin A deficiency.

Nitrites (nitrates):   Compounds of nitrogen and oxygen that occur naturally in many foods and can also be added during processing.

Nitrosamines: Chemical products of certain reactions involving nitrates and nitrites.

Nonheme iron: Iron in the diet other than heme iron that is usually present in milk, eggs, and plant products.

Nouvelle cuisine: A modern style of cooking that emphasizes light sauces and seasonings, shortened cooking times, and new combinations of foods.

Nutrient: A specific substance that must be taken into the body preformed and in sufficient quantity to meet the body's need.

Nutrient density: A measure of nutrients in foods compared with the kcalories it contains.

Nutrition: The interactions between food and a living organism.

Obese: More than 20 percent above ideal body weight.

Offal: Another name for variety meats.

Omelet: A beaten egg mixture cooked rapidly over heat; often filled with a variety of ingredients.

Organ: A specialized body part composed of various types of tissue that work together to perform a particular function or functions.

Organism: Any living thing, whether plant, microorganism, or animal.

Osteoporosis: A condition in which bone mass gradually decreases with age.

Overweight: A term usually used to describe body weight that is generally 10 to 20 percent above ideal body weight.

Oxidation: Energy-producing metabolic processes that take place in cells.

Pan-broil: To cook uncovered in a sauté pan or skillet without fat.

Pan-fry: To cook in a moderate amount of fat in an uncovered pan.

Parboil: To cook partially in a boiling or simmering liquid.

Parfait: A dessert consisting of alternating layers of ice cream and fruit or syrup in a tall, narrow glass.

Pasta: General term for a macaroni product or noodles.

Pasteurization: Heating a food at a temperature below its boiling point for less than a minute to kill pathogens.

Pastry flour: A low-gluten flour often used to make pie crust.

Pellagra: A disease resulting from niacin deficiency.

Peptide bonds: The linkages between amino acids in a protein molecule.

Pernicious anemia: Anemia resulting from the inadequate production of intrinsic factor, which leads to the inadequate absorption of vitamin B_{12} despite its presence in the diet.

pH scale: A measure of the concentration of hydrogen ions in solution.

Phospholipids: Compounds similar to triglycerides but having a phosphorus-containing unit in place of one of the fatty acids.

Phytates: Phosphorus-containing organic compounds found in some plant materials, which decrease mineral absorption.

Pilaf: A rice dish made with herbs and spices.

Pita bread: A thin, soft, flat yeast bread with or without pockets.

Poach: To cook very gently in water or another liquid that is hot but not actually bubbling, at about 160°F to 180°F (71°C to 82°C).

Polysaccharides (complex carbohydrates): Carbohydrates composed of many monosaccharide units linked together, such as starches and dextrins.

Portion control: Control of portion sizes to ensure that the correct amount of an item is used or served.

Pot roast: A large cut of meat cooked by braising.

Precursor: A substance from which another substance is formed.

Produce: Fresh fruits and vegetables.

Proteins: Nitrogen-containing organic substances that have structural, regulatory, and energy-providing functions.

Provitamins: Vitamin precursors that the body can convert into the active form of a vitamin.

Puree: Mashed or strained to a smooth pulp; to make such food product.

Quiche: A tart or pie consisting of a custard baked in a pastry shell.

Quick bread: A bread leavened by chemical leaveners or steam rather than yeast.

Rancidity: Chemical deterioration of fats or oils characterized by a stale, unpleasant taste and smell.

Ratatouille: A vegetable stew made with onions, tomatoes, zucchini, eggplant, and green peppers.

Ravioli: Dumplings consisting of egg noodles filled with any of a variety of fillings.

Recipe: A set of instructions provided for preparing certain foods.

Recommended Dietary Allowances (RDAs): Daily nutrient intake recommendations established by the National Academy of Sciences.

Refining: Separation of the bran and germ from the endosperm early in the milling process.

Relish: A type of appetizer prepared with raw or pickled vegetables.

Ricotta: An Italian-style cheese similar to cottage cheese but smoother, moister, and sweeter in flavor.

Risk factors: Characteristics associated with an increased chance of developing a given health problem.

Roux: A cooked mixture of equal parts of flour and fat.

Saturated fat: A fat that is normally solid at room temperatures.

Saturation: The degree to which hydrogen atoms fill all available positions along the fatty acid skeleton.

Sauce: A flavorful liquid, usually thickened, that is used to season, flavor, and enhance other food.

Sauté: To cook quickly in a small amount of fat.

Scurvy: A disease resulting from vitamin C deficiency.

Sear: To brown the surface of a food quickly at high temperature.

Seasonings: Substances that help enhance the flavor of foods, such as salt, pepper, paprika, and so on.

Semolina: A hard, high-protein flour often used for the best-quality macaroni products.

Shelf life: The length of time a food can be stored without any loss of quality.

Shellfish: Fish that have shells.

Shortening: Any fat used in baking to tenderize the product; fat that can be used in baking, deep-fat frying, and other types of food preparation.

Simmer: To cook in water or another liquid that is bubbling gently at about 185°F to 200°F (85°C to 93°C).

Smoking point: The temperature at which a fat begins to smoke, indicating its chemical breakdown.

Sorbet: A sherbet usually made without milk or milk products.

Soufflé: A light, fluffy baked egg dish consisting of a white sauce mixed with egg yolks and flavoring ingredients into which beaten egg whites are folded just before baking.

Specifications: A detailed statement of the standards required when purchasing different items in an operation.

Standardized recipe: A recipe that has been tested to produce a particular product in a standard form.

Starches: Complex forms of carbohydrates.

Static menu: A menu that offers the same items every day.

Sterols: A class of lipids that includes certain hormones and vitamin D.

Stew: Foods cooked by simmering in liquid; a dish prepared by stewing.

Stock: A clear, thin liquid flavored by soluble substances extracted from meats and vegetables, usually in the presence of herbs and seasonings.

Subcutaneous fat: Adipose tissue located just under the skin.

Sugars: Simple forms of carbohydrates; a common term for simple carbohydrates.

Sweetbreads: Glands of calves and young animals used as food.

Tacos: Corn tortillas filled with meat, vegetables, and other items.

Tamales: Meat mixture wrapped in tortilla dough and corn husks and then steamed.

Tapioca: A starch made from the cassava plant; also used as a thickener.

Tartar sauce: A mixture of mayonnaise, chopped pickles, onions, and other ingredients often used as a garnish for fish.

Thickening agent: A substance that increases the viscosity of a liquid; commonly used agents include gelatin and starches.

Tissue: Similar cells united to perform a particular function.

Tortillas: Round Mexican flat breads made with corn or wheat flour.

Trace minerals: Minerals present in the body in amounts less than 0.01 percent of body weight.

Tripe: The muscular portion of the stomach lining of beef or another meat animal.

Unsaturated fat: A far that is normally liquid at room temperature.

Veins: Vessels that carry blood to the heart.

Vinaigrette: Dressing or sauce made up of oil, vinegar, and flavoring ingredients used on/with foods.

Vitamins: Organic compounds present in small amounts in foods and needed in small amounts by the body as regulators of metabolic functions.

Weak flour: Flour with a low protein or gluten content.

Whey: The watery liquid remaining after milk protein has coagulated.

Whip: To beat foods rapidly in order to incorporate air into them.

Winterized oil: Vegetable oil that stays clear and liquid when refrigerated.

Yield: The quantity of finished product; the number of servings a recipe will provide.

Zest: The colored part of the peel of citrus fruit.

INDEX